For Your Reading Pleasure:

A New and Improved Moon Sign Book!

For over ninety years gardeners, farmers, astrologers, and others have trusted the *Moon Sign Book* to help them choose the best dates for their important activities. No other book on the market tops the *Moon Sign Book* in supplying useful tips for daily success, and now it's easier to use than ever.

- New revised instructions make it simple to know when to start something new for guaranteed results.
- The new expanded Astro Almanac tells you the best dates to begin almost any activity! Now you can find out when to advertise on the internet, hire and fire staff, work with consultants, and more.
- A new, bigger gardening section gives you more how-to articles and advice for master gardeners as well as beginners.

Plus you get our trusted regular features, including accurate weather and earthquake forecasts for all U.S. zones year round, economic predictions that are like money in the bank, tips on planting sumptuous produce with the help of lunar energy, and special feature articles on hot topics that affect us all. As always, you can depend on Gloria Star's accurate Moon sign forecasts to lead you through the ebb and flow of every month.

See why Llewellyn's *Moon Sign Book* has been a bestselling guide to successful living for almost a century!

About the Authors

Donna Cunningham can be considered an expert on the Moon, having written two books about the subject—Ballantine's *Moon Signs* and Weiser's *The Moon in Your Life*. She has over twenty-five years experience as a professional astrologer.

Alice DeVille has been a professional astrologer for over twenty-five years. She runs her own astrological consulting business, focusing on business, career, and personal issues, as well as leading workshops and seminars.

Ronnie Gale Dreyer is an astrological consultant, lecturer, and teacher. She is the author of *Venus: The Evolution of the Goddess and Her Planet* and *Vedic Astrology: A Guide to the Fundamentals of Jyotish*. Ronnie is also a contributor to the anthology *Astrology for Women: Roles and Relationships* (Llewellyn, 1997).

Verna Gates teaches folklore classes at the University of Alabama at Birmingham, and has been featured on NBC *Nightside* as a folklorist. She was a writer for CNN and has been a freelance writer for fourteen years.

Penny Kelly has earned a degree in naturopathic medicine, is working toward a Ph.D. in nutrition, and is the author of the book *The Elves of Lily Hill Farm* (Llewellyn, 1996).

Barbara Koval has been an astrologer since 1970. Her monthly newsletter, *Intelligent Market Insights*, covers stocks, futures, mutual funds, and financial cycles.

Gretchen Lawlor combines twenty-five years as an astrologer with over ten years as a naturopath into her astromedical consultations and teachings. She can be reached for consultations at P.O. Box 753, Langley, WA 98260.

Harry MacCormack is an adjunct assistant professor of theater arts, and owner/operator of Sunbow Farm, which is celebrating a quarter century of operation.

Caroline Moss runs classes and writes articles on herb growing, crafts, cookery, history, and folklore. She lives in England and designs gardens to commission.

Janina Renee holds a degree in anthropology and is a scholar of such diverse subjects as folklore, ancient religions, mythology, magic, and Jungian psychology.

Louise Riotte is a lifetime gardener and the author of several books from Storey Publications, including: *Sleeping with a Sunflower*, *Carrots Love Tomatoes*, *Planetary Planting*, *Astrological Gardening*, and the newly released *Catfish Ponds and Lily Pads*.

Kim Rogers-Gallagher is a professional astrologer and author of *Astrology for the Light Side of the Brain*, from ACS Publications. She also writes monthly columns for the astrology magazines *Welcome to Planet Earth*, *Dell Horoscope*, and *Aspects*.

Bruce Scofield is a professional astrologer certified by the American Federation of Astrologers (AFA) and the National Council for Geocosmic Research (NCGR). His specialties are electional astrology and the astrology of ancient Mexico.

Nancy Soller has been writing weather and earthquake predictions for the *Moon Sign Book* since 1981. She is currently studying the effects of the Uranian planets and the four largest asteroids on the weather.

K. D. Spitzer is an accomplished astrologer and tarot reader, as well as an experienced teacher and workshop leader. Her areas of focus include herbal and musical healing, mystical traditions, and women's mysteries.

Carly Wall is the author of *Naturally Healing Herbs* and *Setting the Mood with Aromatherapy*, from Sterling Publishing. She leads aromatherapy workshops and has a large herb garden.

Moon Sign Book

and Gardening Almanac

Editor/Designer: Cynthia Ahlquist
Cover Illustration: Brian Jensen
Cover Design: Anne Marie Garrison
Lunar Forecasts: Gloria Star

Special thanks to Leslie Nielsen for astrological proofreading.

ISBN 1-56718-933-4

LLEWELLYN PUBLICATIONS
P.O. Box 64383 Dept. 933-4
St. Paul, MN 55164-0383 U.S.A.

Table of Contents

How to Use This Book

Are you ready to harness the power of the Moon? With the *Moon Sign Book* you can do just that. The *Moon Sign Book* provides you with four essential tools to reap the benefits of the Moon. You can use these tools alone or in any combination to help you achieve success in 1998. The first tool is our unique, easy-to-use Astro Almanac: a list of the best dates in 1998 to begin important activities. The second tool is a complete how-to on using the Moon to fine-tune your timing. This takes the Astro Almanac one step further and teaches you *how* to choose the best dates for your activities. The third tool consists of insightful lunar astrological forecasts by astrologer Gloria Star. The fourth tool is informative articles on using the Moon in the home, business, garden, and everywhere you go. Read on to find out more about how to use each of these features.

The Astro Almanac

The simplest method for using the *Moon Sign Book* in lunar timing is to turn straight to the Astro Almanac, beginning on page 12. The Astro Almanac lists the best days to perform sixty different activites, based on the sign and phase of the Moon and on lunar aspects. All you need to do is find the particular activity that you are interested in, and the best dates for each month will be listed across the page. When working with the Moon's energies we consider two things—the inception, or beginning of an activity, and the desired outcome. We begin a project under a certain Moon sign and phase in order to achieve certain results. The results are influenced by the attributes of the sign and phase under which we started the project. Therefore, the Astro Almanac lists the best times to *begin* many activities.

The Moon Tables

The Astro Almanac is a general guide to the best days for the activities listed in it, but for a more in-depth exploration of lunar timing, the *Moon Sign Book* provides the Moon Tables. The Astro Almanac can't take everyone's special needs into account. This is partially because although we can provide generally favorable dates for everyone, not everyone will have the same goal for each activity that they start. Therefore, not everyone will want to start every activity at the same time. For example, let's say you decide to plant a flower garden. Which attributes would you like most in your flowers? Beauty? Then you may want to plant in Libra, because Libra is ruled by Venus, which in turn governs appearance. How about planting for quantity or abundance? Then you might try Cancer or Pisces, the two most fertile signs. What if you were going to be transporting the flowers somewhere, either in pots or as cut blooms? Then you might want to try Scorpio for sturdiness, or Taurus for hardiness. The Astro Almanac also does not take into account retrogrades, Moon void-of-course, or favorable and unfavorable days.

The procedure for using the Moon tables is more complex than simply consulting the Astro Almanac, but we encourage you to try it so that you can tailor the *Moon Sign Book* information to your needs and fully harness the potential of the Moon. The directions for using the tables to choose your own dates are in the section called "Using the Moon Tables," which begins on page 22. Be sure to read all of the directions, paying special attention to the information on the signs, Moon void-of-course, retrogrades, and favorable and unfavorable days. The sections titled "The Moon's Quarters & Signs" (page 52), the Moon Void-of-Course Table (page 55), and "Retrogrades" (page 54) are provided as supplementary material and should be read as well. These sections will give you a deeper understanding of how the process of lunar planning works, and give you background helpful in making use of the articles in this book.

Personal Lunar Forecasts

The third tool for working with the Moon is the Personal Lunar Forecasts section, written by Gloria Star. This section begins on page 329. Here Gloria tells you what's in store for you for 1998, based on your Moon sign. This approach is different than that of other astrology books, including Llewellyn's *Sun Sign Book,* which make forecasts based on Sun sign. While the Sun in an astrological chart represents the basic essence or personality, the Moon represents the internal or private you—your feelings, emotions, and subconscious. Knowing what's in store for your Moon in 1998 can give you great insight for personal growth. If you already know your Moon sign, go ahead and turn to the corresponding section in the back of the book (forecasts begin on page 331). If you don't know your Moon sign, you can figure it out using the procedure beginning on page 62.

Articles, Articles, Articles

Scattered throughout the *Moon Sign Book* are articles on using the Moon for activities from fishing to business. These articles are written by people who successfully use the Moon to enhance their daily lives, and are chosen to entertain you and enhance your knowledge of what the Moon can do for you. The articles can be found in the Home, Health, & Beauty section; the Leisure & Recreation section; the Business section; and the Gardening section. Check the table of contents for specific topics.

Some Final Notes

We get a number of letters and phone calls every year from readers asking the same types of questions. Most of these have to do with how to find certain information in the *Moon Sign Book* and how to use this information.

The best advice we can give is to read the *entire* introduction (pages 5–74), in particular the section on how to use the tables. We provide examples using the current Moon and aspect tables so that you can follow along and get familiar with the process. At first, using the Moon tables may seem confusing because there are several factors to take into account, but if you read the directions carefully and practice a little bit, you'll be a Moon sign pro in no time.

Remember, for quick reference for the best dates to begin an activity, turn to the Astro Almanac. To choose special dates for an activity that are tailor-made just for you, turn to "How to Use the Moon tables." For insight into your personal Moon sign, check out Gloria Star's lunar forecasts. Finally, to learn about the many ways you can harness the power of the Moon, turn to the articles in the Home, Health & Beauty; Leisure & Recreation; Business; Gardening; and Fun with the Moon sections.

Get ready to improve your life with the power of the Moon!

Important!

All times given in the *Moon Sign Book* are set in Eastern Standard Time (EST). You must adjust for your time zone. There is a time zone conversion chart on page 8 to assist you. You must also adjust for Daylight Saving Time where applicable.

Time Zone Conversions

World Time Zones

(Compared to Eastern Standard Time)

(R) EST—Used
(S) CST—Subtract 1 hour
(T) MST—Subtract 2 hours
(U) PST—Subtract 3 hours
(V) Subtract 4 hours
(W) Subtract 5 hours
(X) Subtract 6 hours
(Y) Subtract 7 hours
(Q) Add 1 hour
(P) Add 2 hours
(O) Add 3 hours
(N) Add 4 hours
(Z) Add 5 hours

(A) Add 6 hours
(B) Add 7 hours
(C) Add 8 hours
(D) Add 9 hours
(E) Add 10 hours
(F) Add 11 hours
(G) Add 12 hours
(H) Add 13 hours
(I) Add 14 hours
(K) Add 15 hours
(L) Add 16 hours
(M) Add 17 hours

Important!

All times given in the *Moon Sign Book* are set in Eastern Standard Time (EST). You must adjust for your time zone. You must also adjust for Daylight Saving Time where applicable.

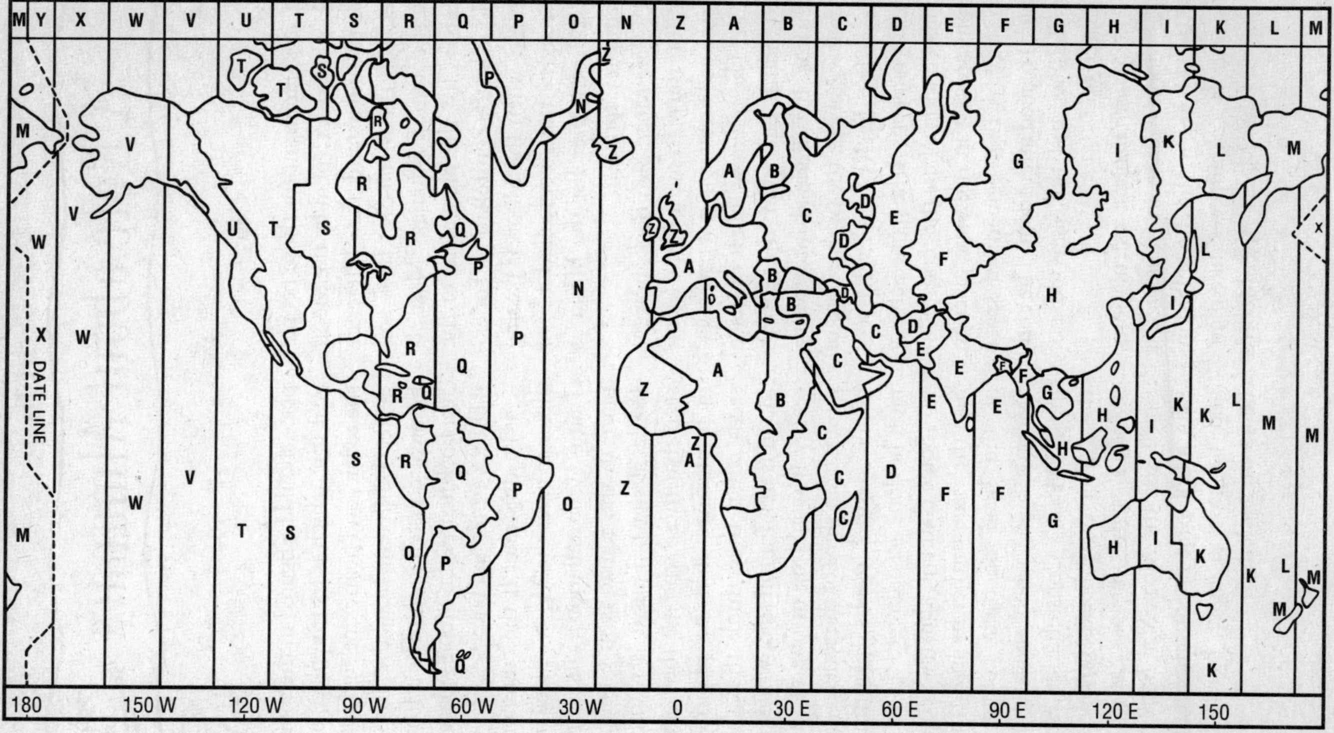
M Y X W V U T S R Q P O N Z A B C D E F G H I K L M
DATE LINE
180
150 W
120 W
90 W
60 W
30 W
0
30 E
60 E
90 E
120 E
150

A Note about Almanacs

It is important for those people who wish to plan by the Moon to understand the difference between the *Moon Sign Book* and most common almanacs. Most almanacs list the placement of the Moon by the constellation. For example, when the Moon is passing through the constellation of Capricorn, they list the Moon as being in Capricorn.

The *Moon Sign Book*, however, lists the placement of the Moon in the zodiac by *sign*, not constellation. The zodiac is a belt of space extending out from the earth's equator. It is divided into twelve equal segments: the twelve signs of the zodiac. Each of the twelve segments happens to be named after a constellation, but the constellations are not in the same place in the sky as the segment of space (sign) named after them. The constellations and the signs do not "match up."

For *astronomical* calculations, the Moon's place in almanacs is given as being in the constellation. For *astrological* purposes, like planning by the Moon, the Moon's place should be figured in the zodiacal *sign*, which is its true place in the zodiac, and nearly one sign (30 degrees) different from the astronomical constellation. The *Moon Sign Book* figures the Moon's placement for *astrological* purposes.

To illustrate: If the common almanac gives the Moon's place in Taurus (constellation), its true place in the zodiac is in Gemini (zodiacal sign). Thus it is readily seen that those who use the common almanac may be planting seeds when they think that the Moon is in a fruitful sign, while in reality it would be in one of the most barren signs of the zodiac. To obtain desired results, planning must be done according to *sign*.

Some common almanacs confuse the issue further by inserting at the head of their columns "Moon's Sign" when they really mean "Moon's Constellation." In the *Moon Sign Book*, however, "Moon's sign" means "Moon's sign"! Use the *Moon Sign Book* to plan all of your important events and to grow a more beautiful, bountiful garden.

Using the Astro Almanac

Llewellyn's unique Astro Almanac (pages 12–21) is provided for quick reference. Use it to find the best dates for anything from asking for a raise to buying a car!

This year, by reader request, we have included several new categories in the Astro Almanac relating to business, from hiring and firing staff to the best time to advertise on the internet. We hope you will find them useful. If you have suggestions for other activities to be added to the Astro Almanac, please write us at the address listed on the title page of this book.

The dates provided are determined from the sign and phase of the Moon and the aspects to the Moon. These are approximate dates only. This year we have removed dates that have long Moon void-of course periods from the list (we did not do this in previous years). Although some of these dates may meet the criteria listed for your particular activity, the Moon void would nullify the positive influences of that day. We have not removed dates with short Moon voids, however, and we have not taken planetary retrogrades into account. To learn more about Moon void-of-course and planetary retrogrades, see pages 54–61.

This year we have also removed days with lots of squares to the Moon, and eclipse dates. Like Moon voids, squares could nullify the "good" influences of a given day. Eclipses lend an unpredictable energy to a day, so we have removed eclipse dates so that you may begin your activites on the strongest footing possible.

Another thing to bear in mind when using the Astro Almanac is that sometimes the dates given may not be favorable for your Sun sign or for your particular interests. The Astro Almanac does not take personal factors into account, such as your Sun and Moon sign, your schedule, etc. That's why it is important for you to learn how to use the entire process to come up with the most beneficial dates for you. To do this, read the instructions under "Using the Moon Tables" (page 22). That way, you can get the most out of the power of the Moon!

Astro Almanac

Activity	Jan.	Feb.	Mar.	Apr.	May	Jun.	Jul.	Aug.	Sep.	Oct.	Nov.	Dec.
Advertise a Sale	25	21	21	15	14	12, 15, 20, 25	6	10, 12, 16, 20, 25, 31	2, 14, 15, 26, 29	4, 8, 10	1, 4, 8, 15, 20, 25, 29	1, 16, 20, 22, 26, 29
Advertise a New Venture	10, 25	5, 7, 21	21	1, 15, 28	14	12, 15, 20, 25	6, 20	4, 16, 31	26	10	24, 29	20, 26, 29
Advertise in the Paper	1, 5, 10, 21, 25, 26, 29, 31	2, 5, 7, 16, 21, 22, 26	3, 6, 8, 21, 24, 28, 30	1, 6, 15, 18, 20, 24, 27, 28	11, 14, 19, 20, 24	3, 12, 15, 20, 25, 30	6, 10, 14, 16, 18, 20, 23, 30	4, 6, 10, 12, 16, 19, 20, 25, 29, 31	2, 14, 15, 20, 25, 26, 29	1, 4, 8, 10, 12, 16, 21, 22, 27, 31	1, 4, 8, 15, 20, 25, 29	1, 11, 15, 20, 22, 26, 29
Advertise on TV, Radio, Internet	9, 28	5, 20, 24	24	1, 15, 20, 28	26	14, 18, 20	6, 11, 19	7, 30	12, 26	1, 9, 28	1, 14, 20, 24, 29	17, 22, 29
Apply for a Job	7, 17	22	30	6, 18, 23	24	12, 21	10, 18, 28	6, 14	2, 11, 29	8, 27	4, 13, 24	1, 20, 29
Apply for Copyrights, Patents	1, 5, 10, 21, 25, 26, 29, 31	5, 7, 21, 22, 26	3, 6, 21, 24, 28, 30	6, 15, 20, 23, 24, 27, 28	11, 14, 19, 20, 24	3, 8, 12, 15, 20, 21, 25, 30	5, 6, 10, 18, 20, 23, 25	1, 6, 10, 12, 14, 16, 20, 25, 29	2, 6, 9, 11, 14, 15, 20, 25, 26, 29	1, 4, 10, 12, 16, 21, 22	1, 4, 8, 15, 18, 25, 29	1, 11, 15, 16, 20, 22, 25, 26, 29

Astro Almanac

Activity	Jan.	Feb.	Mar.	Apr.	May	Jun.	Jul.	Aug.	Sep.	Oct.	Nov.	Dec.
Ask for a Raise	1, 4, 8, 10, 17, 25, 30, 31	7, 16, 22	3, 8, 21, 24, 30	1, 3, 6, 15, 18, 24, 27, 28	2, 27	3, 12, 15, 20, 25	1, 6, 11, 14, 18, 20	1, 10, 14, 15, 20, 25, 29, 31	2, 11, 14, 15, 19, 20, 26, 29	1, 4, 10, 12, 16, 21, 22, 30	1, 4, 8, 15, 24, 25, 29	1, 8, 15, 20, 22, 25, 26, 29
Bid on Contracts	20		14	1, 20		15, 20		20	9	1, 8	10, 18, 25	15, 22, 29
Brewing		26	6	22, 23	20, 21		12, 21	10, 18	6, 14, 15	13	8	25
Buy Stocks		22	2, 21, 30	18, 27	16, 24	12, 20	8, 18	6, 14	1, 2, 29	8, 27	4	1, 20, 29
Buy Animals	1, 2, 28, 29	3, 28	2, 30	1, 3, 30	2, 27, 30	3, 4, 12	1, 23, 25, 26	23–26, 29–31	21, 22, 26	25, 27	8, 13, 20–22, 24, 29	17, 18, 20, 22, 29
Buy Antiques	13, 27	8, 9, 18, 22, 23	8, 20, 23	3, 13, 18, 30	1, 2, 12, 16, 28, 29	11, 12, 25	4, 5, 21	1, 2, 5, 6, 27, 29	1, 2, 14, 15, 25, 29	8, 21–23, 26, 27	8, 18, 29	5, 15, 16, 20, 29

Astro Almanac

Activity	Jan.	Feb.	Mar.	Apr.	May	Jun.	Jul.	Aug.	Sep.	Oct.	Nov.	Dec.
Buy Appliances	4, 9, 18, 23, 28	15, 20, 24, 28	4, 9, 14, 24, 28	1, 15, 24, 28	8, 13, 17, 22, 26	4, 14, 18, 22	1, 6, 11, 15, 19, 29	2, 11, 15, 25, 30	3, 8, 12, 21, 26	1, 5, 9, 18, 23, 28	1, 5, 14, 20, 24, 29	3, 12, 17, 20, 22, 28, 30
Buy Cameras	4, 8, 17, 23, 31	4, 14, 28	4, 13, 31	10, 15, 24, 28	7, 12, 21, 25	3, 30	5, 14, 19, 28	2, 11, 15, 24, 29	7, 11, 20, 25	4, 8, 17, 22	1, 5, 14, 19, 28	2, 11, 16, 25, 30
Buy a Car		5, 21	4, 9, 19	1, 15, 28	14	12	6, 20	16, 31	26	10	8, 19, 29	17, 20, 22
Buy Electronics	4, 9, 18, 23, 28	15, 24, 28	4, 9, 14, 19, 24, 28	15, 20, 24, 28	8, 13, 17, 22, 26	4, 14, 18, 22	1, 6, 11, 15, 19, 29	2, 11, 15, 25, 30	3, 8, 12, 21, 26	1, 5, 9, 13, 28	1, 5, 8, 14, 20, 24, 29	3, 12, 17, 20, 22, 26, 30
Buy a House				3, 30	2, 28, 29	25	18, 21, 25					
Buy Real Estate		1, 22	2, 14, 28	3	1, 2, 29	25	18, 21	19, 25	9, 14, 15		8, 29	15, 20, 29

Astro Almanac

Activity	Jan.	Feb.	Mar.	Apr.	May	Jun.	Jul.	Aug.	Sep.	Oct.	Nov.	Dec.
Canning	13, 16–18	12–14	3, 27	23	20	15	22, 23	18, 19	14, 15, 19, 20	11, 12, 16	8, 13	5
Collect Money		22	2, 9, 10, 24, 30	3, 18	2, 29	12, 25	1, 18	25	2, 14, 15, 29	19, 22	8, 24, 29	14, 20, 29
Cut Hair–Increase Growth	3, 4, 13, 30, 31	8, 26, 27	7, 27	3, 4, 22, 23, 30	1, 20, 28, 29	16, 17, 24, 25	13, 14, 21, 22	9, 10, 17, 18	5, 7, 14, 15	3, 4, 11, 12, 31	7, 8, 27, 28	5, 24
Cut Hair–Decrease Growth	16–18	13, 14	14	24, 25	22	18, 22	15, 16, 19, 20	12, 13, 16	7, 8, 12, 13, 18, 19	5, 6, 9, 10, 16	5, 6, 12, 13	4, 11
Cut Hair for Thickness	10–12	9–11	13, 14	10	11	6		6–8	3, 4		3, 4	7, 28
Cut Timber	14–20, 24, 25	12, 13, 20–25	13–15, 19–24	15–21, 24, 25	13–19, 22–25	10, 18	6, 7, 15, 16	2, 3, 11, 20, 21	7–12, 16–20	5, 13–15	10, 11, 29, 30	7, 8, 17, 18

Astro Almanac

Activity	Jan.	Feb.	Mar.	Apr.	May	Jun.	Jul.	Aug.	Sep.	Oct.	Nov.	Dec.
Dock or Dehorn Animals	21–29	19–25	4–5, 21–25, 31	1–3, 19–21, 28–30	1–3, 18, 26–31	22–27	19–24	15–21	13–17, 28–30	9–14, 26–29	5, 7–10, 24, 25	7, 8, 20–22
End a Relation-ship	13–27	12–26	16–18, 24, 25	20–25	12–25	10–23	10–23	8–21	7–20	6–20	5–18	4–18
Entertain	1, 9, 10, 14, 15, 19, 28, 29	5–7, 10, 11, 15, 16, 24, 25	5, 6, 9–11, 14, 16, 24	1, 2, 5, 10–12, 20, 21, 28, 29	3, 4, 8, 17, 18, 26, 30, 31	4, 5, 14, 22, 26–27	1, 11, 12, 19–21, 24, 25	6, 7, 20, 24, 25	3, 4, 11, 12, 16, 17, 21, 22	1, 9, 10, 13, 14, 18, 19, 29	5, 6, 9, 14, 15, 24, 25	3, 4, 7, 8, 11, 12, 21, 22, 30, 31
Extract Teeth	24, 25	20, 21	5	1, 2, 28, 29	26	2, 22, 29, 30	19, 20, 26 27	15, 16, 22, 23	12, 13, 18–20, 26, 27	16, 23–25	14, 19, 20	11, 17, 18
Get a Perm	7, 8, 14	3, 4, 10, 11	9–10, 30, 31	26	24, 25, 30, 31	20, 21, 26, 27	18, 25	14, 15, 20	9, 10, 16	7, 8, 13, 14	4, 5, 24	1, 2, 7, 8, 29, 30
Fire Staff	13–27	12–26	16, 18, 20, 21, 23, 24	13–18, 20, 21, 23, 25	12, 14, 20–22, 24, 25	10–14, 18–22	10–14, 17–22	8, 10, 11, 14–21	7, 8, 11–17, 19	7–14, 16–19	5, 7, 8, 10, 13–15	4–18

Astro Almanac

Activity	Jan.	Feb.	Mar.	Apr.	May	Jun.	Jul.	Aug.	Sep.	Oct.	Nov.	Dec.
Hire Staff	1, 10, 29, 31	5, 7	2, 3, 8, 28, 30	1, 3, 27	1, 29	4, 25, 30	5, 6, 25	1, 4, 6, 25, 29, 31	2, 25, 26, 29	1, 4, 21, 22, 27, 31	1, 4, 8, 15, 24, 25, 29	1, 20, 22, 26, 29
Legal Matters	1, 5, 10, 25, 29	7, 22	21, 26, 30	3, 18, 23, 27	20, 24	12, 25	14, 18	6, 10, 14	2, 11, 15, 29	4, 8, 12, 27, 31	4, 8, 29	20–29
Marriage Ceremony	1, 3, 4, 7, 8, 10, 17, 23, 25–30	1, 6, 7, 13, 18, 21–23, 27	4, 14, 18, 21, 23, 24, 27, 28	1, 6, 17, 18, 21, 23, 26, 27, 30	1, 5, 24, 25, 27, 29, 30	4, 12, 14, 16, 21, 23	5, 11, 14, 18, 21, 26, 28	2, 10, 15, 16, 25, 29, 31	1, 2, 9, 14, 15, 19, 29	1, 4, 8, 9, 19, 22, 25, 30	8, 13, 18, 19, 24, 29	12, 18, 20, 23, 26, 29
Marry for Happiness	8	7, 27	14, 28	27, 30	1, 2, 24	4, 21, 25, 26	18	15, 25, 29	11, 14, 15	14, 27	8, 29	8, 12, 20, 29
Marry for Longevity			14, 24, 28					20	9			
Mow Lawn for Less Growth	14–27	12–25	13, 14–24, 28–31	12–26	12–25	10–23	10–20	11–16, 19, 20	8–19	6–19	5–18	4–18

Astro Almanac

Activity	Jan.	Feb.	Mar.	Apr.	May	Jun.	Jul.	Aug.	Sep.	Oct.	Nov.	Dec.
Neutering or Spaying Animals	1, 9, 10, 13–15, 27–29	5–11, 22–25	5–11, 22–25	1, 3, 5, 6, 18–21, 28–30	1, 2, 4, 15–17, 25–31	11–14, 23–27	8–11 19–25	5–7, 16–21	1–5, 11, 12, 29, 30	1, 2, 9–14, 26–29	7, 8, 13, 14, 18, 19, 24, 25, 29	3, 7, 8, 20, 22
Open a Business			21, 30		24	12	8, 18	14, 15, 22	1, 2, 29	27	4, 8, 29	1, 20, 29
Paint a House	17	23	4, 24	18	23, 24	21, 26	11	14, 20	9	14	13, 29	8, 29
Pour Concrete	1, 14, 28	10, 25	10, 24	20	31	26, 27	17	7	3, 17	1, 13, 14	11, 26	8, 23
Remodel a Business	1, 4, 5, 9, 10, 13, 14, 16, 20, 23–25, 28–30	1, 2, 10, 15, 17, 20, 22, 24, 28	9, 14, 16, 19, 23–27	1, 3, 5, 6, 10, 15, 18, 23, 24	2, 7, 12, 14, 16, 17, 20, 21, 25	3, 12, 13, 21–25, 26	1, 5, 6, 10, 12–15, 18, 21, 23, 28	1, 2, 6, 7, 10, 11, 14, 17, 19, 24, 29	1, 2, 5, 7, 13, 15, 16, 18, 21, 25, 26, 29	1, 5, 12, 13, 15, 18, 22, 25, 27, 28, 30, 31	1, 8, 9, 11, 14, 18, 19, 24, 29	1, 12, 15, 17, 20, 22, 26, 29
Remodel a House	14, 23, 24	10, 20	9, 10, 14, 16, 19, 23, 24	3, 15	2, 7, 12, 14, 16, 17, 20, 21, 25	10, 26	6, 8, 25	20, 29	16, 18, 26	12, 23, 25	1, 8, 9, 11, 18, 19, 24, 29	7, 12, 17, 20, 26, 29

Astro Almanac

Activity	Jan.	Feb.	Mar.	Apr.	May	Jun.	Jul.	Aug.	Sep.	Oct.	Nov.	Dec.
Repair Electronics	23, 28	10, 24	4, 24	13, 20	25	14, 18, 22	11, 12, 24	2, 7, 14, 15, 29	8, 12, 21, 25, 26, 29	1, 23, 28	4, 8, 13, 24, 29	2, 7, 22
Repair a Car	28	10, 24	4, 24	20, 21	12	12, 14	11	14, 21, 22	9	1, 28	4, 8, 13, 18, 24	7, 22
Roofing	13, 14	24, 25	24	20, 21, 26	17, 25, 30	14, 27	11, 12, 17, 18	13, 14, 20, 21	9	7, 8, 14, 15	4, 10, 11, 18	7, 8, 15, 22, 29
Seek Favors or Credit	1, 3, 4, 25, 28, 29, 30	21, 27	21, 24, 26, 27	3, 18, 23	16, 20, 24	8, 12, 28	11, 14	10, 20, 21, 31	2, 29	4, 25, 30, 31	8, 18, 24, 29	1, 7, 8, 15, 20, 29
Set Fence Posts	1, 14, 28	10, 25	23, 24	20	31	26	25	20, 21	9, 18, 25	15	11, 26	8, 23
Sign Contracts	1		3, 8, 21, 24, 30	18, 20	3, 24	20, 21	18, 25	25	2, 9, 20, 26, 29	1, 2, 8, 10, 12, 16, 22, 27	1, 4, 8, 10, 12, 16, 22, 27	1, 20, 29

Astro Almanac

Activity	Jan.	Feb.	Mar.	Apr.	May	Jun.	Jul.	Aug.	Sep.	Oct.	Nov.	Dec.
Start a Diet	4, 9, 10, 28, 29	6, 7, 27	7, 8	15, 16, 20, 24	12, 13, 21, 24	14, 18, 27	17	20	7, 8, 26, 29	6–8, 13–17	1, 24, 25, 29	7, 8, 22
Start a Savings Account	8		2, 30	18	16, 20, 29	21	18	14	2, 9, 14, 15, 19	8, 25, 27	8, 13, 23, 24	1, 20, 29
Sell Items	8		4, 21, 26, 28	18	16, 22, 29	4, 12, 18, 21	1, 10, 23	11, 24, 25	2, 9, 14, 15, 29		1, 8, 29	8, 20, 29
Sell Real Estate		2	2, 21, 28	3	1, 29	25	5, 8, 12	1, 2, 25	2, 9, 29		1, 8, 29	1, 8, 20, 23
Sporting Activities	25	2	4, 19, 21	1, 6, 17	12	18, 27		2	8, 27	25	19	7, 17
Start Building a House	1, 14, 28	10, 25	10, 24	6	27, 31	25	28	22, 25	2, 9, 29	1, 22, 26	19, 24, 25, 29	8, 23

Astro Almanac

Activity	Jan.	Feb.	Mar.	Apr.	May	Jun.	Jul.	Aug.	Sep.	Oct.	Nov.	Dec.
Stop a Bad Habit	14, 17	10, 13	5, 13		5, 7, 25, 31	21, 30	18, 19, 26	14, 20	18, 20	9, 16	4, 13	7, 8, 11, 15
Travel	9, 15	7, 20	19, 20	1, 15, 28	13, 14, 26	22	6, 19, 20	2, 16, 19, 31	12, 26	9, 10	19	7, 17, 18
Visit a Dentist	1, 14, 28	10, 25	9, 24	6		27	12, 21	1, 14	2, 9, 29	2, 28	11, 24, 25	8, 22, 23
Visit a Doctor			13, 27	17	5, 7, 27	3, 12, 18, 29	26, 28	22–24	2, 8, 18, 19	16, 18, 26, 27	11, 13, 29	22
Work with Consultants	1, 5, 10, 15, 25, 31	5, 16, 21, 22	3, 14, 20, 21, 24, 26, 28, 30	1, 3, 6, 15, 18, 20, 23, 24, 28	8, 14, 16, 19, 20, 24, 29	3, 12, 15, 20, 21, 25, 30	5, 6, 14, 18, 20, 23	16, 25, 29, 31	2, 9, 11, 14, 15, 20, 25, 26, 29	1, 10, 12, 16, 27	1, 4, 8, 15, 18, 25, 29	11, 15, 16, 20, 25, 26, 29
Write Letters	4, 9, 10, 17, 24, 25, 30, 31	5–7, 12–14, 20, 21, 26, 27	4, 6, 12, 13, 19–21, 26, 27	15, 16, 22	13, 20, 25, 26	2, 3, 9, 15, 30	6, 7, 14, 19–21, 28	12, 16, 25, 31	12, 19, 20, 26, 27	3, 4, 9, 10, 16, 17, 24, 30	5, 6, 12, 13, 19–21, 27, 28	3, 9, 10, 11, 17, 18, 24, 30, 31

Using the Moon Tables

Timing by the Moon

Timing your activities is one of the most important things you can do to ensure success. In many Eastern countries, timing by the planets is so important that practically no event takes place without first setting up a chart for it. Weddings have occurred in the middle of the night because that was when the influences were the best. You may not want to take it that far, and you don't really need to set up a chart for each activity, but you can still make use of the influences of the Moon whenever possible. It's easy and it works!

In the *Moon Sign Book* you will find the information you need to plan just about any activity: weddings, fishing, buying a car or house, cutting your hair, traveling, and more. Not all of the things you do will fall on favorable days, but we provide the guidelines you need to pick the best day out of the several from which you have to choose. The primary method in the *Moon Sign Book* for choosing your own dates is to use the Moon Tables, beginning on page 28. Following are instructions for choosing the best dates for your activities using the *Moon Sign Book*, several examples, directions on how to read the Moon Tables themselves, and more advanced information on using the Favorable and Unfavorable Days Tables, Void-of-Course, and Retrograde information to choose the dates that are best for you personally. To enhance your understanding of the directions given below, we highly recommend that you read the sections of this book called "A Note about Almanacs" (page 10), "The Moon's Quarters & Signs" (page 52), "Retrograde Table & Explanation" (page 54), and "Moon Void-of-Course Table & Explanation" (page 55). It is not essential that you read these before you try the examples below, but reading them will deepen your understanding of the date-choosing process.

The Four Basic Steps

Step One: Use the Directions for Choosing Dates

Look up the directions for choosing dates for the activity that you wish to begin. The directions are listed on the second page of each of the following sections of this book: Home, Health, & Beauty; Leisure

& Recreation; Business & Legal; and Farm, Garden, & Weather. Check the Table of Contents to see in which of these sections the directions for your specific activity is listed. The activities contained in each section are listed in italics after the name of the section in the Table of Contents. For example, directions for choosing a good day for canning are listed in the Home, Health, & Beauty Section, and directions for choosing a good day to throw a party are in the Leisure Section. Read the directions for your activity, then go to step two.

Step Two: Check the Moon Tables

Next, turn to the Moon Tables, beginning on page 28. In the Moon Tables section, there are two tables for each month of the year. Use the Moon Tables to determine during which dates the Moon is in the phase and sign listed in the directions for your particular activity. The Moon Tables are the tables on the left-hand pages, and include the day, date, the sign the Moon is in, the element of that sign, the nature of the sign, the Moon's phase, and the times that it changes sign or phase.

If there is a time listed after a date, such as 2 FRI 4:56 am on January 2, that time is the time when the Moon moves into the zodiac sign listed for that day (which in this case would be Pisces). Until then, the Moon is considered to be in the sign for the previous day (Aquarius in this example).

The abbreviation Full signifies Full Moon and New signifies New Moon. The times listed directly after the abbreviation are the times when the Moon changes sign. The times listed after the phase indicate when the Moon changes phase.

If you know the specific month during which you would like to begin your activity, turn directly to that month. When you begin choosing your own dates, you will be using the Moon's sign and phase information most often. All times are listed in Eastern Standard Time (EST). You need to adjust them according to your own time zone. (There is a time zone conversion map on page 8.)

When you have found some dates that meet the criteria for the correct Moon phase and sign for your activity, you may have completed the process. For certain simple activities, such as getting a haircut, the phase and sign information is all that is needed. For other activities, however, we need to meet further criteria in order to choose the best date. If the directions for your activity include information on certain lunar aspects, you should consult the Lunar Aspectarian. An example of this would be if the directions told you that you should not perform a certain activty when the Moon is square Mars.

Step Three: Turn to the Lunar Aspectarian

On the pages opposite the Moon Tables you will find the Lunar Aspectarian and the Favorable and Unfavorable Days Tables. The Lunar Aspectarian gives the aspects (or angles) of the Moon to the other planets. In a nutshell, it tells where the Moon is in relation to the other planets in the sky. Some placements of the Moon in relation to other planets are favorable, while others are not. To use the Lunar Aspectarian, which is the left half of this table, find the planet that the directions for your activity list, and run down the column to the date desired. For example, if you are planning surgery and in the Health & Beauty section it says that you should avoid aspects to Mars, you would look for Mars across the top and then run down that column looking for days where there are no aspects to Mars (these days are signified by empty boxes). If you want to find a favorable aspect (sextile [X] or trine [T]) to Mercury, run your finger down the column under Mercury until you find an X or T; positive or good aspects are signified by these letters. Negative or adverse aspects (square or opposition) are signified by a Q or O. A conjunction, C, is sometimes good, sometimes bad, depending on the activity or planets involved.

Step Four: Use the Favorable and Unfavorable Days Tables

The Favorable and Unfavorable Days Tables are helpful in choosing the best dates for you personally, because it takes your Sun sign into account. The table lists all of the Sun signs. It is the right-hand side of the Lunar Aspectarian table. Once you have determined which days meet the criteria for phase, sign, and aspects for your activity, you can check to see if those days are positive for you personally. To find out if a day is positive for you, find your Sun sign and then look down the column. If it is marked F, it is very favorable. If it is marked f, it is slightly favorable. U means very unfavorable and u means slightly unfavorable.

At this point, you have selected good dates for whatever activity you are about to begin. You can go straight to the examples section beginning on the next page. However, if you are up to the challenge and would like to learn how to fine-tune your selections even further, read on!

Step Five: Check the Moon Void-of-Course and Planetary Retrograde Tables

This last step is perhaps the most advanced portion of the procedure.

It is generally considered a bad idea to make decisions, sign important papers, or start special activities during a Moon void-of-course period or during a planetary retrograde. Once you have chosen the best date for your activity based on steps one through four, you can check the Void-of-Course Table on page 55 to find out if any of the dates you have chosen have void periods. The Moon is said to be void-of-course after it has made its last aspect to a planet within a particular sign, but before it has moved into the next sign. Put simply, during the void-of-course period the Moon is "at rest," so activities initiated at this time generally don't come to fruition. You will notice that there are many void periods during the year, and it is nearly impossible to avoid all of them. Some people choose to ignore these altogether and do not take them into consideration when planning activities.

Next, you can check the Planetary Retrograde Table on page 54 to see what planets are retrograde during your chosen date(s). A planet is said to be retrograde when it appears to move backward in the sky as viewed from the Earth. Generally, the farther a planet is away from the Sun, the longer it can stay retrograde. Some planets will retrograde for several months at a time. Avoiding retrogrades is not as important in lunar planning as avoiding the Moon void-of-course, with the exception of the planet Mercury. Mercury rules thought and communication, so it is important not to sign papers, initiate important business or legal work, or make crucial decisions during these times. As with the Moon void-of-course, it is difficult to avoid all planetary retrogrades when beginning events, and you may choose to ignore this step of the process. Following are some examples using some or all of the steps outlined above.

Using What You've Learned

Example Number One

Let's say you need to make an appointment to have your hair cut. Your hair is thin and you would like it to look thicker. You look in the Table of Contents to see which of the sections of the book lists the directions for hair care. You find that it is in the Home, Health, & Beauty section. Turning to that section you see that for thicker hair you should cut hair while the Moon is Full and in the sign of Taurus, Cancer, or Leo. You should avoid the Moon in Aries, Gemini, or Virgo. We'll say that it is the month of February. Look up February in the Moon Tables (page 30–31). The Full Moon falls on February 11 at 5:23 am. It is in the sign of Leo, so this date meets both the phase and sign criteria.

Example Number Two

That was easy. Let's move on to a more difficult example using the sign and phase of the Moon. You want to buy a house for a permanent home. After checking the Table of Contents to see where the house purchasing instructions are, look in the Home, Health, & Beauty section under House. It says that you should buy a home when the Moon is in Taurus, Leo, Scorpio, or Aquarius (fixed signs). You need to get a loan, so you should also look in the Business & Legal section under Loans. Here it says that the third and fourth quarters favor the borrower (you). You are going to buy the house in January. Look up January in the Moon Tables. The Moon is in the third quarter from January 13–20, and in the fourth quarter from January 20–27. The best days for obtaining a loan would be January 13–14 while the Moon is in Leo or January 20–22 while it is in Scorpio. Just match up the best signs and phases (quarters) to come up with the best dates. With all activities, be sure to check the Favorable and Unfavorable Days for your Sun sign in the table adjoining the Lunar Aspectarian. If there is a choice between several dates, pick the one most favorable for you (marked F under your Sun sign). Because buying a home is an important business decision, you may also wish to check to see if there are Moon voids or a Mercury retrograde during these dates.

Example Number Three

Now let's look at an example that uses signs, phases, and aspects. Our example this time is fixing your car. We will use June as the example month. Look in the Home, Health, & Beauty section under automobile repair. It says that the Moon should be in a fixed sign (Taurus, Leo, Scorpio, or Aquarius) in the first or second quarter and well-aspected to Uranus. (Good aspects are sextiles and trines, marked X and T. Conjunctions are also usually considered good if they are not conjunctions to Mars, Saturn, or Neptune.) It also tells you to avoid negative aspects to Mars, Saturn, Uranus, Neptune, and Pluto. (Negative aspects are squares and oppositions, marked Q and O.) Look in the Moon Tables under June. You will see that the Moon is in the first and second quarters from June 1–9. The Moon is in Scorpio on June 5 from 11:06 pm until 10:35 am on June 8. Obviously you won't fix your car after 11:06 pm, so you should rule out June 5, and you may rule out June 8 if you don't think you can get it done before 10:35 am. Looking to the Lunar Aspectarian we see that neither June 6 nor June 7 has positive aspects to Uranus, and that both have negative aspects to other planets. However, June 7 has a negative aspect to Uranus, so depending on your Sun sign and whether or not these are favorable days for you, June 6 would probably be the better day if you can't wait until another month to fix your car!

Use Common Sense!

Some activities depend on many outside factors. Obviously, you can't go out and plant when there is still a foot of snow on the ground. You have to adjust to the conditions at hand. If the weather was bad during the first quarter when it was best to plant crops, do it during the second quarter while the Moon is in a fruitful sign instead. If the Moon is not in a fruitful sign during the first or second quarter, choose a day when it is in a semi-fruitful sign. The best advice is to choose either the sign or phase that is most favorable when the two don't coincide.

To summarize, in order to make the most of your activities, check with the *Moon Sign Book*. First, look up the activity in the corresponding section under the proper heading. Then, look for the information given in the tables (the Moon Tables, Lunar Aspectarian or Favorable and Unfavorable Days, or all three). Choose the best date according to the number of positive factors in effect. If most of the dates are favorable, then there is no problem choosing the one that will best fit your schedule. However, if there just don't seem to be any really good dates, pick the ones with the least number of negative influences. We know that you will be very pleased with the results if you use nature's influences to your advantage.

Key of Abbreviations for the Moon Tables

X: sextile/positive

T: trine/positive

Q: square/negative

O: opposition/negative

C: conjunction/positive, negative, or neutral depending on planets involved; conjunctions to Mars, Saturn, or Neptune are sometimes negative.

F: very favorable

f: slightly favorable

U: very unfavorable

u: slightly unfavorable

Full: Full Moon

New: New Moon

January Moon Table

Date	Sign	Element	Nature	Phase
1 THU	Aquarius	Air	Barren	1st
2 FRI 4:56 am	Pisces	Water	Fruitful	1st
3 SAT	Pisces	Water	Fruitful	1st
4 SUN 7:44 am	Aries	Fire	Barren	1st
5 MON	Aries	Fire	Barren	2nd 9:19 am
6 TUE 10:53 am	Taurus	Earth	Semi-fruit	2nd
7 WED	Taurus	Earth	Semi-fruit	2nd
8 THU 2:42 pm	Gemini	Air	Barren	2nd
9 FRI	Gemini	Air	Barren	2nd
10 SAT 7:43 pm	Cancer	Water	Fruitful	2nd
11 SUN	Cancer	Water	Fruitful	2nd
12 MON	Cancer	Water	Fruitful	Full 12:24 pm
13 TUE 2:45 am	Leo	Fire	Barren	3rd
14 WED	Leo	Fire	Barren	3rd
15 THU 12:31 pm	Virgo	Earth	Barren	3rd
16 FRI	Virgo	Earth	Barren	3rd
17 SAT	Virgo	Earth	Barren	3rd
18 SUN 12:45 am	Libra	Air	Semi-fruit	3rd
19 MON	Libra	Air	Semi-fruit	3rd
20 TUE 1:35 pm	Scorpio	Water	Fruitful	4th 2:41 pm
21 WED	Scorpio	Water	Fruitful	4th
22 THU	Scorpio	Water	Fruitful	4th
23 FRI 12:26 am	Sagittarius	Fire	Barren	4th
24 SAT	Sagittarius	Fire	Barren	4th
25 SUN 7:40 am	Capricorn	Earth	Semi-fruit	4th
26 MON	Capricorn	Earth	Semi-fruit	4th
27 TUE 11:27 am	Aquarius	Air	Barren	4th
28 WED	Aquarius	Air	Barren	New 1:01 am
29 THU 1:09 pm	Pisces	Water	Fruitful	1st
30 FRI	Pisces	Water	Fruitful	1st
31 SAT 2:21 pm	Aries	Fire	Barren	1st

January

Lunar Aspectatian — Favorable and Unfavorable Days

	Sun	Mercury	Venus	Mars	Jupiter	Saturn	Uranus	Neptune	Pluto	Aries	Taurus	Gemini	Cancer	Leo	Virgo	Libra	Scorpio	Sagittarius	Capricorn	Aquarius	Pisces
1		X			C	X				f	u	f		U		f	u	f		F	
2									Q	f	u	f		U		f	u	f		F	
3	X	Q									f	u	f		U		f	u	f		F
4			X				X	X	T		f	u	f		U		f	u	f		F
5	Q	T		X	X	C				F		f	u	f		U		f	u	f	
6			Q				Q	Q		F		f	u	f		U		f	u	f	
7	T			Q							F		f	u	f		U		f	u	f
8			T		Q			T			F		f	u	f		U		f	u	f
9				T		X	T		0	f		F		f	u	f		U		f	u
10		0			T					f		F		f	u	f		U		f	u
11						Q				u	f		F		f	u	f		U		f
12	0		0							u	f		F		f	u	f		U		f
13							0	0	T	u	f		F		f	u	f		U		f
14				0		T				f	u	f		F		f	u	f		U	
15		T			0					f	u	f		F		f	u	f		U	
16									Q		f	u	f		F		f	u	f		U
17	T		T					T			f	u	f		F		f	u	f		U
18		Q					T		X		f	u	f		F		f	u	f		U
19						0				U		f	u	f		F		f	u	f	
20	Q		Q	T	T			Q		U		f	u	f		F		f	u	f	
21		X					Q				U		f	u	f		F		f	u	f
22			X	Q	Q						U		f	u	f		F		f	u	f
23	X						X	X	C		U		f	u	f		F		f	u	f
24						T				f		U		f	u	f		F		f	u
25				X	X					f		U		f	u	f		F		f	u
26		C	C			Q				u	f		U		f	u	f		F		f
27								C		u	f		U		f	u	f		F		f
28	C					X	C		X	f	u	f		U		f	u	f		F	
29				C	C					f	u	f		U		f	u	f		F	
30			X						Q		f	u	f		U		f	u	f		F
31		X						X			f	u	f		U		f	u	f		F

February Moon Table

Date	Sign	Element	Nature	Phase
1 SUN	Aries	Fire	Barren	1st
2 MON 4:25 pm	Taurus	Earth	Semi-fruit	1st
3 TUE	Taurus	Earth	Semi-fruit	2nd 5:53 pm
4 WED 8:09 pm	Gemini	Air	Barren	2nd
5 THU	Gemini	Air	Barren	2nd
6 FRI	Gemini	Air	Barren	2nd
7 SAT 1:58 am	Cancer	Water	Fruitful	2nd
8 SUN	Cancer	Water	Fruitful	2nd
9 MON 9:57 am	Leo	Fire	Barren	2nd
10 TUE	Leo	Fire	Barren	2nd
11 WED 8:10 pm	Virgo	Earth	Barren	Full 5:23 am
12 THU	Virgo	Earth	Barren	3rd
13 FRI	Virgo	Earth	Barren	3rd
14 SAT 8:18 am	Libra	Air	Semi-fruit	3rd
15 SUN	Libra	Air	Semi-fruit	3rd
16 MON 9:14 pm	Scorpio	Water	Fruitful	3rd
17 TUE	Scorpio	Water	Fruitful	3rd
18 WED	Scorpio	Water	Fruitful	3rd
19 THU 8:56 am	Sagittarius	Fire	Barren	4th 10:27 am
20 FRI	Sagittarius	Fire	Barren	4th
21 SAT 5:30 pm	Capricorn	Earth	Semi-fruit	4th
22 SUN	Capricorn	Earth	Semi-fruit	4th
23 MON 10:10 pm	Aquarius	Air	Barren	4th
24 TUE	Aquarius	Air	Barren	4th
25 WED 11:42 pm	Pisces	Water	Fruitful	4th
26 THU	Pisces	Water	Fruitful	New 12:26 pm
27 FRI 11:42 pm	Aries	Fire	Barren	1st
28 SAT	Aries	Fire	Barren	1st

February

Lunar Aspectatian | Favorable and Unfavorable Days

	Sun	Mercury	Venus	Mars	Jupiter	Saturn	Uranus	Neptune	Pluto	Aries	Taurus	Gemini	Cancer	Leo	Virgo	Libra	Scorpio	Sagittarius	Capricorn	Aquarius	Pisces
1	X		Q			C	X		T	F		f	u	f		U		f	u	f	
2		Q			X			Q		F		f	u	f		U		f	u	f	
3	Q			X			Q				F		f	u	f		U		f	u	f
4			T		Q			T			F		f	u	f		U		f	u	f
5		T		Q			T		0	f		F		f	u	f		U		f	u
6	T					X				f		F		f	u	f		U		f	u
7				T	T					f		F		f	u	f		U		f	u
8			0			Q				u	f		F		f	u	f		U		f
9								0		u	f		F		f	u	f		U		f
10		0				T	0		T	f	u	f		F		f	u	f		U	
11	0				0					f	u	f		F		f	u	f		U	
12									Q		f	u	f		F		f	u	f		U
13			T	0							f	u	f		F		f	u	f		U
14								T			f	u	f		F		f	u	f		U
15						0	T		X	U		f	u	f		F		f	u	f	
16	T	T	Q					Q		U		f	u	f		F		f	u	f	
17					T		Q				U		f	u	f		F		f	u	f
18			X	T							U		f	u	f		F		f	u	f
19	Q	Q			Q			X			U		f	u	f		F		f	u	f
20						T	X		C	f		U		f	u	f		F		f	u
21	X	X		Q						f		U		f	u	f		F		f	u
22					X					u	f		U		f	u	f		F		f
23			C	X		Q		C		u	f		U		f	u	f		F		f
24							C		X	f	u	f		U		f	u	f		F	
25						X				f	u	f		U		f	u	f		F	
26	C	C			C				Q		f	u	f		U		f	u	f		F
27			X	C							f	u	f		U		f	u	f		F
28							X	X	T	F		f	u	f		U		f	u	f	

March Moon Table

Date	Sign	Element	Nature	Phase
1 SUN	Aries	Fire	Barren	1st
2 MON 12:01 am	Taurus	Earth	Semi-fruit	1st
3 TUE	Taurus	Earth	Semi-fruit	1st
4 WED 2:15 am	Gemini	Air	Barren	1st
5 THU	Gemini	Air	Barren	2nd 3:41 am
6 FRI 7:27 am	Cancer	Water	Fruitful	2nd
7 SAT	Cancer	Water	Fruitful	2nd
8 SUN 3:46 pm	Leo	Fire	Barren	2nd
9 MON	Leo	Fire	Barren	2nd
10 TUE	Leo	Fire	Barren	2nd
11 WED 2:36 am	Virgo	Earth	Barren	2nd
12 THU	Virgo	Earth	Barren	Full 11:35 pm
13 FRI 2:59 pm	Libra	Air	Semi-fruit	3rd
14 SAT	Libra	Air	Semi-fruit	3rd
15 SUN	Libra	Air	Semi-fruit	3rd
16 MON 3:51 am	Scorpio	Water	Fruitful	3rd
17 TUE	Scorpio	Water	Fruitful	3rd
18 WED 3:56 pm	Sagittarius	Fire	Barren	3rd
19 THU	Sagittarius	Fire	Barren	3rd
20 FRI	Sagittarius	Fire	Barren	3rd
21 SAT 1:43 am	Capricorn	Earth	Semi-fruit	4th 2:38 am
22 SUN	Capricorn	Earth	Semi-fruit	4th
23 MON 8:02 am	Aquarius	Air	Barren	4th
24 TUE	Aquarius	Air	Barren	4th
25 WED 10:43 am	Pisces	Water	Fruitful	4th
26 THU	Pisces	Water	Fruitful	4th
27 FRI 10:49 am	Aries	Fire	Barren	New 10:14 pm
28 SAT	Aries	Fire	Barren	1st
29 SUN 10:07 am	Taurus	Earth	Semi-fruit	1st
30 MON	Taurus	Earth	Semi-fruit	1st
31 TUE 10:38 am	Gemini	Air	Barren	1st

March

Lunar Aspectatian — Favorable and Unfavorable Days

	Sun	Mercury	Venus	Mars	Jupiter	Saturn	Uranus	Neptune	Pluto	Aries	Taurus	Gemini	Cancer	Leo	Virgo	Libra	Scorpio	Sagittarius	Capricorn	Aquarius	Pisces
1			Q			C				F		f	u	f		U		f	u	f	
2	X				X		Q	Q		F		f	u	f		U		f	u	f	
3		X									F		f	u	f		U		f	u	f
4			T	X	Q		T	T	0		F		f	u	f		U		f	u	f
5	Q					X				f		F		f	u	f		U		f	u
6		Q		Q	T					f		F		f	u	f		U		f	u
7	T					Q				u	f		F		f	u	f		U		f
8		T	0	T				0		u	f		F		f	u	f		U		f
9							0		T	f	u	f		F		f	u	f		U	
10						T				f	u	f		F		f	u	f		U	
11					0				Q	f	u	f		F		f	u	f		U	
12	0										f	u	f		F		f	u	f		U
13								T			f	u	f		F		f	u	f		U
14		0	T	0			T		X	U		f	u	f		F		f	u	f	
15						0				U		f	u	f		F		f	u	f	
16					T			Q		U		f	u	f		F		f	u	f	
17			Q				Q				U		f	u	f		F		f	u	f
18	T							X			U		f	u	f		F		f	u	f
19			X	T	Q		X		C	f		U		f	u	f		F		f	u
20		T				T				f		U		f	u	f		F		f	u
21	Q				X					f		U		f	u	f		F		f	u
22		Q		Q		Q				u	f		U		f	u	f		F		f
23	X							C	X	u	f		U		f	u	f		F		f
24		X	C	X		X	C			f	u	f		U		f	u	f		F	
25									Q	f	u	f		U		f	u	f		F	
26					C						f	u	f		U		f	u	f		F
27	C							X	T		f	u	f		U		f	u	f		F
28		C	X	C		C	X			F		f	u	f		U		f	u	f	
29								Q		F		f	u	f		U		f	u	f	
30					X		Q				F		f	u	f		U		f	u	f
31			Q					T	0		F		f	u	f		U		f	u	f

April Moon Table

Date	Sign	Element	Nature	Phase
1 WED	Gemini	Air	Barren	1st
2 THU 2:10 pm	Cancer	Water	Fruitful	1st
3 FRI	Cancer	Water	Fruitful	2nd 3:19 pm
4 SAT 9:36 pm	Leo	Fire	Barren	2nd
5 SUN	Leo	Fire	Barren	2nd
6 MON	Leo	Fire	Barren	2nd
7 TUE 8:26 am	Virgo	Earth	Barren	2nd
8 WED	Virgo	Earth	Barren	2nd
9 THU 9:05 pm	Libra	Air	Semi-fruit	2nd
10 FRI	Libra	Air	Semi-fruit	2nd
11 SAT	Libra	Air	Semi-fruit	Full 5:24 pm
12 SUN 9:55 am	Scorpio	Water	Fruitful	3rd
13 MON	Scorpio	Water	Fruitful	3rd
14 TUE 9:52 pm	Sagittarius	Fire	Barren	3rd
15 WED	Sagittarius	Fire	Barren	3rd
16 THU	Sagittarius	Fire	Barren	3rd
17 FRI 8:05 am	Capricorn	Earth	Semi-fruit	3rd
18 SAT	Capricorn	Earth	Semi-fruit	3rd
19 SUN 3:42 pm	Aquarius	Air	Barren	4th 2:53 pm
20 MON	Aquarius	Air	Barren	4th
21 TUE 8:07 pm	Pisces	Water	Fruitful	4th
22 WED	Pisces	Water	Fruitful	4th
23 THU 9:31 pm	Aries	Fire	Barren	4th
24 FRI	Aries	Fire	Barren	4th
25 SAT 9:09 pm	Taurus	Earth	Semi-fruit	4th
26 SUN	Taurus	Earth	Semi-fruit	New 6:42 am
27 MON 8:56 pm	Gemini	Air	Barren	1st
28 TUE	Gemini	Air	Barren	1st
29 WED 10:57 pm	Cancer	Water	Fruitful	1st
30 THU	Cancer	Water	Fruitful	1st

April

Lunar Aspectatian — Favorable and Unfavorable Days

	Sun	Mercury	Venus	Mars	Jupiter	Saturn	Uranus	Neptune	Pluto	Aries	Taurus	Gemini	Cancer	Leo	Virgo	Libra	Scorpio	Sagittarius	Capricorn	Aquarius	Pisces
1	X	X		X	Q	X	T			f		F		f	u	f		U		f	u
2			T							f		F		f	u	f		U		f	u
3	Q	Q			T					u	f		F		f	u	f		U		f
4				Q		Q				u	f		F		f	u	f		U		f
5							0	0	T	f	u	f		F		f	u	f		U	
6	T	T		T		T				f	u	f		F		f	u	f		U	
7			0							f	u	f		F		f	u	f		U	
8					0				Q		f	u	f		F		f	u	f		U
9											f	u	f		F		f	u	f		U
10		0					T	T	X	U		f	u	f		F		f	u	f	
11	0					0				U		f	u	f		F		f	u	f	
12				0				Q		U		f	u	f		F		f	u	f	
13			T		T		Q				U		f	u	f		F		f	u	f
14											U		f	u	f		F		f	u	f
15		T	Q				X	X	C	f		U		f	u	f		F		f	u
16					Q	T				f		U		f	u	f		F		f	u
17	T			T						f		U		f	u	f		F		f	u
18		Q	X		X					u	f		U		f	u	f		F		f
19	Q					Q		C		u	f		U		f	u	f		F		f
20		X		Q			C		X	f	u	f		U		f	u	f		F	
21	X					X				f	u	f		U		f	u	f		F	
22				X					Q		f	u	f		U		f	u	f		F
23			C		C						f	u	f		U		f	u	f		F
24		C					X	X	T	F		f	u	f		U		f	u	f	
25						C				F		f	u	f		U		f	u	f	
26	C			C			Q	Q			F		f	u	f		U		f	u	f
27			X		X						F		f	u	f		U		f	u	f
28		X					T	T	0	f		F		f	u	f		U		f	u
29			Q		Q	X				f		F		f	u	f		U		f	u
30	X			X						u	f		F		f	u	f		U		f

May Moon Table

Date	Sign	Element	Nature	Phase
1 FRI	Cancer	Water	Fruitful	1st
2 SAT 4:49 am	Leo	Fire	Barren	1st
3 SUN	Leo	Fire	Barren	2nd 5:04 am
4 MON 2:47 pm	Virgo	Earth	Barren	2nd
5 TUE	Virgo	Earth	Barren	2nd
6 WED	Virgo	Earth	Barren	2nd
7 THU 3:19 am	Libra	Air	Semi-fruit	2nd
8 FRI	Libra	Air	Semi-fruit	2nd
9 SAT 4:10 pm	Scorpio	Water	Fruitful	2nd
10 SUN	Scorpio	Water	Fruitful	2nd
11 MON	Scorpio	Water	Fruitful	Full 9:30 am
12 TUE 3:48 am	Sagittarius	Fire	Barren	3rd
13 WED	Sagittarius	Fire	Barren	3rd
14 THU 1:40 pm	Capricorn	Earth	Semi-fruit	3rd
15 FRI	Capricorn	Earth	Semi-fruit	3rd
16 SAT 9:31 pm	Aquarius	Air	Barren	3rd
17 SUN	Aquarius	Air	Barren	3rd
18 MON	Aquarius	Air	Barren	4th 11:36 pm
19 TUE 3:04 am	Pisces	Water	Fruitful	4th
20 WED	Pisces	Water	Fruitful	4th
21 THU 6:06 am	Aries	Fire	Barren	4th
22 FRI	Aries	Fire	Barren	4th
23 SAT 7:06 am	Taurus	Earth	Semi-fruit	4th
24 SUN	Taurus	Earth	Semi-fruit	4th
25 MON 7:25 am	Gemini	Air	Barren	New 2:32 pm
26 TUE	Gemini	Air	Barren	1st
27 WED 8:58 am	Cancer	Water	Fruitful	1st
28 THU	Cancer	Water	Fruitful	1st
29 FRI 1:38 pm	Leo	Fire	Barren	1st
30 SAT	Leo	Fire	Barren	1st
31 SUN 10:21 pm	Virgo	Earth	Barren	1st

May

Lunar Aspectatian — Favorable and Unfavorable Days

	Sun	Mercury	Venus	Mars	Jupiter	Saturn	Uranus	Neptune	Pluto	Aries	Taurus	Gemini	Cancer	Leo	Virgo	Libra	Scorpio	Sagittarius	Capricorn	Aquarius	Pisces
1		Q			T	Q				u	f		F		f	u	f		U		f
2			T					0	T	u	f		F		f	u	f		U		f
3	Q	T		Q			0			f	u	f		F		f	u	f		U	
4						T				f	u	f		F		f	u	f		U	
5	T								Q		f	u	f		F		f	u	f		U
6				T	0						f	u	f		F		f	u	f		U
7			0					T	X		f	u	f		F		f	u	f		U
8							T			U		f	u	f		F		f	u	f	
9		0				0		Q		U		f	u	f		F		f	u	f	
10							Q				U		f	u	f		F		f	u	f
11	0			0	T						U		f	u	f		F		f	u	f
12								X	C		U		f	u	f		F		f	u	f
13			T		Q		X			f		U		f	u	f		F		f	u
14		T				T				f		U		f	u	f		F		f	u
15			Q							u	f		U		f	u	f		F		f
16	T			T	X	Q				u	f		U		f	u	f		F		f
17		Q					C	C	X	f	u	f		U		f	u	f		F	
18	Q		X	Q		X				f	u	f		U		f	u	f		F	
19		X							Q	f	u	f		U		f	u	f		F	
20					C						f	u	f		U		f	u	f		F
21	X			X				X	T		f	u	f		U		f	u	f		F
22			C				X			F		f	u	f		U		f	u	f	
23						C		Q		F		f	u	f		U		f	u	f	
24		C			X		Q				F		f	u	f		U		f	u	f
25	C			C				T	0		F		f	u	f		U		f	u	f
26					Q		T			f		F		f	u	f		U		f	u
27			X			X				f		F		f	u	f		U		f	u
28										u	f		F		f	u	f		U		f
29		X	Q	X	T	Q		0		u	f		F		f	u	f		U		f
30	X						0		T	f	u	f		F		f	u	f		U	
31		Q				T				f	u	f		F		f	u	f		U	

June Moon Table

Date	Sign	Element	Nature	Phase
1 MON	Virgo	Earth	Barren	2nd 8:45 pm
2 TUE	Virgo	Earth	Barren	2nd
3 WED 10:17 am	Libra	Air	Semi-fruit	2nd
4 THU	Libra	Air	Semi-fruit	2nd
5 FRI 11:06 pm	Scorpio	Water	Fruitful	2nd
6 SAT	Scorpio	Water	Fruitful	2nd
7 SUN	Scorpio	Water	Fruitful	2nd
8 MON 10:35 am	Sagittarius	Fire	Barren	2nd
9 TUE	Sagittarius	Fire	Barren	Full 11:19 pm
10 WED 7:51 pm	Capricorn	Earth	Semi-fruit	3rd
11 THU	Capricorn	Earth	Semi-fruit	3rd
12 FRI	Capricorn	Earth	Semi-fruit	3rd
13 SAT 3:03 am	Aquarius	Air	Barren	3rd
14 SUN	Aquarius	Air	Barren	3rd
15 MON 8:32 am	Pisces	Water	Fruitful	3rd
16 TUE	Pisces	Water	Fruitful	3rd
17 WED 12:23 pm	Aries	Fire	Barren	4th 5:38 am
18 THU	Aries	Fire	Barren	4th
19 FRI 2:47 pm	Taurus	Earth	Semi-fruit	4th
20 SAT	Taurus	Earth	Semi-fruit	4th
21 SUN 4:26 pm	Gemini	Air	Barren	4th
22 MON	Gemini	Air	Barren	4th
23 TUE 6:39 pm	Cancer	Water	Fruitful	New 10:50 pm
24 WED	Cancer	Water	Fruitful	1st
25 THU 11:04 pm	Leo	Fire	Barren	1st
26 FRI	Leo	Fire	Barren	1st
27 SAT	Leo	Fire	Barren	1st
28 SUN 6:55 am	Virgo	Earth	Barren	1st
29 MON	Virgo	Earth	Barren	1st
30 TUE 6:06 pm	Libra	Air	Semi-fruit	1st

June

Lunar Aspectatian | Favorable and Unfavorable Days

	Sun	Mercury	Venus	Mars	Jupiter	Saturn	Uranus	Neptune	Pluto	Aries	Taurus	Gemini	Cancer	Leo	Virgo	Libra	Scorpio	Sagittarius	Capricorn	Aquarius	Pisces
1	Q		T	Q					Q		f	u	f		F		f	u	f		U
2											f	u	f		F		f	u	f		U
3		T			0			T	X		f	u	f		F		f	u	f		U
4	T			T			T			U		f	u	f		F		f	u	f	
5						0				U		f	u	f		F		f	u	f	
6			0					Q			U		f	u	f		F		f	u	f
7							Q				U		f	u	f		F		f	u	f
8					T			X	C		U		f	u	f		F		f	u	f
9	0	0		0			X			f		U		f	u	f		F		f	u
10					Q	T				f		U		f	u	f		F		f	u
11										u	f		U		f	u	f		F		f
12			T		X					u	f		U		f	u	f		F		f
13						Q		C	X	u	f		U		f	u	f		F		f
14	T		Q	T			C			f	u	f		U		f	u	f		F	
15		T				X			Q	f	u	f		U		f	u	f		F	
16			X	Q							f	u	f		U		f	u	f		F
17	Q	Q			C			X	T		f	u	f		U		f	u	f		F
18				X			X			F		f	u	f		U		f	u	f	
19	X					C		Q		F		f	u	f		U		f	u	f	
20		X					Q				F		f	u	f		U		f	u	f
21			C		X			T			F		f	u	f		U		f	u	f
22							T		0	f		F		f	u	f		U		f	u
23	C			C	Q	X				f		F		f	u	f		U		f	u
24										u	f		F		f	u	f		U		f
25		C			T					u	f		F		f	u	f		U		f
26			X			Q	0	0	T	f	u	f		F		f	u	f		U	
27				X						f	u	f		F		f	u	f		U	
28	X		Q			T			Q	f	u	f		F		f	u	f		U	
29											f	u	f		F		f	u	f		U
30		X		Q	0			T			f	u	f		F		f	u	f		U

July Moon Table

Date	Sign	Element	Nature	Phase
1 WED	Libra	Air	Semi-fruit	2nd 1:44 pm
2 THU	Libra	Air	Semi-fruit	2nd
3 FRI 6:46 am	Scorpio	Water	Fruitful	2nd
4 SAT	Scorpio	Water	Fruitful	2nd
5 SUN 6:24 pm	Sagittarius	Fire	Barren	2nd
6 MON	Sagittarius	Fire	Barren	2nd
7 TUE	Sagittarius	Fire	Barren	2nd
8 WED 3:28 am	Capricorn	Earth	Semi-fruit	2nd
9 THU	Capricorn	Earth	Semi-fruit	Full 11:01 am
10 FRI 9:52 am	Aquarius	Air	Barren	3rd
11 SAT	Aquarius	Air	Barren	3rd
12 SUN 2:22 pm	Pisces	Water	Fruitful	3rd
13 MON	Pisces	Water	Fruitful	3rd
14 TUE 5:45 pm	Aries	Fire	Barren	3rd
15 WED	Aries	Fire	Barren	3rd
16 THU 8:33 pm	Taurus	Earth	Semi-fruit	4th 10:14 am
17 FRI	Taurus	Earth	Semi-fruit	4th
18 SAT 11:18 pm	Gemini	Air	Barren	4th
19 SUN	Gemini	Air	Barren	4th
20 MON	Gemini	Air	Barren	4th
21 TUE 2:43 am	Cancer	Water	Fruitful	4th
22 WED	Cancer	Water	Fruitful	4th
23 THU 7:49 am	Leo	Fire	Barren	New 8:44 am
24 FRI	Leo	Fire	Barren	1st
25 SAT 3:34 pm	Virgo	Earth	Barren	1st
26 SUN	Virgo	Earth	Barren	1st
27 MON	Virgo	Earth	Barren	1st
28 TUE 2:15 am	Libra	Air	Semi-fruit	1st
29 WED	Libra	Air	Semi-fruit	1st
30 THU 2:45 pm	Scorpio	Water	Fruitful	1st
31 FRI	Scorpio	Water	Fruitful	2nd 7:05 am

July

Lunar Aspectatian | Favorable and Unfavorable Days

	Sun	Mercury	Venus	Mars	Jupiter	Saturn	Uranus	Neptune	Pluto	Aries	Taurus	Gemini	Cancer	Leo	Virgo	Libra	Scorpio	Sagittarius	Capricorn	Aquarius	Pisces
1	Q		T				T		X	U		f	u	f		F		f	u	f	
2										U		f	u	f		F		f	u	f	
3		Q		T		0		Q		U		f	u	f		F		f	u	f	
4	T						Q				U		f	u	f		F		f	u	f
5					T			X			U		f	u	f		F		f	u	f
6		T	0				X		C	f		U		f	u	f		F		f	u
7					Q					f		U		f	u	f		F		f	u
8				0		T				f		U		f	u	f		F		f	u
9	0									u	f		U		f	u	f		F		f
10					X	Q		C	X	u	f		U		f	u	f		F		f
11		0	T				C			f	u	f		U		f	u	f		F	
12				T		X				f	u	f		U		f	u	f		F	
13									Q		f	u	f		U		f	u	f		F
14	T		Q		C			X			f	u	f		U		f	u	f		F
15				Q			X		T	F		f	u	f		U		f	u	f	
16	Q	T	X					Q		F		f	u	f		U		f	u	f	
17				X		C	Q				F		f	u	f		U		f	u	f
18	X	Q			X						F		f	u	f		U		f	u	f
19							T	T	0	f		F		f	u	f		U		f	u
20		X			Q					f		F		f	u	f		U		f	u
21			C	C		X				f		F		f	u	f		U		f	u
22										u	f		F		f	u	f		U		f
23	C				T	Q		0	T	u	f		F		f	u	f		U		f
24							0			f	u	f		F		f	u	f		U	
25		C				T				f	u	f		F		f	u	f		U	
26			X	X					Q		f	u	f		F		f	u	f		U
27					0						f	u	f		F		f	u	f		U
28	X							T	X		f	u	f		F		f	u	f		U
29			Q	Q			T			U		f	u	f		F		f	u	f	
30		X				0		Q		U		f	u	f		F		f	u	f	
31	Q		T				Q				U		f	u	f		F		f	u	f

August Moon Table

Date	Sign	Element	Nature	Phase
1 SAT	Scorpio	Water	Fruitful	2nd
2 SUN 2:48 am	Sagittarius	Fire	Barren	2nd
3 MON	Sagittarius	Fire	Barren	2nd
4 TUE 12:18 pm	Capricorn	Earth	Semi-fruit	2nd
5 WED	Capricorn	Earth	Semi-fruit	2nd
6 THU 6:31 pm	Aquarius	Air	Barren	2nd
7 FRI	Aquarius	Air	Barren	Full 9:10 pm
8 SAT 10:04 pm	Pisces	Water	Fruitful	3rd
9 SUN	Pisces	Water	Fruitful	3rd
10 MON	Pisces	Water	Fruitful	3rd
11 TUE 12:11 am	Aries	Fire	Barren	3rd
12 WED	Aries	Fire	Barren	3rd
13 THU 2:05 am	Taurus	Earth	Semi-fruit	3rd
14 FRI	Taurus	Earth	Semi-fruit	4th 2:49 pm
15 SAT 4:46 am	Gemini	Air	Barren	4th
16 SUN	Gemini	Air	Barren	4th
17 MON 8:56 am	Cancer	Water	Fruitful	4th
18 TUE	Cancer	Water	Fruitful	4th
19 WED 3:01 pm	Leo	Fire	Barren	4th
20 THU	Leo	Fire	Barren	4th
21 FRI 11:22 pm	Virgo	Earth	Barren	New 9:03 pm
22 SAT	Virgo	Earth	Barren	1st
23 SUN	Virgo	Earth	Barren	1st
24 MON 10:02 am	Libra	Air	Semi-fruit	1st
25 TUE	Libra	Air	Semi-fruit	1st
26 WED 10:25 pm	Scorpio	Water	Fruitful	1st
27 THU	Scorpio	Water	Fruitful	1st
28 FRI	Scorpio	Water	Fruitful	1st
29 SAT 10:55 am	Sagittarius	Fire	Barren	1st
30 SUN	Sagittarius	Fire	Barren	2nd 12:07 am
31 MON 9:23 pm	Capricorn	Earth	Semi-fruit	2nd

August

Lunar Aspectatian — Favorable and Unfavorable Days

	Sun	Mercury	Venus	Mars	Jupiter	Saturn	Uranus	Neptune	Pluto	Aries	Taurus	Gemini	Cancer	Leo	Virgo	Libra	Scorpio	Sagittarius	Capricorn	Aquarius	Pisces
1		Q		T	T						U		f	u	f		F		f	u	f
2	T						X	X	C		U		f	u	f		F		f	u	f
3										f		U		f	u	f		F		f	u
4		T			Q	T				f		U		f	u	f		F		f	u
5										u	f		U		f	u	f		F		f
6			0	0	X			C		u	f		U		f	u	f		F		f
7	0					Q	C		X	f	u	f		U		f	u	f		F	
8		0								f	u	f		U		f	u	f		F	
9						X			Q		f	u	f		U		f	u	f		F
10			T	T	C						f	u	f		U		f	u	f		F
11							X	X	T		f	u	f		U		f	u	f		F
12	T	T		Q						F		f	u	f		U		f	u	f	
13			Q			C	Q	Q		F		f	u	f		U		f	u	f	
14	Q	Q		X	X						F		f	u	f		U		f	u	f
15			X				T	T	0		F		f	u	f		U		f	u	f
16	X	X								f		F		f	u	f		U		f	u
17					Q	X				f		F		f	u	f		U		f	u
18										u	f		F		f	u	f		U		f
19				C	T	Q		0		u	f		F		f	u	f		U		f
20		C	C				0		T	f	u	f		F		f	u	f		U	
21	C									f	u	f		F		f	u	f		U	
22						T			Q		f	u	f		F		f	u	f		U
23											f	u	f		F		f	u	f		U
24				X	0			T	X		f	u	f		F		f	u	f		U
25		X	X				T			U		f	u	f		F		f	u	f	
26								Q		U		f	u	f		F		f	u	f	
27	X			Q		0	Q				U		f	u	f		F		f	u	f
28		Q	Q								U		f	u	f		F		f	u	f
29				T	T			X	C		U		f	u	f		F		f	u	f
30	Q						X			f		U		f	u	f		F		f	u
31		T	T		Q					f		U		f	u	f		F		f	u

September Moon Table

Date	Sign	Element	Nature	Phase
1 TUE	Capricorn	Earth	Semi-fruit	2nd
2 WED	Capricorn	Earth	Semi-fruit	2nd
3 THU 4:21 am	Aquarius	Air	Barren	2nd
4 FRI	Aquarius	Air	Barren	2nd
5 SAT 7:48 am	Pisces	Water	Fruitful	2nd
6 SUN	Pisces	Water	Fruitful	Full 6:22 am
7 MON 8:53 am	Aries	Fire	Barren	3rd
8 TUE	Aries	Fire	Barren	3rd
9 WED 9:17 am	Taurus	Earth	Semi-fruit	3rd
10 THU	Taurus	Earth	Semi-fruit	3rd
11 FRI 10:41 am	Gemini	Air	Barren	3rd
12 SAT	Gemini	Air	Barren	4th 8:58 pm
13 SUN 2:20 pm	Cancer	Water	Fruitful	4th
14 MON	Cancer	Water	Fruitful	4th
15 TUE 8:48 pm	Leo	Fire	Barren	4th
16 WED	Leo	Fire	Barren	4th
17 THU	Leo	Fire	Barren	4th
18 FRI 5:51 am	Virgo	Earth	Barren	4th
19 SAT	Virgo	Earth	Barren	4th
20 SUN 4:57 pm	Libra	Air	Semi-fruit	New 12:01 pm
21 MON	Libra	Air	Semi-fruit	1st
22 TUE	Libra	Air	Semi-fruit	1st
23 WED 5:22 am	Scorpio	Water	Fruitful	1st
24 THU	Scorpio	Water	Fruitful	1st
25 FRI 6:05 pm	Sagittarius	Fire	Barren	1st
26 SAT	Sagittarius	Fire	Barren	1st
27 SUN	Sagittarius	Fire	Barren	1st
28 MON 5:31 am	Capricorn	Earth	Semi-fruit	2nd 4:12 pm
29 TUE	Capricorn	Earth	Semi-fruit	2nd
30 WED 1:54 pm	Aquarius	Air	Barren	2nd

September

Lunar Aspectatian | Favorable and Unfavorable Days

	Sun	Mercury	Venus	Mars	Jupiter	Saturn	Uranus	Neptune	Pluto	Aries	Taurus	Gemini	Cancer	Leo	Virgo	Libra	Scorpio	Sagittarius	Capricorn	Aquarius	Pisces
1	T					T				u	f		U		f	u	f		F		f
2					X					u	f		U		f	u	f		F		f
3				0		Q	C	C	X	u	f		U		f	u	f		F		f
4										f	u	f		U		f	u	f		F	
5		0	0			X			Q	f	u	f		U		f	u	f		F	
6	0				C						f	u	f		U		f	u	f		F
7								X	T		f	u	f		U		f	u	f		F
8				T			X			F		f	u	f		U		f	u	f	
9		T	T			C		Q		F		f	u	f		U		f	u	f	
10	T			Q			Q				F		f	u	f		U		f	u	f
11		Q	Q		X			T	0		F		f	u	f		U		f	u	f
12	Q			X			T			f		F		f	u	f		U		f	u
13					Q	X				f		F		f	u	f		U		f	u
14		X	X							u	f		F		f	u	f		U		f
15	X				T			0		u	f		F		f	u	f		U		f
16						Q	0		T	f	u	f		F		f	u	f		U	
17				C						f	u	f		F		f	u	f		U	
18						T			Q	f	u	f		F		f	u	f		U	
19			C								f	u	f		F		f	u	f		U
20	C	C			0			T			f	u	f		F		f	u	f		U
21							T		X	U		f	u	f		F		f	u	f	
22				X						U		f	u	f		F		f	u	f	
23						0	Q	Q		U		f	u	f		F		f	u	f	
24											U		f	u	f		F		f	u	f
25	X		X	Q	T			X			U		f	u	f		F		f	u	f
26		X					X		C	f		U		f	u	f		F		f	u
27			Q	T	Q					f		U		f	u	f		F		f	u
28	Q	Q				T				f		U		f	u	f		F		f	u
29					X					u	f		U		f	u	f		F		f
30			T			Q		C		u	f		U		f	u	f		F		f

October Moon Table

Date	Sign	Element	Nature	Phase
1 THU	Aquarius	Air	Barren	2nd
2 FRI 6:24 pm	Pisces	Water	Fruitful	2nd
3 SAT	Pisces	Water	Fruitful	2nd
4 SUN 7:32 pm	Aries	Fire	Barren	2nd
5 MON	Aries	Fire	Barren	Full 3:12 pm
6 TUE 6:58 pm	Taurus	Earth	Semi-fruit	3rd
7 WED	Taurus	Earth	Semi-fruit	3rd
8 THU 6:44 pm	Gemini	Air	Barren	3rd
9 FRI	Gemini	Air	Barren	3rd
10 SAT 8:48 pm	Cancer	Water	Fruitful	3rd
11 SUN	Cancer	Water	Fruitful	3rd
12 MON	Cancer	Water	Fruitful	4th 6:11 am
13 TUE 2:25 am	Leo	Fire	Barren	4th
14 WED	Leo	Fire	Barren	4th
15 THU 11:32 am	Virgo	Earth	Barren	4th
16 FRI	Virgo	Earth	Barren	4th
17 SAT 11:02 pm	Libra	Air	Semi-fruit	4th
18 SUN	Libra	Air	Semi-fruit	4th
19 MON	Libra	Air	Semi-fruit	4th
20 TUE 11:37 am	Scorpio	Water	Fruitful	New 5:10 am
21 WED	Scorpio	Water	Fruitful	1st
22 THU	Scorpio	Water	Fruitful	1st
23 FRI 12:17 am	Sagittarius	Fire	Barren	1st
24 SAT	Sagittarius	Fire	Barren	1st
25 SUN 12:05 pm	Capricorn	Earth	Semi-fruit	1st
26 MON	Capricorn	Earth	Semi-fruit	1st
27 TUE 9:45 pm	Aquarius	Air	Barren	1st
28 WED	Aquarius	Air	Barren	2nd 6:46 am
29 THU	Aquarius	Air	Barren	2nd
30 FRI 3:58 am	Pisces	Water	Fruitful	2nd
31 SAT	Pisces	Water	Fruitful	2nd

October

Lunar Aspectatian — Favorable and Unfavorable Days

	Sun	Mercury	Venus	Mars	Jupiter	Saturn	Uranus	Neptune	Pluto	Aries	Taurus	Gemini	Cancer	Leo	Virgo	Libra	Scorpio	Sagittarius	Capricorn	Aquarius	Pisces
1	T	T					C		X	f	u	f		U		f	u	f		F	
2				0		X				f	u	f		U		f	u	f		F	
3									Q		f	u	f		U		f	u	f		F
4					C			X			f	u	f		U		f	u	f		F
5	0		0				X		T	F		f	u	f		U		f	u	f	
6		0		T		C		Q		F		f	u	f		U		f	u	f	
7							Q				F		f	u	f		U		f	u	f
8				Q	X			T			F		f	u	f		U		f	u	f
9	T		T				T		0	f		F		f	u	f		U		f	u
10		T			Q	X				f		F		f	u	f		U		f	u
11			Q	X						u	f		F		f	u	f		U		f
12	Q				T					u	f		F		f	u	f		U		f
13		Q				Q	0	0	T	u	f		F		f	u	f		U		f
14	X		X							f	u	f		F		f	u	f		U	
15				C		T			Q	f	u	f		F		f	u	f		U	
16		X									f	u	f		F		f	u	f		U
17					0			T			f	u	f		F		f	u	f		U
18							T		X	U		f	u	f		F		f	u	f	
19			C							U		f	u	f		F		f	u	f	
20	C					0		Q		U		f	u	f		F		f	u	f	
21		C		X			Q				U		f	u	f		F		f	u	f
22					T			X			U		f	u	f		F		f	u	f
23				Q			X		C		U		f	u	f		F		f	u	f
24					Q					f		U		f	u	f		F		f	u
25	X		X			T				f		U		f	u	f		F		f	u
26				T						u	f		U		f	u	f		F		f
27		X			X	Q		C		u	f		U		f	u	f		F		f
28	Q		Q				C		X	f	u	f		U		f	u	f		F	
29		Q								f	u	f		U		f	u	f		F	
30	T		T			X			Q	f	u	f		U		f	u	f		F	
31				0	C						f	u	f		U		f	u	f		F

November Moon Table

Date	Sign	Element	Nature	Phase
1 SUN 6:27 am	Aries	Fire	Barren	2nd
2 MON	Aries	Fire	Barren	2nd
3 TUE 6:12 am	Taurus	Earth	Semi-fruit	2nd
4 WED	Taurus	Earth	Semi-fruit	Full 12:18 am
5 THU 5:11 am	Gemini	Air	Barren	3rd
6 FRI	Gemini	Air	Barren	3rd
7 SAT 5:39 am	Cancer	Water	Fruitful	3rd
8 SUN	Cancer	Water	Fruitful	3rd
9 MON 9:33 am	Leo	Fire	Barren	3rd
10 TUE	Leo	Fire	Barren	4th 7:29 pm
11 WED 5:38 pm	Virgo	Earth	Barren	4th
12 THU	Virgo	Earth	Barren	4th
13 FRI	Virgo	Earth	Barren	4th
14 SAT 4:58 am	Libra	Air	Semi-fruit	4th
15 SUN	Libra	Air	Semi-fruit	4th
16 MON 5:42 pm	Scorpio	Water	Fruitful	4th
17 TUE	Scorpio	Water	Fruitful	4th
18 WED	Scorpio	Water	Fruitful	New 11:27 pm
19 THU 6:13 am	Sagittarius	Fire	Barren	1st
20 FRI	Sagittarius	Fire	Barren	1st
21 SAT 5:46 pm	Capricorn	Earth	Semi-fruit	1st
22 SUN	Capricorn	Earth	Semi-fruit	1st
23 MON	Capricorn	Earth	Semi-fruit	1st
24 TUE 3:43 am	Aquarius	Air	Barren	1st
25 WED	Aquarius	Air	Barren	1st
26 THU 11:14 am	Pisces	Water	Fruitful	2nd 7:22 pm
27 FRI	Pisces	Water	Fruitful	2nd
28 SAT 3:34 pm	Aries	Fire	Barren	2nd
29 SUN	Aries	Fire	Barren	2nd
30 MON 4:52 pm	Taurus	Earth	Semi-fruit	2nd

November

Lunar Aspectatian — Favorable and Unfavorable Days

	Sun	Mercury	Venus	Mars	Jupiter	Saturn	Uranus	Neptune	Pluto	Aries	Taurus	Gemini	Cancer	Leo	Virgo	Libra	Scorpio	Sagittarius	Capricorn	Aquarius	Pisces
1		T					X	X	T		f	u	f		U		f	u	f		F
2										F		f	u	f		U		f	u	f	
3						C	Q	Q		F		f	u	f		U		f	u	f	
4	0		0	T	X						F		f	u	f		U		f	u	f
5		0					T	T	0		F		f	u	f		U		f	u	f
6				Q	Q					f		F		f	u	f		U		f	u
7						X				f		F		f	u	f		U		f	u
8	T		T	X	T					u	f		F		f	u	f		U		f
9						Q		0	T	u	f		F		f	u	f		U		f
10	Q	T					0			f	u	f		F		f	u	f		U	
11			Q			T				f	u	f		F		f	u	f		U	
12		Q							Q		f	u	f		F		f	u	f		U
13	X		X	C	0						f	u	f		F		f	u	f		U
14							T	T	X		f	u	f		F		f	u	f		U
15		X								U		f	u	f		F		f	u	f	
16						0		Q		U		f	u	f		F		f	u	f	
17							Q				U		f	u	f		F		f	u	f
18	C			X	T						U		f	u	f		F		f	u	f
19			C					X	C		U		f	u	f		F		f	u	f
20		C			Q		X			f		U		f	u	f		F		f	u
21				Q		T				f		U		f	u	f		F		f	u
22										u	f		U		f	u	f		F		f
23					X	Q				u	f		U		f	u	f		F		f
24	X		X	T			C	C	X	u	f		U		f	u	f		F		f
25		X								f	u	f		U		f	u	f		F	
26	Q					X				f	u	f		U		f	u	f		F	
27		Q	Q		C				Q		f	u	f		U		f	u	f		F
28				0				X			f	u	f		U		f	u	f		F
29	T	T	T				X		T	F		f	u	f		U		f	u	f	
30						C		Q		F		f	u	f		U		f	u	f	

December Moon Table

Date	Sign	Element	Nature	Phase
1 TUE	Taurus	Earth	Semi-fruit	2nd
2 WED 4:30 pm	Gemini	Air	Barren	2nd
3 THU	Gemini	Air	Barren	Full 10:20 am
4 FRI 4:28 pm	Cancer	Water	Fruitful	3rd
5 SAT	Cancer	Water	Fruitful	3rd
6 SUN 6:56 pm	Leo	Fire	Barren	3rd
7 MON	Leo	Fire	Barren	3rd
8 TUE	Leo	Fire	Barren	3rd
9 WED 1:22 am	Virgo	Earth	Barren	3rd
10 THU	Virgo	Earth	Barren	4th 12:54 pm
11 FRI 11:44 am	Libra	Air	Semi-fruit	4th
12 SAT	Libra	Air	Semi-fruit	4th
13 SUN	Libra	Air	Semi-fruit	4th
14 MON 12:17	Scorpio	Water	Fruitful	4th
15 TUE	Scorpio	Water	Fruitful	4th
16 WED 12:47 pm	Sagittarius	Fire	Barren	4th
17 THU	Sagittarius	Fire	Barren	4th
18 FRI 11:55 pm	Capricorn	Earth	Semi-fruit	New 5:42 pm
19 SAT	Capricorn	Earth	Semi-fruit	1st
20 SUN	Capricorn	Earth	Semi-fruit	1st
21 MON 9:17 am	Aquarius	Air	Barren	1st
22 TUE	Aquarius	Air	Barren	1st
23 WED 4:45 pm	Pisces	Water	Fruitful	1st
24 THU	Pisces	Water	Fruitful	1st
25 FRI 10:04 pm	Aries	Fire	Barren	1st
26 SAT	Aries	Fire	Barren	2nd 5:46 am
27 SUN	Aries	Fire	Barren	2nd
28 MON 1:05 am	Taurus	Earth	Semi-fruit	2nd
29 TUE	Taurus	Earth	Semi-fruit	2nd
30 WED 2:22 am	Gemini	Air	Barren	2nd
31 THU	Gemini	Air	Barren	2nd

December

Lunar Aspectatian | Favorable and Unfavorable Days

	Sun	Mercury	Venus	Mars	Jupiter	Saturn	Uranus	Neptune	Pluto	Aries	Taurus	Gemini	Cancer	Leo	Virgo	Libra	Scorpio	Sagittarius	Capricorn	Aquarius	Pisces
1					X		Q				F		f	u	f		U		f	u	f
2				T				T			F		f	u	f		U		f	u	f
3	0	0			Q		T		0	f		F		f	u	f		U		f	u
4			0	Q		X				f		F		f	u	f		U		f	u
5										u	f		F		f	u	f		U		f
6		T			T	Q		0		u	f		F		f	u	f		U		f
7	T			X			0		T	f	u	f		F		f	u	f		U	
8			T			T				f	u	f		F		f	u	f		U	
9		Q							Q	f	u	f		F		f	u	f		U	
10	Q				0						f	u	f		F		f	u	f		U
11		X	Q					T			f	u	f		F		f	u	f		U
12				C			T		X	U		f	u	f		F		f	u	f	
13	X					0				U		f	u	f		F		f	u	f	
14			X				Q	Q		U		f	u	f		F		f	u	f	
15					T						U		f	u	f		F		f	u	f
16		C						X			U		f	u	f		F		f	u	f
17				X			X		C	f		U		f	u	f		F		f	u
18	C				Q	T				f		U		f	u	f		F		f	u
19			C	Q						u	f		U		f	u	f		F		f
20					X					u	f		U		f	u	f		F		f
21						Q		C		u	f		U		f	u	f		F		f
22		X		T			C		X	f	u	f		U		f	u	f		F	
23	X					X				f	u	f		U		f	u	f		F	
24		Q	X						Q		f	u	f		U		f	u	f		F
25					C			X			f	u	f		U		f	u	f		F
26	Q	T					X		T	F		f	u	f		U		f	u	f	
27			Q	0		C				F		f	u	f		U		f	u	f	
28	T						Q	Q		F		f	u	f		U		f	u	f	
29			T		X						F		f	u	f		U		f	u	f
30							T	T	0		F		f	u	f		U		f	u	f
31		0		T	Q	X				f		F		f	u	f		U		f	u

The Moon's Quarters & Signs

Everyone has seen the Moon wax and wane through a period of approximately twenty-nine and a half days. This circuit from New Moon to Full Moon and back again is called the lunation cycle. The cycle is divided into parts, called quarters or phases. There are several methods by which this can be done, and the system used in the *Moon Sign Book* may not correspond to those used in other almanacs.

The Quarters

First Quarter

The first quarter begins at the New Moon, when the Sun and Moon are in the same place, or conjunct. (This means that the Sun and Moon are in the same degree of the same sign.) The Moon is not visible at first, since it rises at the same time as the Sun. The **New Moon** is the time of new beginnings, beginnings of projects that favor growth, externalization of activities, and the growth of ideas. The first quarter is the time of germination, emergence, beginnings, and outwardly directed activity.

Second Quarter

The second quarter begins halfway between the New Moon and the Full Moon, when the Sun and Moon are at right angles, or a 90 degree square to each other. This half Moon rises around noon and sets around midnight, so it can be seen in the western sky during the first half of the night. The second quarter is the time of growth, development, and articulation of things that already exist.

Third Quarter

The third quarter begins at the Full Moon, when the Sun and Moon are opposite one another and the full light of the Sun can shine on the full sphere of the Moon. The round Moon can be seen rising in the east at sunset, and then rising a little later each evening. The **Full Moon** stands for illumination, fulfillment, culmination, completion, drawing inward, unrest, emotional expressions, and hasty actions leading to failure. The third quarter is a time of maturity, fruition, and the assumption of the full form of expression.

Fourth Quarter

The fourth quarter begins about halfway between the Full Moon and New Moon, when the Sun and Moon are again at 90 degrees, or square. This decreasing Moon rises at midnight, and can be seen in the east during the last half of the night, reaching the overhead position just about as the Sun rises. The fourth quarter is a time of disintegration, drawing back for reorganization and reflection.

The Signs

Moon in Aries

Good for starting things, but lacking in staying power. Things occur rapidly, but also quickly pass.

Moon in Taurus

Things begun now last the longest and tend to increase in value. Things begun now become habitual and hard to alter.

Moon in Gemini

An inconsistent position for the Moon. Things begun now are easily changed by outside influence. A lot of talk.

Moon in Cancer

Stimulates emotional rapport between people. Pinpoints need, supports growth and nurturance.

Moon in Leo

Showmanship, favors being seen, drama, recreation, and happy pursuits. May be overly concerned with praise and subject to flattery.

Moon in Virgo

Favors accomplishment of details and commands from higher up while discouraging independent thinking.

Moon in Libra

Increases self-awareness, favors self-examination and interaction with others, but discourages spontaneous initiative.

Moon in Scorpio

Increases awareness of psychic power. Precipitates psychic crises and ends connections thoroughly.

Moon in Sagittarius

Encourages expansionary flights of imagination and confidence in the flow of life.

Moon in Capricorn

Increases awareness of the need for structure, discipline, and organization. Institutional activities are favored.

Moon in Aquarius

Favors activites that are unique and individualistic, concern for the humanitarian needs, society as a whole, and improvements that can be made.

Moon in Pisces

Energy withdraws from the surface of life, hibernates within, secretly reorganizing and realigning for a new day.

Retrogrades

When the planets cross the sky, they occasionally appear to move backward as seen from Earth. When a planet turns "backward" it is said to be *retrograde*. When it turns forward again, it is said to go *direct*. The point at which the movement changes from one direction to another is called a *station*.

When a planet is retrograde, its expression is delayed or out of kilter with the normal progression of events. Generally, it can be said that whatever is planned during this period will be delayed, but usually it will come to fruition when the retrograde is over. Of course, this only applies to activities ruled by the planet that is retrograde. Mercury and Venus retrogrades are easy to follow.

Mercury Retrograde

Mercury rules informal communications—reading, writing, speaking, and short errands. Whenever Mercury goes retrograde, personal communications get fouled up or misunderstood. The general rule is *when Mercury is retrograde, avoid informal means of communication*.

Planetary Stations for 1998 (EST)

Planet	Begin		End	
Venus	12/26/97	4:15 pm	02/05/98	4:26 pm
Pluto	03/10/98	7:19 pm	08/15/98	11:14 pm
Mercury	03/27/98	2:37 pm	04/20/98	2:28 am
Neptune	05/04/98	12:26 am	10/11/98	7:10 am
Uranus	05/17/98	5:54 am	10/18/98	1:46 pm
Jupiter	07/17/98	7:55 pm	11/13/98	7:33 am
Mercury	07/30/98	9:23 pm	08/23/98	5:30 pm
Saturn	08/15/98	12:17 pm	12/29/98	10:14 am
Mercury	11/21/98	6:40 am	12/11/98	1:24 am

Moon Void-of-Course

By Kim Rogers-Gallagher

The Moon makes a loop around the Earth in about twenty-eight days, moving through each of the signs in two and a half days (or so). As she passes through the 30 degrees of each sign, she "visits" with the planets in numerical order by forming angles or aspects with them. Because she moves one degree in just two to two and a half hours, her influence on each planet lasts only a few hours, then she moves along. As she approaches the late degrees of the sign she's passing through, she eventually reaches the planet that's in the highest degree of any sign, and forms what will be her final aspect before leaving the sign. From this point until she actually enters the new sign, she is referred to as void-of-course, or void.

Think of it this way: The Moon is the emotional "tone" of the day, carrying feelings with her particular to the sign she's "wearing" at the moment. After she has contacted each of the planets, she symbolically "rests" before changing her costume, so her instinct is temporarily on hold. It's during this time that many people feel "fuzzy" or "vague"—scattered, even. Plans or decisions we make now will usually not pan out. Without the instinctual "knowing" the Moon provides as she touches each planet, we tend to be unrealistic or exercise poor judgment. The traditional definition of the void Moon is that "nothing will come of this," and it seems to be true. Actions initiated under a void Moon are often wasted, irrelevant, or incorrect—usually because information is hidden or missing, or has been overlooked.

Now, although it's not a good time to initiate plans, routine tasks seem to go along just fine. However, this period is really ideal for what the Moon does best: reflection. It's at this time that we can assimilate what the world's tossed at us over the past few days.

On the lighter side, remember that there are other good uses for the void Moon. This is the time period when the universe seems to be most open to loopholes. It's a great time to make plans you don't want to fulfill or schedule things you don't want to do. See the table on pages 56–61 for a schedule of the 1998 void-of-course Moons.

Moon Void-of-Course

Last Aspect		Moon Enters New Sign		
Date	Time	Date	Sign	Time
		January		
1	4:08 pm	2	Pisces	4:56 am
4	6:09 am	4	Aries	7:44 am
6	9:25 am	6	Taurus	10:53 am
8	1:22 pm	8	Gemini	2:42 pm
10	3:45 pm	10	Cancer	7:43 pm
13	1:37 am	13	Leo	2:45 am
15	3:23 am	15	Virgo	12:31 pm
17	11:54 pm	18	Libra	12:45 am
20	12:57 pm	20	Scorpio	1:35 pm
23	12:00 am	23	Sagittarius	12:26 am
25	3:27 am	25	Capricorn	7:40 am
27	11:22 am	27	Aquarius	11:27 am
29	10:54 am	29	Pisces	1:09 pm
31	9:06 am	31	Aries	2:21 pm
		February		
2	3:46 pm	2	Taurus	4:25 pm
4	12:08 am	4	Gemini	8:09 pm
6	2:58 am	7	Cancer	1:58 am
8	12:28 pm	9	Leo	9:57 am
11	5:23 am	11	Virgo	8:10 pm
13	11:21 am	14	Libra	8:18 am
16	5:15 pm	16	Scorpio	9:14 pm
19	5:26 am	19	Sagittarius	8:56 am
21	1:08 am	21	Capricorn	5:30 pm
23	12:01 pm	23	Aquarius	10:10 pm
25	3:41 am	25	Pisces	11:42 pm
27	6:25 pm	27	Aries	11:42 pm
		March		
1	8:57 pm	2	Taurus	12:01 am

Moon Void-of-Course

Last Aspect		Moon Enters New Sign		
Date	**Time**	**Date**	**Sign**	**Time**
4	1:45 am	4	Gemini	2:15 am
6	12:09 am	6	Cancer	7:27 am
7	6:33 pm	8	Leo	3:46 pm
10	5:06 am	11	Virgo	2:36 am
12	11:35 pm	13	Libra	2:59 pm
15	7:04 am	16	Scorpio	3:51 am
18	11:45 am	18	Sagittarius	3:56 pm
20	7:29 am	21	Capricorn	1:43 am
22	3:29 pm	23	Aquarius	8:02 am
24	7:51 pm	25	Pisces	10:43 am
26	6:03 am	27	Aries	10:49 am
28	8:59 pm	29	Taurus	10:07 am
31	12:30 am	31	Gemini	10:38 am
		April		
2	7:23 am	2	Cancer	2:10 pm
4	9:35 am	4	Leo	9:36 pm
6	11:41 pm	7	Virgo	8:26 am
8	2:30 pm	9	Libra	9:05 pm
12	9:15 am	12	Scorpio	9:55 am
13	6:10 pm	14	Sagittarius	9:52 pm
17	2:33 am	17	Capricorn	8:05 am
19	2:53 pm	19	Aquarius	3:42 pm
21	10:32 am	21	Pisces	8:07 pm
23	2:35 am	23	Aries	9:31 pm
25	1:06 pm	25	Taurus	9:09 pm
27	9:47 am	27	Gemini	8:56 pm
29	3:21 pm	29	Cancer	10:57 pm
		May		
2	1:38 am	2	Leo	4:49 am
4	6:49 am	4	Virgo	2:47 pm

Moon Void-of-Course

Last Aspect		Moon Enters New Sign		
Date	**Time**	**Date**	**Sign**	**Time**
6	8:11 am	7	Libra	3:19 am
9	9:19 am	9	Scorpio	4:10 pm
11	11:06 am	12	Sagittarius	3:48 am
14	12:43 pm	14	Capricorn	1:40 pm
16	4:54 pm	16	Aquarius	9:31 pm
21	2:45 am	21	Aries	6:06 am
23	4:13 am	23	Taurus	7:06 am
24	9:15 pm	25	Gemini	7:25 am
27	6:43 am	27	Cancer	8:58 am
29	1:09 pm	29	Leo	1:38 pm
31	9:24 pm	31	Virgo	10:21 pm
		June		
3	12:08 am	3	Libra	10:17 am
5	10:29 pm	5	Scorpio	11:06 pm
8	2:01 am	8	Sagittarius	10:35 am
10	12:08 pm	10	Capricorn	7:51 pm
12	8:04 pm	13	Aquarius	3:03 am
14	9:39 pm	15	Pisces	8:32 am
17	6:34 am	17	Aries	12:23 pm
19	11:48 am	19	Taurus	2:47 pm
21	11:24 am	21	Gemini	4:26 pm
23	1:46 pm	23	Cancer	6:39 pm
25	6:11 pm	25	Leo	11:04 pm
27	8:05 pm	28	Virgo	6:55 am
30	5:58 pm	30	Libra	6:06 pm
		July		
3	2:35 am	3	Scorpio	6:46 am
5	2:09 pm	5	Sagittarius	6:24 pm
7	11:34 pm	8	Capricorn	3:28 am
10	6:15 am	10	Aquarius	9:52 am

Moon Void-of-Course

Last Aspect		Moon Enters New Sign		
Date	**Time**	**Date**	**Sign**	**Time**
11	10:48 pm	12	Pisces	2:22 pm
16	2:51 pm	16	Taurus	8:33 pm
18	8:01 pm	18	Gemini	11:18 pm
20	11:20 pm	21	Cancer	2:43 am
23	4:14 am	23	Leo	7:49 am
25	9:57 am	25	Virgo	3:34 pm
27	10:03 pm	28	Libra	2:15 am
30	11:13 am	30	Scorpio	2:45 pm
		August		
1	11:02 pm	2	Sagittarius	2:48 am
4	7:45 am	4	Capricorn	12:18 pm
6	1:59 pm	6	Aquarius	6:31 pm
8	1:47 pm	8	Pisces	10:04 pm
10	7:25 pm	11	Aries	12:11 am
13	1:53 am	13	Taurus	2:05 am
14	11:18 pm	15	Gemini	4:46 am
17	2:56 am	17	Cancer	8:56 am
19	1:48 pm	19	Leo	3:01 pm
21	9:03 pm	21	Virgo	11:22 pm
24	9:58 am	24	Libra	10:02 am
26	10:14 PM	26	Scorpio	10:25 pm
29	10:38 AM	29	Sagittarius	10:55 am
31	11:57 am	31	Capricorn	9:23 pm
		September		
3	3:56 am	3	Aquarius	4:21 am
5	4:56 am	5	Pisces	7:48 am
7	8:23 am	7	Aries	8:53 am
9	8:43 am	9	Taurus	9:17 am
11	10:03 am	11	Gemini	10:41 am
13	2:47 am	13	Cancer	2:20 pm

Moon Void-of-Course

Last Aspect		Moon Enters New Sign		
Date	**Time**	**Date**	**Sign**	**Time**
15	7:59 pm	15	Leo	8:48 pm
17	5:57 am	18	Virgo	5:51 am
20	3:57 pm	20	Libra	4:57 pm
23	4:18 am	23	Scorpio	5:22 am
25	4:59 pm	25	Sagittarius	6:05 pm
27	10:42 pm	28	Capricorn	5:31 am
30	1:27 pm	30	Aquarius	1:54 pm
		October		
2	1:28 pm	2	Pisces	6:24 pm
4	6:35 pm	4	Aries	7:32 pm
6	6:26 pm	6	Taurus	6:58 pm
8	5:44 pm	8	Gemini	6:44 pm
10	5:36 pm	10	Cancer	8:48 pm
13	1:17 am	13	Leo	2:25 am
14	6:54 pm	15	Virgo	11:32 am
17	9:50 pm	17	Libra	11:02 pm
20	10:25 am	20	Scorpio	11:37 am
22	11:07 pm	23	Sagittarius	12:17 am
24	1:58 pm	25	Capricorn	12:05 pm
27	9:24 pm	27	Aquarius	9:45 pm
30	3:20 am	30	Pisces	3:58 am
		November		
1	5:59 am	1	Aries	6:27 am
3	5:28 am	3	Taurus	6:12 am
5	4:29 am	5	Gemini	5:11 am
7	4:01 am	7	Cancer	5:39 am
9	8:52 am	9	Leo	9:33 am
11	3:06 pm	11	Virgo	5:38 pm
14	4:22 am	14	Libra	4:58 am
16	5:11 pm	16	Scorpio	5:42 pm

Moon Void-of-Course

Last Aspect		Moon Enters New Sign		
Date	**Time**	**Date**	**Sign**	**Time**
19	5:49 am	19	Sagittarius	6:13 am
21	1:52 pm	21	Capricorn	5:46 pm
24	3:33 am	24	Aquarius	3:43 am
26	7:10 am	26	Pisces	11:14 am
27	7:56 pm	28	Aries	3:34 pm
30	12:53 pm	30	Taurus	4:52 pm
		December		
1	10:43 pm	2	Gemini	4:30 pm
4	12:08 pm	4	Cancer	4:28 pm
6	2:09 pm	6	Leo	6:56 pm
8	8:02 pm	9	Virgo	1:22 am
11	11:31 am	11	Libra	11:44 am
13	6:11 pm	14	Scorpio	12:17 am
15	4:33 pm	16	Sagittarius	12:47 pm
18	5:50 pm	18	Capricorn	11:55 pm
21	3:18 am	21	Aquarius	9:17 am
23	10:56 am	23	Pisces	4:45 pm
25	6:23 am	25	Aries	10:04 pm
27	7:42 pm	28	Taurus	1:05 am
29	2:22 pm	30	Gemini	2:22 am

Find Your Moon Sign

Every year we give tables for the position of the Moon during that year, but it is more complicated to provide tables for the Moon's position in any given year because of its continuous movement. However, the problem was solved by Grant Lewi in *Astrology for the Millions* (available from Llewellyn).

Grant Lewi's System

1. Find your birth year in the Natal Moon Tables (pages 64–74).

2. Run down the left-hand column and see if your date is there.

3. If your date is in the left-hand column, run over this line until you come to the column under your birth year. Here you will find a number. This is your base number. Write it down, and go directly to the direction under the heading "What to Do with Your Base Number" on the next page.

4. If your birth date is not in the left-hand column, get a pencil and paper. Your birth date falls between two numbers in the left-hand column. Look at the date closest after your birth date; run across this line to your birth year. Write down the number you find there, and label it "top number." Having done this, write directly beneath it on your piece of paper the number printed just above it in the table. Label this "bottom number." Subtract the bottom number from the top number. If the top number is smaller, add 360 to it and then subtract. The result is your difference.

5. Go back to the left-hand column and find the date before your birth date. Determine the number of days between this date and your birth date. Write this down and label it "intervening days."

6. In the table of difference below, note which group your difference (found at 4, above) falls in.

Difference	Daily Motion
80–87	12 degrees
88–94	13 degrees
95–101	14 degrees
102–106	15 degrees

Note: If you were born in a leap year and use the difference between February 26 and March 5, use the following table:

Difference	Daily Motion
94–99	12 degrees
100–108	13 degrees
109–115	14 degrees
115–122	15 degrees

7. Write down the "daily motion" corresponding to your place in the proper table of difference above. Multiply daily motion by the number labeled "intervening days" (found at step 5).

8. Add the result of step 7 to your bottom number (under step 4). This is your base number. If it is more than 360, subtract 360 from it and call the result your base number.

What to Do with Your Base Number

Turn to the Table of Base Numbers and locate your base number in it. At the top of the column you will find the sign your Moon was in. At the left you will find the degree the Moon occupied at 7 am of your birth date if you were born under Eastern Standard Time (EST); 6 am of your birth date if you were born under Central Standard Time (CST); 5 am of your birth date if you were born under Mountain Standard Time (MST); 4 am of your birth date if you were born under Pacific Standard Time (PST).

If you don't know the hour of your birth, accept this as your Moon's sign and degree. If you do know the hour of your birth, get the exact degree as follows:

If you were born after 7 am Eastern Standard Time (6 am Central Standard Time, etc.), determine the number of hours after the time that you were born. Divide this by two. Add this to your base number, and the result in the table will be the exact degree and sign of the Moon on the year, month, date, and hour of your birth.

If you were born before 7 am Eastern Standard Time (6 am Central Standard Time, etc.), determine the number of hours before the time that you were born. Divide this by two. Subtract this from your base number, and the result in the table will be the exact degree and sign of the Moon on the year, month, date, and hour of your birth.

Following is a key for the astrological symbols found on the Table of Base Numbers:

♈ Aries
♉ Taurus
♊ Gemini
♋ Cancer
♌ Leo
♍ Virgo
♎ Libra
♏ Scorpio
♐ Sagittarius
♑ Capricorn
♒ Aquarius
♓ Pisces

Table of Base Numbers

	♈ (13)	♉ (14)	♊ (15)	♋ (16)	♌ (17)	♍ (18)	♎ (19)	♏ (20)	♐ (21)	♑ (22)	♒ (23)	♓ (24)
0°	0	30	60	90	120	150	180	210	240	270	300	330
1°	1	31	61	91	121	151	181	211	241	271	301	331
2°	2	32	62	92	122	152	182	212	242	272	302	332
3°	3	33	63	93	123	153	183	213	243	273	303	333
4°	4	34	64	94	124	154	184	214	244	274	304	334
5°	5	35	65	95	125	155	185	215	245	275	305	335
6°	6	36	66	96	126	156	186	216	246	276	306	336
7°	7	37	67	97	127	157	187	217	247	277	307	337
8°	8	38	68	98	128	158	188	218	248	278	308	338
9°	9	39	69	99	129	159	189	219	249	279	309	339
10°	10	40	70	100	130	160	190	220	250	280	310	340
11°	11	41	71	101	131	161	191	221	251	281	311	341
12°	12	42	72	102	132	162	192	222	252	282	312	342
13°	13	43	73	103	133	163	193	223	253	283	313	343
14°	14	44	74	104	134	164	194	224	254	284	314	344
15°	15	45	75	105	135	165	195	225	255	285	315	345
16°	16	46	76	106	136	166	196	226	256	286	316	346
17°	17	47	77	107	137	167	197	227	257	287	317	347
18°	18	48	78	108	138	168	198	228	258	288	318	248
19°	19	49	79	109	139	169	199	229	259	289	319	349
20°	20	50	80	110	140	170	200	230	260	290	320	350
21°	21	51	81	111	141	171	201	231	261	291	321	351
22°	22	52	82	112	142	172	202	232	262	292	322	352
23°	23	53	83	113	143	173	203	233	263	293	323	353
24°	24	54	84	114	144	174	204	234	264	294	324	354
25°	25	55	85	115	145	175	205	235	265	295	325	355
26°	26	56	86	116	146	176	206	236	266	296	326	356
27°	27	57	87	117	147	177	207	237	267	297	327	357
28°	28	58	88	118	148	178	208	238	268	298	328	358
29°	29	59	89	119	149	179	209	239	269	299	329	359

		1901	1902	1903	1904	1905	1906	1907	1908	1909	1910
Jan.	1	55	188	308	76	227	358	119	246	39	168
Jan.	8	149	272	37	179	319	82	208	350	129	252
Jan,	15	234	2	141	270	43	174	311	81	213	346
Jan.	22	327	101	234	353	138	273	44	164	309	84
Jan.	29	66	196	317	84	238	6	128	255	50	175
Feb.	5	158	280	46	188	328	90	219	359	138	259
Feb.	12	241	12	149	279	51	184	319	90	221	356
Feb.	19	335	111	242	2	146	283	52	173	317	94
Feb.	26	76	204	326	92	248	13	136	264	60	184
Mar.	5	166	288	57	211	336	98	229	21	147	267
Mar.	12	249	22	157	300	60	194	328	110	230	5
Mar.	19	344	121	250	24	154	293	60	195	325	105
Mar.	26	86	212	334	116	258	22	144	288	69	192
Apr.	2	175	296	68	219	345	106	240	29	155	276
Apr.	9	258	31	167	309	69	202	338	118	240	13
Apr.	16	352	132	258	33	163	304	68	204	334	115
Apr.	23	96	220	342	127	267	31	152	299	77	201
Apr.	30	184	304	78	227	354	114	250	38	164	285
May	7	267	40	177	317	78	210	348	126	249	21
May	14	1	142	266	42	172	313	76	212	344	124
May	21	104	229	350	138	275	40	160	310	85	210
May	28	193	313	87	236	2	123	259	47	172	294
Jun.	4	277	48	187	324	88	219	358	134	258	30
Jun.	11	11	151	275	50	182	322	85	220	355	132
Jun.	18	112	238	359	149	283	48	169	320	93	218
Jun.	25	201	322	96	245	11	133	267	57	180	304
Jul.	2	286	57	197	333	97	228	8	142	267	40
Jul.	9	21	160	283	58	193	330	94	228	6	140
Jul.	16	121	247	7	159	291	57	178	330	102	226
Jul.	23	209	332	105	255	18	143	276	66	188	314
Jul.	30	295	66	206	341	105	239	17	151	275	51
Aug.	6	32	168	292	66	204	338	103	237	17	148
Aug.	13	130	255	17	168	301	65	188	339	111	234
Aug.	20	217	341	113	265	27	152	285	76	197	323
Aug.	27	303	77	215	350	113	250	25	160	283	62
Sep.	3	43	176	301	75	215	346	111	246	27	157
Sep.	10	139	263	27	176	310	73	198	347	121	242
Sep.	17	225	350	123	274	35	161	294	85	205	331
Sep.	24	311	88	223	358	122	261	33	169	292	73
Oct.	1	53	185	309	85	224	355	119	256	35	166
Oct.	8	149	271	36	185	320	81	207	356	130	250
Oct.	15	233	359	133	283	44	169	305	93	214	339
Oct.	22	319	99	231	7	130	271	42	177	301	83
Oct.	29	62	194	317	95	233	5	127	266	44	176
Nov.	5	158	279	45	193	329	89	216	5	139	259
Nov.	12	242	6	144	291	53	177	316	101	223	347
Nov.	19	328	109	239	15	140	280	50	185	311	91
Nov.	26	70	203	325	105	241	14	135	276	52	185
Dec.	3	168	288	54	203	338	98	224	15	148	268
Dec.	10	251	14	155	299	61	185	327	109	231	356
Dec.	17	338	118	248	23	150	289	59	193	322	99
Dec.	24	78	213	333	115	249	23	143	286	61	194
Dec.	31	176	296	61	213	346	107	232	26	155	277

		1911	1912	1913	1914	1915	1916	1917	1918	1919	1920
Jan.	1	289	57	211	337	100	228	23	147	270	39
Jan.	8	20	162	299	61	192	332	110	231	5	143
Jan.	15	122	251	23	158	293	61	193	329	103	231
Jan.	22	214	335	120	256	23	145	290	68	193	316
Jan.	29	298	66	221	345	108	237	32	155	278	49
Feb.	5	31	170	308	69	203	340	118	239	16	150
Feb.	12	130	260	32	167	302	70	203	338	113	239
Feb.	19	222	344	128	266	31	154	298	78	201	325
Feb.	26	306	75	231	353	116	248	41	164	286	60
Mar.	5	42	192	317	77	214	2	127	248	26	172
Mar.	12	140	280	41	176	311	89	212	346	123	259
Mar.	19	230	5	136	276	39	176	308	87	209	346
Mar.	26	314	100	239	2	124	273	49	173	294	85
Apr.	2	52	200	326	86	223	10	135	257	35	181
Apr.	9	150	288	51	184	321	97	222	355	133	267
Apr.	16	238	14	146	286	48	184	318	96	218	355
Apr.	23	322	111	247	11	132	284	57	181	303	96
Apr.	30	61	208	334	96	232	19	143	267	43	190
May	7	160	296	60	192	331	105	231	4	142	275
May	14	246	22	156	294	56	192	329	104	227	3
May	21	331	122	255	20	141	294	66	190	312	105
May	28	69	218	342	106	240	29	151	277	51	200
Jun.	4	170	304	69	202	341	114	240	14	151	284
Jun.	11	255	30	167	302	65	200	340	112	235	11
Jun.	18	340	132	264	28	151	304	74	198	322	114
Jun.	25	78	228	350	115	249	39	159	286	60	209
Jul.	2	179	312	78	212	349	122	248	25	159	293
Jul.	9	264	39	178	310	74	209	350	120	244	20
Jul.	16	349	141	273	36	161	312	84	206	332	123
Jul.	23	87	237	358	125	258	48	168	295	70	218
Jul.	30	187	321	86	223	357	131	256	36	167	302
Aug.	6	272	48	188	319	82	219	360	129	252	31
Aug.	13	359	150	282	44	171	320	93	214	342	131
Aug.	20	96	246	6	133	268	57	177	303	81	226
Aug.	27	195	330	94	234	5	140	265	46	175	310
Sep.	3	281	57	198	328	90	229	9	138	260	41
Sep.	10	9	158	292	52	180	329	102	222	351	140
Sep.	17	107	255	15	141	279	65	186	312	91	234
Sep.	24	203	339	103	244	13	149	274	56	184	319
Oct.	1	288	68	206	337	98	240	17	148	268	52
Oct.	8	18	167	301	61	189	338	111	231	360	150
Oct.	15	118	263	24	149	290	73.	195	320	102	242
Oct.	22	212	347	113	254	22	157	284	65	193	326
Oct.	29	296	78	214	346	106	250	25	157	276	61
Nov.	5	26	177	309	70	197	348	119	240	7	161
Nov.	12	129	271	33	158	300	81	203	329	112	250
Nov.	19	221	355	123	262	31	164	295	73	202	334
Nov.	26	305	88	223	355	115	259	34	165	285	70
Dec.	3	34	187	317	79	205	359	127	249	16	171
Dec.	10	138	279	41	168	310	89	211	340	120	259
Dec.	17	230	3	134	270	40	172	305	81	211	343
Dec.	24	313	97	232	3	124	267	44	173	294	78
Dec.	31	42	198	325	87	214	9	135	257	25	181

		1921	1922	1923	1924	1925	1926	1927	1928	1929	1930
Jan.	1	194	317	80	211	5	127	250	23	176	297
Jan.	8	280	41	177	313	90	211	349	123	260	22
Jan.	15	4	141	275	41	175	312	86	211	346	123
Jan.	22	101	239	3	127	272	51	172	297	83	222
Jan.	29	203	325	88	222	13	135	258	34	184	306
Feb.	5	289	49	188	321	99	220	359	131	269	31
Feb.	12	14	149	284	49	185	320	95	219	356	131
Feb.	19	110	249	11	135	281	60	181	305	93	230
Feb.	26	211	334	96	233	21	144	266	45	191	314
Mar.	5	297	58	197	343	107	230	8	153	276	41
Mar.	12	23	157	294	69	194	328	105	238	6	140
Mar.	19	119	258	19	157	292	68	190	327	104	238
Mar.	26	219	343	104	258	29	153	275	70	200	323
Apr.	2	305	68	205	352	115	240	16	163	284	51
Apr.	9	33	166	304	77	204	337	114	247	14	149
Apr.	16	130	266	28	164	303	76	198	335	115	246
Apr.	23	227	351	114	268	38	161	285	79	208	331
Apr.	30	313	78	214	1	123	250	25	172	292	61
May	7	42	176	313	85	212	348	123	256	23	160
May	14	141	274	37	173	314	84	207	344	125	254
May	21	236	359	123	277	47	169	295	88	217	339
May	28	321	88	222	11	131	259	34	181	301	70
Jun.	4	50	186	321	94	220	358	131	264	31	171
Jun.	11	152	282	45	182	324	93	215	354	135	263
Jun.	18	245	7	134	285	56	177	305	96	226	347
Jun.	25	330	97	232	20	139	268	44	190	310	78
Jul.	2	58	197	329	103	229	9	139	273	40	181
Jul.	9	162	291	54	192	333	101	223	4	144	272
Jul.	16	254	15	144	294	65	185	315	104	236	355
Jul.	23	338	106	242	28	148	276	54	198	319	87
Jul.	30	67	208	337	112	238	20	147	282	49	191
Aug.	6	171	300	62	202	341	110	231	15	152	281
Aug.	13	264	24	153	302	74	194	324	114	244	4
Aug.	20	347	114	253	36	157	285	65	206	328	95
Aug.	27	76	218	346	120	248	29	156	290	59	200
Sep.	3	179	309	70	213	350	119	239	25	161	290
Sep.	10	273	32	162	312	83	203	332	124	252	13
Sep.	17	356	122	264	44	166	293	75	214	337	105
Sep.	24	86	227	354	128	258	38	165	298	70	208
Oct.	1	187	318	78	223	358	128	248	35	169	298
Oct.	8	281	41	170	322	91	212	340	134	260	23
Oct.	15	5	132	274	52	175	303	85	222	345	115
Oct.	22	97	235	3	136	269	46	174	306	81	216
Oct.	29	196	327	87	232	7	137	257	44	179	307
Nov.	5	289	50	178	332	99	221	349	144	268	31
Nov.	12	13	142	283	61	183	313	93	231	353	126
Nov.	19	107	243	12	144	279	54	183	315	91	225
Nov.	26	206	335	96	241	17	145	266	52	189	314
Dec.	3	297	59	187	343	107	230	359	154	276	39
Dec.	10	21	152	291	70	191	324	101	240	1	137
Dec.	17	117	252	21	153	289	63	191	324	99	234
Dec.	24	216	343	105	249	28	152	275	60	199	322
Dec.	31	305	67	197	352	115	237	9	162	285	47

		1931	1932	1933	1934	1935	1936	1937	1938	1939	1940
Jan.	1	60	196	346	107	231	8	156	277	41	181
Jan.	8	162	294	70	193	333	104	240	4	144	275
Jan.	15	257	20	158	294	68	190	329	104	239	360
Jan.	22	342	108	255	32	152	278	67	202	323	88
Jan.	29	68	207	353	116	239	19	163	286	49	191
Feb.	5	171	302	78	203	342	113	248	14	153	284
Feb.	12	267	28	168	302	78	198	339	113	248	8
Feb.	19	351	116	266	40	161	286	78	210	332	96
Feb.	26	77	217	1	124	248	29	171	294	59	200
Mar.	5	179	324	86	213	350	135	256	25	161	306
Mar.	12	276	48	176	311	86	218	347	123	256	29
Mar.	19	360	137	277	48	170	308	89	218	340	119
Mar.	26	86	241	10	132	258	52	180	302	69	223
Apr.	2	187	334	94	223	358	144	264	34	169	315
Apr.	9	285	57	185	321	95	227	355	133	264	38
Apr.	16	9	146	287	56	178	317	99	226	349	128
Apr.	23	96	250	18	140	268	61	189	310	80	231
Apr.	30	196	343	102	232	7	153	273	43	179	323
May	7	293	66	193	332	103	237	4	144	272	47
May	14	17	155	297	64	187	327	108	235	357	139
May	21	107	258	28	148	278	69	198	318	90	239
May	28	205	351	111	241	17	161	282	51	189	331
Jun.	4	301	75	201	343	111	245	13	154	280	55
Jun.	11	25	165	306	73	195	337	117	244	5	150
Jun.	18	117	267	37	157	288	78	207	327	99	248
Jun.	25	215	360	120	249	28	169	291	60	200	339
Jul.	2	309	84	211	353	119	254	23	164	289	64
Jul.	9	33	176	315	82	203	348	125	253	13	160
Jul.	16	126	276	46	165	297	87	216	336	108	258
Jul.	23	226	8	130	258	38	177	300	69	210	347
Jul.	30	317	92	221	2	128	262	33	173	298	72
Aug.	6	41	187	323	91	211	359	133	261	21	170
Aug.	13	135	285	54	175	305	97	224	346	116	268
Aug.	20	237	16	138	267	49	185	308	78	220	355
Aug.	27	326	100	232	10	136	270	44	181	307	80
Sep.	3	49	197	331	100	220	8	142	270	31	179
Sep.	10	143	295	62	184	314	107	232	355	125	278
Sep.	17	247	24	147	277	58	194	317	89	228	4
Sep.	24	335	108	243	18	145	278	55	189	316	88
Oct.	1	58	206	341	108	229	17	152	278	40	188
Oct.	8	151	306	70	193	322	117	240	4	134	288
Oct.	15	256	32	155	287	66	203	324	100	236	13
Oct.	22	344	116	253	27	154	287	64	198	324	98
Oct.	29	68	214	350	116	239	25	162	286	49	196
Nov.	5	161	316	78	201	332	126	248	12	145	297
Nov.	12	264	41	162	298	74	212	333	111	244	22
Nov.	19	353	125	262	36	162	296	73	207	332	108
Nov.	26	77	222	0	124	248	33	172	294	58	205
Dec.	3	171	325	87	209	343	135	257	19	156	305
Dec.	10	272	50	171	309	82	220	341	120	253	30
Dec.	17	1	135	271	45	170	306	81	217	340	118
Dec.	24	86	231	10	132	256	43	181	302	66	214
Dec.	31	182	333	95	217	354	142	265	27	167	313

		1941	1942	1943	1944	1945	1946	1947	1948	1949	1950
Jan.	1	325	88	211	353	135	258	22	165	305	68
Jan.	8	50	176	315	85	219	348	126	256	29	160
Jan.	15	141	276	50	169	312	87	220	340	123	258
Jan.	22	239	12	133	258	52	182	303	69	224	352
Jan.	29	333	96	221	2	143	266	32	174	314	75
Feb.	5	57	186	323	95	227	358	134	265	37	170
Feb.	12	150	285	58	178	320	96	228	349	131	268
Feb.	19	250	20	142	267	62	190	312	78	234	359
Feb.	26	342	104	231	11	152	274	43	182	323	83
Mar.	5	65	196	331	116	236	8	142	286	46	179
Mar.	12	158	295	66	199	328	107	236	10	139	279
Mar.	19	261	28	150	290	72	198	320	102	243	8
Mar.	26	351	112	242	34	161	281	53	204	332	91
Apr.	2	74	205	340	125	244	16	152	294	55	187
Apr.	9	166	306	74	208	337	117	244	19	148	289
Apr.	16	270	36	158	300	81	206	328	112	252	17
Apr.	23	360	120	252	42	170	290	63	212	340	100
Apr.	30	83	214	350	133	254	25	162	302	64	195
May	7	174	316	82	217	346	127	252	27	158	299
May	14	279	45	166	311	90	215	336	123	260	26
May	21	9	128	261	50	179	299	72	221	349	110
May	28	92	222	1	141	263	33	173	310	73	204
Jun.	4	184	326	91	226	356	137	261	36	168	307
Jun.	11	287	54	174	322	98	224	344	134	268	34
Jun.	18	17	137	270	60	187	308	81	231	357	119
Jun.	25	102	231	11	149	272	42	183	318	82	213
Jul.	2	194	335	99	234	7	145	269	44	179	316
Jul.	9	296	63	183	332	106	233	353	144	277	43
Jul.	16	25	147	279	70	195	318	89	241	5	129
Jul.	23	110	240	21	157	280	52	192	327	91	224
Jul.	30	205	343	108	242	18	153	278	52	190	324
Aug.	6	304	71	192	341	115	241	3	153	286	51
Aug.	13	33	156	287	80	203	327	98	251	13	138
Aug.	20	119	250	30	165	289	63	201	336	99	235
Aug.	27	216	351	117	250	28	162	287	61	200	332
Sep.	3	314	80	201	350	125	249	13	161	296	59
Sep.	10	41	165	296	90	211	336	108	260	21	146
Sep.	17	127	261	39	174	297	74	209	345	107	246
Sep.	24	226	359	126	259	38	170	295	70	209	341
Oct.	1	323	88	211	358	135	257	22	170	306	67
Oct.	8	49	174	306	99	220	344	118	269	30	154
Oct.	15	135	272	47	183	305	84	217	353	116	256
Oct.	22	236	8	134	269	47	180	303	80	217	351
Oct.	29	333	95	220	7	144	265	31	179	315	75
Nov.	5	58	181	317	107	229	352	129	277	39	162
Nov.	12	143	283	55	192	314	94	225	1	125	265
Nov.	19	244	18	141	279	55	189	311	90	225	0
Nov.	26	343	104	229	16	153	274	39	189	323	84
Dec.	3	67	189	328	115	237	360	140	284	47	171
Dec.	10	153	292	64	200	324	103	234	9	136	274
Dec.	17	252	28	149	289	63	199	319	100	234	9
Dec.	24	351	112	237	27	161	282	47	199	331	93
Dec.	31	76	198	338	123	246	9	150	293	55	180

		1951	1952	1953	1954	1955	1956	1957	1958	1959	1960
Jan.	1	194	336	115	238	6	147	285	47	178	317
Jan.	8	297	67	199	331	107	237	9	143	278	47
Jan.	15	30	150	294	70	200	320	104	242	9	131
Jan.	22	114	240	35	161	284	51	207	331	94	223
Jan.	29	204	344	124	245	17	155	294	55	189	325
Feb.	5	305	76	207	341	116	246	18	152	287	56
Feb.	12	38	159	302	80	208	330	112	252	17	140
Feb.	19	122	249	45	169	292	61	216	340	102	233
Feb.	26	215	352	133	253	27	163	303	63	199	333
Mar.	5	314	96	216	350	125	266	27	161	297	75
Mar.	12	46	180	310	91	216	351	121	262	25	161
Mar.	19	130	274	54	178	300	86	224	349	110	259
Mar.	26	225	14	142	262	37	185	312	72	208	356
Apr.	2	324	104	226	358	135	274	37	169	307	83
Apr.	9	54	189	319	100	224	360	131	271	34	170
Apr.	16	138	285	62	187	308	97	232	357	118	269
Apr.	23	235	23	150	271	46	194	320	82	217	5
Apr.	30	334	112	235	6	146	282	48	177	317	91
May	7	62	197	330	109	232	8	142	279	42	177
May	14	146	296	70	196	316	107	240	6	127	279
May	21	243	32	158	280	54	204	328	91	225	15
May	28	344	120	244	15	155	290	55	187	326	100
Jun.	4	71	205	341	117	241	16	153	288	51	186
Jun.	11	155	306	79	204	325	117	249	14	137	288
Jun.	18	252	42	166	290	63	214	336	101	234	25
Jun.	25	354	128	253	26	164	298	63	198	335	109
Jul.	2	80	214	351	125	250	24	164	296	60	195
Jul.	9	164	315	88	212	335	126	259	22	147	297
Jul.	16	260	52	174	299	72	223	344	110	243	34
Jul.	23	3	137	261	37	173	307	71	209	343	118
Jul.	30	89	222	2	134	258	33	174	304	68	205
Aug.	6	174	324	97	220	345	134	268	30	156	305
Aug.	13	270	62	182	308	82	232	353	118	254	42
Aug.	20	11	146	269	48	181	316	79	220	351	126
Aug.	27	97	232	11	143	267	43	183	314	76	215
Sep.	3	184	332	107	228	355	143	278	38	166	314
Sep.	10	280	71	191	316	92	241	2	127	265	50
Sep.	17	19	155	278	58	189	325	88	230	359	135
Sep.	24	105	242	20	152	274	54	191	323	84	225
Oct.	1	193	341	116	237	4	152	287	47	174	324
Oct.	8	291	79	200	324	103	249	11	135	276	58
Oct.	15	27	163	287	68	198	333	98	239	8	143
Oct.	22	113	252	28	162	282	64	199	332	92	235
Oct.	29	201	350	125	245	12	162	295	56	182	334
Nov.	5	302	87	209	333	114	256	19	144	286	66
Nov.	12	36	171	297	76	207	341	109	247	17	150
Nov.	19	121	262	37	171	291	73	208	341	101	244
Nov.	26	209	0	133	254	20	173	303	65	190	345
Dec.	3	312	95	217	342	124	265	27	154	295	75
Dec.	10	45	179	307	84	216	348	119	255	27	158
Dec.	17	129	271	46	180	299	82	218	350	110	252
Dec.	24	217	11	141	263	28	184	311	73	199	355
Dec.	31	321	103	225	352	132	273	35	164	303	84

		1961	1962	1963	1964	1965	1966	1967	1968	1969	1970
Jan.	1	96	217	350	128	266	27	163	298	76	197
Jan.	8	179	315	89	217	350	126	260	27	161	297
Jan.	15	275	54	179	302	86	225	349	112	257	36
Jan.	22	18	141	264	35	189	311	74	207	359	122
Jan.	29	105	225	1	136	275	35	173	306	85	206
Feb.	5	188	323	99	225	360	134	270	35	171	305
Feb.	12	284	64	187	310	95	235	357	121	267	45
Feb.	19	26	150	272	46	197	320	81	218	7	130
Feb.	26	113	234	11	144	283	45	182	315	93	216
Mar.	5	198	331	109	245	9	142	280	54	180	313
Mar.	12	293	73	195	332	105	244	5	142	277	54
Mar.	19	34	159	280	71	205	329	90	243	15	139
Mar.	26	122	243	19	167	291	54	190	338	101	226
Apr.	2	208	340	119	253	18	151	290	63	189	323
Apr.	9	303	82	204	340	116	252	14	150	288	62
Apr.	16	42	167	288	81	213	337	99	253	23	147
Apr.	23	130	253	28	176	299	64	198	347	109	235
Apr.	30	216	349	128	261	27	161	298	71	197	333
May	7	314	90	213	348	127	260	23	158	299	70
May	14	51	176	298	91	222	345	109	262	32	155
May	21	137	263	36	186	307	74	207	357	117	245
May	28	225	359	137	270	35	172	307	80	205	344
Jun.	4	325	98	222	357	137	268	31	168	309	78
Jun.	11	60	184	308	99	231	353	119	270	42	163
Jun.	18	146	272	45	195	315	82	217	6	126	253
Jun.	25	233	10	145	279	43	183	315	89	214	355
Jul.	2	336	106	230	6	147	276	40	178	318	87
Jul.	9	70	191	318	108	241	1	129	279	51	171
Jul.	16	154	281	56	204	324	91	227	14	135	261
Jul.	23	241	21	153	288	52	193	323	98	223	5
Jul.	30	345	115	238	16	156	286	47	188	327	97
Aug.	6	79	200	327	116	250	10	138	288	60	180
Aug.	13	163	289	66	212	333	99	238	22	144	270
Aug.	20	250	32	161	296	61	203	331	106	233	14
Aug.	27	353	124	246	27	164	295	55	199	335	106
Sep.	3	88	208	336	126	259	19	147	297	68	189
Sep.	10	172	297	77	220	342	108	249	30	152	279
Sep.	17	260	41	170	304	72	212	340	114	244	23
Sep.	24	1	134	254	37	172	304	64	208	344	115
Oct.	1	97	217	344	136	267	28	155	308	76	198
Oct.	8	180	306	88	228	351	117	259	38	161	289
Oct.	15	270	50	179	312	82	220	350	122	254	31
Oct.	22	10	143	262	47	182	313	73	217	353	123
Oct.	29	105	226	352	146	275	37	163	318	84	207
Nov.	5	189	315	97	237	359	127	268	47	168	299
Nov.	12	281	58	188	320	93	228	359	130	264	39
Nov.	19	19	151	271	55	191	321	82	225	3	131
Nov.	26	113	235	1	157	282	45	172	328	92	215
Dec.	3	197	326	105	245	7	138	276	55	176	310
Dec.	10	291	66	197	328	102	237	7	139	273	48
Dec.	17	30	159	280	63	202	329	91	234	13	139
Dec.	24	121	243	11	167	291	53	183	337	101	223
Dec.	31	204	336	113	254	14	149	284	64	184	320

		1971	1972	1973	1974	1975	1976	1977	1978	1979	1980
Jan.	1	335	109	246	8	147	279	56	179	318	90
Jan.	8	71	197	332	108	243	6	144	278	54	176
Jan.	15	158	283	69	207	328	93	240	18	139	263
Jan.	22	244	20	169	292	54	192	339	102	224	4
Jan.	29	344	117	255	17	156	288	64	188	327	99
Feb.	5	81	204	342	116	253	14	153	287	63	184
Feb.	12	167	291	79	216	337	101	251	26	147	271
Feb.	19	252	31	177	300	62	203	347	110	233	14
Feb.	26	353	126	263	27	164	297	72	199	334	109
Mar.	5	91	224	351	124	262	34	162	296	72	204
Mar.	12	176	312	90	224	346	122	262	34	156	203
Mar.	19	261	55	185	309	72	226	356	118	243	37
Mar.	26	1	149	270	37	172	320	80	208	343	130
Apr.	2	100	233	360	134	270	43	170	307	80	213
Apr.	9	184	320	101	232	355	131	273	42	164	302
Apr.	16	271	64	194	317	82	235	5	126	254	46
Apr.	23	9	158	278	47	181	329	88	217	352	139
Apr.	30	109	242	8	145	278	52	178	318	88	222
May	7	193	329	111	240	3	141	282	50	173	312
May	14	281	73	203	324	92	243	14	134	264	54
May	21	19	167	287	55	191	337	97	226	3	147
May	28	117	251	16	156	286	61	187	328	96	231
Jun.	4	201	339	120	249	11	151	291	59	180	323
Jun.	11	291	81	213	333	102	252	23	143	273	63
Jun.	18	29	176	296	64	201	346	106	234	13	155
Jun.	25	125	260	25	167	295	69	196	338	105	239
Jul.	2	209	349	129	258	19	162	299	68	188	334
Jul.	9	300	90	222	341	111	261	32	152	282	72
Jul.	16	40	184	305	72	212	354	115	243	24	163
Jul.	23	133	268	35	176	303	78	206	347	114	248
Jul.	30	217	0	137	267	27	172	308	77	197	344
Aug.	6	309	99	230	350	120	271	40	161	290	83
Aug.	13	51	192	314	81	223	2	124	252	34	171
Aug.	20	142	276	45	185	312	86	217	356	123	256
Aug.	27	225	10	146	276	36	182	317	86	206	353
Sep.	3	317	109	238	360	128	281	48	170	299	93
Sep.	10	61	200	322	90	232	10	132	262	43	180
Sep.	17	151	284	56	193	321	94	228	4	132	264
Sep.	24	234	20	155	284	45	191	326	94	215	2
Oct.	1	325	120	246	9	136	291	56	179	308	103
Oct.	8	70	208	330	101	241	19	140	273	51	189
Oct.	15	160	292	66	202	330	102	238	12	140	273
Oct.	22	243	28	165	292	54	199	336	102	225	10
Oct.	29	334	130	254	17	146	301	64	187	318	112
Nov.	5	79	217	338	112	249	27	148	284	59	197
Nov.	12	169	300	76	210	339	111	247	21	148	282
Nov.	19	253	36	175	300	63	207	347	110	234	18
Nov.	26	344	139	262	25	156	310	73	195	329	120
Dec.	3	87	226	346	122	257	36	157	294	67	206
Dec.	10	177	310	84	220	347	121	255	31	156	292
Dec.	17	261	45	185	308	72	216	356	118	242	28
Dec.	24	355	148	271	33	167	318	81	203	340	128
Dec.	31	95	235	355	132	265	44	166	303	76	214

		1981	1982	1983	1984	1985	1986	1987	1988	1989	1990
Jan.	1	226	350	129	260	36	162	300	71	205	333
Jan.	8	315	89	225	346	126	260	36	156	297	72
Jan.	15	53	188	309	73	225	358	119	243	37	168
Jan.	22	149	272	35	176	319	82	206	348	129	252
Jan.	29	234	0	137	270	43	172	308	81	213	343
Feb.	5	324	98	234	354	135	270	44	164	306	82
Feb.	12	64	196	317	81	236	6	128	252	48	175
Feb.	19	157	280	45	185	328	90	217	356	138	260
Feb.	26	242	10	145	279	51	182	316	90	222	353
Mar.	5	332	108	242	15	143	280	52	185	313	93
Mar.	12	74	204	326	104	246	14	136	275	57	184
Mar.	19	166	288	55	208	337	97	227	19	147	268
Mar.	26	250	20	154	300	60	191	326	111	230	1
Apr.	2	340	119	250	24	151	291	60	194	322	103
Apr.	9	84	212	334	114	255	22	144	286	66	192
Apr.	16	175	296	66	216	346	106	237	27	156	276
Apr.	23	259	28	164	309	69	199	336	119	240	9
Apr.	30	349	130	258	33	160	302	68	203	331	113
May	7	93	221	342	124	264	31	152	297	75	201
May	14	184	304	75	225	355	114	246	36	165	285
May	21	268	36	175	317	78	207	347	127	249	18
May	28	358	140	266	41	170	311	76	211	341	122
Jun.	4	102	230	350	135	272	40	160	307	83	210
Jun.	11	193	313	84	234	3	123	255	45	173	294
Jun.	18	277	45	185	325	87	216	357	135	258	27
Jun.	25	8	149	275	49	180	320	85	219	352	130
Jul.	2	110	239	359	146	281	49	169	317	92	219
Jul.	9	201	322	93	244	11	133	263	55	181	304
Jul.	16	286	54	196	333	96	225	7	143	266	37
Jul.	23	19	158	284	57	191	328	94	227	3	138
Jul.	30	119	248	7	155	290	57	178	327	101	227
Aug.	6	210	331	101	254	19	142	272	66	189	313
Aug.	13	294	64	205	341	104	236	16	152	274	48
Aug.	20	30	166	293	66	202	337	103	236	13	147
Aug.	27	128	256	17	164	299	65	187	335	111	235
Sep.	3	218	340	110	264	27	151	281	75	197	321
Sep.	10	302	75	214	350	112	247	24	160	282	59
Sep.	17	40	174	302	74	212	345	112	245	23	156
Sep.	24	138	264	26	172	309	73	197	343	121	243
Oct.	1	226	349	119	274	36	159	292	84	206	329
Oct.	8	310	86	222	359	120	258	32	169	291	70
Oct.	15	50	183	310	84	220	354	120	255	31	165
Oct.	22	148	272	35	181	319	81	206	352	130	251
Oct.	29	234	357	130	282	44	167	303	92	214	337
Nov.	5	318	96	230	8	129	268	40	178	300	79
Nov.	12	58	193	318	93	229	4	128	265	39	175
Nov.	19	158	280	44	190	329	90	214	2	139	260
Nov.	26	243	5	141	290	53	175	314	100	223	345
Dec.	3	327	106	238	16	139	277	49	185	310	88
Dec.	10	66	203	326	103	237	14	136	274	48	185
Dec.	17	167	288	52	200	337	98	222	12	147	269
Dec.	24	252	13	152	298	62	184	324	108	232	355
Dec.	31	337	114	248	24	149	285	59	193	320	96

		1991	1992	1993	1994	1995	1996	1997	1998	1999	2000
Jan.	1	111	242	15	145	281	53	185	317	92	223
Jan.	8	206	326	108	244	16	136	279	56	186	307
Jan.	15	289	54	210	337	99	225	21	147	270	37
Jan.	22	18	158	299	61	190	329	110	231	2	140
Jan.	29	119	252	23	155	290	62	193	326	101	232
Feb.	5	214	335	116	254	24	145	287	66	193	315
Feb.	12	298	63	220	345	108	235	31	155	278	47
Feb.	19	29	166	308	69	201	337	119	239	12	148
Feb.	26	128	260	32	164	299	70	202	335	111	240
Mar.	5	222	356	124	265	32	166	295	76	201	337
Mar.	12	306	87	229	354	116	259	39	164	285	72
Mar.	19	39	189	317	77	211	360	128	248	22	170
Mar.	26	138	280	41	172	310	90	212	343	121	260
Apr.	2	230	5	133	275	40	175	305	86	210	345
Apr.	9	314	98	237	3	123	270	47	173	294	83
Apr.	16	49	198	326	86	220	9	136	257	31	180
Apr.	23	148	288	50	180	320	98	221	351	132	268
Apr.	30	238	13	143	284	48	183	315	95	218	353
May	7	322	109	245	12	132	281	55	182	302	93
May	14	57	207	335	95	228	18	144	267	39	190
May	21	158	296	59	189	330	106	230	1	141	276
May	28	247	21	154	292	57	191	326	103	227	1
Jun.	4	330	119	253	21	141	291	64	190	311	102
Jun.	11	66	217	343	105	236	28	152	276	48	199
Jun.	18	168	304	68	199	340	114	238	11	150	285
Jun.	25	256	29	165	300	66	199	337	111	236	10
Jul.	2	339	129	262	29	150	300	73	198	321	111
Jul.	9	74	227	351	114	245	38	160	285	57	209
Jul.	16	177	313	76	210	348	123	246	22	158	293
Jul.	23	265	38	175	309	75	208	347	120	245	19
Jul.	30	349	137	272	37	160	308	83	206	331	119
Aug.	6	83	237	359	123	255	48	169	293	67	218
Aug.	13	186	322	84	221	356	132	254	33	166	302
Aug.	20	273	47	185	318	83	218	356	129	253	29
Aug.	27	358	146	282	45	169	317	93	214	340	128
Sep.	3	93	246	7	131	265	56	177	301	78	226
Sep.	10	194	331	92	231	4	141	263	43	174	311
Sep.	17	281	56	194	327	91	228	5	138	261	39
Sep.	24	8	154	292	53	178	326	102	223	349	137
Oct.	1	104	254	16	139	276	64	186	310	89	234
Oct.	8	202	339	101	241	13	149	273	53	183	319
Oct.	15	289	66	202	337	99	238	13	148	269	49
Oct.	22	16	164	301	61	187	336	111	231	357	148
Oct.	29	115	262	25	148	287	72	195	318	100	242
Nov.	5	211	347	111	250	22	157	283	61	193	326
Nov.	12	297	76	211	346	107	247	22	157	277	58
Nov.	19	24	174	309	70	194	346	119	240	5	159
Nov.	26	126	270	33	156	297	80	203	328	109	251
Dec.	3	220	355	121	258	31	165	293	69	202	334
Dec.	10	305	85	220	355	115	256	31	165	286	67
Dec.	17	32	185	317	79	203	357	127	249	13	169
Dec.	24	135	278	41	166	306	89	211	338	117	260
Dec.	31	230	3	131	266	41	173	303	78	211	343

Home, Health, &
Beauty
☽ How to Choose the Best Dates for Home, Health, & Beauty Activities
☽ Surgery & the Zodiac
The Secrets of Beer Making • Hops • Drying Food by the Moon • Holiday Herbs • Lunar Fertility • Your Moon Sign & Your Link to Mother • The Moon & Relationships • New Moon, New Start • Healing with Fire, Earth, Air, & Water • Exercise, Diet, & Weight Loss by the Moon • The Cell Salts • Love Under a Moon Spell

Home, Health, & Beauty

How to Choose the Best Dates

Automobile Purchase

The Moon is helpful when in favorable aspect to Mercury and Uranus and in the signs of Gemini or Sagittarius, which correspond to travel. Also try the fixed signs (Aquarius, Taurus, Leo, and Scorpio), which correspond to reliable purchases.

Automobile Repair

The Moon should be in favorable aspect to Uranus and in the signs of Taurus, Leo, Aquarius, or Virgo. The first and second quarters are best. Avoid any unfavorable aspects between the Moon and Mars, Saturn, Uranus, Neptune, or Pluto.

Baking

Baking should be done when the Moon is in Cancer. Bakers who have experimented say that dough rises higher and bread is lighter during the increase of the Moon (first or second quarter). If it is not possible to bake under the sign of Cancer, try Aries, Libra, or Capricorn.

Beauty Care

For beauty treatments, skin care, and massage, the Moon should be in Taurus, Cancer, Leo, Libra, or Aquarius, and sextile, trine, or conjunct Venus and/or Jupiter.

Plastic surgery should be done in the increase of the Moon, when the Moon is not square or opposite (Q or O) Mars. Nor should the Moon be in the sign ruling the area to be operated on. Avoid days when the Moon is square or opposite Saturn or the Sun.

Fingernails should be cut when the Moon is not in any aspect with Mercury or Jupiter. Saturn and Mars must not be marked Q or O because this makes the nails grow slowly or thin and weak. The Moon should be in Aries, Taurus, Cancer, or Leo. For toenails, the Moon should not be in Gemini or Pisces. Corns are best cut in the third or fourth quarter.

Brewing

It is best to brew during the Full Moon and the fourth quarter. Plan to have the Moon in Cancer, Scorpio, or Pisces.

Building

Turning the first sod for the foundation of a home or laying the cornerstone for a public building marks the beginning of the building. Excavate, lay foundations, and pour cement when the Moon is Full and in Taurus, Leo, or Aquarius. Saturn should be aspected, but not Mars, which indicates accidents.

Canning

Can fruits and vegetables when the Moon is in either the third or fourth quarter, and when it is in Cancer or Pisces. For preserves and jellies, use the same quarters but see that the Moon is in Cancer, Pisces, or Taurus.

Cement and Concrete

Pour cement and concrete during the Full Moon in Taurus, Leo, or Aquarius.

Dental Work

Pick a day that is marked favorable for your Sun sign. Mars should be marked X, T, or C and Saturn, Uranus, and Jupiter should not be marked Q or O.

Teeth are best removed during the increase of the Moon in the first or second quarter in Gemini, Virgo, Sagittarius, Capricorn, or Pisces. Avoid the Full Moon! The day should be favorable for your lunar cycle, and Mars and Saturn should be marked C, T, or X.

Fillings should be done in the third or fourth quarters in the signs of Taurus, Leo, Scorpio, or Aquarius. The same applies for plates.

Dieting

Weight gain occurs more readily when the Moon is in a water sign (Cancer, Scorpio, Pisces). Experience has shown that weight may be lost if a diet is started when the Moon is decreasing in light (third or fourth quarter) and when it is in Aries, Leo, Virgo, Sagittarius, or Aquarius. The lunar cycle should be favorable on the day you wish to begin your diet.

Dressmaking

Design, cut, repair, or make clothes in Taurus, Leo, or Libra on a day marked favorable for your Sun sign. First and second quarters are best. Venus, Jupiter, and Mercury should be aspected, but avoid Mars or Saturn aspects. William Lilly wrote in 1676, "Make no new clothes, or first put them on when the Moon is in Scorpio or afflicted by Mars, for they will be apt to be torn and quickly worn out."

Eyeglasses

Eyes should be tested and glasses fitted on a day marked favorable for your Sun sign and on a day that falls during your favorable lunar cycle. Mars should not be in aspect with the Moon. The same applies for any treatment of the eyes, which should also be started during the increase of the Moon (first or second quarter).

Fence Posts and Poles

Set the posts or poles when the Moon is in the third or fourth quarters. The fixed signs Taurus, Leo, and Aquarius are best for this.

Habits

To end any habit, start on a day when the Moon is in the third or fourth quarter and in a barren sign. Gemini, Leo, or Virgo are the best times, although Aries and Capricorn may be suitable as well. Make sure your lunar cycle is favorable. Avoid lunar aspects to Mars or Jupiter. Aspects to Neptune or Saturn are helpful. These rules apply to smoking.

Hair Care

Haircuts are best when the Moon is in a mutable (Gemini, Sagittarius, Pisces) or earthy sign (Taurus, Capricorn), well placed and aspected, but not in Virgo, which is barren. For faster growth, hair should be cut when the Moon is in Cancer or Pisces in the first or second quarter. To make hair grow thicker, cut it when the Moon is Full or in opposition to the Sun (marked O in the Lunar Aspectarian) in the signs of Taurus, Cancer, or Leo up to and at, but not after, the Full Moon. However, if you want your hair to grow more slowly, the Moon should be in Aries, Gemini, or Virgo in the third or fourth quarter, with Saturn square or opposite the Moon.

Permanents, straightening, and hair coloring will take well if the Moon is in Taurus or Leo and Venus is marked T or X. You should avoid doing your hair if Mars is marked Q or O, especially if heat is to be used. For permanents, a trine to Jupiter is helpful. The Moon also should be in the first quarter, and check the lunar cycle for a favorable day in relation to your Sun sign.

Health

Diagnosis is more likely to be successful when the Moon is in a cardinal sign (Aries, Cancer, Libra, Capricorn), and less so when in a mutable sign (Gemini, Sagittarius, Pisces, Virgo). Begin a program for recuperation when the Moon is in a cardinal or fixed sign and the day is favorable to your sign. Enter hospitals at these times. For surgery, see Surgical Procedures. Buy medicines when the Moon is in Virgo or Scorpio.

House Furnishings

Days when Saturn is aspected make things wear longer and tend to a more conservative purchase. Saturn days are good for buying, and Jupiter days are good for selling.

House Purchasing

If you desire a permanent home, buy when the Moon is in Taurus,

Leo, Scorpio, Aquarius, or Cancer, preferably when the Moon is New. If you're buying for speculation and a quick turnover, be certain that the Moon is not in a fixed sign, but in Aries, Cancer, or Libra.

Lost Articles

Search for lost articles during the first quarter and when your Sun sign is marked favorable. Also check to see that the planet ruling the lost item is trine, sextile, or conjunct the Moon. The Moon governs household utensils, Mercury letters and books, and Venus clothing, jewelry, and money.

Marriage

The best time for marriage to take place is during the increase of the Moon, just past the first quarter, but not under the Full Moon. Good signs for the Moon to be in are Taurus, Cancer, Leo, and Libra. The Moon in Taurus produces the most steadfast marriages, but if the partners later want to separate they may have a difficult time. Avoid Aries, Gemini, Virgo, Scorpio, and Aquarius. Make sure that the Moon is well aspected (X or T), especially to Venus or Jupiter. Avoid aspects to Mars, Uranus, or Pluto.

Moving

Make sure that Mars is not aspected to the Moon. Try to move on a day that is favorable to your Sun sign, or when the Moon is conjunct, sextile, or trine the Sun.

Mowing the Lawn

Mow the lawn in the first or second quarter to increase growth. If you wish to retard growth, mow in the third or fourth quarter.

Painting

The best time to paint buildings is during the decrease of the Moon (third and fourth quarter).

If the weather is hot, do the painting while the Moon is in Taurus; if the weather is cold, paint while the Moon is in Leo. Another good sign for painting is Aquarius. By painting in the fourth quarter, the wood is drier and the paint will penetrate; when painting around the New Moon the wood is damp and the paint is subject to scalding when hot weather hits it. It is not advisable to paint while the Moon is in a water sign if the temperature is below 70 degrees, as it is apt to creep, check, or run.

Pets

Take home new pets when the date is favorable to your Sun sign, or the Moon is well aspected by the Sun, Venus, Jupiter, Uranus, or Neptune. Avoid days when the Moon is badly aspected (Q or O) by the Sun, Mars, Saturn, Uranus, Neptune, or Pluto.

Train pets starting when the Moon is in Taurus. Neuter them in any sign but Virgo, Libra, Scorpio, or Sagittarius. Avoid the week before and after the Full Moon.

Declaw cats in the dark of the Moon. Avoid the week before and after the Full Moon and the sign of Pisces.

When selecting a new pet it is good to have the Moon well aspected by the planet that rules the animal. Cats are ruled by the Sun, dogs by Mercury, birds by Venus, horses by Jupiter, and fish by Neptune.

Predetermining Sex

Count from the last day of menstruation to the day next beginning, and divide the interval between the two dates into halves. Pregnancy occurring in the first half produces females, but copulation should take place when the Moon is in a feminine sign.

Pregnancy occurring in the latter half, up to within three days of the beginning of menstruation, produces males, but copulation should take place when the Moon is in a masculine sign. This three-day period to the end of the first half of the next period again produces females.

Romance

The same principles hold true for starting a relationship as for marriage. However, since there is less control over when a romance starts, it is sometimes necessary to study it after the fact. Romances begun under an increasing Moon are more likely to be permanent, or at least satisfying. Those started on the waning Moon will more readily transform the participants. The general tone of the relationship can be guessed from the sign the Moon is in. For instance, those begun when the Moon is in Aries may be impulsive and quick to burn out. Those begun in Capricorn will take greater effort to bring them to a desirable conclusion, but they may be very rewarding. Good aspects between the Moon and Venus are excellent influences. Avoid Mars, Uranus, and Pluto aspects. Ending relationships is facilitated by a decreasing Moon, particularly in the fourth quarter. This causes the least pain and attachment.

Sauerkraut

The best tasting sauerkraut is made just after the Full Moon in a fruitful sign (Cancer, Scorpio, or Pisces).

Shingling

Shingling should be done in the decrease of the Moon (third or fourth quarter) when it is in a fixed sign (Taurus, Leo, Scorpio, or Aquarius). If shingles are laid during the New Moon, they have a tendency to curl at the edges.

Surgical Procedures

The flow of blood, like the ocean tides, appears to be related to the Moon's phases. *Time* magazine (page 74, June, 6, 1960) reported that on 1,000 tonsillectomy case histories analyzed by Dr. Edson J. Andrews, only 18 percent of associated hemorrhaging occurred in the fourth and first quarters. Thus, an astrological rule: To reduce hemorrhage after a surgical procedure, plan to have the surgery within one week before or after the New Moon. Avoid surgery within one week before or after the Full Moon.

Also select a date when the Moon is not in the sign governing the part of the body involved in the operation. The further removed the Moon sign from the sign ruling the afflicted part of the body, the better for healing. The signs and the body parts they rule are as follows:

Aries: Head

Taurus: Neck, throat

Gemini: Lungs, nerves, arms, shoulders, hands, fingers

Cancer: Breast, chest, stomach

Leo: Heart, spine, back

Virgo: Nervous system, intestines

Libra: Kidneys

Scorpio: Reproductive organs

Sagittarius: Thighs, hips, liver

Capricorn: Knees, bones, teeth

Aquarius: Circulatory system, shins, ankles

Pisces: Feet

More information on surgery can be found on page 82. For successful operations, there should be no lunar aspects to Mars, and favorable aspects to Venus and Jupiter should be present.

Cosmetic surgery should be done in the increase of the Moon, when the Moon is not in square or opposition to Mars. Avoid days when the Moon is square or opposite Saturn or the Sun.

Weaning Children

This should be done when the Moon is in Sagittarius, Capricorn, Aquarius, or Pisces. The child should nurse for the last time when the Moon is in a fruitful sign. Venus should then be trine, sextile, or conjunct the Moon.

Wine and Drinks Other Than Beer

It is best to start when the Moon is in Pisces or Taurus. Good aspects (X or T) to Venus are favorable. Avoid aspects with Mars or Saturn.

Surgery & the Zodiac

By Louise Riotte

Following is a list of rules for surgical operations using astrology. For more information, see the surgery section on page 81.

1. Operate in the increase of the Moon if possible, but not during the week before the Full Moon.
2. Do not operate at the exact time of the Full Moon, as the fluids are running high at this time.
3. Never operate when the Moon is in the same sign as at the patient's birth (the person's Sun sign).
4. Never operate on that part of the body ruled by the sign through which the Moon is passing at the time, but wait a day or two until the Moon passes into the next sign. Better yet, wait until the Moon is in the sign that rules the body part farthest away from the part to be operated on. (See chart, facing page.)
5. Let the Moon be in a fixed sign, but not in the same sign as the patient's ascendant (rising sign).
6. Do not operate when the Moon is applying to (moving toward) any aspect of Mars, which tends to promote inflammation and complications after the operation. (See the Lunar Aspectarian, pages 28–51 to determine which days have Mars aspects.)
7. There should be good aspects to Venus and Jupiter (X or T in the Lunar Aspectarian).
8. Avoid operations when the Sun is in the sign ruling the body part to be operated on.
9. The Moon should be free of all manner of impediment. There should be no Q or O aspects in the Lunar Aspectarian, and the Moon should not be void-of-course. (See pages 28–51.)
10. Do not cut a nerve when Mercury is afflicted (marked Q or O in the Lunar Aspectarian).
11. When the Moon is conjunct or opposed the Sun (C or O) or when it is opposed by Mars (O), avoid amputations.
12. Good signs for abdominal operations are Sagittarius, Capricorn, or Aquarius.

Zodiac Signs &

Their Corresponding Body Parts

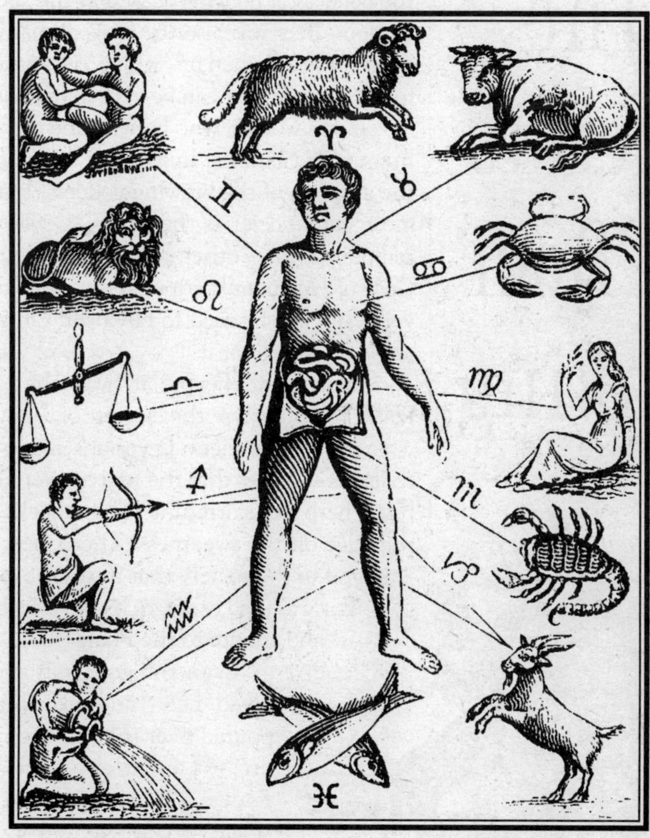

♈	= Aries	♎	= Libra
♉	= Taurus	♏	= Scorpio
♊	= Gemini	♐	= Sagittarius
♋	= Cancer	♑	= Capricorn
♌	= Leo	♒	= Aquarius
♍	= Virgo	♓	= Pisces

The Secrets of Beer Making

By K. D. Spitzer

The Elba Beer advertisement at right was found on a cuneiform tablet from Sumeria, dated at least 1500 years BCE. Also found were hundreds of recipes for beer, and prayers to the goddess Siduri in praise of beer. Siduri was the goddess of brewing as well as the goddess of wisdom. Beer was also the basis of many medicines for the Sumerians, which is not surprising for a beverage that can be very nutritious.

It was women who brewed and served beer in ancient Sumeria, living and working under the auspices of the brewing goddess. Indeed, in most early societies, beer was brewed in the temple. Unlike other cultures, however, the *Code of Hammurabi* stipulated that gold or silver could not be used to buy beer. Only barley could be traded for it.

In ancient Egypt, it was the goddess Hathor who gave the secret of brewing to women. The ancient Egyptians made a beer that was so sweet that the natives would tuck a bitter herb like skirret into their cheeks to take the edge off the sweetness. There, beer was so integral to the society that it was the currency that was used as wages for workers or taxes and tribute to the Pharaoh.

Even the gods and goddesses loved beer, and libations were poured over their statues in tribute. As a matter of fact, drunkenness was regarded as a deeply spiritual state in Egypt, which makes one wonder how they managed to get anything done. Cabbage juice was their chief line of defense against a swollen head. Interestingly enough, in recent years research has shown that the cabbage cure was a smart move, as it neutralized the effects of the alcohol.

The Vikings were another society built on brewing and drinking ale; they often served their ale with garlic to ward off the evil spirits. Indeed, using their runes, they wrote magical inscriptions to throw into their flagons to ward off the effects of poisons and the evil designs of women. Although women were the brewers, in this macho society men felt they needed added protection from female importunities. Drunkenness was not a legal plea, and any statements, pledges, or behavior when drunk were held binding, so you can see that any help from the gods was advantageous.

Drink Ebla—the beer with the heart of a lion

The daughters of Hathor no longer make beer in the temple, but anybody can make beer in a clean kitchen, with or without incantations. It's a very simple process, and you really don't need any great skills to produce a palatable beverage.

Beer Ingredients

Like good Italian or French bread, beer is made with four ingredients: water, fermentable sugars, hops, and yeast. The fermentable sugars are actually grains, with malted barley the traditional one. To malt the grain, the barley (seed) is soaked in water until it sprouts; then it is dried. In this first step, the sugars are developed in the grain, along with soluble starches. (This same process is used to add natural sweetening to bread. The malted barley is ground into flour in this case.)

In a procedure called mashing, these starches are then converted to usable sugars that will ferment. To do this, the grain is again immersed in water, this time at selected temperatures to control the enzymes that convert starches to sugars. It is these sugars that will ferment into alcohol.

Hops has been used in beer for at least a thousand years. Hops is an herb that lends its bitterness to the brew to offset the sweetness of the malt. Hops also helps to retard spoilage.

Water as an ingredient also affects the taste of beer. Although Madison Avenue has managed to convince most Americans of danger in drinking tap water, most municipal water supplies are fine for quality beer making. If you like the flavor of your drinking water, then use it for brewing.

The last of the basic beer ingredients is yeast. Yeast is the catalyst that starts the conversion of sugar to alcohol. Yeasts are living microorganisms that live on sugar during their life cycle. Wild yeasts (those not introduced into the mixture by the brewer) are everywhere, and can also be harmful to the final flavor of the beer, so brewers protect their products from these uninvited guests. A special yeast called brewer's yeast is used for beer making, just as bread is made with baker's yeast. Mainly, two kinds of yeast are cultured for beer making; one for lagers and one for ales.

Brewing Equipment

Beer making is a simple procedure for anyone, as long as they mutter the proper incantations and observe the first law of food preservation: All equipment must be scrubbed clean and sterilized!

Probably it would be wise to start your brewing career with a beer-making kit, moving on to malting your own barley and growing your own hops. Even using a kit for your first batch, you will need to invest in several pieces of equipment.

- 1 four-gallon enameled or stainless steel canning kettle
- 1 glass carboy about 5 or 6 gallons in size
- 1 (10-gallon) plastic trash pail
- 1 (6') length of ⅜" (inside diameter) plastic hose
- 1 fermentation lock and rubber stopper with a hole for the lock
- 1 (2½') length of clear plastic hose, 5⁄16" inside diameter
- 1 plastic funnel
- 1 thermometer
- 1 beer hydrometer
- 1 bottle capper
- 60 new bottle caps
- 60 (12-ounce) beer bottles that do not have screwtops; or fewer larger bottles

Most kits make about five gallons of beer. The toughest decision will be to choose which kit to purchase, as they come in a range of "flavors," from extra pale to very dark.

Preparing to Brew

The instructions below assume that you will be using a brewing kit for your first batch of beer, and that the brewing kit comes with instructions.

First, make sure that all equipment is clean and sanitized. Use a couple ounces of household bleach to five gallons of cold water to rinse the equipment. Make sure that you rinse the mild bleach solution from the equipment so it doesn't affect the flavor of the beer.

Brewing

Follow the directions that come with the beer kit to combine and dissolve the malt extracts in 1½ gallons of water in your canning kettle. Keep the mixture at a slow boil for fifteen minutes. The kits often don't recommend the boiling, but a better beer results. Also, the kits suggest using sugar in an equal amount to the malt extract. The sugar can be eliminated or substituted with a pound of light dried malt extract, and this will make a superior beer.

The malt will be easier to handle if you warm it by sticking the can in hot water before opening. The malt is actually a thick, heavy syrup, thicker than molasses, and stickier than honey.

Next, fill the carboy with 3 gallons of cold water. Then add the hot malt extracts and hot water to the carboy. Cap and agitate to stir the contents. Once the water and malt mixture is well blended, add enough extra water to make 5 gallons. If you have used hops, be sure and strain them out before adding water.

Using the sanitized thermometer, take the temperature of your beer. If it's between 68°F and 78°F, now is the first opportunity to use the new hydrometer, which you have also sanitized. This is an instrument for measuring the density of liquids in relation to water to arrive at specific gravity. At this point comes rule number two: Always keep accurate notes of your methods and recipes.

Fill the hydrometer flask with some of the mixture, insert the hydrometer, and read the density scale. Record this number and the temperature in your notebook. Discard the unfermented beer from the flask. Never return it to the carboy, which could introduce wild yeasts (or bacteria) into the batch. If the temperature is below 78°F, now is the time to add the brewer's yeast. Higher temperatures will kill the yeast.

Place the fermentation lock in the carboy and fill it with water. The period of the most activity occurs now. The first two to three days will be quite exciting as bubbles form in the active fermentation of your brew. Within eight to fourteen days fermentation will slowly diminish and sediment will settle to the bottom of the carboy. The brew will appear darker. Using your hydrometer you can measure the density. If the readings stay the same for three days, you can begin to bottle.

Remember to sanitize all equipment that will come in contact with the beer, i.e. the hoses, the bottle caps, and the bottles.

Once the hydrometer reading has been the same for three days, boil the corn sugar (¾ cup) or dried malt extract (1¼ cup) in 2 cups of cold water for five minutes. Pour this priming sugar into the sanitized plastic pail, and then siphon the beer into the pail with the least amount of agitation, both in you and with the beer. (Put the pail on the floor and the carboy over it on the counter.) Be careful not to disturb or siphon the sediment.

Take another hydrometer reading and record it in your journal. Then carefully siphon the beer/sugar mixture from the bucket into the bottles, filling them within 1 inch from the top. Cap with the sanitized bottle caps and store in a dark cool place. After about fourteen days, the yeasts will drop to the bottom of the bottles and the beer will be ready to drink. Chill, and decant into a glass or pitcher leaving the bottom untouched.

Once you have gained confidence as a brewer, you will want to spread your wings and try different methods and different ingredients until you can formulate your own recipes. Before you know it, you'll need another refrigerator!

Because of the increased demand for beer making information, you'll find several magazines on the shelves, including *Zymurgy*, *World Beer Review*, and *All About Beer*. If you are looking for a comprehensive, clear, and humorous approach to brewing, you'll want to own *The New Complete Joy of Home Brewing* by Charlie Papazian, Avon Books, 1991, ISBN: 0-380-76366-4.

Hops

By K. D. Spitzer

In home gardens, *Humulus lupulus*, or hops, is largely grown as an ornamental vine. Each winter it dies back to the ground, and then in the spring it starts growing again, reaching some twenty to thirty feet in length.

While hops have antiseptic qualities and have been used as a liver tonic, their most important use medicinally is as a sedative. Hop "flowers" are sewn into a pillow and then dampened with water or alcohol so they dodn't "shush" in your ear. It is this sedative quality in the hops that may contribute to beer's reputation for inducing sleep. Indisputably, hops have been used to flavor and preserve beer since at least the ninth century.

There are male and female hops plants, but it is the female that is desirable for commercial as well as home use. The "flowers" resemble a soft, yellow-green hemlock cone, and it is this part of the plant that is useful.

Since the plant is a perennial vine, you'll want to plant yours after the Full Moon and before the fourth quarter. The Moon in Scorpio is the most propitious time. Although hops can be grown from seed, it is better to plant a rooted cutting or a sucker taken from a healthy, older plant. Dig deeply before planting and be sure the soil is hummusy. If you are planning on using the hops for brewing homemade beer, be sure that your plant is not just an ornamental, but a beer hops variety.

Don't be surprised if it takes three years for the plant to produce its flowers. The first year it will just settle in, the second year it will do some vigorous growing, so cut off any flowers that appear and then, in the fall, cut it back to the ground when the Moon is in Capricorn. The third year will mark the beginning of the productive years of the plant.

If you are going to use the hops for beer, then they must be dried as soon as possible. Pick them when they have just turned brown. If you don't have a dehydrator, then dry them in a 125°F oven. For medicinal purposes, it is best to make a tincture of them. Hops lose their flavor quite rapidly and should be used within six months. Be sure to store in a dry and dark place.

Drying Food by the Moon

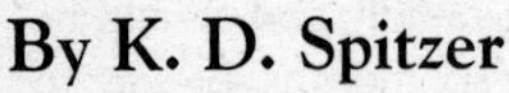

By K. D. Spitzer

If you are one of those who succumbed to late-night hucksters in the frenzy of insomnia, you may have a food dehydrator sitting in baleful reproach in your kitchen. In self-defense, you may have already sent it to the farthest reaches of the cellar. Well, dust it off, because it's time you put it to work.

Fruit for Crafting

If you are a crafter, the dehydrator can be cranking out orange and apple slices for various wreaths, swags, and kitchen ornaments. Combined in various permutations with cinnamon sticks, nutmegs, bay leaves, red chili peppers, and a little natural raffia, you can cover every wall and window in your kitchen. Slice up one of the two boxes of oranges Aunt Edith sent from Florida and you can decorate the walls in your friends' kitchens as well, especially if you were good at stringing beads in kindergarten.

Visit a health food store to buy herbs and spices economically. Using your imagination, you can redecorate your kitchen with a country theme. Buy a glue gun and you can apply your dried fruits to every surface that doesn't move. Having visited craft shows around New England this past season, I can tell you that it's obvious that there can't be enough dried fruit swag!

Drying fruit for crafting is relatively easy. Just slice the citrus or apples a tad less than a quarter inch thick, arrange neatly, without overlapping, in the trays of the dehydrator, and plug it in. Dip apples into a citric acid solution beforehand to avoid browning. You'll need to keep an eye on things and rotate the trays every so often so the fruit dries evenly.

You'll also want to pull the plug before the slices get too dark—they'll actually have a scorched look to them if you let them go too long, and they will continue to darken!

You may have a food dehydrator sitting in baleful reproach in your kitchen…dust it off, because it's time you put it to work

Drying Food to Eat

Food that you are actually going to eat requires a little pre-treatment before drying, and unless you are a hiker (in which case you have probably been using the machine since you bought it) it really isn't very practical to dry most vegetables if you can freeze them. Of course, if you have a garden and surplus of veggies, it might be worthwhile to dehydrate some instead of freezing them in a couple of particular circumstances.

Uses for Dried Vegetables

Dried veggies can be ground finely and later reconstituted to make a healthy and nutritious pureed baby food. Use 2 teaspoons ground veggies to a scant cup of water. Sprinkle a couple teaspoons into a soup or stew for additional flavor and vitamins. Spinach is the one exception to this rule of thumb; it becomes wonderfully concentrated when dried, and ½ teaspoon of powdered spinach is more than enough to add great flavor to the soup pot.

If veggies are not ground but used whole or sliced, their best use is in the soup or stew pot. They don't need to be reconstituted and add wonderful, robust flavor. If you are desperate to use dried veggies in a side dish, plan on about 1 cup of dried veggies for four servings. Reconstitute vegetables by pouring 1½ cups boiling water or broth over 1 cup of dried veggies and let them sit about twenty to thirty minutes. More water can be added. Cook them in whatever liquid wasn't absorbed.

Astrological Signs for Dehydration

Harvest and dehydrate vegetables and fruit when the Moon is in Sagittarius or Aries. They will dry better and store longer. Harvest in the morning after the dew has dried, and choose mature and perfect specimens. A bad spot can ruin the flavor and storage quality of the whole batch.

Preparing for Dehydration

To prepare vegetables for dehydration, tail and tip the green beans, and peel, slice and dice the rest of the vegetable family according to how you use them. Blanch by immersing in boiling water for the time prescribed. (Check the *Ball Blue Book* for guidelines.) Even better, using one of the adjustable metal steamers (and don't overload it), steam blanch for the prescribed time. The same water can be used for all the batches of the same vegetable. Onions, garlic, tomatoes, and herbs do not need to be blanched.

Arrange the veggies in the dehydrator mostly in single layers for maximum air circulation. Herbs like parsley or shredded veggies like cabbage can be piled a little thicker. If your dehydrator doesn't have a fan to move the heated air through the trays, then you'll need to rotate the trays. Vegetables can be dried to an almost brittle state. Again, you'll want to consult the table in a good book on food preserving for the exact moment to remove. The big thing is to avoid scorching.

Let the dried vegetables cool, and then bag or jar accordingly. It is most critical to store them promptly in an airtight container so they don't re-absorb moisture. If you are using a heavy plastic bag, then remove as much air as possible before sealing. Store in a cool, dry, and dark place; the cooler and drier the better, with absolutely no light! This is most important; without any one of these requirements, you will have wasted your efforts and the vegetables. The vegetables are best used in less than six to eight months, or before the next harvest.

If dehydration is done properly, then just the water content is removed from fruits and vegetables, leaving a nutritional powerhouse. When reconstituted, the flavor is about the same as the frozen version and superior to that of canned.

Soup Mix

You can make a homestyle version of "Cup of Soup" using your own dried vegetables, with this adapted and updated recipe from an old hiker's trail soup. Mix up the following just after breakfast.

- 4 tablespoons mixed dried vegetables
- 2 teaspoons red lentils (use only the red as other dried legumes cannot rehydrate quickly enough)
- 1 tablespoon alphabet pasta or any other small pasta, or 1 tablespoon instant couscous, or 1 tablespoon instant rice
- 1 teaspoon parmesan or romano grated cheese
- 1 pinch each of dried basil and dried oregano and dried parsley
- Ground black pepper
- Several drops soy sauce
- 1½ cups boiling vegetable or meat stock

Seal in an insulated container or thermos and enjoy at lunch time.

Dried Tomatoes in Oil

Wash plum tomatoes and slice them in half lengthwise. Place them in the dehydrator cut side up, and sprinkle them with sea salt. Dry them until most of the moisture is gone, but before the tomatoes are brittle. They should seem leathery. You should be able to twist the shrunken tomato half without expressing juice or cracking it. Pack the dried tomatoes in sterilized, wide-mouth half-pint jars. The tomatoes can be layered in a wide-mouth jar, whereas they have to stand on end in a regular jar.

Alternate the layers with fresh basil leaves and slices of garlic. Slide a bay leaf decoratively into the jar alongside the glass. Cover with a good quality olive oil to a quarter inch from the top. Wipe the rim carefully and seal. Process half pint jars in a boiling water bath for twenty minutes.

These tomatoes keep well if stored in a cool, dark place. Refrigerate after opening. Use as you would purchased sun-dried tomatoes, saving the flavored olive oil for salad dressing.

Tomatoes can be reconstituted in wine as well as water and broth. Cut up, they can be added to a fresh tomato sauce for extra zip.

Dried Fruit

Everyone has enjoyed the pleasures of dehydrated fruit, whether eating it out of hand in a trail mix, or as the candied sweet in dessert cakes and cookies. Muffins especially are particularly adaptable to the addition of dried fruit. While dried fruits are more readily available than vegetables, they are easily prepared at home.

Again it is critical to choose perfect, unblemished fruit. Apples should be late fall harvest varieties. Stone fruits should be tree-ripened, and of varieties that can take some handling. Slightly unripe pears can be picked and held a week until ripening, but need to be quite firm for drying. The whole process will be more successful if the fruit is harvested when the Moon is in Aries or Sagittarius.

Preparing Fruit for Dehydration

The preparation for preserving fruit is slightly different than that of vegetables. Certain fruits, when cut open and exposed to the air, turn brown. This process is called oxidation, and contributes to loss of flavor, color, and vitamins. Apples, apricots, bananas, and peaches, which are popular fruits for drying, need a little extra help to halt this process.

The easiest method is to soak fruit slices in a bath with ascorbic acid or lemon juice. Use 1 tablespoon ascorbic acid to 1 quart of water, or juice from half a lemon to 1 quart of water. You only need to soak the fruit for two minutes. Longer soaking will require longer drying time and result in a poorer product. Fruit prepared in this manner will keep quite satisfactorily for six to eight months.

To preserve flavor longer, you'll need to employ a technique copied from the commercial fruit industry, which is sulfuring. This helps fruit to maintain nutrition, shape, color, and pliability. It also fights insects or, of more importance in long-term home preserving, resists mold. Describing this process is beyond the scope of this article, so you'll need to consult another source if you elect to go this route. This must be done out of doors and requires another piece of equipment.

Fruit should be peeled, sliced, halved, seeded and stoned according to your requirements. Plums, cherries, grapes, rhubarb, and berries do not need to be treated before drying. Just stone the fruit and cut up as desired. Various fruits can be mixed during the dehydration process as long as each fruit is placed on its own shelf. Do not mix fruit and vegetables in the dryer.

For a change, you can sprinkle fruit with cinnamon sugar or coconut that has been ground to a powder. You can even sprinkle fruits with dry powdered gelatin for additional flavor. As with vegetables, you need to keep an eye on the fruit, rotating trays as necessary or removing in a timely fashion. Cool and package in airtight containers. Store as for vegetables in a cool, dry, and dark place.

Dried fruit can be eaten as is or reconstituted to add to entrees or baked goods.

Fruit Leather

Fruit leathers are an ancient method to not only preserve fruits, but to make them conveniently portable.

Apple Leather

5 pounds apples, peeled, cored, and chopped

1 cup apple cider

¼ cup sugar

Cinnamon, nutmeg, and cloves to taste

Place apples and cider in a pot with a heavy bottom. Using low heat so the apples don't scorch, bring mixture to a boil. If necessary, add more cider or water to prevent this. Reduce heat, and let apples thicken. Remove from heat and purée with a food mill or food processor. Taste for sweetness and add sugar as needed. Add ground cinnamon, nutmeg, and cloves for spicy flavor, and return to heat to thicken further.

Meanwhile, cut brown paper or parchment paper to fit dehydrator trays without affecting the main circulation of air. If you have a dehydrator with a center hole, do not cover it. When apples are dense enough to spread, cover paper about a quarter inch thick with the apple mixture. Rotate trays as necessary during drying process. When it is dry enough to peel from the paper in one solid sheet, return it to the racks so it will dry on both sides. It should remain pliable, so keep a sharp eye on it at this point. Sprinkle finished fruit leather with corn starch. Store in a cool, dark place.

You can substitute peaches, apricots, or nectarines for the apples and use unsweetened pineapple juice for the cider. Use the same spices or others of your choice to flavor the leather.

Here's a tasty recipe to offer relief from the ubiquitous chili pepper and cilantro flavored dish.

Pot Roast with Dried Fruits

5 pounds beef for pot roast

Olive oil

2 cups water

½ cup red wine

2 tablespoons mixed pickling spice in a spice ball or muslin bag

1 small diced onion

2 teaspoons sea salt

1 pound dried mixed fruit

Brown pot roast in olive oil in a heavy kettle. Drain off any fat and return pot roast to kettle. Add pickling spice, onion, wine, and water. Cover and simmer for two and a half hours. Add salt and fruit and simmer for another hour until meat is tender. Make a gravy as you wish. Slice meat, garnish with fruit and pan juices or gravy.

Recommended Reading

Stocking Up III. Rodale Press, Inc. ISBN: 0-87857-613-4.

Canning, Freezing, and Drying. Sunset Press. ISBN: 0-37602213-2.

Holiday Herbs

Christmas Lore, Gifts, & Crafts

By Caroline Moss

Many herbs and plants have Christian and pre-Christian legends that associate them with the holiday season. It is a pleasant thing to include them in your decorations and holiday gifts.

Holly

(Ilex opaca)

English holly (*Ilex aquifolium*) is similar to the native American holly (*Ilex opaca*), and was originally used in Pagan Winter Solstice celebrations and by the Romans during Saturnalia festivals. It was also used by the Druids, who decorated their homes with evergreens during the winter to provide an abode for sylvan (wood) spirits. Legend states that the holly sprung from Jesus' footprints as he walked on the earth. The berries symbolized blood, and thus his suffering, from the associations with the crown of thorns.

Ivy

(Hedera helix)

In ancient Greek legend, Ivy so loved Dionysus that she danced around him until she dropped dead at his feet. He was so distressed that he turned her into an evergreen vine and always wore a crown of it on his head. Ivy is a symbol of friendship. It has also been considered the wily female to the rumbustuous male holly—whichever is brought first into the home at Christmas (the holly or the ivy) denotes whether the man or the woman will rule the house in the coming year.

Mistletoe

(Viscum album)

Mistletoe is another Pagan herb. In Norse legend, Balder, the son of Odin, was killed by a mistletoe spear thrown by the blind god Hodr, who was deceived by the evil Loki. Balder was revived, and the mistletoe swore never to harm another soul. Mistletoe is symbol of both peace and fertility, either of which may account for our custom of kissing under it. Originally, with each kiss, a berry was removed from the bunch, and when all the berries were gone, the kissing stopped. It is called *herbe de la croix* in parts of France, as legend has it that Jesus' Cross was made of its wood. This is the reason given for mistletoe's "demotion" from a strong tree into a parasite—from shame. Mistletoe is rarely seen decorating churches due to the Pagan associations. Some thought it bad luck to cut mistletoe, and instead pulled it from the tree with sticks.

Many herbs and plants have Christian and pre-Christian legends that associate them with the holiday season

Bay

(Laurus nobilis)

Bay is the herb of Apollo, and was used in winter festivals through the ages. It is a symbol of victory and honor.

Pine

(Pinus picea)

Pine was introduced as a Christmas tree from Germany. Legend has it that the tree custom started when Martin Luther saw how beautiful real stars were shining through the pine trees in a forest. He then decorated a small pine tree with lights and trinkets. The Lutheran connection is the reason trees were slow to travel to Catholic countries. One of the earliest written accounts of a decorated tree was by a visitor to Strasbourg in 1605, "For Christmas they have fir trees in their rooms, all decorated with paper roses, apples, sugar, gold, and wafers." It is believed, however, that both the Romans and Norse peoples decorated trees for their winter feasts.

Rosemary

(Rosmarinus officinalis)

Legend has it that all rosemaries were originally white, but acquired blue flowers when the virgin Mary hung her heavenly blue cloak on a rosemary bush to dry. As a sign of its sympathy, the rosemary bush did not rustle its leaves as the Holy Family hid within it during their flight to Egypt. The twigs are soft and silent to touch today. Rosemary is reputed to bring happiness to the family who uses it to decorate and perfume the home on Christmas night, and it was popular as a Christmas evergreen until the nineteenth century.

Craft Idea

Try making a table top wreath using only rosemary sprigs. This is very effective and fragrant. Highlight the wreath with ribbons or miniature fir cones. Add candles for an Advent wreath.

Pennyroyal

(Mentha pulegium)

Pennyroyal is another manger herb. The children of Sicily believe it blooms on Christmas Day. They use it in their nativity scenes.

Ladies' Bedstraw

(Galium verum)

Sometimes known as cradlewort, indicating its former use, this herb formed the main "mattress" that Jesus lay upon in the manger, and was also found in Mary's bed. Until the first Christmas this was a scentless plant with white flowers. After Joseph cleared out the animal fodder and placed fresh grasses and herbs in the manger, the flowers turned to brilliant gold and a beautiful fragrance filled the air.

Thyme

(Thymus vulgaris)

A manger herb, found among the grasses in the stable, thyme symbolizes bravery and strength.

Horehound

(Ballota nigra)

This native to the Middle East was one of the five bitter herbs of Passover, symbolizing good health. It was said to have been included with the mixture of herbs and grasses in Jesus' manger. It was also sacred to the major Egyptian god Horus, and thus it is traditionally linked with the Holy Family's flight to Egypt.

Chamomile

(Anthemis nobilis)

Chamomile is the symbol of patience and energy in adversity, and is native to Palestine. It is also the symbol of St. Ann, mother of Mary.

Gift Idea

If you can get hold of them, why not give a plant of each of the "manger herbs" together with a written legend (copy out the above notes) for a lasting holiday present?

Sweet Woodruff

(Galium odoratum)

The final manger herb (along with bedstraw, horehound, chamomile, and thyme), sweet woodruff is a symbol of humility. Interestingly, we can appreciate its lovely fragrance only when it is wilted or dried.

Craft Idea

Use as many of the "manger herbs" as you can find in decorating a nativity scene. If you don't use a nativity in your holiday decorations, try incorporating the herbs into a nonreligious winter village scene for an original touch.

Juniper

(Juniperus communis)

Another bush that sheltered the Holy Family en route to Egypt. They hid in the soft, fragrant depths of the tree while the juniper protected them by turning its spiny branches to outsiders. This is the herb that flavors gin!

Lavender

(Lavandula officinalis)

This plant was scentless until Mary dried the infant Jesus' clean clothes on it. Then it took on a wonderful perfume, which it retains to this day. Also said by some to be a manger herb. The herb represents purity, cleanliness, and virtue.

Craft Idea

Make tiny posies of lavender, tied with narrow ribbon (mauves, purples, or greens work well), and tie them onto your tree.

Star of Bethlehem

(Ornithogalum umbellatum)

After the star guided the three kings to the stable, it exploded. The fragments fell to earth and turned into these tiny white star-shaped flowers. This may not be strictly true! It may be that the plant was a simple grass in the manger and the flowers came to form a wreath around Jesus' head.

Rue

(Ruta graveolens)

Shakespeare's "herb of grace" is the symbol of virginity and repentance. It is particularly linked to St. Lucia, whose feast day is celebrated on December 13 in Scandinavian countries, and by many Scandinavian families in America. This festival of light and fire starts the holiday season. Traditionally on that day, the youngest daughter in the household must serve her family a breakfast in bed of coffee and sweet breads—a custom well worth cultivating, I would have thought! The young girl should wear a long white gown with a red sash, and a wreath of lighted candles on her head.

Craft Idea

Add rue to your Holiday wreaths. The gray-green leaves make an attractive addition to arrangements. Take care when handling rue, as some are allergic. Use rubber gloves if you are unsure.

Costmary/Alecost

(Tanacetum balsamita)

Used by Mary Magdalen to make ointment, costmary was used to flavor ale in medieval England. The wassail bowl was a vital part of ancient winter festivals and the early Christmas.

Christmas Rose

(Helleborus niger)

Christmas rose is a garden flower that blooms in December. The flowers were said to have been black originally. A little shepherd girl followed the three kings to the stable. However, when she saw them present their wondrous gifts of gold, frankincense, and myrrh, she held back, ashamed, as she had nothing to offer. As she prayed for a gift, the insignificant black herbs at her feet turned to a mass of waxen white flowers, which she gathered for the baby Jesus. A similar tale is told about that other holiday flower, the poinsettia (*Euphorbia pulcherrima*), which is said to have blushed red in the presence of the baby Jesus.

Frankincense

(Boswellia sacra)

One of the gifts of the Magi, along with gold and myrrh. Frankincense is a shrub that grows in North Africa and the Middle East. The frankincense in use as an incense is formed from the resin, collected from cuts in the bark, in a similar way to maple.

Myrrh

(Commiphora myrrha)

Myrrh is a small, thorny tree that only bears leaves in the short rainy season. Again, a resin is collected from cuts in the trunk.

Craft Idea

Make a potpourri Advent calendar. Collect ingredients for a suitably seasonal potpourri, but do not mix. Collect twenty-four little boxes and cover with fabric or paper if they are not already decorative. Put a little of the potpourri ingredients in each box, minus the essential oils. In the last box, include a tiny vial of the essential oils (old perfume sample bottles are idea). Attach decoratively written instructions and a bowl to put it all in and you have a beautiful and original gift. Make sure you give it before December 1 so a box can be opened each day and emptied into the bowl.

Craft Idea

Make a batch of frankincense and myrrh potpourri to give as gifts.

- ¼ cup orris root mixed with 1 teaspoon frankincense essential oil
- ¼ cup orris root mixed with 1 teaspoon lavender essential oil
- ⅛ cup orris root mixed with ½ teaspoon myrrh essential oil.
- 12 cups dried rose petals
- 1 cup vetiver, sandalwood, or cedar
- 2 cups dried lavender
- ⅛ cup ground cloves
- ⅛ cup ground cinnamon
- 1 finely chopped vanilla pod
- ¼ cup myrrh
- ½ cup frankincense

Mix oils and orris root first, and let stand for a few days before adding all other ingredients. Don't worry about being too precise—vary the above with the addition of cinnamon, pine, bayberry, balsam, small cones, or dried citrus.

Lunar Fertility

By K. D. Spitzer

Since antiquity, the Moon has been associated with women and femininity; it has also been the symbol of fertility throughout the animal world. Of course, the effect of the Moon on menstruation is such an ingrained idea that most languages call the process, in part or in full, by the term for the Moon: Moon madness, Moon change, Moon sickness, time of the Moon, or just Moon.

Astrologers have long known of a specific lunar influence on conception, contraception, and the determination of gender in humans. It is possible to astrologically calculate the maximum period of fertility in a woman's cycle. Of course, it must be a woman's natural cycle and not one set artificially by oral contraceptives.

If a regular menstrual cycle is established, a woman is fertile during the natural ovarian fertility cycle, which accounts for 30 percent of all pregnancies. A woman also experiences maximum fertility each month at the same time as her natal lunar phase, regardless of where this falls in her menstrual cycle. This is accurate 97 percent of the time. In 1970, fifteen scientists, doctors, and technicians examined the records of 1,252 women who used astrological birth control charts for at least one year. The percentage of women who did not get pregnant was 97.7 percent. This test has been duplicated with the same superior results.

A woman's natal lunar phase is determined by the angle between the Sun and Moon at the moment of her birth. Calculations are made using the date, time, and place of birth and result in a degree somewhere between 0 degrees and 360 degrees. This can be conveniently done by an astrological computer software program. If the woman has moved away from her place of birth, a relocation chart must be done, and calculations will be based on the longitude and latitude of her current residence. This is especially important if contraception is the goal!

Lunar Contraception

A woman born on June 30, 1950, has the Moon in Capricorn, one day past the Full Moon at 198 degrees. (More people are born at the

Full Moon than any other phase.) Every lunar month the Moon returns to this degree and the computerized astrology program that determined the natal lunar phase can also project the days and times that the Moon will cyclically return there.

Because sperm (female-producing sperm) can live for three days, the period of fertility starts three days before this moment and lasts for another day afterward, for a maximum of four fertile days. It is a simple matter to count back exactly seventy-two hours from the exact time of the natal lunar degree for the beginning of the fertile period and then to count forward twenty-four hours from the exact time to complete it. The maximum fertile time each month can be calculated reliably with the help of the Lady Moon and used for conception and contraception. Using autosuggestion techniques, it is possible to synchronize the hormonally fertile time with the lunar fertile phase. While it is of course true that men are always fertile, some preliminary testing shows that their sperm count is significantly higher at their own natal lunar phase.

Determining Sex

The Moon can also aid in determining the sex of the child. Many astrologers differ over how. Some examine the gender of the father's natal Moon, not to mention the gender of the rising sign, the sign on the cusp of the Fifth House, and some other indicators in the mother's chart. This will help to point out any fertility problems.

All of them agree, however, and have since the ancient Babylonians and Sumerians, that the gender of the zodiac sign the Moon is passing through at the moment of conception pure and simply determines the gender of the baby. Thus if the Moon is in Aries, Gemini, Leo, Libra, Sagittarius, or Aquarius at conception, then the baby will be a boy, and it will be a girl if the Moon is in Taurus, Cancer, Virgo, Scorpio, Capricorn, or Pisces. The gender of the signs alternate around the zodiac. Preliminary tests indicate that the Moon influences the acidity/alkalinity of the womb, which of course determines which sperm (male- or female-producing) reach the desired goal.

So, generally speaking, if you wish to get pregnant, you have a good chance of doing so during your natal lunar fertility phase. Because of the Moon's influence, this cyclic measurement marks the reaffirmation of one's psychic roots, not to mention one's social capacity for personal relationships, of which sex is an extension. A woman's subconscious urge to reproduce correlates to this time frame.

Your Moon Sign & Your Link to Mother

By Kim Rogers-Gallagher

The Moon is the ultimate feminine energy. She's the head of the department of feelings. Her subtle power is apparent in the tides, as she calls the ocean to her and sends it away, but we feel her influence ebb and flow through our bodies, too.

In our charts, the Moon is just as much of an enigma. She prefers to react rather than act, as she stands back and watches from her vantage point in our bellies. She offers her silent counsel to our Sun as it charges through life gobbling up experiences. She's where we keep our instinct and our ability to express our feelings. The Moon in your chart represents all these issues and more. She is the lady who decides what makes you feel secure—and what doesn't. Amazingly enough, all these subtle reactions were instilled in you before you were born, which brings me to the subject of your Moon sign and your mom.

Consider the incredible bond we share with our mothers—the humans whose bodies we actually lived in for nine months. During that time, we learned all about emotions. We felt everything, for better or worse, that she felt. If our mom spent a majority of her pregnancy in fear, we've "recorded" that emotion as a permanent state of expectation. If she was safe and happy, we learned to expect that from the world, too. Now, our emotions affect us both physically and psychologically. They're a subtle undercurrent that flows through each of our days, powerfully influencing our reactions to what life offers—so it's very important to understand our own Moons, and what was passed on to us via our moms. One of the best ways to start to get to know our Moons is to consider the sign the Moon was passing through when we were born.

The sign a planet is "wearing" is like a costume or an outfit that shows the style of behavior this planet will display as it goes about its business. Our Moon sign, then, shows the emotional climate that was present when we made our planetary debut, as well as our expectations of how the world will treat us. Regardless of whether she raised us or not, our Moon signs are also an indication of our relationship with our mother, and therefore the type of mother (whether we're male or female) we'll be. Let's take a look at the Moon in each of the signs, then, to better understand our connection with our moms, as well as what to expect from ourselves when the issue of expressing emotions arises.

Moon sign is also an indication of our relationships with our mothers, and therefore the type of mothers (whether we're male or female) we'll be

Aries

The sign Aries is feisty and argumentative, bold and courageous—not likely to let anyone step on its blue suede shoes and get away with it. This is the first sign, the sign of the newborn, full of energy, life, and awareness of its own needs. It's impulsive, assertive, and can be a bit stress-oriented.

If you were born with the Moon in Aries, then God help anyone who hurts you. They'll be conjuring the wrath of the energetic war-god, Aries—and he's no lightweight. Your mom was your first introduction to this energy. She may have been extremely active—or overly stressed— during her pregnancy with you. She may have spent the time angry with someone. She most likely had to take care of herself, too. As a result, in typical Aries style, you learned to fire first and ask questions later when you feel as if you're under attack emotionally. You learned to defend yourself first—under all circumstances. You also learned that

if your needs were going to be taken care of, you'd have to do it yourself. Needless to say, you folks are the true survivors of the zodiac, even more so than Aries Suns. Remember, this is a Moon/Mars combination—so no matter what it is you're feeling, it's going to come out passionately. You may also have learned to "do battle" with women to defend yourself, another common Moon/Mars "symptom." At any rate, you probably saw your mom as a fighter—an independent, fiery woman who stood up for herself and taught you to do the same. Of course, you're in equally fiesty company. Just take a look at these examples of Aries Moons: Marlon Brando, Ellen Burstyn, Jimmy Cagney, Grace Jones, Lily Tomlin, and Jerry Garcia.

Taurus

The Moon in Taurus garb is in her earthiest finery, all done up in rich browns and fertile greens. This Moon sign is the lady at her most solid and sensual, feeling secure and well rooted in her sister Venus' garb. There's no need to stress or hurry—and definitely no need to change anything. That's how you'll feel most of the time if you're born with the Moon in this sign—that all is quite well in your world, thank you. You learned stability from your mom, who you may have seen as quite resistant to change—any kind of change, but most especially those changes that came from the outside world. In a nutshell, your mom was probably an earthy type who taught you the magic of enjoying life on this planet, with all its sensory delights. As a result, you'd rather sit still, have a wonderful dinner, and listen to good music than do just about anything else—except maybe have a backrub.

If you were born with the Moon in this sign—lucky you! Your Moon is one of the happiest around. You may have seen your mom literally as a rock—the very soul of constancy. From her, you learned to handle emotions of any kind by simply hanging tough. Nothing, but nothing, rocks you. In times of turmoil, just as she did, you put up, bear up, and stay put. You may even be a bit too constant, in fact. Watch for a tendency to fall into an emotional rut, because once you start feeling, it's difficult for you to stop. Your mom probably taught you to love quality in all things—friends and possessions included. Your soul comes alive when there's quality music playing and at least one bottle of hundred-year-old scotch or very fine wine on the premises. Just look at the company you keep: Glen Campbell, Mick Jagger, Elton John, Vincent Price, Lee Iacocca, and Diana Ross.

Gemini

Gemini Moons are built for activity. This is a mutable air sign, so it likes to move around—quickly—and if you were born with the Moon here, you probably like to travel quickly, too. Since Gemini is ruled by Mercury, the head of the communications department, your mom may have been a witty conversationalist, and an expert at puzzles, riddles, and word games. If you have the Moon here, your fondest memories of mom may be of her as a great communicator, too. You probably inherited the innate instincts of a writer, and the mind of a coyote. You may want two—at least two—of everything, and you're a bit more restless than the average bear, since this Moon's costume is a coat of many colors, appropriate to her motto: "variety is the spice of life." Emotionally, variety brings change, so this Moon sign can be a bit on the scattered side, especially since Gemini is mutable air—which literally means changing your mind. Is this Moon sign fickle? Well, maybe, but only if you're bored.

If you were born with the Moon in this sign, you probably saw your mom as an expert at flexibility and mobility—so you might even move a lot. In fact, if you own a Gemini Moon, you may have moved so much in childhood that you can't comfortably stay put for long. Since Mercury rules communication, and the Moon is in charge of yor domestic life, you will most likely "communicate in your home." Yes, that may mean that you'll teach classes in your living room, but it might also mean that you'll spend a lot of time on the phone.

In keeping with Gemini's fondness for more than one, you may also have had two moms—an adopted mom and your natural mother, or just someone who nurtured you through youth as if she were your mom. You learned movement, words, wit, and "flight" of some kind from both your biological mom and your other mother, and they're planted deep in your soul. Here's the company you keep: Fred Astaire, George Carlin, John Delorean, Erle Stanley Gardner, Goldie Hawn, Buddy Holly, and Amelia Earhart.

Cancer

Here's the Moon at her most emotional and most nurturing. The Moon rules Cancer, so when she's here she's home, lounging casually in her sea-greens and blues. Here the Moon's concerns turn to home, family, children, and mothers. There's no doubt that even in your adult life, home and family are your main concerns—regardless of whether or not you actually choose to start a family of your own. Growing up with a Cancer Moon is being taught that's it's okay to express emotions, to be sympathetic and understanding to others. So if you were born with the Moon in this sign, you're among the best nurturers out there—and you're also undeniably one of the best huggers around. Now, this Moon sign also learned to express love by cooking or cuddling dear ones. You're expert at making a house a home, and at choosing just the right food, fabrics, and furnishings to create a safe, secure nest. All this makes you a very natural caregiver, but be careful. The greatest danger in this wonderful quality is that you'll become so fond of that role that you'll need others to need you in order to feel worthy—in other words, avoid codependence at all costs. It's important to watch out for becoming over-sensitive, dependent, or needy, too. You're probably also the most private of the private, guarding your extremely sensitive little heart very, very cautiously. Because the Moon operates so purely here, you're driven primarily by your emotions—by how something "hits" you on a gut level. You're in the record books with the most amazing caregivers around: Dr. Benjamin Spock, Eleanor Roosevelt, and Dr. Elizabeth Kubler-Ross.

Leo

Leo is the sign that rules drama, with a capital D. This theatrical sign has long been known for its big entrances, love of display, and need for attention. If you were born with the Moon in this sign, you just might have a bit of a flair for the dramatic yourself. This Moon tends to display her emotions, regardless of what they are. That means you're liable to throw a tantrum when you're mad, and an elaborate cocktail party in someone's honor when you're not. Leo is ruled by the Sun, the center of the Universe, the creative force, so you were probably taught by your mom that it's perfectly okay to expect recognition, applause, and appreciation from your world. Most Leo Moons tend to think of their mothers as the queen, in fact, and of themselves as the royal heirs. Now, all that inner pride and dramatic emotion can turn into histrionics and melodrama in the blink of an eye, so Leo Moons need to be careful of overreacting or being excessively vain.

Like the other fire Moons, your mom somehow taught you to stop whatever was hurting you from hurting you. You want your feelings to be noticed, above all else, but you also want to be appreciated for what you are on the inside. More than anything, your mom probably taught you pride. Speaking of Leo's love for drama, check out this roster of Leo Moons: Clint Eastwood, David Bowie, Kris Kristofferson, Jane Fonda, Peter

O'Toole, Marlene Dietrich, Dolly Parton, and Barbra Streisand.

Virgo

Here's the Moon at her most discriminating. Wearing an efficient, tailored outfit that's specially designed for work, she's ready to take care of whatever needs it—no matter what it needs. This is the most detail-oriented sign out there, the sign most concerned with fixing, fussing, and tending to. Your mom probably taught you the virtues of scouring, scrubbing, sorting out, and trouble shooting. Virgo is the most helpful of all the signs. Often, Virgo Moons see their mom as a shining example of neatness and organization. No matter how much you protest that it's not true, your Moon in Virgo really does love her home to be clean and orderly, so you'll think about cleaning places most of us wouldn't even look at, much less touch. Your mom taught you to appreciate surroundings that were clean and orderly, and you probably need your own home environment to be that way, too—because it makes you feel orderly, like all's well with the world. This is a tough Moon to own. If you've got one, you probably beat yourself up on a regular basis. Virgo is a sign long associated with a critical eye—so you may have seen your mom as rather particular herself. Of course, you're also undoubtedly very, very good at whatever you do—because being good, accurate, and precise is what you inherited from mom. Remember your finer qualities next time you're feeling like you'll just never be good enough—like the gentleness, compassion, attention to detail, and willingness to help you're famous for. Sean Connery, Dustin Hoffman, Shirley MacLaine, Jack Nicholson, Robert Redford, Madonna, and Emily Post share your Virgo Moon.

Libra

Folks born with this Moon know instinctively how to avoid conflict because they probably grew up with it around them. If you own this Moon, your mom was probably quite good at sensing what the other needed, regardless of who the other was, or what type of social situation she happened to be invloved in. As a result, you feel unhappy in unbalanced situations, and you're an expert at how to fix them. When you find yourself in situations of emotional unbalance that require a delicate tap of the scales to set them right, you set to work finding compromises—just like mom taught you. In general, this is a social, polite, friendly Moon, always ready to extend a hand to others, to be cooperative, and to agree more easily to compromise. Libra is the second Venus-ruled sign, and Libra just loves people—so your mom probably taught you that relationships, partnerships, and being with someone are very important things. Libra Moons also usually have moms who prompt us to make our surroundings beautiful, or to put ourselves in situations where beauty is all around us. She probably was fond of decorating, shopping for the home, or visiting places of elegant beauty.

In a nutshell, owning this Moon means you were raised to be a cruise director, out to keep everyone happy—except possibly yourself. Like Mercury in this sign, the Moon here is a natural-born mediator, arriving on the planet with the built-in curse/blessing of being able to understand—and make a case for—both sides of an issue. Libra Moons also look heavily to their primary relationships to keep them feeling happy and secure, so when they don't have one, they can be absolutely forlorn. Take a peek at these Libra Moons, all of whom have a spouse who's strongly associated with them: George Bush, Burt Reynolds, and Don Johnson.

Scorpio

Here's a Moon that can love just as intensely as she can hate—at the same time, too. This fixed, feminine water sign is co-ruled by Mars and Pluto, so this Moon doesn't mess around. If you own one, you're a natural-born firewalker, ready to do that and more to prove your feelings for someone. Scorpio is the most intense sign out there, so this Moon sign feels everything to the absolute degree. The intensity of your feelings, in fact, is what makes you know you're alive. You stew and smolder, and own a passion that's just barely concealed. Others wonder why they're so drawn to you. Needless to say, if you were born with the Moon in this sign, passion, joy, jealousy, betrayal, love, and desire were probably all a part of your mom's emotional repertoire, and you probably learned from your Mother that all emotions were intense emotions. Be careful of a tendency to become secretive, suspicious, or to brood or "stew" over an offense that was not intended.

Your mom was probably the best friend and the worst enemy to have. You probably watched your mom successfully get through even the hardest emotional times, and so you're built for endurance, too. Now, the other side of endurance is obsession, so watch yourself for the possibility of re-running every situation, and wondering (all night long) "what they really meant by that." Remember, Scorpio loves to play detective, to investigate a mystery, to do research, to dig—both figuratively and literally—and to allow intimacy with an "other." If you were born with this

Moon sign, you can use that natural detective ability you inherited from mom to understand the people around you and become an excellent judge of character. Prince Andrew, Warren Beatty, Mario Cuomo, James Dean, David Frost, Quincy Jones, and Bruce Lee share your Scorpio Moon.

Sagittarius

Here's the Moon at her most optimistic, non-judgmental, and positive. Sagittarius is ruled by benevolent Jupiter, so if you were born with a Sag Moon, you were born believing that everything will work out just fine, no matter what. It was your mom who taught you all this—how to shrug things off, let them go, and laugh about it. Your mom probably always had a smile on her face, and may have been a true emotional optimist, a real giver who somehow always landed on her feet. As a result, you inherited the soul of a comedian, a philosopher, and a preacher. You have a gift for teaching, and for lending this same optimism out to those who really need it. Your innate faith in the universe seldom lets you down.

Your mom probably taught you to love spending time outdoors, to be spontaneous, and that there was no such thing as laughing too loudly. Of course, Jupiter's also the planet of long-distance travel and educating the higher mind, so she may have also given you a love for two-day adventures and seminars on a topic you've always been interested in—say, philosophy or religion. Sag loves to collect knowledge, experiences, and wisdom, so when the Moon's in this sign, she's dressed for any adventure. Your mom may have taught you to be quite at home on the road, and that includes foreign countries.

Now Jupiter can get too big for his britches, as can Sag, his very own sign. So watch out for a tendency toward excess, waste, and overdoing. Since your Moon is Jupiter-powered, no matter what you feel, you feel it hugely—as your mom may have. Watch for a tendency to be a bit too Pollyanna in your expectations of others, and for the possibility of leaning toward overindulging in something to pick you up when you're having that unusually blue kind of day. John Belushi, Liberace, Mozart, Christopher Reeve, and Oprah Winfrey share your Moon sign.

Capricorn

Capricorn Moon owners have the driest, funniest senses of humor out there. That's because they tend to see things as they really are, and people as they really are—just the facts, ma'am. If you own this Moon, you have a no-nonsense attitude toward life, as did your mom. You were definitely raised on patriotism, family values, and the work ethic—and you may even have been raised on the road by military parents. Regardless of what your mom did for work, this sign is more concerned than any other with conforming to set rules and following orders. This is the Moon at her most organized, practical, and business-like. Capricorn is dutiful, cautious, and a bit pessimistic at times, and may prefer to work rather than play—all of which may be characteristics you learned from your mother. Mom may have placed a great emphasis on goals for the future, too, and undoubtedly taught you that the right thing to do is the only thing to do. As a result, you learned to take charge of your own life, and to immediately organize any part of your life that becomes scattered or disrupted. Mom probably also taught you to set down your own rules and guidelines, to sit patiently, listen, and learn. Watch for the possibility of acting in too business-like a way—at the expense of others' emotions. Remember that contrary to popular opinion, Capricorn planets aren't "cold," they're starved—for love, affection, and security. If you own this Moon, you probably cry a lot more than you'd ever let anyone see. Johnny Carson, Merv Griffin, General George Patton, and David Letterman have Capricorn Moons.

Aquarius

The Moon in Aquarius is a rebel—for better or worse. Dressed in electric blue, in something outrageous, eccentric, and far too futuristic, this Moon is ready to break free from the past, to "just say no" to all the rules we just set in place in Capricorn. Your mom may have taught you not to be afraid to break out of a rut, to try something different, and to make sure everyone sees you for the unique individual you are. Folks born with restless Aquarian Moons came here to break the family tradition, no matter what that was. If you've got one you'll undoubtedly renounce your family's traditions, broadcast their secrets, and deliberately set out to shock everyone. You have an innate emotional need to be different, to separate yourself from everyone you're related to, and to make sure they know just how different you are. If you own this Moon, you've probably become an expert at coming off "cold" when you're hurt, rather than showing your emotions. That doesn't mean you don't have any, only that you tend to *think* your feelings, rather than experience them—something you may also feel you learned from your mom. Like the Moon in Capricorn, you'll have a hard time crying for yourself, but you'll cry a river for an underdog.

You may have seen your mom as an expert at extreme, sudden, and abrupt actions, so you'll surprise even yourself at what you'll say. You may also be prone to complete reversals and changing your mind at the last minute. This sign is ruled by Uranus, so personal freedom and individuality are more important than anything else. Watch for a tendency to become fanatical, act deliberately rebellious without a reason, or break tradition just for the sake of breaking it. Remember, you were raised to have the soul of a rebel and the spirit of a nonconformist. Here are some famous members of the pack you run with: Merle Haggard, John Lennon, Princess Diana, Angela Davis, Shirley Chisholm, and Margaret Mead.

Pisces

Here's the Moon at her most sensitive and most intuitive. There are no walls between your Pisces planets and what's out there. If you own this Moon, on some level, you understand this, and you may be in touch with your ability to feel everything that's happening around you—for better or worse. You may have seen your mom as someone who absorbed the emotions of others, or confused them as her own. As a result, you could have learned rather than talking about what you're feeling, to withdraw and hide your feelings—even from yourself. In truth you may have problems finding your emotions. Pisces Moon folks sometimes find the world such an emotionaly abusive place that they shut their feelings down in self-defense. Remember, this sign belongs to the planet Neptune, the ruler of sensitivity and altered states of reality. If you were born with the Moon in this sign, you're extremely susceptible to emotional assaults of any kind. When you're feeling fuzzy, vague, dreamy, nostalgic, wistful, or impressionable, then you may do what you perceived your mom doing, and seek solace and sanctuary through sleep, meditation, prayer, drugs, or alcohol—whatever induces a trance-like state that will allow you to escape.

On the other hand, you may also have a mom who's amazingly compassionate, and who taught you to be generous to "strays" of any kind. Of course, you may also have seen your mom as a most spiritual creature, who used her ability to lower her boundaries to its best. In this case, you learned to trust your intuition, and to be sensitive to those less fortunate. You probably inherited the soul of a poet and the ability to tap into the collective unconscious and bring back the images for the rest of us. Other Pisces Moons include: Leonardo Da Vinci, Robert DeNiro, Michaelangelo, Martin Luther King, and Edgar Allan Poe.

The Moon & Relationships

Taking Inventory of Emotional Needs

By Alice DeVille

How well do you get along with others? Are you able to share your innermost thoughts and desires with close contacts, and communicate easily with your peer group, business colleagues, and other associates? Do you feel energized by close encounters with the people you have drawn into your circle? Are you experiencing abundance, love, and enthusiasm in your relationships, or do they resemble melodramatic misfits that cloud your life with turmoil and uncertainty? If you feel good about your answers to these questions, you are most likely attuned to the emotional drawing power of your natal Moon. If not, it is time to take inventory and find the right connections.

Each relationship you have with another person reflects the relationship you have with yourself. The degree to which you get along with yourself is directly mirrored by how well (or poorly) you get along with others. Your Moon sign reveals a great deal about your choice of friends and companions and the emotional needs you are looking to fulfill. The more you understand these needs, the greater your chances of attracting the best people to aid you in fulfilling your life's purpose. Take a look at your Moon sign and see if you are on the mark in measuring your relationship needs.

Aries Moon

When picking a partner for either business or personal reasons, you need a good listener. You have plenty of great ideas and want someone to hear what you have to say. No one will be bored by your ideas, but they may have to wait for you to follow through as you talk a good game but are short on delivery. Your brainstorm often falls apart when you are pushed for a plan or timeline because you haven't thought about details. Your boss loves your innovation and puts it to good use. You are easily selected for positions of leadership. If you stay with the same company, you hold positions for extremely long periods of time since you probably peaked and there is no place else to go. Instead you get to head up new projects and draw new audiences who appreciate your talent.

Career success is important to you, Aries. If you have not achieved it or don't feel in charge, you may fall into a series of romantic relationships, often ill-fated, to prove that the power of attraction works for you. You must be careful not to select fragile partners, as such a mate will almost always fall in love with you first due to the sensational vibes you send out. You enjoy the chase and often go to great lengths to mesmerize the object of your affections. Some of you who do give your energy to the partner may find you have misread their intentions and feel like you woke up from a bad dream when a major crisis in the relationship occurs.

Each relationship you have with another person reflects the relationship you have with yourself

If you do experience considerable monetary and career success, you can be a bit rigid at home, feeling that material accouterments came from your efforts and genius. You'll never balk at taking credit from an appreciative partner for each and every accomplishment. You need a partner who is understanding and patient, as your Aries Moon comes with a short temper. At least you get over it quickly, even if you are a bit self-centered and don't always consider your partner's perspective. Your partner must understand your impulsiveness to act on what you know and feel at the moment.

The least appealing partner is one who is stuck in a rut or who throws pity parties to brood over their own or your setbacks. Your partner must pay close attention to you, otherwise you will stray. You much prefer people who build your ego and nurture your fragile self-esteem. Your recipe for successful relationships is simple, Aries. Find partners who resonate to your upbeat and fun-loving nature, and you will enthusiastically contribute creative ideas to the world.

Taurus Moon

You are reasonable, practical, and down-to-earth, and search for a soulmate who appreciates a little bit of heaven on earth. Indeed you are grounded in a need for security and want financial matters out on the table before any serious love talk begins. You want every romantic frill to be a part of your romancing ritual—the flowers, wine, love notes, impeccable grooming, and chocolate kisses. Even if your head does inevitably rule your heart, you are devoted to partners and feel that nothing is too good for them. In turn, you appreciate these special touches and fill your romantic scrapbook with sentimental memorabilia from intimate encounters.

Status matters, so you will not be receptive to a date who wants to treat you to a hot dog on the run or invites you to a microwave dinner served at the kitchen bar. The setting is of utmost importance to you in dating and courtship. Should your date arrive in scruffy clothing, you will find a way to terminate the evening or make them change, regardless of who did the inviting. Instinctively, you know how to orchestrate the ideal climate to get to know a prospective partner, and need appreciation for your efforts.

You collect contacts in business and social endeavors the way others collect stamps. People of importance seem to gravitate to you, yet you must derive mutual benefit from these relationships or you lose interest. You know how to make money work for you, yet you are very generous with social causes that improve conditions for people in your local environment and the world in general. Business partners must hold up their end of the deal or you will find the legal loophole to remove them. Meticulous financial plans appeal to your sense of security.

Whether you work on commission or draw a salary, you enjoy seeing the numbers come out ahead and know the greater whole benefits from your meticulous performance. If the boss keeps the books a secret, you will lose interest quickly as you want to be trusted and dislike the insecurity of an obscure financial base. You would enjoy working with colleagues who dress appropriately for the environment, speak with conviction about their roles in the work place, and demonstrate resourcefulness.

To attract the best people into your circle, rely on your innate common sense when it comes to selecting life and work partners, Taurus Moon. You'll reap big dividends in the department of fulfillment.

Gemini Moon

You meet new people everywhere you go, Gemini Moon, and feel good about your eclectic mix of friends. Initially you can get along with just about anyone because you know a little about many subjects. Consequently, you mean different things to different people, and often form shallow rather than deep friendships. Not that you are incapable of forming close friendships—you just have so much energy you want to spread it around. You take inventory in relationships automatically and have few hangers-on from "the good old days" because you book yourself solidly in new ventures and ignore people you think you no longer need.

When it comes to employer relationships, you work best in environments where someone else organizes priorities and sets the timeline. With multiple tasks, you get sidetracked by a type of workload wanderlust and often stray from the main assignment. Your colleagues may not understand the focus of your work, or you may lose interest in the work altogether. Then things get dicey. Either you make up stories about why you could not accomplish the work or think nothing of blaming others for the delays. Relationships suffer because people see through your embellishments.

You have a deep need to respect your boss' professionalism and prefer working for someone who respects your need for freedom in shaping the final product. A strong, organized partner is the perfect match for your creative, imaginative drive. If you are in business for yourself, you may need someone who can help you manage the finances and curb your tendency to spend on products that satisfy your latest whim.

In the romance department, you need someone who vibrates to your youthful charm, energetic ideas, and compulsion to talk. Look for someone who enjoys spontaneity and a sense of adventure. If you flirt, and most of you do, you will not be adored for long by an insecure partner. Find someone long on understanding and short on temper or your ego could be bruised. You hate to be nagged, so reminders of any bad habits by "shape 'em up" types will leave you cold. If you remember to let your mate get a word in every now and then, you may experience the relationship of a lifetime. Trust your feelings and your glorious gift of gab and your walk down the aisle will be one of permanent bliss.

Cancer Moon

Both male and female Cancer Moons thrive on relationships with people who appreciate the attention you so willingly lavish on them. Your life force revolves around nurturing. The more receptive your audience, the more you want to please. Partners always know their special place in your universe, and your children know you are lovingly looking out for them, even if you do hover a bit. Friends and co-workers feel like family. If you have siblings, they hear your frequent dissertations "for their own good" on living a better life. No matter who receives your special attention, you will be sure to tell them how much you have sacrificed on their behalf.

Your emotional barometer calls for personal interactions with others. It is unnatural for you to be without a significant other in your life. If a woman, you need someone who brings out your maternal instincts and appreciates the affection you want to lavish. You know how to make your mate feel like the most important person on earth. If a man, you need a love who thrills to the way you cater to her every wish. Both of you need to avoid the detached type of lover or you will suffer from rejection and spend lots of time licking emotional wounds. An overly critical partner will hurt your feelings and may seriously damage your self-esteem. You belong in the married state and need a deeply evolved partner who shares the bonds of commitment and abiding love.

Since you excel at drawing others out of their shells and promoting their talents, you make an excellent counselor or personnel person. Bosses often seek your advice in handling problem employees. You relate well to others and are able to put people at ease in almost any setting. If you own the business, you are quick to spot trouble and will go out of your way to solve the problem. The work place is enhanced by your reverence for family values.

Let your intuition guide you in opening your heart to sensitive partners with a loony sense of humor and a craving for homemade chicken soup. Then put your Cancer claws around them and make them your obsessions for life.

Leo Moon

You magnanimous Leo Moons like to stay ahead of the pack, so you do best in relationships that let you grow and spread your sunny wings. You look for ways to mix business with pleasure, equating "socialize" with "status rise" via a bigger and better paycheck. Spending becomes you, so you rarely take positions where the income bottoms out quickly or the boss might be a tightwad. Although you need a fair amount of feedback from an employer, you must avoid being fooled by the old pat on the back routine. Some employers are slicker than others, so you probably have your own timetable for expecting cash for a job well done.

The power game appeals to you, especially if you understand the odds. Heading up a team is right up your alley, especially when you develop a winning strategy. You like competition and must have enough people around you to feel like you are coming out on top. Your work world revolves around taking charge and organizing the environment. When you strut around handing out procedural change bulletins, you need to make sure your diplomatic barometer is in high gear, or your domineering attitude may isolate the troops.

Leo Moons are idealistic and must have heroes. Whether they are your lifelong friends, famous sports figures, or the love of your life, you need someone to place upon a pedestal. Psychologically, you want to be there yourself, and like to compare your actions with those you revere. You have blind spots where your loved ones are concerned and get burned more easily than most of the other Moon signs. In love relationships, you are often the last to know your partner has strayed or fallen from grace because no one wants to mess with your Leo pride. Then bitterness sets in and you woefully withdraw your affections from the world until the wounds heal.

You follow your heart when you foster relationships with people who adore your exuberance and generosity, share your sense of drama, appreciate your affectionate nature, and insist that you handle responsibility.

Virgo Moon

You like people who keep your mind sharp and your body fit. You Virgo Moons hang around the library or the health club hoping to give yourself the ultimate workout. You're not merely building your I.Q. or toning your muscles, you are going for the self-confidence bonanza. The promise of meeting the love of your life at a place of mutual interest appeals to your practical nature. You may be able to convert your workout into a romantic romp without adjusting your schedule. If the relationship endures, the two of you may be eligible for a reduced membership rate.

You thrive in a work setting where your employer gives you lots of latitude to solve problems and be of service. Since communication is your strong suit, employers must understand your need to express your opinions, write, or give presentations. With your magic green thumb as the bait, you could meet a love interest or prospective boss at the local nursery, the garden club, or the horticultural society. You stay on good terms with work group peers when you criticize less. A boss who gives clear directions and has a handle on the "big picture" is your idea of perfection. When parameters are vague, you worry about performance outcomes and upset your delicate nervous system. Once they are defined, nothing deters you from accomplishing your goals, and business partners appreciate your determination.

Although you are shy and rarely take the lead in romantic relationships, you feel incomplete without a partner. Many of you settle for inferior matches because you fear being alone and figure you can't have it all. Your fragile ego has lots of doubts about partners' motives and responses to your attractive presence. You feel at one with a partner who ignores your critical tongue and understands your need to dissect just about everything. Develop intellectual rapport and an appreciation for the finer qualities of prospective partners and you will easily fulfill your dreams for everlasting love and affection.

Libra Moon

Tactile Libra needs physical contact with both business and romantic partners. You want business associates to shake your hand often in recognition for your good work, and you want them to cross your palm with silver several times a year to nurture incentive. You care about what's "fair" in work place dynamics and complain to bosses if you think the workload is unbalanced. You excel in career fields that allow you to shine in collaboration with others. Teamwork, either structured or unstructured, suits you better than solo endeavors, because you enjoy the creative sparks that fly when people put their heads together. Group energy inspires you to be extremely fair in giving others credit for their accomplishments. Some Libra Moons excel in mediating disputes. You make an excellent "front man" or "marketer" for your firm's message, and need bosses who appreciate your diplomatic skills and charming manners.

If ever there was a sign who needed to do a relationship inventory, Libra, it is you. You Libra Moons love the social life and have a large cadre of friends and associates from all walks of life to share your hobbies and preferences. Professional acquaintances, like your attorney, accountant, and home builder often attend your parties. You usually have ongoing relationships with these folks and like to give them an opportunity to network.

In the romance department you want moonlight and magic with all the bells and whistles. A truly attuned partner knows you want the honeymoon to last forever. Your greatest challenge may be selecting the perfect mate as you meet more than your share of eligible partners. To some observers, you seem afraid of making a marriage mistake. Surprisingly, you can be very demanding with partners underneath your calm exterior, especially if you are the jealous type. Male Libra Moons like refined, feminine women who appreciate a full-blown courtship, while female Libra Moons expect to marry well and manage a healthy checkbook. Look for companions who like to hold hands and share your love for a harmonious home life. Be perceptive in assessing mutual needs and enjoy life's bliss with the mate of your dreams.

Scorpio Moon

Sugar and spice and everything sexy—that's what makes Scorpio Moon's romantic relationships sizzle. You seek true love and loyal mates. Once you stop hiding your feelings and testing your intended, you expect the relationship to intensify quickly. You may sting a few prospects with your sarcastic slang, but underneath that bitter breath you long to be loved. You need physical and psychological synchronicity to experience the passion unique to your sign. Shallow types frustrate you, Scorpio, so pick spunky mates with deep psyches and be responsive to the cadence of love.

When you have something on your mind, you are inclined to keep it to yourself. Friends look at your eyes and catch the shift in your energy. They are baffled by the way you clam up, yet nothing they do pries the gist of your hurt from your lips. Should you decide to share a tidbit, you leave out important facts, usually because your pain would show if you disclosed the whole truth. In contrast, these friends break down and tell all with one quick glance at your radar eyes. Your knack for ferreting out the truth is fueled by your genuine desire to help the troubled transform their lives. You need a few good friends who are patient with your bouts of silence, share your love of sports and competition, and help you put away exotic foods at trendy restaurants.

You need deep space and a quiet environment to do your best work. Employers who push you into frenetic situations and want instant results are sorely disappointed. You become rigid and your brain goes numb. Your boss should appreciate the thorough approach you use in searching for facts and your strong business savvy. While you thrive in large organizations, employers need to realize that you prefer to work alone. To achieve maximum career satisfaction, look for employers who value your professional integrity, encourage your autonomy, and ignore your habitual sniping.

Constant reporting before a product is ready drives you straight to the bat cave. You may threaten insecure bosses with your craving for new challenges and use of strategic planning methods, especially if you make no secret of your intention to orchestrate a hostile takeover—the work group, the department, or the firm. Accept positions with employers who give your project-driven mindset a workout.

Sagittarius Moon

Life is a lark and you like to hear its music in faraway places with your sweetheart, your best friend, or your favorite boss. You are blessed with boundless energy and want it reinforced by enthusiastic employers and capricious companions. You need a boss who appreciates your optimism. After you've made the silk purse, you'll get plenty of comments from the doubters' corner about how they knew you could do it, but few associates will realize how much self-control it took to complete your goal.

Astute employers sense your high level of dedication and allow you plenty of latitude in managing the details. Bosses make your day when they send you on long trips or ask you to accompany them on plum assignments to foreign countries. You need employers who are tolerant of your brutal honesty and are unflappable when you tell them their reorganization proposal is headed for disaster. Rigid types will not appreciate it when you serve up theories like sunny-side eggs and want to fund them with most of the available grant money. Secure your destiny with employers who invest in further education of the staff, recruit for language skills, and promote diversity.

In the love department, you seldom have trouble attracting a mate and enjoy the chase, but not all of you are keepers of the flame. The duality of Sagittarius suggests that very different romantic types represent your Moon sign. Some of you have a romantic interest in every port like the proverbial sailor. You set up territorial sideboards and let your partner know you will bail out if emotions override your need for freedom. Others of your Moon sign love deeply and tenderly, yet your atypical jealousy curdles Cupid's caresses. Then you decide you want more independence from your partner and the fire goes out. Others are incredibly cautious in love matters, but once you validate your heart's decision, you are faithful to the end.

Both male and female Sagittarius Moons procrastinate when it comes to making a serious love commitment. Whether you decide to marry or not, you will find your greatest bliss with partners who share your sense of adventure and love of intellectual stimulation. Aim your flaming arrows at the truthful type and you may capture the love of your life.

Capricorn Moon

At the top of your list of prerequisites for emotional fulfillment is an employer who offers long-term career stability and a generous benefits package. When considering employment offers, you look at the parameters of the signing bonus and negotiate ways to spread the wealth for as many years as possible. You have to know that prospective bosses promote from within the organization and that your rise to the top will be rapid and rewarding. You are mesmerized by organization charts and quickly assess the paths you might take to achieve the highest status possible.

Although your leadership style may be either authoritarian or participatory, you expect respect for workplace ethics. Trust issues are important. You want colleagues to know that your word counts. Some of you start looking for another job if the organization threatens worker security and falls from grace in your eyes. Others grumble incessantly and curl up in a blanket of gloom that can permanently curb their ambition or ruin their health. Find your sense of humor and look for opportunities with employers who let you demonstrate your workhorse panache and make lots of money.

The Moon in Capricorn is in the sign of its detriment, and is associated with emotional repression that surfaces in your adult life. Some of your psychological inhibition may stem from a poor relationship with dear old mom. These hangups affect your perspective about love. When romance strikes you Capricorn Moons, you may date the boss' children or marry the employer. Your choice of friend or partner may include those who share your sense of community. Some of you meet prospective mates at fund raisers, where you have a chance to assess their net. You can be very passionate or very aloof and need a partner who understands your self-protective reserve. A mature mind appeals to you and you could marry someone who has a few years on you. Your loved one needs to understand that you will spend a lot of time on the job, but the material rewards are a shared resource that fulfills fantasies and practical needs for both of you.

Loyalty and longevity are your signature traits. Marry a partner who can advance your career and you may celebrate a golden anniversary together.

Aquarius Moon

You are the innovative channelers of the universe, Aquarius Moon, and find emotional gratification through exciting assignments, unique lifestyles, and intelligent companions. The ideal work climate should provide latitude for your independent thinking. You thrill with assignments that involve human resources development, problem solving, and the high-paced work of a change agent. You have a knack for making major decisions that generate a win-win environment for the greater whole. Bosses should not give you the "hatchet man" assignment as your compassion runs deep—you'll be looking for new positions for those you have to fire. Employers must respect your need for privacy as you tend to be reserved about disclosing too much of your personal life and don't like being put on the spot before you are ready to talk. You have a deep psyche and give body language specialists a workout.

You are seldom a clock watcher and bosses appreciate your commitment to work until the task is finished. They sometimes spot your need for a break before you do—you get cranky and crotchety from mental anxiety and lack of food. Most of you Aquarian Moons have a creative flair for consulting businesses of all types. Find employers who charge you with creating a climate of positive change or start your own business. Look for relationships with people who advocate broad-minded change for society's good.

Your powerful charisma attracts a variety of friends, yet very few are your true intimates. Potential mates need to give you a lot of space or you balk and drop out of sight. If they have a problem, you enjoy rescuing them by offering constructive solutions. Although you are reluctant to make commitments until you feel you know everything about the person, you make a loyal partner once you give your heart away. If you are a male with an Aquarius Moon, get used to the idea that your soulmate may not want to be treated like your child once the relationship gels. If a female Aquarius Moon, pick partners who tell the truth, for you seldom forgive them when you catch them in a lie. Search for partners who savor your magnetic personality and share your interest in unusual topics. Let your independent spirit fall in love with commitment to your cherished goals and expect the blessings of a glorious partnership.

Pisces Moon

Lunar Pisceans enjoy the work scene and pitch in feverishly when crunch time hits. More than most signs, you environmentally sensitive Pisceans need to enjoy the work itself and the people who work with you. Bosses must show appreciation for the way you go beyond the call of duty to please them, or you get resentful. Coworkers usually benefit from your kindness and helpfulness in coordinating workloads. You can fall into dangerous self-pity traps when less productive types dump their unfinished work on you. With your innate compassion, you easily fall for a sob story, even when you see through the details. You need an astute supervisor to oversee the workload balance.

While money feeds your security gene, you are much more concerned with finding work you love and need a good fit to stay motivated and involved. Nothing is worse than an unfulfilled Pisces Moon. You may daydream excessively or fall into a downward spiral instead of organizing your life for meaningful change. You need work that offers variety and vision because forced routines are actually adverse to your delicate Piscean nature. Employers who offer flexible workplace programs help you break the cycle of monotony that often frustrates you. A few guidelines and a quiet alcove and you're on a productive roll.

Most of you experience problems with authority figures at some point in your career. Restore balance in your life by critically examining your attitudes, rewriting your resume to match your career preferences, and cultivating partnerships with people who have a positive effect on your self-confidence.

With your dynamic psychic insight, partners often feel vulnerable that you are tuning in to their innermost thoughts. You seem to know what is on their mind before they speak, and answer their questions before they ask. Actually, you give so much to those you love because you genuinely want to please them and secretly long for the same depth of devotion. Unless you have strong fire placements in your natal chart, you go out of your way not to hurt your partner. That means stuffing your true feelings when you really need to unload. Pick partners whose hearts palpitate to the passionate rhythm you so potently propagate.

New Moon, New Start

By Donna Cunningham, M.S.W.

The day after the New Moon is viewed by many classically trained astrologers as an excellent time to start an enterprise. The seed of a new project is planted at that time to grow with the waxing Moon, reach a point of fruition at the Full Moon, and then wind down and tie up loose ends as the Moon wanes. The dark of the Moon is best used to contemplate what has been accomplished and to plan for the next lunar cycle. This highly productive technique of working with the Moon's rhythm can be enhanced by paying attention to the sign of the New Moon and any planets that aspect it, as we will do in this article. Combined, these factors highlight the types of issues or projects that are likely to respond well to focused attention in any given month. Below I will give an overview of each of the New Moons of 1998. If you know your birth chart, or even just the rising sign, personalize the capsule readings that follow by tracking the New Moons through your own chart. (You can order a printout of your natal chart through Llewellyn at 1-800-THE MOON.) Pay attention to the houses they fall into, for those represent the areas of life where monthly projects would especially bear fruit. A Ninth House New Moon, for instance, is an excellent time to begin some course of study, while a Second House lunation is timely for a new financial plan, and a Sixth House New Moon would be good for establishing a new health regimen.

The degrees of the New Moons are given here. If they fall within three degrees of a planet in your chart, that planet and its issues are highlighted for at least a month. If a New Moon occurs within three days of your birthday, then the concerns of that lunation may well be with you all year. If a solar eclipse—which occurs once or twice a year on the New Moon—is conjunct (within 3 degrees of) one of your planets, it is highlighted for at least six months. *Editor's Note: The listings of the degrees and minutes of each New Moon in this article have been rounded off to the nearest degree.*

I will also be giving some information about using flower essences in the capsule readings. The choice of whether or not to use this information is, of course, entirely up to you.

If you use this one-year cycle diligently, you will notice a gradual improvement on all fronts

A Note about Flower Essences

Some of you may already be using the flower remedies made by Bach, the Flower Essence Society, and other companies, but you may not know how well they support your work with lunar cycles. I will suggest remedies (also known as essences) for the issues each of the New Moons evokes. Similar in some respects to homeopathy, flower remedies are natural substances that stimulate our consciousness to work through issues and release thought patterns that hold us back. If you are unfamiliar with these tools, keep an open mind, and one or more of the ones described here may touch on issues you'd like to improve. If so, give them a try.

You may order these liquids in concentrate form (called stock level) or a dosage-level mixture. Mix the concentrates with an ounce of water in the type of dropper bottle pharmacies use for eye drops, and shake a hundred times. Starting at the New Moon if possible, take four drops of the mixture four times a day until you feel complete with the process. Those who need more details about the remedies might wish to order my *Flower Remedies*

Handbook from the publisher, Sterling, at 1-800-548-0075.

While you can order directly from the companies mentioned, many will find it more convenient to order from two handy sources that carry a vast number of remedies from companies around the world: Flower Essence Pharmacy (1-800-343-8693) and Flower Vision Research (1-800-298-4434). Both companies can mix several of the concentrates together for you in a dosage bottle. If you want the concentrates, the Bach remedies are available at many health or New Age stores or from the sources above. The Flower Essence Society (shortened here to FES) can be reached directly at 1-800-548-0075, and Desert Alchemy at (602) 325-1545. Ask for a catalog, as I will only mention a few of the multitudes of remedies available. (If you aren't ready to work with the remedies, just skip that part of the monthly reading.)

The Impact of the New Moon

There were two Capricorn New Moons in 1997, as the collective—and Capricorns in particular—struggled to establish new structures in the face of important shifts by three of the outer planets into new signs. In 1998, by contrast, there are no Capricorn New Moons, signifying that, in general, structures are more solidly established this year. This, combined with Neptune's shift from Capricorn into Aquarius, is likely to give those people with Capricorn highlighted a much needed breather, after nearly a decade of intense stress and change. (Capricorn is highlighted in your chart if the Sun, Moon, rising sign, or several planets are in that sign.)

On the other hand, many Leos will be challenged by this year's lunar pattern, because there are two New Moons in Leo. The first, on July 23, opposes Neptune in Aquarius and the second, on August 22, is a solar eclipse. Those with Leo strong in their charts—the Sun, Moon, or rising sign—are constrained to reexamine outmoded self-concepts and to take a less egocentric view of the world's rapidly changing contours. They will be asked to let go of the "what does that mean for me" goggles and look at the universal implications of events that are, essentially, out of their control. The galaxy no longer revolves around them—not that it ever did, but Leos like to dream.

The 1998 New Moons

January

The New Moon is at 1:02 am EST on January 28. (10:02 pm PST on January 27) It is at 8 degrees of Aquarius, with the Sun and Moon both conjunct Uranus within hours of the New Moon.

Because of the close conjunction to Uranus, this is perhaps the most Aquarian New Moon of the century, for Uranus is the planetary ruler of Aquarius and last entered its own sign in 1912. Thus, as a collective, we kick off 1998 by a visionary look at where we are now and what the future holds. Spend some time this month contemplating your own future and honing your personal vision of what you can create in the world. Look beyond personal concerns to glimpse how you fit into the universal needs of our increasingly interconnected world. Where will you be at the millennium? What new technology do you need to join the fast pace of progress? Flower remedies to help with this visionary process are FES's Shooting Star (for a feeling of fitting into humanity), Desert Alchemy's Fulfilling Your Divine Mission, or their Sacred Datura, the flower essence based on a plant Native Americans used for vision quests.

February

There is a total eclipse of the Sun at 8 degrees Pisces on February 26 at 12:27 pm EST/9:27 am PST. Jupiter in Pisces is only two degrees away from the conjunction.

Fittingly, the combination of Sun, Moon, and Jupiter in Pisces extends last month's search for a longer view by zeroing in on spiritual, psychic, and creative development. It is more a month for dreaming than for doing, but those dreams will contain the seeds of future action. With Jupiter in the picture, it is a wonderful month for learning or teaching inspirational materials—the best of all possible times for a workshop being at the New or Full Moon this month. Lotus, the sacred flower, is also a potent flower essence, helpful with all meditative and spiritual pursuits, and is especially relevant to this month's lunation. FES's St. John's Wort, for faith, Angelica for connecting with the angels and higher realms, or Mugwort for dreamwork, would also be wonderful spiritual "booster shots."

March

The New Moon at 7 degrees Aries is at 10:27 pm EST/7:15 pm PST on March 27. It forms a close trine to Pluto in Sagittarius.

Finally, after all that drifting and dreaming, the potent moment for action presents itself. Not only have we just entered the astrological new year, the New Moon in Aries is also a focused flame that can be an important new beginning in some area of your life. Go for it! That trine to Pluto will help you persevere toward your goal. This is an excellent month to initiate activities that require drive, confidence, and concentrated bursts of energy—even physically demanding ones. Bach's Larch helps if you hold back because of fear of failure. FES's Cayenne spurs you out of lethargy, and their Blackberry helps you put ideas into action. Bach's Gentian strengthens those who become easily discouraged after a setback—like when the Sun hits Saturn on April 13.

April

The New Moon at 6 degrees Taurus occurs at 7:42 am EDT/4:42 am PDT on April 26. It forms right angles to both Uranus and Neptune in Aquarius.

This month's lunation highlights your financial life, and especially any addictive spending or debt patterns. It's time to turn over a new leaf, taking in hand any spaciness or willfulness where money is concerned. Take stock of your assets and debts and make a reasonable budget. At the same time, the aspects to Uranus and Neptune suggest that you also share some of your abundance with charitable or social causes. This is a good month for starting projects that require careful financial planning, practicality, and groundedness. Four Leaf Clover by Pegasus Products can help those who take foolhardy financial risks, while abundance consciousness can be enhanced by Abundance Essence by Pacific Essences or Celebration of Abundance by Desert Alchemy.

May

On May 25 at 3:33 pm EDT/12:33 pm PDT, there is a New Moon at 4 degrees Gemini, conjunct Mars and opposite Pluto and trine Uranus.

An emphasis on communication, writing, study, or travel can make this an interesting and exciting month, so design a project to meet some of your heart's desires in these areas. Gemini's tendency toward glibness or staying on the surface may be challenged by the opposition to Pluto, which urges you to dig in deeper, do your research, and analyze hidden meanings. Madia, Cosmos, Rabbitbrush, and Indian Pink are all FES essences that help with various forms of difficulty in concentration. Shasta Daisy helps synthesize ideas coming from diverse perspectives.

June

The New Moon is on June 23 at 11:51 pm EDT/8:51 pm PDT at 2 degrees Cancer.

This is the month to tend the home fires and any family ties you may have been yearning to renew. If you have a home improvement project in mind, working on it now can help you feel better grounded and nurtured by your nest. If there are painful family-of-origin wounds, use this month to lift and heal some of the residues, for family is bound to be on your mind anyway. Two of the most potent healers are FES's Golden Eardrops, for releasing the pain associated with unhappy childhood memories, and Mariposa Lily, for feelings of alienation resulting from a poor bond with the mother. For homesickness or nostalgia, try Bach's Honeysuckle.

July

The first of two New Moons in Leo this year occurs on July 23 at 9:45 am EDT/6:45 am PDT. It falls at 1 degree of Leo, opposite Neptune at 1 degree Aquarius and square Saturn at 3 degrees Taurus.

Falling just at the peak of vacation time, this combination challenges us to walk a tightrope between our desires for fun, glamour, and fantasy (Leo, Neptune in Aquarius) and the very real financial constraints (Saturn in Taurus) we all face from time to time. The challenge here is to find fun and exciting activities that don't leave a lasting hole in the budget. Use your imagination—rent videos of your favorite old movies, throw a party where you all dress as your favorite stars, or pile in the car and hold a midnight beach cookout. FES's California Wild Rose can help with the end-of-summer blahs, and their Hound's Tooth can help those who think money is a prerequisite for fulfillment. Those who yearn for glamour can find a real-world balance with FES's California Poppy.

August

The second New Moon in Leo occurs at 29 degrees Leo and is an eclipse of the Sun. (It occurs just past midnight on August 22 Eastern Time, or at 9:07 pm Pacific.)

Both Leo New Moons may challenge those with Leo prominent in their charts to examine their self-concepts, discarding those that are outmoded, and to find a realistic self-esteem. All of us could productively use this eclipse period in nurturing self-worth and gaining a realistic assessment of our postive and not so postive qualities. Where available, use a personality test or inventory of skills and abilities. Those who are well versed in astrology could use the houses of the birth chart to assess how they are currently functioning in all the major areas of life. Such self-examination can sometimes lead us to be hard on ourselves, so flower remedies for self-esteem can be valuable tools in this process. FES's Sunflower is the quintessential Sun-remedy, for it balances self-esteem, neither undervaluing or overestimating one's contributions. Their Buttercup helps you to cherish your talents and abilities.

September

At 1:03 pm EDT/10:03 am PDT on September 20, there will be a New Moon at 28 degrees Virgo, opposing Jupiter in Pisces.

In the hey-day of autumn, the month of Virgo is always a great time to streamline work operations and day-to-day routine. Take a look at what is and is not working, revamp procedures to be more efficient, toss out clutter, and give your work site a good cleaning. The connection with Jupiter in Pisces asks you to balance work with spiritual pursuits and to temper criticism with compassion, especially around this month's Full Moon. Desert Alchemy's Staghorn Cholla is a wonder for times of reorganization—take it and watch those closets or files sort themselves out! The FES remedy Filaree helps Virgos and other worry-warts move from obsessing about small details into a larger perspective.

October

On October 20, at 6:10 am EDT/3:10 am PDT, there will be a New Moon at 27 degrees Libra squaring Neptune.

With the connection to Neptune, this Libra New Moon is an important time to examine your relationships and to tackle and change patterns that are codependent. You might especially want to examine ways you are allowing yourself to be taken advantage of in your relationships. Cantaury, by Bach, is an important remedy in changing the ways you volunteer for victimization, while Desert Alchemy's Ephedra mobilizes the will to extricate yourself from abusive situations. If you don't feel your relationships are codepedent or abusive, but would like instead to enhance your capacity for emotional and physical intimacy, try FES's Pink Monkeyflower. If your relationships are happy, congratulate yourself and spend the month on beautification projects—whether your home or your personal image. FES's Iris, for creativity, can give you inspiration in such efforts.

November

The New Moon at 27 degrees Scorpio will be on November 18 at 11:28 pm EST/8:28 pm PST.

Scorpio is the sign of transformation and rebirth, so this sometimes intense month can be an excellent time to identify healing issues, especially old emotional baggage that you want to be liberated from. It would be a good time to begin body work, attend a self-help group, or take a workshop that focuses on some of your issues. An especially powerful transformation can come from letting go of long-standing resentments, for that rekindles your zest for life, as it releases energy that had gone into brooding and makes it available for more constructive pursuits. Bach's Willow and Holly are excellent for sorting out resentments and letting go of the tendency to accumulate them. If the wounds have gone deep, forgiveness work can literally transform a life. If you are willing to give it a try, Salal by Pacific Essences and Mountain Wormwood are amazing supports.

December

The New Moon on December 18 falls at 27 degrees Sagittarius, in a stablilizing trine to Saturn in Aries (5:43 pm EST/2:43 pm PST).

"Joy to the World" is an old carol that could well be the theme for this month's New Moon in optimistic Sag. As you have followed the course of the year's New Moons and designed projects for each month, a myriad of accomplishments, both large and small, may well have given you a new perpective and new hope in your life. Focus this month on such positive thinking tools as visualizations and affirmations. An excellent combination of remedies to support you in the process of changing your mind-set for a more positive outcome is FES's so-called "manifestation formula," consisting of Blackberry, Iris, and Madia. If you are discouraged, Bach's Gentian or Gorse can improve your attitude and lift your spirits.

The Yearly Lunation Cycle: A Tool for Life

If you use this one-year cycle diligently, you will notice a gradual improvement on all fronts, for the cycle of New Moons covers every house in your chart, and thus causes you to focus on and tackle issues in every major area of your life. The capsule readings given here have been based not just on the New Moon's sign but on planets in aspect to it, which change every year. Still, the process is one you may become hooked on and wish to consider using every year.

Healing with Fire, Earth, Air, & Water

By Gretchen Lawlor

Just as the elements fire, earth, air, and water are the building blocks of life, to an astrologer they provide the foundations and vital indicators for the health and well-being of an individual. Each of us has a dominant element in our makeup. When we identify it we've got an excellent tool for improving our health.

How do you identify your dominant element? Start with your Sun sign for an indicator of your essential vitality. The fire signs, Aries, Leo, and Sagittarius, are the most radiant and vital of the signs. Next are the air signs, Gemini, Libra, and Aquarius. The water signs, Cancer, Scorpio, and Pisces, are more dense. They are a more difficult medium through which to manifest, and take longer to charge up again. Earth signs, Taurus, Virgo, and Capricorn, are the most dense, giving tenacity rather than vitality.

Fire signs are conductors. They like to spread their energy around. Air signs are curious and ready to relate. Water is more self-protective and indirect. Earth is cautious and conservative. Water is accented in childhood, while fire is strongest in adolescence. The air element increases with age, and earth strengthens with maturity.

The Fire Constitution

(Aries, Leo, Sagittarius)

Fire rules the function of internal combustion, or digestion, in the body. Fire is needed to burn up and absorb foods cleanly and efficiently. Fire is purifying; it is necessary for removing toxins, viruses, bacteria, and fungus from the system.

Fire signs have the ability to burn off viruses and fight diseases more aggressively than any of the other signs. The extremely high temperatures and sudden acute inflammations that are natural for a fire sign can be terrifying without the knowledge that this is quite the norm for them.

The fire element is strongest from puberty to middle age, in the summer, and daily at noon. Fire has good recuperative abilities from ailments that are extreme and short-lived. Fire sign people tend to ignore warning signals from their bodies. If injured, they will attempt to stay mobile, seeing no reason to stop to recuperate.

Each of us has a dominant element in our makeup...When we identify it we've got an excellent tool for improving our health

The Earth Constitution

(Taurus, Virgo, Capricorn)

The earth element rules the skeletal and eliminatory systems. The earth element is essential to growth, reproduction, and repair of tissue. Like water, the earth element is vital and active in childhood, becoming more dense with age. Earth signs know how to conserve themselves, and have a natural instinct as to which foods are right or wrong for them.

Earth is more accomplished at building up than breaking down, hence there is a tendency toward weight problems, tumor growth, and glandular disorders (especially involving the thyroid). Overeating and a diet of heavy foods create excess earth, which is aggravated by sedentary habits and lack of exercise.

The earth signs have strong sense impressions and thrive on contact with the earth. Theirs is a strength of endurance and persistence. They are more resistant than fire or air to transient colds and flu, but find it harder to throw off bugs once they have taken hold.

The Air Constitution

(Gemini, Libra, Aquarius)

Air rules the nervous and circulatory systems, and the function of movement, i.e. peristalsis, urination, and breathing. Air people are easily stimulated, with quick and extremely sensitive minds that are easily stressed.

The air constitution tends to catch and throw off health problems quickly, but can suffer from lingering after-effects because of impatience and inconsistency, and unwillingness to slow down or remain focused long enough to recover fully. They tend to have a low threshold for pain.

The air element is accentuated between 2:00 and 6:00 am, by dry or windy weather, excess sunlight, x-rays, computer and TV radiation, loud sounds, and by shock and fear. The air element strengthens with age, which works to your advantage if you are naturally low in air.

The Water Constitution

(Cancer, Scorpio, Pisces)

The water element rules the reproductive and lymphatic systems, and all the liquids of the body. Water lubricates and cools the body. Water signs are exceptionally sensitive to their environment, particularly to fungi, bacteria, and viruses. They are sturdier than they look because of their accentuated ability to flush toxins from the system. Their body type tends to be well rounded and full, with good skin. The water element is strongest during childhood.

Health issues for water signs generally have a strong emotional component, though it is not necessarily their own emotions they are responding to. They easily pick up negativity from others. They tend to brood on their health and imagine problems to be greater than they are. Frequently there is a periodicity to their health problems, which they can use to their advantage if they learn to anticipate these periods of lowered vitality. They respond well to a practitioner who is sympathetic, cheerful, and optimistic, and willing to spend time with them to ferret out underlying emotional issues.

Types of Constitutions

Division of human constitutions into different classifications has been around for thousands of years. In the fifth century BCE Hippocrates developed four basic types, which he correlated from the elements of astrology. There's the phlegmatic or earthy constitution, valued for its unemotional calm, and the cheerful optimism of the sanguine, or air constitution. The melancholic, or water constitution, has its emotional sensitivity, and the choleric, or fire sign type, has a hot temper.

This methodology was developed and widely used by physicians into the nineteenth century. There is currently a revival of interest in constitutional types by many practitioners in the mainstream and alternative health fields. Conventional medicine has ignored the unique makeup of each individual when recommending treatment, and yet we all know we respond differently to illnesses, stresses, and even to medications. By identifying the constitution of individuals we can have an idea of the progression of their illness and choose the best form of treatment for them. The information gained is focused on what sort of patient has the disease rather than what sort of disease the patient has.

Sun Types and Moon Types

The Sun by element in your astrological chart is indicative of your underlying essence, the dominant theme or orientation of your life. Therefore it is an excellent indicator of the life force available to you. Much more detail and accuracy can be gathered if the full horoscope is available. Here you will have information on ten planets plus the ascendant.

In times of stress it is often the element of the Moon that will give you the most information in terms of tonic support to the system. The position of the Moon indicates instinctive habits or coping mechanisms that you return to for emotional support during times of difficulty; what you need in order to feel safe and secure.

For example, a Moon in Scorpio prefers to move an uncomfortable situation into crisis rather than to leave it simmering. Only in that way do they feel they can move on—by bringing it to a head and moving through it, *now*. Comfort foods for Scorpio Moon will be found in the information for the water signs below, and are useful in supporting their need for emotional discharge.

A Taurus Moon, in contrast, is extremely discomforted by emotional outbursts and will prefer to ignore them. As an earth sign, these people may pretend nothing is going on, plodding on despite the explosions around them. They use food as a panacea, or extra girth as a buffer to difficult environments. They are more emotionally unshaken, but need to be careful that they don't suppress difficult emotions entirely, as these suppressed emotions can develop into toxic tissue.

Identifying Excessive and Weak Elements

If you have access to your full horoscope, you have the tools for a more comprehensive picture of your health. By categorizing the planets and Ascendant into the four elements, you will come up with more details about the strengths and weaknesses of your unique constitution.

Here is an example of a horoscope broken down into fire, earth, air, and water for a person born August 3, 1987, at 4:30 am. This person has Sun in Leo (fire); Moon in Scorpio (water); Ascendant in Cancer (water); Mercury in Cancer (water); Venus in Leo (fire); Mars in Leo (fire); Jupiter in Aries (fire); Saturn in Sagittarius (fire); Uranus in Sagittarius (fire); Neptune in Capricorn (earth); and Pluto in Scorpio (water).

If each planet is categorized by element, and if you give two points each to Sun, Moon, and Ascendant to reflect their greater influence, you have seven fire planets; six water planets; one earth planet; and no air planets. This gives an excess of fire and a deficiency in air and earth.

If this were your horoscope, how would we describe your vitality, your elemental constitution? Immediately we know that you have high natural life force, are prone to sudden inflammations and high fevers when you are ill, and that you recover quickly. You tend to stretch yourself to the maximum and ignore your body's warnings, and need to take care not to burn yourself out. You tend toward headaches due to energy blockages that keep your energy high in your body. This could be rectified with acupuncture treatment. Your digestive function is extremely active, you have a voracious appetite, and are hungry again soon after eating.

Grains, potatoes, squash, yams, sweet potatoes, and dairy products—heavy nutritious foods that take a long time to digest—are particularly beneficial. Reasonable amounts of sugars, butter, and oil are also good for your constitutional type.

Helpful herbs would be mineral-rich ones like seaweed, nettles, and Siberian ginseng for tonic support and steady grounding energy.

Balancing Your Elements

Few people are born with a perfect balance of elements in their makeup, and life is constantly presenting challenges that require adaptation. Health is not a constant state, but a perpetually shifting interaction between outer circumstances and inner constitution. Each time we eat a meal there is a complex interaction of elements as we adjust to the intake and adapt the materials presented by the meal to our unique needs. Moments of balance occur between periods of readjustment.

Each element interacts with each other in nature, and also in our own bodies. Earth grounds air, water moistens fire, fire warms and dries out water, and air stimulates and aerates earth.

To Balance Fire

Low Fire

With a deficiency of the fire element, it may be hard to burn off or fight disease. The digestion and absorption of food are inadequate and need stimulation, but must be done gradually to prevent irritation. Eat foods that are light, hot, dry, and aromatic, and avoid cold foods. Hot spices and sour food, such as lemons and yogurt, are good, as are whole grains cooked in oil, spices, and even salt. Keep dairy and meat to a minimum, and frequent light meals are best. Midday is a good time to eat your main meal, as the maximum amount of fire your body can marshal is available at this time.

Headaches are frequently caused by low fire, where the only partially digested food begins to ferment. Physical exercise helps strengthen the fire element.

Low fire is strengthened by digestive stimulants such as cayenne, ginger, mustard, and cloves. Use circulatory stimulants such as cinnamon, garlic, and ginger.

Excess Fire

Excessive fire has a tendency to burn out as fire people find it difficult to conserve energy or pace themselves. They are prone to skin problems, acne, and have a strong body odor.

Fire is hot, light, and dry, and is therefore balanced by foods that are cold, moist, and heavy, or slow-burning foods that ground energy. A voracious appetite reflects excess fire. Anything that stimulates this should be avoided, particularly if you are thin and wiry. If this is the case, eat bland foods, avoid stimulating spices, consume little oil, meat, nuts, and beans. Raw or steamed vegetables are good, as is fruit (avoid sour fruits, peaches, and bananas). Milk is good, but not yogurt, as it is too sour.

Excess fire should avoid spicy herbs. Goldenseal, aloe, and milk thistle help detoxify the liver. Blood purifiers, such as yellow dock, reduce inflammations.

To Balance Earth

Excess Earth

Excess earth is prone to heaviness in the body and sluggishness in the system, with dullness and lethargy. Digestion and metabolism are slow, increasing density of body tissue, i.e. thick skin, sclerosis, calcium deposits, tumors, and increased body hair. Excess earth eats too much, too frequently.

Light foods such as fruit, salads, sprouts, and steamed vegetables with spices are advised. Meals that consist of liquids, juices, soups, and teas are better than heavier diets. If possible, the main meal should be taken at midday, when digestive fire is strongest. Meals should be simple. Keep combinations to a minimum, with no desserts and plenty of time to digest. Avoid dairy and fried foods. Fasting helps as earth tends to retain toxins.

Use bitter tonics such as gentian or Swedish bitters, and hot spices such as ginger, black pepper, and cayenne.

Low Earth

Low earth needs grounding. Low-earth people tend to ignore the body and are not instinctive about what they need. They need activities and routines that stabilize their lives and give a sense of security. Foods need to be heavy and nutritious, such as potatoes, unrefined grains, and dairy. Use vegetables steamed and served with cheese and butter. Reasonable amounts of sugar, butter, and oil are well tolerated. Keep fruits and raw foods to a minimum. To improve the digestion, cook with plenty of spices.

Low earth should use demulcents such as licorice, slippery elm, seaweed, and minerals. Ginseng is grounding, as is astragalus and the auryvedic herb ashwaganda.

To Balance Air

Excess Air

Restlessness, excessively dry hair and skin, dry mucus membranes, nervous disorders, problems with balance, and even Alzheimer's disease are associated with too much air. Excessive air tends toward insomnia from an inability to turn it all off, as well as memory loss from systemic overload. Air benefits from a schedule with intervals of relaxation with minimal stimulation (not even television or radio), to allow the nervous system to recharge itself.

Dancing, any slow and rhythmic exercise, yoga or yoga breathing, or any breath meditations are particularly helpful for air signs. The wearing of warm colors and the adoption of consistent daily routines will bring out the best of air's vivacious and versatile nature.

Excess Air benefits from digestive enzymes or swedish bitters and small, frequent meals. There is a tendency toward gas, and the bowels evacuate quickly.

Air is cold and very drying and needs to be balanced by moisture and heat. In terms of diet use dairy (especially yogurt), cooked rice and oats, vegetables cooked in oil, nuts, and seeds.

Air energy tends to collect high in the body and gains from any opportunity to connect with earth, to be drawn or enticed downward. Grains and root crops are particularly helpful. Raw foods aggravate the naturally cold quality of air. Raw salads should be kept to a minimum, though are easier to tolerate in the warm summer months. Otherwise use plenty of dressing, and add or replace with lightly steamed vegetables, nuts or croutons to ground the energy. Avoid yeasty foods, mushrooms, refined sugars, beans, and too much cabbage and broccoli.

Herbs for excessive air signs include nervines such as skullcap, passionflower, or even valerian. These can be particularly soothing to the anxiety of the air type.

Low Air

For those lacking air there may be problems with the flow of body energy. Circulatory stimulants such as garlic and ginger are good. Anything that is light, dry, and stimulating will be helpful. Nervines can also be helpful, but specifically those that are tonic but not particularly sedating, such as skullcap or oats.

To Balance Water

Excess Water

Excess water manifests as excess weight, in the form of water and fat. Even without an excessive appetite, these people have sluggish digestion, poor assimilation, and slow metabolism. Stagnant excess water may manifest as mucus, cysts, tumors, and swellings, as well as systemic candida. It is seldom helpful to decrease dietary intake alone; better results come from increasing the metabolic rate, decreasing the liquid intake, changing the diet, and increasing physical activity.

Excess water is balanced by foods that are hot, dry, and light. Vegetables are well tolerated, steamed and spicy, with minimal salt. Sweets increase water and fat; if eaten, they should be eaten separately. Excess water is cold, wet, and heavy. Avoid heavy, oily foods, dairy, sweets, yeasty foods, breads, and salt. Beans and fruit are good, but avoid large quantities of melon.

Excess water should use digestive stimulants and expectorants such as sage, basil, and thyme. Diuretics such as parsley, uva ursi, and juniper berries help drain excess water from boggy tissue.

Low Water

Low water constitutions have trouble flushing toxins from their systems, and lack lubrication to their systems. They tend to be stiff and dehydrated and have difficulty sleeping. They suffer from conditions similar to excess air, such as skin and hair dryness and difficult absorption of nutrients. They find it hard to receive emotional nourishment. Add baths, drink plenty of liquids, and live near water. Use wheat, rice, oats, seaweed, dairy products, and natural sugars. Avoid beans and natural diuretics such as carrots, celery, cabbage, and asparagus. Don't fast. Take care with extreme exposure to heat or sunlight, and take extra salt with exertion or warm weather.

Exercise, Diet, & Weight Loss by the Moon

By Janina Renee

There are many ways that we can improve our health by attuning ourselves to the cycles of the Moon. One thing that we can do is apply her phases of increase and decrease to the building of muscle and loss of fat through diet and exercise. Following is an outline for a health program that emphasizes building lean muscle mass with the waxing Moon, and then shifting focus to diet and the burning of fat with the waning Moon.

First Quarter

Start a program of exercise on the first day of the New Moon. This program should require that you do at least twenty minutes of outdoor exercise each day, though you can choose the type of exercise you prefer. This enables you to connect with the life force, and will stimulate the vibrant health that is so important to radiant beauty. It also takes you out into the realm of nature, which has such an affinity with the Moon's powers. I recommend brisk walking, as it has aerobic qualities and enables you to see what's going on in nature. If it is not possible to be outdoors, then indoor exercise is okay. Also, do a moderate amount of weight lifting—perhaps about ten minutes a day to start with. During the Moon's first quarter, just ease into your exercise routine and don't push yourself too hard, especially if you have not been exercising regularly. Do visualize yourself building muscle: picture yourself becoming more taut and toned with the Moon's daily increase.

Do not get into any serious diets at this stage, the first quarter phase, as you will need energy as you adjust to your program of exercise, but keep your consumption moderate so that you are not consuming more than you need. This is a good time to concentrate on learning about and preparing more nutritious foods—foods that are very fresh so that your own vitality can increase with that of the Moon. It is important to eat a decent breakfast and adequate meals, and your meals (and snacks) should contain at least two hundred calories just to get your metabolic furnace going and keep it burning. If you consume fewer than two hundred calories, your metabolic burner won't kick in, making the calories more likely to go to fat. Also, do drink lots of liquid (astrologically, liquids are ruled by the Moon), as the body requires a larger than normal amount of liquid to process the breakdown and elimination of fat.

Although you'll be tempted to check your scale each day, don't weigh yourself until you've followed your program through an entire Moon cycle. Exercise will build lean muscle mass, which is denser and therefore heavier than fat. Thus, you may actually gain weight while losing inches and clothing sizes. Fortunately, the lean muscle you will have created has enzymes that cause you to metabolize at a higher rate, so weight loss will eventually follow.

Start a program of exercise on the first day of the New Moon

Second Quarter

As the Moon progresses into this and the next two quarters, you can make your exercise more strenuous. You can also increase the amount of time spent exercising, perhaps adding an extra ten minutes with each following quarter. (If you have the time and are really determined, you could add twenty minutes with each new quarter.) As far as diet goes, continue to keep your consumption moderate. You can start learning about different types of diets, and make plans to go on one of them after the night of the Full Moon.

Full Moon

For the night of the Full Moon, plan something special to celebrate having come this far, and to renew your commitment to carrying out the rest of your program. Go somewhere or do something that you enjoy. Consider buying yourself a garment that's one size too small, to affirm that you will soon be able to wear it.

Third Quarter

By sticking with daily exercise during the waxing Moon phase, you will have acquired some lean muscle, which will cause you to start burning calories at a higher rate. You should continue to exercise, increasing the amount or difficulty of the exercise, with special emphasis on aerobic activities. However, the waning Moon phase is the time for releasing the things we want gone from our lives, so now you can turn your focus to weight loss. Therefore, on the first day after the Full Moon, shift your attitude and mental images to seriously trimming some fat. As you watch the Moon decrease (it will be visible later at night and early in the morning), visualize a more lithe and slender you.

While you're doing your daily exercise, visualize yourself burning fat. Take a positive rather than a negative approach to it: don't think of that fat as ugly flab. Think of it as stored energy. It may have served some practical or psychological purpose at one time, but now you are ready to release it. Think of your exercise as burning that stored energy, releasing it into the atmosphere for planet earth to metabolize. To reinforce this visualization, you can burn incense. (The kind of incense that you have to smolder on a brazier over a special charcoal briquette is ideal, because this type of incense produces especially impressive clouds of smoke.) Contemplate the rising smoke, then retain its image in your mind when you are ready to proceed with your exercise. The Egyptians, Aztecs, and other ancient peoples sometimes burned incense in astonishing quantities as part of very special celebrations. On the same note, think of this phase of your exercise as a big burn-off in celebration of the shaping of a newer and more beautiful you. Introduce a serious but sensible diet at this point. The diet should be one of your own choosing, determined by what is practical and realistic for your lifestyle.

Also, during this phase, you may want to consider whether any psychological factors or feelings have contributed to your being overweight. For example, attitudes that make for bad eating habits and the retention of weight can include seeking comfort and insulation from the harshness of the world. If you're thinking "I'm so thin-skinned" because you have problems dealing with difficult people, your unconscious mind, which takes the things you say and think literally, can respond by adding an additional layer of fat in order to "protect" you.

Fourth Quarter

Carry your program of diet and exercise through the remaining lunar quarter. While being mindful of your own body's needs so that you don't overdo anything, see if you can get used to eating less during the last quarter. It will probably not be possible for you to view the Moon's further decrease, as she rises later each evening, and you would have to stay up too late to see her—although you may sometimes be able to catch a glimpse of her during the day. Honor the last day and night of the old Moon (the Dark Moon) as a time of fast and contemplation.

Afterward

If you haven't lost poundage by the end of one Moon cycle, don't despair. Judge by how you feel and whether you're looking more trim and toned, not by what the scale says. Also, bear in mind that the muscle gained will continue to keep your metabolism higher, even after the Moon cycle is over. Of course, exercise should continue to be a part of your daily life. However, if you increased your amount of exercise intensively during the last quarter or quarters, once this program is over, you can drop back to just twenty minutes a day, or whatever is comfortable for you. Also, once you have gone through an entire Moon cycle, give yourself a break from the dieting. Continue to eat modestly enough so that you won't gain, but don't try to starve to lose more. You must take a break from dieting so that your body won't think you're weathering a long famine and lower your metabolism to retain more weight. If you want to lose more weight, then repeat this program every other Moon cycle, or just do your dieting during the Moon's waning phases.

The Cell Salts

Astrological Tonics for Healing

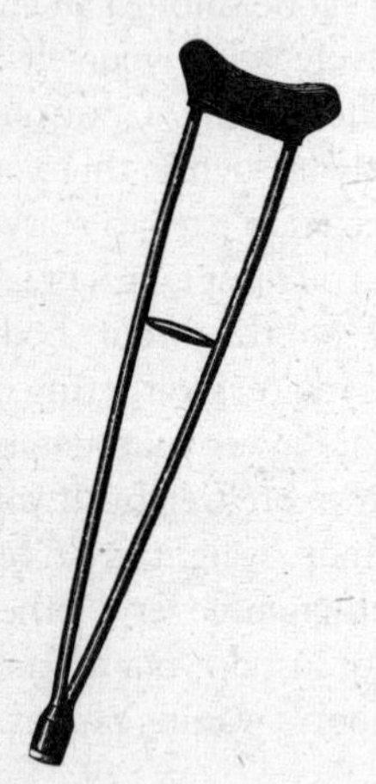

By Gretchen Lawlor

Homeopathy and astrology have colluded to provide an extraordinary series of tonic medicines particularly suited to each of the twelve astrological signs. These are called "homeopathic cell salts" or "biochemical cell salts," and can be used by people who have no medical background to improve the quality of health for themselves, their families, and friends.

These cell salts are readily available in most health food stores, and are inexpensive and easy to take. They are very popular with children and with their parents, because children are happy to take these tiny, sweet pellets that easily dissolve in the mouth. They are also used extensively with elderly people because of the gentleness of their action and the tonic support to tissues and functions that are beginning to falter. In adolescence the cell salts are invaluable, as they are easily depleted during the rapid growth and hormonal activity of the maturing body.

You might ask, "Why haven't I heard about them before?" Cell salts are a form of homeopathic medicine. Homeopathy is a system of medicine that is becoming increasingly popular in the United States, and is widely practiced throughout much of the rest of the world. It has proved itself in many settings, from pregnancy, where it is one of the only safe forms of medicine, to epidemics and viral conditions, where antibiotics and the modern "arsenal" of western medicine have little influence.

Homeopathic cell salts are made from minute amounts of minerals that are highly diluted and processed in such a way that they become highly energized. They activate the body's own natural healing force. They are compatible with most conventional medications and have no side effects.

Cell salts are not drugs, but rather highly purified compounds of naturally occurring minerals that are normal constituents of the human body. They are found in trace amounts in foods, and like vitamins are used up in the complex chemical reactions of the cells. They therefore must be replenished in order to maintain healthy cells and tissues.

As astrologers know, people born under different signs are prone to particular health problems. Virgo is liable to suffer from digestive and intestinal difficulties, Cancer has an easily disturbed stomach, and Taurus has a sensitive throat. A medical astrologer knows that the full picture, drawn from the complete horoscope, with all the planets and their interactions delineated, is a fuller, more accurate picture of an individual's unique constitution.

As astrologers know, people born under different signs are prone to particular health problems

However, even the beginner, possessing the date of birth, can make a considerable contribution to the health of those around them by suggesting the use of a cell salt, based on a correlation with the Sun sign.

The Cell Salts

Aries: Kali phos. (potassium phosphate)
Taurus: Nat sulph. (sodium phosphate)
Gemini: Kali mur. (potassium chloride)
Cancer: Calc fluor. (calcium flouride)
Leo: Mag phos. (magnesium phosphate)
Virgo: Kali sulph. (potassium sulphate)
Libra: Nat phos. (sodium phosphate)
Scorpio: Calc sulph. (calcium sulphate)
Sagittarius: Silica (silicon oxide)
Capricorn: Calc phos. (calcium phosphate)
Aquarius: Nat mur. (sodium chloride)
Pisces: Ferrum phos. (iron phosphate)

Each person uses more of their birth salt than any other salt. Use it in times of stress as a tonic to prevent a crisis or a lingering debility. Cell salts can also be used for specific conditions, from acute first aid to more chronic conditions. For example, Kali mur. is used to clear the residual effects of colds and flu, such as fluid in the ear or excessive mucus in the nose and throat. Calc fluor. is useful by people prone to varicose veins for helping the veins regain their elasticity. Ferrum phos. is a source of iron to fight anemia.

Although the most common use of cell salts is based on correlation with the Sun sign, there are times when one would choose to use the cell salt that correlates with the Moon sign, and supports its function. Although the cell salts can have a significant effect on physical problems, they also profoundly influence the subtle energy bodies, including the emotional, mental, etheric, and spiritual.

When there is tremendous emotional stress people use more of the cell salt associated with the Moon sign. When the body becomes depleted of this salt, symptoms manifest such as anxiety, panic attacks, depression, and fearfulness about even the most simple daily circumstances. Use of the cell salt related to the Moon sign will restore their sense of safety and emotional resilience.

Lunar cell salts are based on the position of the Moon in the individual's horoscope, which is frequently placed in a sign other than that of the Sun sign. However, the correlation is still the same. For example, Calc fluor. is the salt for those born while the Sun is in Cancer. Calc fluor. is also used to support a Moon in Cancer, with its tendency to emotional hypersensitivity and armoring. In this situation, Calc fluor. adds emotional resiliency and decreases the instinctive tendency of the Cancer Moon to isolate themselves or to feign indifference to slights or assaults.

In the first seven years of life, when the Moon is the most influential planet, the lunar cell salts are the most appropriate choice as a tonic. If a specific health problem is present, take both the salt of the Moon and the salt that pertains to the specific condition.

Aries

Kali phos. (potassium phosphate) is the Aries cell salt. It is a nerve nutrient with a significant effect on the nerve cells, especially the brain cells. It is used for all forms of mental fatigue, as well as for depression, insomnia, irritability, hysteria, and headaches. Nervous disorders and fatigue from long hours of concentration and overwork are particularly responsive to treatment with Kali phos.

Aries rules the external, internal and structural parts of the head and brain. Kali phos. creates the gray matter of the brain.

The cycle of Saturn through the twelve signs (two and a half years in each sign) reflects a pattern of universal deficiency that can be rectified with the use of the corresponding cell salt. For example, between May 1996 and June 1998, the planet Saturn is in the sign of Aries, creating a general deficiency of Kali phos. Many people will experience periods of impaired circulation to the head and brain during this time, causing irritability, sleeplessness, inability to think efficiently, or memory problems. This may be remedied by a course of Kali phos.

Taurus

Nat sulph. (sodium sulfate) is the Taurus cell salt, and the first to use when a person born under Taurus becomes ill. Its main function is to remove excess fluids from the body. It is one of the most important salts affecting the digestive organs. The bile of the liver, the pancreatic juices, and the secretions of the kidneys are all regulated by Nat sulph. A deficiency of Nat sulph. is shown by symptoms such as tiredness and sluggishness upon waking, gall stones, constipation, and jaundice. Complaints caused or aggravated by living in damp conditions, such as rheumatism or asthma, benefit from use of this cell salt, known traditionally as "Glauber's Salt."

Taurus rules the throat, tonsils, thyroid, lower jaw, and metabolic system. Colds and sore throats occur with increased frequency when the digestive organs are not functioning harmoniously, and can be eliminated from their tendency to recur with every minor stress.

Gemini

Kali mur. (potassium chloride) is the cell salt for those born when the Sun is in the sign of Gemini. Gemini rules the lungs, bronchial tree, shoulders, arms and hands, the tubes of the body, and the central nervous system. Kali mur. is essential to the formation of most cells in the body except the bone cells, and helps the cells retain their shape.

Symptoms of a deficiency of Kali mur. are congestion of the bronchial tubes, excessive mucus in nose and sinuses, and swollen glands, including mumps and tonsillitis. Chronic inflammation of the mucus membranes can occur when the body is unable to break down nutrients and they are being run off in the form of mucus. Kali mur. breaks down mucus and allows the body to effectively create new tissue from dietary intake.

Cancer

Calc flour. (calcium fluoride) is the Cancer cell salt. It is an important constituent of the hard tissue of the body—the teeth, bones, fingernails—the lens of the eye, and the elastic fibers in muscle tissue. Deficiency of Calc flour. causes loss of elasticity in tissue and malnutrition of the bones.

Cancer rules the stomach, breasts, body fluids, and mucus membranes. Calc fluor. provides nourishment to the structures that contain and support the body. It also provides the flexibility needed for optimum function of the Cancer-ruled organs. It keeps abdominal and breast tissue supple, and restores resilience to boggy or fissured mucus membranes. Emotionally it prevents the armoring Cancerians are prone to in their desire to protect their natural sensitivity.

Leo

Mag phos. (magnesium phosphate) is the cell salt for Leo. Physiologically Leo rules the heart, upper back, diaphragm, and cardiac system. Magnesium has recently been identified in allopathic medicine as a critical mineral for the prevention of heart attacks. In naturopathic medicine, the cell salt Mag phos. has a longstanding tradition of use in situations involving cramps, convulsions, spasms, or paralysis.

Mag phos. is the great antipain salt, a natural aspirin without side effects, and is indicated in all conditions of cramp and spasm—headaches, angina, neuralgias, menstrual cramps, and even the bronchial spasms of an acute asthma attack.

Virgo

Kali sulph. (potassium sulfate) is the salt attributed to those born under the sign of Virgo. Virgo rules the small intestine, the spleen, and the lower alimentary system.

Kali sulph. improves the body's ability to take up nutrition efficiently, and particularly to make and distribute oils throughout the system. As we age, our decreasing ability to effectively use what we eat shows up in dryness of the skin and hair. Insufficient Kali sulph. causes decreased spleen function, specifically blood filtration, as well as clogging of the pores of the skin and intestinal tract.

Kali sulph. (with another cell salt, ferrum phos.) assists in the oxygenation of skin cells, and is the lubricant that keeps the body machinery functioning. A deficiency of Kali sulph. can cause eczema, dandruff, psoriasis, and any diseases where there has been a rash or scaling of the skin.

Libra

Nat phos. (sodium phosphate) is the Libra cell salt. Libra rules the kidneys and lower back, and the acid/alkaline balance of the body.

Nat phos. prevents excess acidity or alkalinity, especially in the bloodstream. It assists the kidneys in their function and is used to treat gout, kidney stones, ulcers, and stomach acidity.

The function of Libra is to keep the balance in the system by separating out poisons that are carried off in the urine. Emotionally, Nat phos. is helpful in restoring emotional equilibrium, especially after mental exertion, or exposure to extremely stressful or tense environments. Nat phos. can be used in the early stages of many health conditions.

Scorpio

Calc sulph. (calcium sulphate) is the Scorpio cell salt. Calcium sulphate is an important constituent of all connective tissue and essential to the healing process as a purifying agent. All ailments in which the process of discharge continues too long will be helped by Calc sulph.

Scorpio rules the colon, sexual organs, large intestine, eliminative channels and outlets, and the prostate gland. Calc sulph. provides a protective coating to these organs. When it is lacking we get boils, skin eruptions, fistula, chronic constipation, or diarrhea. Another manifestation is barrenness or impotence, as the body is incapable of providing a competent protective coating for the egg and sperm. In conditions where something must be eliminated from the body, such as tumors or tonsillitis, a course of calc sulph. can be useful (it is often used with the sagittarian salt silica).

Sagittarius

Silica (silicon oxide) is the cell salt for those born under the sign of Sagittarius. Silica is called "nature's knife" by naturopaths. It is of use whenever there is pus to be discharged, such as in boils, abscesses, or splinters. Taking silica after surgery helps minimize scar formation, and can assist the body to expel foreign objects such as splinters.

Sagittarius rules the liver, hips, thighs, sciatic nerve, and autonomic nervous system. Sagittarians under stress use up their silica, leaving themselves prone to chronic problems involving liver function or hip degeneration later on in life. Silica is an important constituent of the cells of the connective tissue and the epidermis, of the bones, teeth, and even the lens of the eye. Inadequate silica can make the teeth susceptible to decay, the hair dull, and the nails brittle.

Capricorn

Calc phos. (calcium phosphate) is the cell salt of Capricorn. It is an important constituent of the bones. Capricorn rules the skeletal system, especially the teeth, knees, and joints. It also rules the gall bladder and the skin. The Capricorn body requires larger amounts of Calc phos. than any other salt, especially during childhood and growth spurts, or when recovering from broken bones. Skeletal problems such as rickets, curvature of the spine, and tooth decay respond well to this cell salt.

Elderly people are particularly responsive to Calc phos. because it not only adds calcium to the system, but improves gastric digestive function so all vitamins and minerals are better assimilated. Pregnant women find this form of calcium gentle and well received by the body, as do children, who can develop overly strong bones too early if given supplemental calcium in other forms.

Aquarius

Nat mur. (natrum muriaticum, sodium chloride) is the cell salt of Aquarius. Nat mur. has the effect of attracting or drawing away water from affected parts of the body to redistribute it wherever it is needed

Symptoms of insufficient Nat mur. are associated with watery colds, dryness, or excessive salivation of the mouth, constipation, malaria, even herpes or any watery blisters on the skin or mucus membranes. Aquarius rules the blood and circulation, the ankles, the spinal cord, and the electrical force of the nerves. Nat mur. supports the smooth and even flow of electricity through and across the nerves. Lack of Nat mur. can cause sleeplessness and prevent proper nerve synapse firing with consequent learning and speaking difficulties, and intermittent nerve pains.

Pisces

Ferrum phos. (iron phosphate) is the cell salt for Pisces. It is the only common metal salt among the twelve cell salts, and is critically important in its function of making all of the other cell salts more effective. It is required for healthy red blood cells, and lack of it can cause anemia.

Pisces rules the lymphatic system and the feet. Ferrum phos. distributes oxygen to all body organs and tissues, and is indicated in all cases of inflammation and fever. It enables the blood and the lymph to carry waste and poisons away from affected tissue. It is especially indicated for people who are nervous and sensitive, who come down with every transient cold or flu.

How to Take Cell Salts

It is perfectly acceptable to take more than one cell salt at a time. Some practitioners will recommend the use of both the cell salt of the Sun and of the sign opposite to strengthen a fragile constitution. In such a situation, you would take a standard dose of each cell salt together. You may instead choose to alternate first one and then the other during the day.

How do you take cell salts and when? The tablets come in several sizes, depending on the source. The number of pellets also varies. Generally there are two to four pellets per dose. They dissolve almost immediately in the salivary juices of the mouth. They are best taken without water, and need to be taken at least ten minutes away from any other food, because of their high purity and potency.

For babies, very small, soft pellets can be obtained. One pellet tucked gently into the inside cheek will dissolve before it could possibly cause choking. Otherwise it can be dissolved in a small amount of water and given by spoon.

The optimum frequency for a chronic or long-standing condition would be to take one dose four times a day. In our busy world this is often impossible. I find I get more compliance from my clients if I suggest they take them twice a day, morning and evening, at least ten minutes away from food or toothpaste. Toothpaste has been known to counteract homeopathic medicines in some people. If you feel you are not benefiting from your regime of cell salts, consider using baking soda or salt as a toothpaste for a few weeks while you are using the cell salts.

If someone has an acute condition, repeat the dose every two hours for two to three days, and then reduce the frequency to four times a day to support the resolution of the problem. In acute conditions, people are more likely to find the time to take their tablets with greater frequency, at least for a while.

The response to the cell salt tonic can be nearly immediate, or it may take weeks to see a significant change. If you are dealing with a condition that has taken a long time to develop, it will take time to return the body to its healthy state. Unlike other homeopathic remedies, the cell salts can be taken for weeks or months at a time, in a manner similar to a vitamin.

The cell salts should never be used as a substitute for competent medical attention when a disease condition is present. They are natural substances with a profound tonic effect—to prevent disease and maintain good health.

Love Under a Moon Spell

By Carly Wall

Scent has a strong connection with attraction and romance. When we look at the most scented of the flowers, we see that many are tropical in nature, and most are night-blooming too. Though there are plants that are richly scented that grow in all areas of the world, the connection with the strongest scents of night lingers warmly, and most people are attracted to these night scents. No wonder the Full Moon has always been associated with love.

To understand the depths of scent and romance, we can get to know a little about aromatherapy and see how we can use it in our lives to enhance our love relationships. That way, we can have some control over the Moon's magic spell.

Aromatherapy Uncovered

It's strange how scent can evoke memories. Science tells us that all scent has its purpose. Only now are we beginning to realize how important that purpose is. At birth, mother and child bond through odor; in the business world, experts are finding that certain scents can induce us to work more efficiently. In Tokyo, Shimizu Corporation, an architectural engineering construction firm, has found that diffusing the scented oils of lavender, jasmine, or lemon in the areas where computer and keypunch operators work reduces their stress levels.

In the medical fields, technicians are experimenting with scent to relax people undergoing magnetic resonance imaging (MRI), a diagnostic procedure that isn't painful, but is lengthy and confining, triggering a claustrophobic reaction in many that makes the procedure hard to complete. It has been found that the scent of lavender diminishes their feelings of panic.

Although it has taken the American scientific community a while to recognize the benefits of scent, Europeans have been incorporating it in their health care practices for decades, using rooms in spas where specific essences and perfumes are piped in. In France, the practice of scent therapy is actually covered by most health insurances. Here in the United States, we have known about scent and its effects on the mind, although it has been a somewhat unconcious enterprise. How else can we explain the billion-dollar perfume industry? We know that odors can attract mates or turn people off. You can dab on some perfume if you are in a romantic mood, and it changes everything, altering perception. Studies have found that fragrance can stimulate or calm us, shape positive or negative memories, or induce sweet dreams.

To understand the depths of scent and romance, we can get to know a little about aromatherapy

Our sensitivity to odor is both genetic and learned as we relate to our environment. Studies by Hilary J. Schmidt at the Monell Chemical Senses Center in Philadelphia, Pennsylvania, show that babies are born having odor preferences. Later in life, as experiences and memories are built up, smell associations are stored in the brain so that we associate memories with smell.

The term "aromatherapy" is used to describe the contemporary version of the ancient healing art of scent—using scent for healing through inhalation, massage, or bath. The ancients knew that scent helped restore harmony among body, mind, and spirit. It has been used to restore energy, vitality, and sexuality, as well as being used medically for everything from acne and headaches to high blood pressue or gout. The ancients used fragrance in sacred ritual as well as in their daily lives. Today, we can do the same by looking into practices that were used and found to be of value.

R. M. Gattefosse, a French chemist, first coined the word *aromatherapy* in 1928. He built an essential oil house that produced oils for cosmetics and fragances. One day, while working in his lab, he burned his hand. Remembering that lavender was supposed to heal burns and reduce inflammation, he immersed his hand in a container of pure lavender that he had on his workbench. The burn quickly lost its redness and began to heal. He was so impressed that he began to research the curative powers of essential oils. He found that the nose and skin conduct the rejuvenating benefits of the oils to other parts of the body. This research led to his classification of the different essences and their specific effects on the body through metabolism, nerves, digestion, and the endocrine glands.

Essential Oils

It is quite impressive to see what it takes for a plant to produce scent. In order to concentrate its scent "chemical," many scented plants require a dry climate. The ones that are most aromatic need plenty of bright sunshine. Solar activity, then, is important to the manifestation of "essential oil." This essential oil is what I call the lifeblood of the plant. Actually, it is the liquid produced by the plant, containing many healing chemicals. This essential oil is extracted from the plant, through the distillation process or with solvents.

These essential oils can be purchased at most health food stores or through mail order companies that specialize in aromatherapy.

Scent and Sex

Every time we inhale, we smell. To detect scent we require scent molecules. These molecules stimulate receptors in our nose, which has a direct link the the limbic portion of our brain. This limbic brain, often called the old brain, controls and directs our moods and emotions. The odor stimulation, according to what scents have been detected, can cause our bodies to release neurotransmitters like encephaline, endorphins, serotonin, and others. This means that pain can be reduced, euphoric sensations and feelings of well-being can be enhanced, and we can relax and calm ourselves, all with the sniff of the right scent.

Our erotic lives depend on scent. Our bodies produce hormones called pheromones, a personal body scent that influences our choice of partners. Rarely will anyone become intimate with anyone whose body odor is disliked or that they are not attracted to. It is a simple matter of biology. This is seen most readily in the animal kingdom. The male butterfly can smell a female from as far away as six miles, and a male dog can smell a female in heat from a distance of almost two miles. This shows us how we are all biologically programmed to assure survival of the species through scent messages we send out. Our personal scents change according to our mood, state of health or illness, and sexual inclinations. We smell different when we are happy and peaceful than when we are angry, aggressive, or under stress. In this way, we can use essential odors to change our moods, thereby changing our body scent—and attract mates and enhance passion, love and romance!

Essential Oils of Love

Here is a list of essential oils that aromatherapists have found to be especially good aphrodisiacs. Remember, essential oils are concentrated, and caution must be taken when using them. Never use undiluted essential oils on the skin as they can cause irritation and harmful reactions. Also, never ingest essential oils unless directed by an aromatherapist. Also test for allergic reactions to your homemade products by rubbing a small amount on your wrist. If redness appears, do not use.

You can make perfumes by adding 20 drops of essential oil to 1 ounce of vodka, with 8 drops of castor oil. Let this sit for two weeks to blend thoroughly.

You can make a massage oil by adding 10 drops per 1 ounce of base oil (use sweet almond, sunflower, or peanut oil), along with a vitamin E capsule squeezed in as a preservative.

The scents are lovely by themselves, but the effect is enhanced if you learn to blend a variety of scents to create your own personal and effective smell. Experimentation is fun, and I recommend you start out by blending only 3 essential oils at a time, using this formula: Main scent: half of the drops accordingly (for perfume this would be 10 drops, for massage oil 5 drops), second scent: 6 drops for perfume, 3 drops for massage oil, third scent: 4 drops for perfume, 2 drops for massage oil. Of course, it is all up to your nose. Find out what you like and become the creator of your own sexy scent. You will be surprised how much scent affects your life. There are many essential oils to choose from, but to spice up your love life, be sure you add one or two of these scents listed below that are specific to enhancing romance!

Essential Oils of Love

Ambrette seed: musky aphrodisiac.

Atlas cedarwood: stimulant.

Black pepper: use sparingly, a hot essential oil, warms.

Cananga: men favor it, relaxes.

Cardomon: warming fragrance, stimulant.

Cassie: helpful in reducing frigidity, nervous exhaustion.

Cinnamon leaf: use sparingly, a hot essential oil, warms.

Clary sage: revitalizes, helps reduce frigidity, impotence.

Coriander: spicy, helps reduce exhaustion.

Cumin: spicy, musky, eases debility, headaches.

Galbanum: green-woody scent.

Gardenia: exotic oriental scent.

Jasmine: helps self-esteem, highly stimulating.

Narcissus: narcotic scent, has sedative qualities.

Neroli: calming and balancing, helps fear and eases stress.

Nutmeg: exciting.

Orange: enhances sensuality.

Patchouli: antidepressant, helps relieve stress, improves with age.

Rockrose: eroticizing.

Rose: affects the heart, strengthens love, makes one happy.

Rosemary: Avoid in pregnancy, stimulating, good for depression.

Rosewood: stimulant, deodorant.

Sandalwood: awakens love emotions from within.

Tuberose: sweet/spicy, narcotic.

Vetiver: regenerates and balances women's hormones.

Ylang Ylang: powerful aphrodisiac, good for depression too.

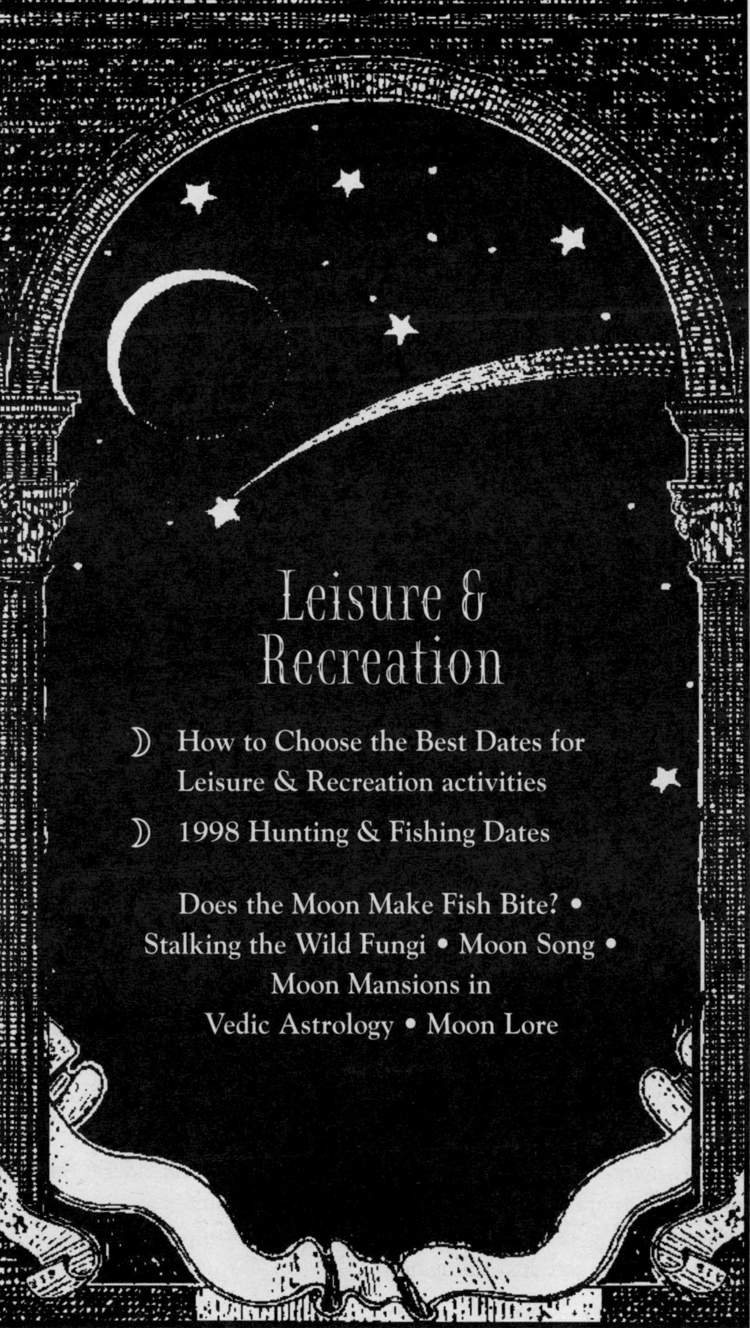
Leisure &
Recreation
☽ How to Choose the Best Dates for Leisure & Recreation activities
☽ 1998 Hunting & Fishing Dates
Does the Moon Make Fish Bite? •
Stalking the Wild Fungi • Moon Song •
Moon Mansions in
Vedic Astrology • Moon Lore

Leisure & Recreation

How to Choose the Best Dates

Everyone is affected by the lunar cycle. Your lunar high occurs when the Moon is in your Sun sign, and your lunar low occurs when the Moon is in the sign opposite your Sun sign. The handy Favorable and Unfavorable Dates Tables on pages 28–51 give the lunar highs and lows for each Sun sign for every day of the year. This lunar cycle influences all your activities: your physical strength, mental alertness, and manual dexterity are all affected.

By combining the Favorable and Unfavorable Dates Tables and the Lunar Aspectarian Tables with the information given below in the list of astrological rulerships, you can choose the best time for a variety of activities.

The best time to perform an activity is when its ruling planet is in favorable aspect to the Moon—that is, when its ruling planet is trine, sextile, or conjunct the Moon (marked T, X, or C in the Lunar Aspectarian), or when its ruling sign is marked F in the Favorable and Unfavorable Days tables. Another option is to check when the Moon is in the activity's ruling sign.

For example, if you wanted to find a good day to train your dog, you would look under animals, and find that the sign corresponding to animal training is Taurus, and that the planet that rules this activity is Venus. Then, you would consult the Favorable and Unfavorable Days Tables to find a day when Venus (the ruling planet) is trine, sextile, or conjunct (T, X, or C) the Moon; or when Taurus (the ruling sign) is marked F in the Favorable and Unfavorable Days table; or when the Moon is in Taurus.

Animals and Hunting

Animals in general: Pisces, Neptune; Sagittarius, Jupiter; Virgo, Mercury

Animal training: Taurus, Venus

Cats: Leo, Sun, Virgo, Mercury

Dogs: Virgo, Mercury

Fish: Pisces, Neptune; Moon, Cancer

Birds: Gemini, Mercury; Libra, Venus

Horses, trainers, riders: Sagittarius, Jupiter

Hunters: Sagittarius, Jupiter

Arts

Acting, actors: Pisces, Neptune; Sun, Leo

Art in general: Libra, Venus

Ballet: Pisces, Neptune; Libra, Venus

Ceramics: Capricorn, Saturn

Crafts: Virgo, Mercury; Libra, Venus

Dancing: Taurus, Venus; Pisces, Neptune

Drama: Taurus, Venus; Pisces, Neptune

Embroidery: Libra, Venus

Etching: Aries, Mars

Films, filmmaking: Pisces, Neptune; Sun, Leo; Aquarius, Uranus

Literature: Gemini, Mercury

Music: Libra, Taurus, Venus

Painting: Libra, Venus

Photography: Pisces, Neptune; Aquarius, Uranus

Printing: Gemini, Mercury

Theaters: Sun, Leo; Libra, Venus

Fishing

During the summer months the best time of the day for fishing is from sunrise to three hours after, and from about two hours before sunset until one hour after. In cooler months, the fish are not biting until the air is warm. At this time the best hours are from noon to 3:00 pm. Warm and cloudy days are good. The most favorable winds are from the south and southwest. Easterly winds are unfavorable. The best days of the month for fishing are those on which the Moon changes quarters, especially if the change occurs on a day when the Moon is in a watery sign (Cancer, Scorpio, Pisces). The best period in any month is the day after the Full Moon.

Friends

The need for friendship is greater when Uranus aspects the Moon, or the Moon is in Aquarius. Friendship prospers when Venus or Uranus is trine, sextile, or conjunct the Moon. The chance meeting of acquaintances and friends is facilitated by the Moon in Gemini.

Other Entertainments

Barbecues: Moon, Cancer; Aries, Mars

Casinos: Taurus, Venus; Leo, Sun; Sagittarius, Jupiter

Collections: Moon, Cancer

Festivals: Taurus, Libra, Venus

Parades: Jupiter, Sagittarius; Libra, Venus

Parties

The best time for parties is when the Moon is in Gemini, Leo, Libra, or Aquarius, with good aspects to Venus and Jupiter. There should be no aspects (positive or negative) to Mars or Saturn.

Sports

The Sun rules physical vitality, Mars rules coordination and competition, and Saturn rules strategy but hinders coordination. Plan activities to coincide with good aspects (X or T in the Lunar Aspectarian) from the planets. Accidents are associated with squares or oppositions (Q or O in the Lunar Aspectarian) to Mars, Saturn, or Uranus. Specific sports are ruled by specific planets, from which they benefit. Below is a list of sports and the planets and signs that rule them.

Acrobatics: Aries, Mars

Archery: Sagittarius, Jupiter

Ball games in general: Venus

Baseball: Aries, Mars

Bicycling: Gemini, Mercury; Aquarius, Uranus

Boxing: Aries, Mars

Calisthenics: Aries, Mars; Pisces, Neptune

Chess: Gemini, Mercury; Aries, Mars

Competitive sports: Aries, Mars

Coordination: Aries, Mars

Deep-sea diving: Pisces, Neptune

Exercising: Leo, Sun

Football: Aries, Mars

Horse racing: Sagittarius, Jupiter

Jogging: Gemini, Mercury

Physical vitality: Leo, Sun

Polo: Aquarius, Uranus; Sagittarius, Jupiter; Taurus, Venus; Capricorn, Saturn

Racing (other than horse): Leo, Sun; Aquarius, Uranus

Ice skating: Pisces, Neptune

Roller skating: Gemini, Mercury

Sporting equipment: Sagittarius, Jupiter

Sports in general: Sun, Leo

Strategy: Capricorn, Saturn

Swimming: Neptune, Pisces; Moon, Cancer

Tennis: Gemini, Mercury; Taurus, Venus; Aquarius, Uranus; Aries, Mars

Wrestling: Aries, Mars

Travel

Air travel: Gemini, Mercury; Sagittarius, Jupiter; Aquarius, Uranus

Automobile travel: Gemini, Mercury

Boating: Moon, Cancer; Pisces, Neptune

Camping: Sun, Leo

Helicopters: Aquarius, Uranus

Hotels: Moon, Cancer; Taurus, Venus

Journeys in general: Leo, Sun

Long journeys: Sagittarius, Jupiter

Parks: Sun, Leo

Picnics: Taurus, Venus; Sun, Leo

Rail travel: Aquarius, Uranus; Gemini, Mercury

Restaurants: Moon, Cancer; Virgo, Mercury; Sagittarius, Jupiter

Short journeys: Gemini, Mercury

Vacations, holidays: Pisces, Neptune; Taurus, Venus

Short journeys are ruled by Mercury, long ones by Jupiter. The Sun rules the actual journey itself. Long trips that threaten to exhaust the traveler are best begun when the Sun is well aspected to the Moon, and the date is favorable for the traveler. If traveling with other people, good aspects from Venus are desirable. For enjoyment, aspects to Jupiter are profitable. For visiting, aspects to Mercury are good. To avoid accidents, avoid squares or oppositions to Mars, Saturn, Uranus, or Pluto.

For air travel, choose a day when the Moon is in Gemini or Libra, and well aspected by Mercury and/or Jupiter. Avoid adverse aspects of Mars, Saturn, or Uranus.

Writing

Write for pleasure or publication when the Moon is in Gemini. Mercury should be direct. Favorable aspects to Mercury, Uranus, and Neptune promote ingenuity.

Hunting & Fishing Dates

From/To	Quarter	Sign
January 2, 4:56 am—January 4, 7:44 am	1st	Pisces
January 10, 7:43 pm—January 13, 2:45 am	2nd	Cancer
January 20, 1:35 pm—January 23, 12:26 am	3rd	Scorpio
January 29, 1:09 pm—January 31, 2:21 pm	1st	Pisces
February 7, 1:58 am—February 9, 9:57 am	2nd	Cancer
February 16, 9:14 pm—February 19, 8:56 am	3rd	Scorpio
February 25, 11:42 pm—February 27, 11:42 pm	4th/1st	Pisces
March 6, 7:27 am—March 8, 3:46 pm	2nd	Cancer
March 16, 3:51 am—March 18, 3:56 pm	3rd	Scorpio
March 25, 10:43 am—March 27, 10:49 am	4th	Pisces
April 2, 2:10 pm—April 4, 9:36 pm	1st/2nd	Cancer
April 12, 9:55 am—April 14, 9:52 pm	3rd	Scorpio
April 21, 8:07 pm—April 23, 9:31 pm	4th	Pisces
April 29, 10:57 pm—May 2, 4:49 am	1st	Cancer
May 9, 4:10 pm—May 12, 3:48 am	2nd	Scorpio
May 19, 3:04 am—May 21, 6:06 am	4th	Pisces
May 27, 8:58 am—May 29, 1:38 pm	1st	Cancer
June 5, 11:06 pm—June 8, 10:35 am	2nd	Scorpio
June 15, 8:32 am—June 17, 12:23 pm	3rd	Pisces
June 23, 6:39 pm—June 25, 11:04 pm	4th/1st	Cancer
July 3, 6:46 am—July 5, 6:24 pm	2nd	Scorpio
July 12, 2:22 pm—July 14, 5:45 pm	3rd	Pisces
July 21, 2:43 am—July 23, 7:49 am	4th	Cancer
July 30, 2:45 pm—August 2, 2:48 am	1st	Scorpio
August 8, 10:04 pm—August 11, 12:11 am	3rd	Pisces
August 17, 8:56 am—August 19, 3:01 pm	4th	Cancer
August 26, 10:25 pm—August 29, 10:55 am	1st	Scorpio
September 5, 7:48 am—September 7, 8:53 am	2nd	Pisces
September 13, 2:20 pm—September 15, 8:48 pm	4th	Cancer
September 23, 5:22 am—September 25, 6:05 pm	1st	Scorpio

Hunting & Fishing Dates

From/To	Quarter	Sign
October 2, 6:24 pm—October 4, 7:32 pm	2nd	Pisces
October 10, 8:48 pm—October 13, 2:25 am	3rd	Cancer
October 20, 11:37 am—October 23, 12:17 am	1st	Scorpio
October 30, 3:58 am—November 1, 6:27 am	2nd	Pisces
November 7, 5:39 am—November 9, 9:33 am	3rd	Cancer
November 16, 5:42 pm—November 19, 6:13 am	4th	Scorpio
November 26, 11:14 am—November 28, 3:34 pm	1st	Pisces
December 4, 4:28 pm—December 6, 6:56 pm	3rd	Cancer
December 14, 12:17 am—December 16, 12:47 pm	4th	Scorpio
December 23, 4:45 pm—December 25, 10:04 pm	1st	Pisces

Editor's Note: This chart lists the best hunting and fishing dates for this year, but not the only possible dates. To accomodate your own schedule, you may wish to try dates other than those listed above. To learn more about choosing good fishing dates, see the fishing information on page 161. To learn more about hunting dates, see the animal and hunting information on page 160.

Does the Moon Make Fish Bite?

By Bruce Scofield

The best times to fish have long been a part of annual almanacs and sports magazines. The *Moon Sign Book* that you hold in your hand lists the best fishing and hunting days on pages 164–5. Nearly every fishing and hunting magazine has some sort of graph or table that promises the best time to fish or hunt. The standard methods used to determine these dates are fairly simple. Most astrological almanacs simply list the days when the Moon is in one of the water signs (Cancer, Scorpio, and Pisces). It makes perfect astrological sense, since water is the element in which fish live. It also suggests that fish, or other animals for that matter, may be more reactive when the Moon is in these signs. People are certainly more reactive during these times.

Another standard technique for locating the best fishing times is to fish near the phases of the Moon—the New Moon, Full Moon and the second and fourth quarters. Again, this makes some sense because of the agitation that these four points in the Sun/Moon cycle generate. The tension of the phases quite possibly makes fish agitated and more likely to strike. I know these alignments work on people.

A third rule, and one that nearly any fisherman knows, is to fish around the time of sunrise or sunset. When I was in my teens I used to start my bass fishing just as the Sun would set, and stay with it for an hour or two. It always amazed me that if I started to fish too early, nothing would happen. Most of the time, when the Sun was near the horizon, I'd start getting bites. The same was true for morning fishing, though I did that less often (I've always been more of a night person and I love to sleep late). I didn't know how to explain what was happening at these times, I just knew I could catch more fish then.

My experiences with fishing were nothing in comparison with those of John Alden Knight, the developer of the solunar theory.

John Alden Knight was a great fisherman and prolific author. He wrote numerous articles and books on many aspects of sports fishing including fly casting, freshwater angling theory and technique, bird hunting, and bass fishing. What drew my attention, however, was his writing on his solunar theory of fishing, which is really a kind of astrology.

The tension of the phases quite possibly makes fish agitated and more likely to strike

As Knight told it, he once fished with an old man named Bob in Florida who told him that fish bite when the Moon is overhead or directly beneath the Earth. "Moon up, Moon down" was what he said. Proof that this idea worked came that same day when the fish bit wildly around 3:00 pm when the Moon was at its noon position. There was also another period of good fishing that day at sunset. This was a day Knight never forgot.

Knight became curious, perhaps even obsessed, by his experience in Florida, and he put his strong investigative skills to work in hopes of discovering what exactly was making these fish bite at those times. As he lived in the New York/New Jersey area, he did his field work saltwater fishing along New Jersey's coastline and freshwater fishing in Pennsylvania and New York State. He considered all sorts of possible reasons that fish bite, including temperature and barometric pressure fluctuations, but eventually realized that the one constant was the rising, setting, culmination, and lower culmination of the Sun and Moon, essentially the two driving forces behind the tides.

Most serious fishermen know that saltwater fish have active feeding times roughly near low tide. Knight was sharp enough to notice that low tide varied greatly along the coast where there were natural obstructions, like inlets. He also noticed that feeding times in parts of the shore where the tide acted more immediately were right with the Moon's position in the sky. More observations showed that the fish out in the tidal inlets also fed strongly then, even though low tide hadn't yet occurred for them. In other words, the fish were eating with the Sun and Moon, not just with the tide. The next step was a big one. Knight calculated where the actual tide would be in Pennsylvania and tried fishing at those times—with excellent results. This was a radical insight and Knight first published an article on this theory of "inland tides" back in 1935. Because tides are caused by the Sun and Moon, he named his theory the "solunar theory."

The initial response to Knight's theory was strong. So many people wanted him to tell them when to fish that he was forced to produce a set of tables that allowed any fisherman to calculate when the feeding periods would occur for their locality. The tables were printed up in book form and were sold for fifty cents by mail order. Over 1,000 copies were sold in the first five weeks!

To Knight's credit, he didn't stop with this money-making idea. He keep thinking, observing, and speculating as to how his solunar theory actually worked. He thought that it was not just the gravitation of the Sun and Moon on the fish or the level of the water (which isn't changed in fresh water) that was behind the feeding periods. Knight believed that the effects of the Sun and Moon on the Earth are quite complex. He speculated that the gravitational force of these bodies disturbed the flow of cosmic rays and the patterns of terrestrial magnetism. He never came up with a final theory, but he believed that someday, one would be found.

One of Knight's observations was that fish feeding periods seemed to be driven by the Sun near Full and New Moons, and by the Moon at the quarters. At the New or Full Moon, the Sun and Moon are traveling together. At the New Moon, both are "up" or "down" at the same time. At the Full Moon, one is "up" while the other is "down." With the Moon at the first quarter, it is "up" when the Sun is setting and "down" when the Sun is rising. At the third quarter it is "down" at sunset and up at sunrise. Knight worked throughout his life to perfect his tables, particularly the times between the main phases of the Moon and a "minor" point of activity between the "major" times when the luminaries were "up" or "down." These are listed in his tables.

Another of Knight's observations was that insect and worm activity (the bugs that the fish wanted to eat) was very precisely timed to the inland tidal period. When the Moon was overhead, the bugs started squirming, and it was only a matter of time before the fish started biting. He observed this same effect with the feeding habits of birds and other animals. His health failing, Knight quit his bank job in New York City and moved to Williamsport, Pennsylvania. There he devoted himself entirely to writing, fishing, and studying nature. His observations extended to all sorts of wildlife, and he adapted his tables for hunting. Knight even went so far as to observe the effects of the solunar periods on human life. He may just have been one of this century's great astrological pioneers, even though he probably never thought of himself in this way. In his mind he was a student of nature, a close observer who was always looking for a scientific explanation. Like all astrologers, he had to settle for his experiential evidence that was not backed up by a scientifically provable theory. Still, if there were an astrological hall of fame, I'd like to nominate him for it.

Readers interested in learning more about how John Alden Knight developed his solunar theory should read his book *Moon Up—Moon Down*, published by Solunar Sales Co. His solunar tables appear bimonthly in *Field and Stream* magazine.

Stalking The Wild Fungi

By Carly Wall

Wild fungi are the most prized mushrooms for cooks. These mushrooms and their amazing tastes have caught on in popularity. Restaurants serve wild mushroom specialties, cooking shows feature them in dishes they whip up, and cookbooks have "mushroomed" on the scene with amazing recipes. With wild mushrooms, you can go from appetizer to main course and add a bit of adventure to tantalize your taste buds.

Perhaps what fascinates and tantalizes us most is that the mushroom isn't wholly understood—we don't quite know exactly how they grow. Fungi are a large class, and have a structure similar to plants, but they lack chlorophyll, which other plants manufacture with help from sunlight. Instead, they obtain their food ready-made, from other plants, living or decayed. That's why we associate them with the night, saying the Moon is the light they lean on. In reality, it remains a mystery how they do grow. We see them popping up here and there where we least expect it. They are very unpredictable.

We know that the mushroom is the reproductive part of the fungus organism, developed to distribute the spores (their type of "seed"). To develop, they need a rare combination of factors to come about. Humidity and temperature must be just right, and the spores must have the right food nearby, so the soil has to have the right condition for certain types of spores. To top it all off, it is hard to get wild mushrooms to grow in artificial environments—even if all the factors for growth are present. No one knows why. That's why I like to believe the moonlight has a part to play.

The mysterious nature of mushrooms makes them elusive characters. Perhaps that is why they are so fun and exciting to hunt for—and why there are so many mushroom-hunting clubs and organizations springing up all over. There is a pleasure and satisfaction when you stumble upon a grove of twenty-five morels playing hide and seek among a stand of mayapples, or to spy a magnificent fairy ring in field or meadow. Not only is there the fun of the discovery, but if you find the right kind of mushroom, you can eat it, too.

Not only is there the fun of the discovery, but if you find the right kind of mushroom, you can eat it, too

Mushroom Hunting

To become a mushroom hunter, first and foremost to remember is never eat anything you can't identify. If you aren't sure, don't eat it. You have to be absolutely positive that the mushroom you are eating is safe, because there are dangerous mushrooms out there that can cause much misery, and even death. As a beginner, it is a good idea to collect with an experienced group. There are many local organizations nationwide, and about seventy amateur societies in North America. They publish newsletters, organize hunting forays, and give beginners a safe opportunity for learning to identify. Membership fees are often quite reasonable. There is one national group you can contact that can help answer questions, and tell you about the groups in your area. Write to: Executive Secretary, North American Mycological Association, 3556 Oakwood, Ann Arbor, MI 48104-5213 and enclose a self-addressed stamped envelope.

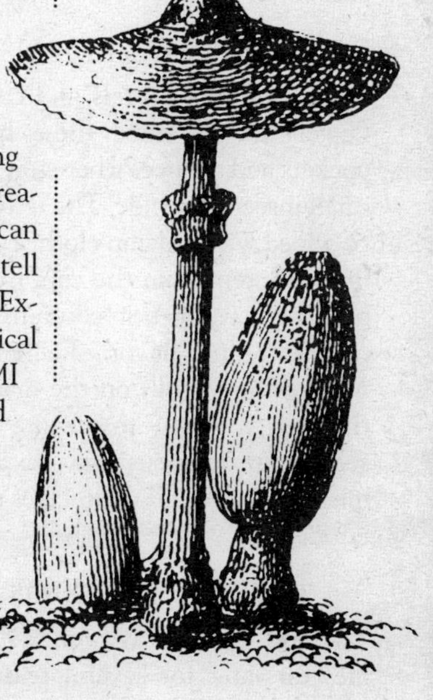

If you think you have to get up at the crack of dawn to be a mushroom hunter, think again. You can track them any time of day. Advantages to early morning forays include the ability to grab your fungi before anyone else has the chance to nab them, and you can get to them before insects discover them, too.

Take along your expert or group of friends, a good field guide, and a flat-bottomed container or basket to put your finds in. Try to avoid plastic bags as they sweat and ruin the mushrooms, as well as causing them to disintegrate. Paper bags work better. Pick fresh, firm mushrooms. Note cap shape, size, color, and texture. Check the underside. Smell each mushroom, as all mushrooms have their own distinct odors. When you are a hundred percent certain that what you have found is edible, your next step is to take your fungi home and prepare for a feast.

Cleaning Mushrooms

Wash only the morels and cauliflower fungus, since these have pockets and crevices where soil and small insects can hide. The rest can be wiped with a damp cloth. Separate the stem from the cap. Don't peel them, as the skin contains the nutrition and flavor. There are many recipe books on the market that tell you how to prepare and serve your delicious finds. Experiment and savor all the recipes that entice you.

Storing Mushrooms

You may want to save your delicacies for later for several reasons; you are either overwhelmed by a good find of mushrooms—some years are better than others for whatever reason—or as happens often, you find more than you can eat in a few days. Do not despair, for though you can only store the mushrooms in the refrigerator fresh for several days, you have at your disposal two other methods to ensure you can enjoy every bit of your wild harvest. The first is freezing. This isn't the best method, for some flavor can be lost, but it is handy. Clean the mushrooms, using fresh, firm ones only. Freeze them in a single layer uncovered on a cookie sheet until solid. Then pack them in plastic bags. These will keep about a month. The second method involves drying. Clean the mushrooms well, and cut them in thin slices leaving the small ones like the fairy rings whole. Dry them on a wire rack in a warm oven (under 140°F, with the door kept ajar). Make sure you don't over-dry them as they will blacken and lose their flavor. Then simply let them cool after they become completely brittle, and pack in airtight containers. I love to see dried mushrooms as they look exotic. Some people thread slices on string to hang in a warm place to dry. They decorate a kitchen wonderfully and are useful as well. To use them, reconstitute them with a soak in warm water thirty minutes, drain them, and add to recipes, or grind the dried mushrooms into a powder to use as seasonings for soups and casseroles.

Introducing the Wild and Wooly Fungi

Here is a list of the most common edible wild fungi that you may want to keep an eye out for in future hunts (remember to use your identifying field guides).

Cep (*Boletus edulis*): Yellow-brown to orange-brown caps. Firm white flesh. It is delicious. Found in the Northern parts of North America, July through October.

Meadow (*Agaricus campestris*): The best known wild mushroom, found in pastures, favoring dense clumps of grass, appearing midsummer through fall (or in California, from fall through winter). Silky white, turning cream-colored, with pale pink gills that turn reddish. Taste and smell are pleasant.

Fairy Ring (*Marasmius oreades*): Found growing in large numbers in pastures and lawns. You must not confuse this type with others that grow in rings and are poisionous. These are slender, with straw-colored stems. Smells haylike. Interesting flavor. Appears late spring until winter. In California, appears year round.

Chanterelle (*Cantharellus cibarius*): Bright yellow to pale yellow. Flesh firm, white to yellow. Smells slightly of apricot, tastes mild and peppery. In eastern states appears July to August, in the northwest September through November.

Oyster (*Pleurotus ostreatus*): Variable in color from bluish gray to gray-brown. Found in large clusters on logs and trunks of deciduous trees. Quite delicious. Found late October through January, or through winter if weather is mild.

Yellow Morel (*Morchella esculenta*): Sponge-like, yellow-brown. Crisp, pleasant odor and taste that is highly prized. Found April through May. Favors ground under dead apple and elm trees.

Black Morel (*Morchella elata*): Sponge-like, but black or dark brown. Good taste, eat when cooked. Seems to have an affinity to grow under pine and conifer trees.

Chicken of the Woods (*Laetiporus sulphureus*): Also called sulphur shelf. Fan-shaped, thick and fleshy, lemon orange fading to straw brown. Found growing on downed trees in clusters. A fungusy odor, very pleasant eating when fresh and cooked.

Shaggy Mane (*Coprinus comatus*): A tall, white ovoid, becoming cylindrical as it expands, with a very shaggy, scaly cap. Delicious when young. Found in large numbers on roadsides, lawns, and other urban sites, sometimes in spring, but usually July through November.

Moon Song

Bird Watching by the Moon

By Louise Riotte

When we moved into our new house in the spring of 1939, we did not know that a mockingbird was nesting in the big old hackberry tree about thirty feet from our bedroom window. As we settled down for the night we were quite surprised to hear the little musician burst into song. Now, a mockingbird that near can be a source of delight or provocation. To us, it was the perfect touch, welcoming us to our new home. My husband not only loved birds, but they loved him. He knew many bird calls, and often birds would come to rest on his head or shoulders and eat out of his hands. We would lie there in the dark, entranced, and he would identify the different notes of the various birds our mockingbird imitated.

The mockingbird is a star performer in the group of lively singers. His love song is entrancing. When the moonlight sheds a silvery radiance everywhere, the mockingbird sings to his mate such delicious music as only the European nightingale can rival. Perhaps the stillness of the hour and the beauty and fragrance of the place increase the magic of his almost pathetically sweet voice; but surely there is no lovelier sound in nature on this side of the sea. Like the sound of the sea, he lulled us to sleep night after night. Alas, he was indeed a fleeting pleasure, for in time he left and did not return again.

The mockingbird is ever alert, and can no more suppress the music within him, night or day, than he can keep his slim, neat, graceful, nervous, high-strung body at rest. As might be expected, he is a bird of Venus. He is about the size of a robin and gray above, with brownish wings and a wedge-shaped tail. His upper wing feathers are tipped with white, his outer tail quills are white, conspicuous in flight; and his chin is white on top, with gray underneath, shading to whitish. He is peculiar to the torrid and temperate zones of the two Americas, has no fixed migrations, and is usually resident where seen. He has been immortalized in the old song "Listen to the Mockingbird," which was once very popular.

From his restlessness you might suspect the mockingbird is a cousin of the catbird and the wrens, or the brown thrasher. Flitting from perch to perch (fluttering is one of his chief amusements, even in a cage); taking short flights from tree to tree, hopping lightly, swiftly, gracefully over the ground; bounding into the air, or the next minute shooting his ashy gray body far across the garden and leaving a wake of rippling music behind him as he flies, he seems to be perpetually in motion. If you live in the South you can encourage no more delightful and amusing neighbor than the mockingbird.

With all his virtues, it must be added, however, that this charming bird is a sad tease. There is no sound, whether made by bird or beast about him, that he cannot imitate so clearly as to deceive everyone but himself. Very rarely can you find a mockingbird without intelligence and mischief enough to appreciate his ventriloquism.

The Whippoorwill

The whippoorwill, ruled by Venus and the Moon, is a queer, shadowy bird that sleeps all day in the woods and flies about through open country after dark with uncanny softness, like an owl. This bird would likely pass unnoticed were it not for the weird, snappy triplets of notes that tell its name. The whippoorwill is a long-winded bird, mottled all over with reddish brown, grayish black, and dusky white; with numerous bristles fringing his large

Mockingbird sings to his mate such delicious music as only the European nightingale can rival

mouth. A narrow white band runs across his breast and the ends of his outer tail-quills are white.

Everyone knows the whippoorwill better by sound than by sight. "*Whip-poor-will (chuck) whip-poor-will (chuck) whip-poor-will (chuck)*," he calls rapidly for about two hours, just after sunset or just after sunrise. He is a crepuscular, or twilight-loving bird. He calls from some low place, fluttering his wings at each announcement. You must be near him to hear the "chuck" at the end of each vigorous triplet; most listeners don't. In the southern states a similar whippoorwill is known as "Chuck Will's Widow," the name it calls itself at nightfall.

You might be very close indeed without seeing the plump bird, who has flattened himself lengthwise against a lichen-covered branch until you cannot tell bird from bark. He has a little short beak, but his large mouth stretches from ear to ear, and when he flies low above the fields at sunset, this trap is kept open, like the swift's and the swallow's, to catch any night-flying insects—mosquitos, June bugs, gnats, and little moths—that cross his path. Long, stiffened bristles at the ends of his mouth prevent the escape of a victim past the gaping trap.

Relying on the protective covering of her soft plumage, the mother whippoorwill builds no nest, but lays a pair of mottled eggs in an old stump or directly on the ground in the dark woods, where concealment is perfect.

The Nighthawk

When the nightjar, bull-bat, nighthawk, or mosquito hawk is coursing low above the fields, with quick, erratic, bat-like turns, notice the white spots almost forming a bar across the wings, for they, together with the white band near the end of his forked tail, will help to distinguish him from the whippoorwill, who carries his white signals on the outer feathers of his tail.

I love to sit on my front porch late in the summer evenings, watching the nighthawks who live in the large hackberry trees across the street from my home. They fly about, catching dusk-flying insects. It is the nighthawk who makes the rushing, whirring, booming sound that one hears on still summer evenings. The bird is such a high flyer that in the dusk of late afternoon when he sails abroad to get his dinner, one cannot always see him; but as he coasts on his half-closed wings with tremendous speed, the rush of air through his stiff, long wing feathers makes an uncanny, aeolian music that superstitious people have declared is a bad omen. This bird of the Moon is not as nocturnal in his habits as the whippoorwill, and often, toward the end of summer, he may be seen coursing over open country at almost any hour of the day. Once in a while, as he hunts, he calls "peent"—a sharp cry that reminds one of the meadowlark's nasal call note.

The female nighthawk makes no nest, but deposits her two speckled treasures in some sunny spot on the bare ground, a rock, or even the flat roof of a house. Since electric lights attract so many insects to the streets of towns and villages, the enterprising nighthawk mother often forsakes the country to rear her children where they may enjoy the benefits of modern improvements.

The Mourning Dove

Not really a night bird, I am going to include the mourning dove because here in southern Oklahoma I usually hear him just at the break of dawn—a time when I am often in the garden gathering dew-fresh vegetables before the early morning Sun has a chance to dry them. Locally, the mourning dove is also popularly known as the "rain bird." I think this is because we can hear him so well in the still of early morning before the wind comes up, and we seem to be perpetually hoping for rain in the dry Southwest.

That mourning cry is deceiving, however, and we need waste no sympathy on this incessant love-maker that slowly sings, "*coo-o-o, ah-coo-o-o-ooo-o-o-ooo-o-o*," in a sweetly sad voice. Really he is not melancholy at all, but, on the contrary, is so happy in his love that his devotion has passed into a proverb. Nevertheless, his song sounds more like a dirge than a rapture—but while his mate lives there is no more contented bird. The dove is a bird of Venus.

Unlike pigeons, who depend on friends for their happiness and like to live in large flocks, doves scatter in couples over a wide area—from Panama in winter as far north as Ontario in warm weather. Not until nursery duties, which begin in early spring or late summer, do they give up their shy, unsociable habits to enjoy the company of a few friends.

Only the cuckoo builds so flimsy a nest as the dove's. She is a slack, incompetent housekeeper, but evidently her lover is blind to her every fault. It is a wonder that the dove's two white eggs do not fall through the rickety, rimless, unlined lattice she builds, but somehow, year after year, the hatchlings seem to thrive. Like pigeons, hummingbirds, flickers, and some other feathered parents, doves feed their fledglings by pumping partly digested food—"pigeon's milk"—from their own crops into those of the babies. Mourning doves are bluish, fawn-colored birds, about one foot long.

The Owls

Not all of the birds of the night have a moonsong as delightful as the mockingbird's, but their cries are nevertheless the "Moon music" of their particular species, and in their own way meaningful. Owls are no exception. They may not be great singers, but these nocturnal birds of the Moon are among the farmers' and gardeners' best friends because the owls do the same work by night that other birds do during the day—eating insects and small rodents that otherwise might destroy crops.

Owls are very interesting. They have a peculiarly flexible, reversible hind toe; eyes set firmly in the sockets, necessitating the turning of the head to see in different directions; feathered discs around the eyes; and loose, mottled plumage. Some species sport feathered ear tufts (horns). Others have hooked beaks and muscular feet for perching and for grasping prey, and the ability to fly almost silently. Owls are birds of the woodland, more rarely of grassy marshes and plains, and are nearly all nocturnal in habits. Since their food consists mostly of small mammals that steal abroad at night to destroy the farmer's crops, the owls are among the most valuable of birds to the agriculturist. Unless it is too large, the owl's prey is bolted entire.

The Screech Owl

The little screech owl, which is about as long as a robin, is a permanent resident of eastern North America, and his cry is not a screech at all, but rather a mournful wail. This little fellow likes to make his home near those of humans. His weird, sweet, shivering tremolo emitting from under our windows may startle us, as the uncanny voices of all owls do, however familiar we may be with the little screecher. Owls, totally innocent, have probably been the subject of more superstitions than any other bird. Because it makes its home so near ours, often in some crevice of our houses, a hollow of a tree, or around the barn lofts, this is probably the most familiar owl to the majority of Americans and Canadians.

Owl Superstitions

Owl superstitions may be only that, nevertheless they are interesting. Patricia Telesco, writing in *Folkways*, tells us that images of Athena, the Goddess of Wisdom, show her with an owl for a companion. Because of this, the owl has strong associations with sagacity.

Hopi folklore claims that if you give someone an owl feather, they will be unable to lie to themselves. Thus the plumage makes an excellent addition to your medicine pouch to keep yourself honest.

Navaho tradition tells us that if an owl hoots three times within your hearing, or flies near you, it is a sign to check your motivation.

The Barred Owl

The barred owl, grayish brown, recognizable by his feathers, each of which has two or three white or buff bars, ranges the Eastern United States to Nova Scotia and Manitoba, west to Minnesota, Nebraska, Kansas, and Texas; nesting throughout the range. "*Whoo-whoo-too-whoo-too-o-o*," he calls, with endless variation, a deep-toned, guttural, weird, startling sound, like the wail of some lost soul asking its way through the dark.

The Hoot Owl

The sound, "*haw-haw-hoo-hoo*," like a coarse, mocking laugh, comes from the noisy hoot owl between dusk and midnight, rarely at sunrise, more rarely still by day. Sometimes the sound comes from a solitary hooter, sometimes a duet sung out of tune! Everyone knows the hoot, but few people who know its voice will ever see its smooth, round head and bland, almost human face. Its diet consists of mice and other rodents, as well as birds, frogs, lizards, and insects. In Texas it is often found in the sagebrush area. When it makes its own home it is usually in the hollow of a tree. It is popularly known as the "hoot owl."

The Barn Owl

The barn owl, fifteen to eighteen inches long, is said to be the American counterpart of "wise Minerva's only fowl." It is known best by its startling scream. It keeps its odd, triangular face, its speckled and mottled down feathers, and its body well concealed by day, and so silently does it move at night that only in the moonlight can one hope for a passing glimpse as the barn owl sails about.

The Horned Owl

Horned owls have always captured our imaginations. The bold and powerful great horned owl is one of the largest of the owls, measuring a good two feet in length. Its white-barred chest distinguishes a generally sooty brown plumage mottled with grayish white. Called the "tiger of the air," its courage and rapacity cause it to be dreaded by even so comparatively large an animal as the woodchuck. Of 146 great horned owl stomachs examined, only thirty-one contained poultry, eight contained other birds, and the majority contained the remains of various mammals and insects. It is one of the few birds that have no objection to feeding on the remains of a skunk. It has a shriek that will make your blood curdle.

Found in the eastern States, it has often been known to lay its eggs while the snow still flies.

These are laid one at a time at successive intervals of days in the nest of grasses, twigs, and roots. The nest is usually destroyed once the young are able to fly in order to avoid attracting other hunting birds to the vicinity. While its most familiar cry is a hoot, it also indulges in feline and canine noises. The horned owl is ruled by the Moon and Uranus.

The Pygmy Owl

Pygmy owls, or gnome owls of the western United States, are the dwarves of the tribe. Although it is only six and a- half inches long, the pygmy owl has no hesitation about attacking larger birds or mammals. Unlike all the other American owls, its wings make a whistling noise in flight. It also hunts more often during the day than other owls, its body blending with the pine trees on which it is usually perched. The reddish gnome owl, ruled by Venus, is among the handsomest of the owls.

The Elf Owl

The Moon-ruled elf owls are no larger than a sparrow, being only six inches. These southern California owls are the smallest members of the owl family. They like to nest high above the ground, but when large trees are not handy, they will occupy a hole in a giant cactus.

Whitney's elf owl is now found only in southern Arizona and New Mexico in the United States. It likes to skim across the hot, dry river bottoms. The Texas elf owl frequents the lower Rio Grande Valley. A third subspecies inhabits lower California.

Have You Thanked a Bird Today?

It is a bit breathtaking to realize just how much birds, both of the day and night, do for us. Neltje Blanchan, writing in *Birds*, tells us, "One class of tireless workers is bidden to sweep the air and keep down the small gauzy-winged pests such as mosquitos, gnats, and midges. Swallows, purple martins, whippoorwills, nighthawks, and swifts all ply the air for hours at a time."

The black-billed cuckoo has been an invaluable ally to farmers in destroying the gypsy moth, an alarming pest introduced from Europe. Then there are the birds, like the woodpecker, in charge of the bark, where insects and their eggs are often hidden. The red-headed woodpecker also varies his diet with grasshoppers. He is aided in his search for insects by the nuthatches, brown creepers, chickadees, kinglets, and other tireless helpers.

Some birds are caretakers of the ground floor, consuming white grubs, may beetles, or june bugs and the wireworms that attack the roots of grasses. The meadowlarks, bobwhites or quail, blackbirds, robins, native sparrows, chewinks, ovenbirds, brown thrushes, ground warblers, woodcock, arotise, plovers, and the yellow-winged woodpecker or flicker are among those rushing to the rescue.

Weeds produce a lot of seeds. Were it not for the weed destroyers we would be overrun. Sparrows and finches, and even the despised English sparrow help out.

In autumn, noisy flocks of the little gamins settle on our lawns and clean off seeds of crabgrass, dandelions, plantain, and other upstarts in the turf. Because of his special preferences, the little black and yellow goldfinch is an unequaled destroyer of the composite weeds. Sometimes we think of the hawks and owls as both saints and sinners, but they also do the work nature intended for them, admirably supplementing each other's work. One group hunts while the other sleeps. The owls usually remain in a chosen neighborhood through the winter, while the hawks go south. We are never left unprotected. In consideration of the overwhelming amount of good these unthanked friends do us, can we not afford to be a little blind to their faults?

Bibliography

Bills, Rex. *The Rulership Book*. Richmond, VA: Macoy Publishing Company and Masonic Supply Co., 1971.

Birds and Mammals of North America. New York: The Works Progress Administration in the City of New York, 1946.

Blanchan, Neltje. *Birds*. Garden City, NY: The Nature Library, Doubleday & Co., Inc., 1917.

Cornell, H. L., M.D. *Encyclopedia of Medical Astrology*. St. Paul: Llewellyn, 1972.

Telesco, Patricia. *Folkways*. St. Paul: Llewellyn, 1995.

World Book Encyclopedia. Chicago: Field Enterprises Educational Corp., 1963.

Moon Mansions in Vedic Astrology

By Ronnie Dreyer

Based on the sidereal, or fixed, zodiac, which uses 0 degrees of the actual constellation Aries and not the spring equinox as its starting point, vedic (Hindu) astrology, the astrology of India, is a soli-lunar system that places more emphasis on the Moon than on the Sun. Of course, this stems in part from the fact that in India, like most ancient agricultural societies, planting was calculated according to the waxing and waning phases of the Moon. Called *chandra* or *soma* in Sanskrit, the Moon, which represents the mind, is the most important heavenly body in Indian astrology and mythology. According to Vedic philosophy, if one's mind is disciplined and well directed, then one's emotions and physical well-being, also ruled by the Moon, will be under control, healthy, and at peace. It is for this reason that the twenty-seven Moon Mansions, or fixed star clusters, called *asterisms*, into which the zodiac is divided, have such an important place in Vedic Astrology.

Beginning at 0 degrees of Aries, each of these twenty-seven asterisms, called *Nakshatras*, span 13 degrees 20 minutes of the 360-degree zodiac. Each is ruled by one of the nine *grahas*, or planets used in jyotish astrology (See Table 2). Moon Mansions are a fundamental feature of most lunar-based astrological systems such as Chinese, Egyptian and, of course, Indian. In fact, according to Vedic legend, the Nakshatras represent the Moon God's twenty-seven individualistic wives, each of whom provided him domicile during his monthly journey through the zodiac.

Find Your Moon Mansion

Just as we define the positions of the planets in their signs and houses, Indians commonly delineate the planets according to the Nakshatra in which they are placed. Most important is the *Janma Nakshatra*, the mansion in which your natal Moon is placed. To calculate your Janma Nakshatra, first determine the position of your sidereal Moon by subtracting the *ayanamsa* (the difference between the equinox and 0 degrees of Aries, see Table 1) for your birth year from your tropical Moon (the degree of your Moon in a "regular" tropical astrological birthchart).

The Moon is the most important heavenly body in Indian astrology and mythology

Table 1: Krishnamurti Ayanamsa

Year	Ayanamsa
1900	22 degrees 22 minutes
1910	22 degrees 31 minutes
1920	22 degrees 39 minutes
1930	22 degrees 47 minutes
1940	22 degrees 54 minutes
1950	23 degrees 04 minutes
1960	23 degrees 12 minutes
1970	23 degrees 20 minutes
1980	23 degrees 29 minutes
1990	23 degrees 37 minutes
2000	23 degrees 46 minutes

According to the tropical zodiac, Bill Clinton's Moon is situated at 20 degrees 18 minutes Taurus. If we subtract the ayanamsa of 23 degrees (22 degrees 54 minutes rounded off) for his birth year of 1946, we arrive at a sidereal Moon position of 27 degrees 18 minutes of Aries. His Janma Nakshatra, therefore, is the fourth Nakshatra of Krittika, which is ruled by the Sun. (See Table 2.) *Editor's Note: When subtracting, remember that each sign of the zodiac has 30 degrees. Therefore, when we subtract Clinton's ayanamsa (23 degrees) from his tropical Moon placment (20 degrees 18 minutes of Taurus), the Janma Nakshatra ends up in Aries, the sign before Taurus.* Hillary Rodham

Table 2

Mansion	Degrees	Planet	Gana
Aswini	00° 00' Aries–13° 20' Aries	South Node	Divine
Bharani	13° 20' Aries–26° 40' Aries	Venus	Human
Krittika	26° 40' Aries–10° 00' Taurus	Sun	Diabolical
Rohini	10° 00' Taurus–23° 20' Taurus	Moon	Human
Mrigsira	23° 20' Taurus–06° 40' Gemini	Mars	Divine
Ardra	06° 40' Gemini–20° 00' Gemini	North Node	Human
Punarvasu	20° 00' Gemini–03° 20' Cancer	Jupiter	Divine
Pushya	03° 20' Cancer–16° 40' Cancer	Saturn	Divine
Aslesha	16° 40' Cancer–00° 00' Leo	Mercury	Diabolical
Magha	00° 00' Leo–13° 20' Leo	South Node	Diabolical
Purvaphalguni	13° 20' Leo–26° 40' Leo	Venus	Human
Uttraphalguni	26° 40' Leo–10° 00' Virgo	Sun	Human
Hasta	10° 00' Virgo–23° 20' Virgo	Moon	Divine
Chitra	23° 20' Virgo–06° 40' Libra	Mars	Diabolical
Svati	06° 40' Libra–20° 00' Libra	North Node	Divine
Vishakha	20° 00' Libra–3° 20' Scorpio	Jupiter	Diabolical
Anuradha	03° 20' Scorpio–16° 40' Scorpio	Saturn	Divine
Jyeshtha	16° 40' Scorpio–0° 00' Sagittarius	Mercury	Diabolical
Mula	00° 00' Sagittarius–13° 20' Sagittarius	South Node	Diabolical
Purvashadya	13° 20' Sagittarius–26° 40' Sagittarius	Venus	Human
Uttrashadya	26° 40' Sagittarius–10° 00' Capricorn	Sun	Human
Shravana	10° 00' Capricorn–23° 20' Capricorn	Moon	Divine
Dhanishtha	23° 20' Capricorn–06° 40' Aquarius	Mars	Diabolical
Shatbisha	06° 40' Aquarius–20° 00' Aquarius	North Node	Diabolical
Purvaphadrapada	20° 00' Aquarius–03° 20' Pisces	Jupiter	Human
Uttraphadrapada	03° 20' Pisces–16° 40' Pisces	Saturn	Human
Revati	16° 40' Pisces–00° 00' Aries	Mercury	Divine

Clinton's tropical Moon is posited at 29 degrees 11 minutes Pisces. Subtracting the ayanamsa of 23 degrees 1 minute for her birth year of 1947, we get the sidereal position for her Moon as 6 degrees 10 minutes Pisces, in the Saturn-ruled Nakshatra of Uttraphadrapada.

Whichever planet rules your Janma Nakshatra determines the planetary period, or *Dasa*, in which you were born; the remaining planetary periods then follow in sequential order. According to Table 2, Bill Clinton's Moon in Krittika indicates that its ruler, the Sun, was the first period of his life, with the remaining sequential periods following suit. He is presently in Jupiter's Mahadasa, Sanskrit for "great age." Hillary Rodham Clinton's Moon is in Uttraphadrapada. Saturn ruled the first period of her life, and now she is in the Dasa ruled by Venus.

Moon Mansions and Marriage

Since he is called on to arrange marriages, the Indian astrologer often utilizes the ancient Gana Kuta system, which determines compatibility through a comparison of the bride and groom's Janma Nakshatras. As seen from Table 2, each Moon Mansion is categorized as divine (*deva*), human (*manusha*) or diabolical (*rakshasa*). Don't take the classifications of these *Ganas* (Sanskrit for "temperaments") too literally! In fact, divine refers to someone who is unselfish and kindhearted, human is someone both well-meaning and willful, and diabolical describes someone who is self-willed and assertive—traits that may be detrimental in Hindu society, but are admired here in the West. According to this system, the most ideally suited couple will share the same temperament, as this will bestow them with similar hopes, goals, and outlooks on life. If the man and woman are of different ganas (which is quite common) the difficulty will be cancelled if the woman's Janma Nakshatra is more than fourteen signs past that of the man's.

Bill and Hillary Clinton

Let's see how this works with a few celebrity couples. Bill Clinton's Janma Nakshatra is Krittika, a demonic Moon Mansion, while Hillary Rodham Clinton's Janma Nakshatra is Uttraphadrapada, a human Moon Mansion. The twenty-sixth asterism of Uttraphadrapada, however, is twenty-three Nakshatras past the third Mansion of Krittika, where Bill Clinton's natal Moon lies. Though the Clintons have very different temperaments, they would still be considered to have common goals according to this system.

Prince Charles and Princess Diana

Princess Diana's tropical Moon lies at 25 degrees 2 minutes of Aquarius. Subtracting the ayanamsa for 1961 gives her a sidereal Moon of 1 degree 50 minutes of Aquarius. Prince Charles' Moon is 0 degrees 26 minutes Taurus. Subtracting the ayanamsa for 1948 gives him a sidereal Moon of 7 degrees 24 minutes Aries. Charles' Janma Nakshatra is the first Mansion of Aswini which is divine, while Diana's Janma Nakshatra is the twenty-fifth Mansion of Purvaphadrapada, which is human. Even though their temperaments are different, Diana's birth asterism is more than fourteen past that of Charles. They may have gotten divorced, but Charles and Diana still have similar hopes and dreams. An astrologer would probably not have objected to this union based on the Janma Kuta system alone. It must be remembered, however, that this is only one system out of many. Other methods, such as *Yoni Kuta*, measure sexual and emotional harmony, and it is quite possible that in these other areas Diana and Charles would not have passed the marriage test.

Paul Newman and Joanne Woodward

Paul Newman and Joanne Woodward's compatibility rating shows why they are one of the most enduring married couples in Hollywood. Paul Newman's sidereal Moon is located at 8 degrees 55 minutes Aquarius, in Shatbisha, the twenty-fourth Nakshatra, while Joanne Woodward's sidereal Moon is situated at 2 degrees 2 minutes Aquarius, which is also in Shatbisha. Not only does each have an Aquarius Moon, but they both share the same diabolical temperament. Because this makes them both independent and assertive, we can only assume that their mutual respect has helped the duo maintain such a long lasting, happy union.

Electional Charts

Because it takes approximately one month for the Moon to travel through the entire zodiac, the Nakshatra that the Moon transits is used extensively for setting up the electional, or event, chart. Electional astrology is the branch of astrology devoted to determining the best most favorable times to begin activities. Much of the astrology in the *Moon Sign Book* is electional. Known in Sanskrit as *muhurta*, the event chart favors certain Nakshatras over others for marriages, contract signing, automobile or home purchases, journeys, and even surgery. Setting up the best electional chart is a complex process, but the first step simply involves identifying which Moon Mansion is best suited for the enactment of a particular event.

Before planning a specific ritual, project, or event, first review which Moon Mansions are most conducive and then select a day on which the sidereal Moon passes through that particular Nakshatra. Table 3 lists which Nakshatras the Moon will be passing through during 1998 according to Eastern Standard Time (EST). Since each Nakshatra spans 13 degrees 20 minutes and the Moon travels approximately 12 degrees per day, note how rapidly each Mansion changes.

According to *Brihat Samhita*, the classic work by Hindu sage Varahamihira, the following summarizes which Nakshatras are best suited for starting specific events.

Weddings

When deciding on a wedding date, the best asterisms for marriage and sexual union include Rohini, Mrigsira, Magha, Uttraphalguni, Hasta, Svati, Anuradha, Mula, Uttrashadya, Uttraphadrapada, and Revati, except for the first quarter of Magha and Mula and the last quarter of Revati. Of course, choosing a wedding date is more complex, but it is advisable to at least begin by narrowing it down to the aforementioned suitable constellations.

Buying a Home

The best asterisms for buying a home are Mrigsira, Aslesha, Magha, Purvaphalguni, Vishakha, Mula, Punarvasu, and Revati. Buying land on which to build a house should take place when the Moon is in Aswini, Rohini, Mrigsira, Punarvasu, Pushya, Uttraphalguni, Hasta, Svati, Anuradha, Uttrashadya, Shravana, Dhanishtha, Shatbisha, or Uttraphadrapada. Purchasing land or property for purposes of agriculture, business, commerce, or anything other than personal use should take place when the Moon is in Aswini, Rohini, Mrigsira, Punarvasu, Pushya, Uttrashadya, Shravana, Shatbisha, and Uttraphadrapada. No renovations should take place under Krittika, Magha, Purvaphalguni, Pushya, Hasta, Mula, and Revati.

Long-Term Activities

If you wish to begin long-term activities and permanent operations like buying a house, accepting a new position, or starting college, the Moon should occupy one of the fixed Nakshatras such as Rohini, Uttraphalguni, Uttrashadya, Uttraphadrapada. It is advisable to begin a business trip when the Moon is in Mrigsira, Aswini, Pushya, Punarvasu, Hasta, Anuradha, Shravana, Mula, Dhanishtha, and Revati. No journeys should commence when the Moon is in Krittika, Bharani, Aslesha, Vishakha, Purvashadya, Purvaphadrapada, and Ardra. Beginning a lawsuit or filing for divorce should begin when the Moon is in Aswini, Rohini, Mrigsira, Pushya, Uttraphalguni, Hasta, Chitra, Anuradha, Dhanishtha, and Revati.

Lighter Asterisms

When the Moon passes through lighter asterisms, such as Aswini, Pushya, Hasta, Chitra, Anuradha, Mrigsira and Revati, the recommended activities include taking a vacation, participating in sporting events, attending a fine arts performance, making love, or doing anything creative, sensual, and enjoyable. For spiritual activities, Mula, Jyeshtha, Ardra, and Aslesha are the best placements for the Moon.

Moveable Mansions

Buy a new vehicle and begin planning a garden during one of the moveable Mansions such as Punarvasu, Svati, Shravana, Dhanishtha, Shatbisha. Krittika and Vishakha are good for mundane day-to-day activities while Pushya is favorable for any activity except for marriage.

As a rule, it is a good idea not to begin any projects when the Moon is in Bharani, which is considered to be generally destructive. Last but not least, do not begin any projects for which you may be misunderstood, or for which you may be caught like cheating on your income taxes under Purvaphalguni, Purvashadya, Purvaphadrapada, Bharani and Magha since they will are well known for harboring evil deeds.

Bibliography

Braha, James. *Ancient Hindu Astrology for the Modern Western Astrologer*. Hollywood: Hermetician Press, 1986.

Braha, James. *Astro-Logos: Revelations of a Hindu Astrologer*. Longboat Key: Hermetician Press, 1996.

Braha, James. *How to Predict Your Future*. Hollywood: Hermetician Press, 1994.

DeFouw, Hart. *Light on Life: An Introduction to the Astrology of India*. London: Arkana Books, 1996.

Dreyer, Ronnie Gale. *Vedic Astrology: A Guide to the Fundamentals of Jyotish*. York Beach: Samuel Weiser Inc., 1997.

Frawley, David. *The Astrology of the Seers*. Salt Lake City: Passage Press, 1990.

Raman, B.V. *Muhurtha or Electional Astrology*. Bangalore: IBH Prakashana, 1986.

Table 3: 1998 Moon Mansions

Mansion	Date	Mansion	Date
Shravana	Dec. 31, 8:20 am	Dhanishtha	Jan. 1, 7:01 am
Shatbisha	Jan. 2, 5:35 am	Purvaphadrapada	Jan. 3, 4:08 am
Uttraphadrapada	Jan. 4, 2:43 am	Revati	Jan. 5, 1:22 am
Aswini	Jan. 6, 12:07 am	Bharani	Jan. 6, 10:59 pm
Krittika	Jan. 7, 10:00 pm	Rohini	Jan. 8, 9:12 pm
Mrigsira	Jan. 9, 8:39 pm	Ardra	Jan. 10, 8:25 pm
Punarvasu	Jan. 11, 8:35 pm	Pushya	Jan. 12, 9:14 pm
Aslesha	Jan. 13, 10:26 pm	Magha	Jan. 15, 12:12 am
Purvaphalguni	Jan. 16, 2:30 am	Uttraphalguni	Jan. 17, 5:16 am
Hasta	Jan. 18, 8:18 am	Chitra	Jan. 19, 11:25 am
Svati	Jan. 20, 2:21 pm	Anuradha	Jan. 22, 6:47 pm
Jyeshtha	Jan. 23, 7:59 pm	Mula	Jan. 24, 8:25 pm
Purvashadya	Jan. 25, 8:06 pm	Uttrashadya	Jan. 26, 7:10 pm
Shravana	Jan. 27, 5:41 pm	Dhanishtha	Jan. 28, 3:51 pm
Shatbisha	Jan. 29, 1:46 pm	Purvaphadrapada	Jan. 30, 11:37 am
Uttraphadrapada	Jan. 31, 9:30 am	Revati	Feb. 1, 7:32 am
Aswini	Feb. 2, 5:49 am	Bharani	Feb. 3, 4:24 am
Krittika	Feb. 4, 3:22 am	Rohini	Feb. 5, 2:43 am
Mrigsira	Feb. 6, 2:29 am	Ardra	Feb. 7, 2:40 am
Punarvasu	Feb. 8, 3:17 am	Pushya	Feb. 9, 4:21 am
Aslesha	Feb. 10, 5:52 am	Magha	Feb. 11, 7:48 am
Purvaphalguni	Feb. 12, 10:09 am	Uttraphalguni	Feb. 13, 12:52 pm
Hasta	Feb. 14, 3:51 pm	Chitra	Feb. 15, 6:57 pm
Svati	Feb. 16, 10:00 pm	Vishakha	Feb. 18, 12:49 am
Anuradha	Feb. 19, 3:11 am	Jyeshtha	Feb. 20, 4:57 am
Mula	Feb. 21, 5:59 am	Vishakha	Jan. 21, 4:53 pm
Purvashadya	Feb. 22, 6:13 am	Uttrashadya	Feb. 23, 5:42 am
Shravana	Feb. 24, 4:27 am	Dhanishtha	Feb. 25, 2:37 am
Shatbisha	Feb. 26, 12:20 am	Purvaphadrapada	Feb. 26, 9:44 pm
Uttraphadrapada	Feb. 27, 7:00 pm	Revati	Feb. 28, 4:18 pm
Aswini	Mar. 1, 1:47 pm	Bharani	Mar. 2, 11:36 am
Krittika	Mar. 3, 9:52 am	Rohini	Mar. 4, 8:40 am
Mrigsira	Mar. 5, 8:06 am	Ardra	Mar. 6, 8:09 am
Punarvasu	Mar. 7, 8:50 am	Pushya	Mar. 8, 10:07 am
Aslesha	Mar. 9, 11:54 am	Magha	Mar. 10, 2:07 pm
Purvaphalguni	Mar. 11, 4:41 pm	Uttraphalguni	Mar. 12, 7:31 pm
Hasta	Mar. 13, 10:31 pm	Chitra	Mar. 15, 1:36 am

Svati	Mar. 16, 4:38 am	Vishakha	Mar. 17, 7:31 am
Anuradha	Mar. 18, 10:07 am	Jyeshtha	Mar. 19, 12:17 pm
Mula	Mar. 20, 1:54 pm	Purvashadya	Mar. 21, 2:50 pm
Uttrashadya	Mar. 22, 3:02 pm	Shravana	Mar. 23, 2:30 pm
Dhanishtha	Mar. 24, 1:15 pm	Shatbisha	Mar. 25, 11:21 am
Purvaphadrapada	Mar. 26, 8:56 am	Uttraphadrapada	Mar. 27, 6:09 am
Revati	Mar. 28, 3:10 am	Aswini	Mar. 29, 12:10 am
Bharani	Mar. 29, 9:20 pm	Krittika	Mar. 30, 6:35 pm
Rohini	Mar. 31, 4:50 pm	Mula	Apr. 16, 8:05 pm
Mrigsira	Apr. 1, 3:28 pm	Ardra	Apr. 2, 2:51 pm
Punarvasu	Apr. 3, 3:02 pm	Pushya	Apr. 4, 3:59 pm
Aslesha	Apr. 5, 5:39 pm	Magha	Apr. 6, 7:55 pm
Purvaphalguni	Apr. 7, 10:36 pm	Uttraphalguni	Apr. 9, 1:34:10 am
Hasta	Apr. 10, 4:39:27 am	Chitra	Apr. 11, 7:44:34 am
Svati	Apr. 12, 10:43:29 am	Vishakha	Apr. 13, 1:31:20 pm
Anuradha	Apr. 14, 4:03:55 pm	Jyeshtha	Apr. 15, 6:16:59 pm
Purvashadya	Apr. 17, 9:26 pm	Uttrashadya	Apr. 18, 10:12 pm
Shravana	Apr. 19, 10:22 pm	Dhanishtha	Apr. 20, 9:53 pm
Shatbisha	Apr. 21, 8:45 pm	Purvaphadrapada	Apr. 22, 7:01pm
Uttraphadrapada	Apr. 23, 4:46 pm	Revati	Apr. 24, 2:07 pm
Aswini	Apr. 25, 11:14 am	Bharani	Apr. 26, 8:17 am
Krittika	Apr. 27, 5:28 am	Rohini	Apr. 28, 2:58 am
Mrigsira	Apr. 29, 12:58 am	Ardra	Apr. 29, 11:37 pm
Punarvasu	Apr. 30, 11:04 pm	Pushya	May 1, 11:21 pm
Aslesha	May 3, 12:29 am	Magha	May 4, 2:22 am
Purvaphalguni	May 5, 4:53 am	Uttraphalguni	May 6, 7:47 am
Hasta	May 7, 10:54 am	Chitra	May 8, 2:00 pm
Svati	May 9, 4:58 pm	Vishakha	May 10, 7:39 pm
Anuradha	May 11, 10:02 pm	Jyeshtha	May 13, 12:03 am
Mula	May 14, 1:42 am	Purvashadya	May 15, 2:59:11 am
Uttrashadya	May 16, 3:51 am	Shravana	May 17, 4:17 am
Dhanishtha	May 18, 4:16 am	Shatbisha	May 19,, 3:44 am
Purvaphadrapada	May 20 2:43 am	Uttraphadrapada	May 21, 1:12 am
Revati	May 21, 11:15 pm	Aswini	May 22, 8:58 pm
Bharani	May 23, 6:28 pm	Krittika	May 24, 3:54 pm
Rohini	May 25, 1:28 pm	Mrigsira	May 26, 11:19 am
Ardra	May 27, 9:38 am	Punarvasu	May 28, 8:35 am
Pushya	May 29, 8:17 am	Aslesha	May 30, 9:14 am
Magha	May 31, 10:10 am	Purvaphalguni	Jun. 1, 12:14 pm

Uttraphalguni	Jun. 2, 2:52 pm	Hasta	Jun. 3, 5:51 pm
Chitra	Jun. 4, 8:55 pm	Svati	Jun. 5, 11:53 pm
Vishakha	Jun. 7, 2:34 am	Anuradha	Jun. 8, 4:50 am
Jyeshtha	Jun. 9, 6:40 am	Mula	Jun. 10, 8:03 am
Purvashadya	Jun. 11, 9:00 am	Uttrashadya	Jun. 12, 9:34 am
Shravana	Jun. 13, 9:47 am	Dhanishtha	Jun. 14, 9:39 am
Shatbisha	Jun. 15, 9:13 am	Purvaphadrapada	Jun. 16, 8:27am
Uttraphadrapada	Jun. 17, 7:22 am	Revati	Jun. 18, 5:59 am
Aswini	Jun. 19, 4:21 am	Bharani	Jun. 20, 2:30 am
Krittika	Jun. 21, 12:33 am	Rohini	Jun. 21, 10:37 pm
Mrigsira	Jun. 22, 8:49 pm	Ardra	Jun. 23, 7:19 pm
Punarvasu	Jun. 24, 6:16 pm	Pushya	Jun. 25, 5:47 pm
Aslesha	Jun. 26, 5:59 pm	Magha	Jun. 27, 6:55 pm
Purvaphalguni	Jun. 28, 8:34 pm	Uttraphalguni	Jun. 29, 10:51 pm
Hasta	Jul. 1 ,1:35 am	Chitra	Jul. 2, 4:34 am
Svati	Jul. 3, 7:33 am	Vishakha	Jul. 4, 10:19 am
Anuradha	Jul. 5, 12:40 pm	Jyeshtha	Jul. 6, 2:29 pm
Mula	Jul. 7, 3:46 pm	Purvashadya	Jul. 8, 4:29 pm
Uttrashadya	Jul. 9, 4:42 pm	Shravana	Jul. 10, 4:29 pm
Dhanishtha	Jul. 11, 3:54 pm	Shatbisha	Jul. 12, 3:03 pm
Purvaphadrapada	Jul. 13, 1:59 pm	Uttraphadrapada	Jul. 14, 12:45 pm
Revati	Jul. 15, 11:23 am	Aswini	Jul. 16, 9:57 am
Bharani	Jul. 17, 8:29 am	Krittika	Jul. 18, 7:01 am
Rohini	Jul. 19, 5:38 am	Mrigsira	Jul. 20, 4:24 am
Ardra	Jul. 21, 3:24 am	Punarvasu	Jul. 22, 2:44 am
Pushya	Jul. 23, 2:30 am	Aslesha	Jul. 24, 2:47 am
Magha	Jul. 25, 3:39 am	Purvaphalguni	Jul. 26, 5:08 am
Uttraphalguni	Jul. 27, 7:10 am	Hasta	Jul. 28, 9:42 am
Chitra	Jul. 29, 12:33 pm	Svati	Jul. 30, 3:33 pm
Vishakha	Jul. 31, 6:26 pm	Anuradha	Aug, 1 9:01 pm
Jyeshtha	Aug 2, 11:05 pm	Mula	Aug 4, 12:33 am
Purvashadya	Aug 5, 1:21 am	Uttrashadya	Aug 6, 1:30 am
Shravana	Aug 7, 1:03 am	Dhanishtha	Aug 8, 12:05 am
Shatbisha	Aug 8, 10:44 pm	Purvaphadrapada	Aug, 9 9:06 pm
Uttraphadrapada	Aug 10, 7:17 pm	Revati	Aug 11, 5:26 pm
Aswini	Aug 12, 3:36 pm	Bharani	Aug 13, 1:54 pm
Krittika	Aug 14, 12:24 pm	Rohini	Aug 15, 11:09 am
Mrigsira	Aug 16, 10:13 am	Ardra	Aug 17, 9:37 am
Punarvasu	Aug 18, 9:25 am	Pushya	Aug 19, 9:37 am

Aslesha	Aug 20, 10:16 am	Magha	Aug 21, 11:23 am
Purvaphalguni	Aug 22, 12:58 pm	Uttraphalguni	Aug 23, 3:01 pm
Hasta	Aug 24, 5:28 pm	Chitra	Aug 25, 8:15 pm
Svati	Aug 26, 11:14 pm	Vishakha	Aug 28, 2:14 am
Anuradha	Aug 29, 5:03 am	Jyeshtha	Aug 30, 7:31 am
Mula	Aug 31, 9:26 am	Purvashadya	Sep. 1, 10:40 am
Uttrashadya	Sep. 2, 11:10 am	Shravana	Sep. 3, 10:55 am
Dhanishtha	Sep. 4, 9:59 am	Shatbisha	Sep. 5, 8:27 am
Purvaphadrapada	Sep. 6, 6:27 am	Uttraphadrapada	Sep. 7, 4:08 am
Revati	Sep. 8, 1:38 am	Aswini	Sep. 8, 11:07 pm
Bharani	Sep. 9, 8:45 pm	Krittika	Sep. 10, 6:39 pm
Rohini	Sep. 11, 4:57 pm	Mrigsira	Sep. 12, 3:43 pm
Ardra	Sep. 13, 3:02 pm	Punarvasu	Sep. 14, 2:55 pm
Pushya	Sep. 15, 3:21 pm	Aslesha	Sep. 16, 4:18 pm
Magha	Sep. 17, 5:45 pm	Purvaphalguni	Sep. 18, 7:37 pm
Uttraphalguni	Sep. 19, 9:51 pm	Hasta	Sep. 21, 12:25 am
Chitra	Sep. 22, 3:12 am	Svati	Sep. 23, 6:10 am
Vishakha	Sep. 24, 9:12 am	Anuradha	Sep. 25, 12:10 pm
Jyeshtha	Sep. 26, 2:55 pm	Mula	Sep. 27, 5:17pm
Purvashadya	Sep. 28, 7:06 pm	Uttrashadya	Sep. 29, 8:15 pm
Shravana	Sep. 30, 8:38 pm	Dhanishtha	Oct. 1, 8:13 pm
Shatbisha	Oct. 2, 7:03 pm	Purvaphadrapada	Oct. 3, 5:13 pm
Uttraphadrapada	Oct. 4, 2:50 pm	Revati	Oct. 5, 12:04 pm
Aswini	Oct. 6, 9:05 am	Bharani	Oct. 7, 6:05 am
Krittika	Oct. 8, 3:16 am	Rohini	Oct. 9, 12:47 am
Mrigsira	Oct. 9, 10:49 pm	Ardra	Oct 10, 9:29 pm
Punarvasu	Oct. 11, 8:52 pm	Pushya	Oct. 12, 9:00 pm
Aslesha	Oct. 13, 9:52 pm	Magha	Oct. 14, 11:21 pm
Purvaphalguni	Oct. 16, 1:23 am	Uttraphalguni	Oct. 17, 3:49 am
Hasta	Oct. 18, 6:32 am	Chitra	Oct. 19, 9:26 am
Svati	Oct. 20, 12:25 pm	Vishakha	Oct. 21, 3:25 pm
Anuradha	Oct. 22, 6:21 pm	Jyeshtha	Oct. 23, 9:09 pm
Mula	Oct. 24 11:43 pm	Purvashadya	Oct. 26, 1:54 am
Uttrashadya	Oct. 27, 3:36 am	Shravana	Oct. 28, 4:41 am
Dhanishtha	Oct. 29, 5:03 am	Shatbisha	Oct. 30, 4:15 am
Purvaphadrapada	Oct. 31, 3:30 am	Uttraphadrapada	Nov. 1, 1:39 am
Revati	Nov. 1, 11:13 pm	Aswini	Nov. 2, 8:21 pm
Bharani	Nov. 3, 5:15 pm	Krittika	Nov. 4, 2:05 pm
Rohini	Nov. 5, 11:05 am	Mrigsira	Nov. 6, 8:26 am

Ardra	Nov. 7, 6:19 am	Punarvasu	Nov. 8, 4:54 am
Pushya	Nov. 9, 4:17 am	Aslesha	Nov. 10, 4:31 am
Magha	Nov. 11, 5:35 am	Purvaphalguni	Nov. 12, 7:22 am
Uttraphalguni	Nov. 13, 9:43 am	Hasta	Nov. 14, 12:29 pm
Chitra	Nov. 15, 3:27 pm	Svati	Nov. 16, 6:30 pm
Vishakha	Nov. 17, 9:28 pm	Anuradha	Nov. 19, 12:19 am
Jyeshtha	Nov. 20, 2:59 am	Mula	Nov. 21, 5:25 am
Purvashadya	Nov. 22, 7:35 am	Uttrashadya	Nov. 23, 9:23 am
Shravana	Nov. 24, 10:47 am	Dhanishtha	Nov. 25, 11:40 am
Shatbisha	Nov. 26, 11:57 am	Purvaphadrapada	Nov. 27, 11:36 am
Uttraphadrapada	Nov. 28, 10:35 am	Revati	Nov. 29, 8:57 am
Aswini	Nov. 30, 6:46 am	Bharani	Dec. 1, 4:10 am
Krittika	Dec. 2, 1:19 am	Rohini	Dec. 2, 10:24 pm
Mrigsira	Dec. 3, 7:36 pm	Ardra	Dec. 4, 5:07 pm
Punarvasu	Dec. 5, 3:08 pm	Pushya	Dec. 6, 1:49 pm
Aslesha	Dec. 7, 1:18 pm	Magha	Dec. 8, 1:38 pm
Purvaphalguni	Dec. 9, 2:47 pm	Uttraphalguni	Dec. 10, 4:42 pm
Hasta	Dec. 11, 7:11 pm	Chitra	Dec. 12, 10:03 pm
Svati	Dec. 14, 1:05 am	Vishakha	Dec. 15, 4:06 am
Anuradha	Dec. 16, 6:55 am	Jyeshtha	Dec. 17, 9:29 am
Mula	Dec. 18, 11:42 am	Purvashadya	Dec. 19, 1:35 pm
Uttrashadya	Dec. 20, 3:07 pm	Shravana	Dec. 21, 4:17 pm
Dhanishtha	Dec. 22, 5:05 pm	Shatbisha	Dec. 23, 5:28 pm
Purvaphadrapada	Dec. 24, 5:26 pm	Uttraphadrapada	Dec. 25, 4:57 pm
Revati	Dec. 26, 3:59 pm	Aswini	Dec. 27, 2:35 pm
Bharani	Dec. 28, 12:48 pm	Krittika	Dec. 29, 10:42 am
Rohini	Dec. 30, 8:26 am	Mrigsira	Dec. 31, 6:07 am

Moon Lore

By Verna Gates

Shakespeare's wise Juliet chides Romeo, "Swear not by the Moon, the inconstant Moon that monthly changes in her circled orb." The Moon's mysterious changes fascinated our ancestors and make romantics of our contemporaries. Even science bows to the Moon's majesty when it comes to controlling the tides of this planet and the tides of humanity. So does the historian.

Caesar defeated the feared Germans when they suddenly stopped in the middle of a battle and retreated back to camp. A seer had foreseen that the Germans could not claim victory since the battle had begun before the waxing of the Moon. They were right. Caesar saw their weakness and routed them. Even the warlike Spartans considered it a waste of time to make war before the Moon peaked at fullness, a fact that caused great concern to neighboring Athens when it was facing a New Moon invasion.

In the fifth century BCE, Hippocrates, the father of modern medicine, said that no physician should practice without studying the Moon. Many studies have shown excessive bleeding from wounds and during surgery when the Moon is waxing. On the flip side, Moon lore tells us that most living things are stronger during the Full Moon.

The Full Moon is the perfect time to harvest medicinal herbs, which reach their potency with the full lunar face shining up on them. However, it's best to start taking medicines with a new Moon, when most diseases are easiest to cure. Diseases must also gain strength in the Full Moon.

The Druids believed in harvesting the mistletoe, a gift from the lightning, six days after the New Moon. At this time, two white bulls would be sacrificed and other rituals performed.

Once the mistletoe was properly prepared, it would make potent medicines to cure infertility, poisons, ulcers, and epilepsy. As a child of lightning, it could also quench fire, and was used as a fire extinguisher.

If you suspect death is at all close, beware the ebb tide. People are most likely to die near the time of the closest ebb tide. The wise Aristotle believed in this concept. This was a common concern during Dickens' day as well. He wrote in *David Copperfield* that Mr. Barkis would die at ebb tide—so says the character of Mr. Peggoty to the book's main character. The Dutch believe that thin people die during ebb, and fat people during flood. Since there are fewer floods, perhaps a little weight could be a good thing.

If you want to live long, try this Hindu ritual. Place the evening meal on your rooftop in the month of Kuar (September/October). Let it absorb plenty of Full-Moon beams. Then divide your meal among the family members who you want to bless with long life (don't invite the brother-in-law who borrows money). With moonbeams inside them, your family members will be able to regenerate, just like their lunar dinner companion.

It is true, according to psychiatrists and social workers, that the Full Moon brings out a certain lunacy. Don't worry; you can cure it by making snake meatballs and eating them under the Full Moon. The only problem is that the snake itself is a native of Egypt, which for most of us is quite a long journey.

Is That a Face We See?

Back in the old days, people lived much more closely together than they do now. Farms housed extended family. Villages often contained two hundred or fewer people, who spent

Swear not by the Moon, the inconstant Moon that monthly changes in her circled orb

—Shakespeare

their whole lives together. Under these conditions, people could get on your nerves. Often, the man, or woman, on the Moon has some very annoying habits. As in all folklore, there is a method to the madness—a reason for telling a story. Old wives used them to teach the lessons of life.

Night people and day people have never gotten along. In Tahiti, there was a woman who insisted on working at night, but she was not a quiet sort who hummed quietly over gentle tasks. No, she would beat tapa with a mallet all night long. (Tahitians beat the bark of the paper-mulberry tree to make tapa, a cloth used to make clothing.) As Hina, the woman, beat the tapa, it was so loud, it even reached the sensitive ears of the god Tangaroa. The god sent Pani to Hina to tell her to stop that racket. He said the harbor of the gods was noisy. Pani told Hina to stop. He told her again. He told her a third time. Since Hina was making the cloth for Tangaroa, she refused to believe she was annoying him. At the third time, instead of Hina beating tapa with the mallet, Pani began to beat Hina with the mallet. In her appeal for escape, she was carried up to the Moon, where she can beat tapa all night long, if she wants to.

Another woman from Tahiti was caught cracking jokes with her girlfriends about her husband's aroma. For this disrespectful gossip, he punished her with banishment. Since no place is more desolate than the Moon, this is where he suggested she should go. She took her son, Marama (moonlight), with her to a place far from her husband's sensitive feelings.

Another Moon goddess of the South Seas area lives on the Moon not because she was annoying, but because she was annoyed. It seemed that some taboo forced her to carry her children's diaper contents to the far side of her land. As her husband worked hard, they owned more and more land. They had more and more children. She had to travel farther and farther to the latrine for her many offspring. She wearied of this task and one night, went up to a high ridge and leaped to the Moon, as many a woman has been tempted to do. Her husband tried to foil her escape and grabbed her leg, which broke off. Because of her one leg, she is called Lono-muku.

A couple of versions of this diaper/Moon story indicate that arguments over the less pleasant child-rearing duties have long been a part of husband and wife relations. On the island of Maui, legend has it that the husband is left to tend the child and, unaccustomed to such duties, soon wearies of crying and diapers. He uses gourds as parachutes to float over to the Moon. A story from New Zealand tells of a god who marries an earthling. When she has a very human child, he complains about the diaper messes. She takes her child and steps off the roof to jump to the Moon.

One lunar dweller got there strictly by cussedness. Rona was a hard-working Maori woman, but she had a bad habit of cussing—not very ladylike. One night, she was preparing the fires for her husband to bring home his catch of fish, caught under the Full Moon. As his arrival time drew near, she realized that she had no water to steam the fish. She grabbed her bags and dashed to the river, guided only by the light of the Full Moon. When a cloud covered the Moon, she stumbled, not once but twice, giving her toes a good stub. She not only cried out in pain, but here she made a fatal error. She looked up and cursed the Moon, calling it "Pokokohua!" (cooked head) which is apparently the Maaori equivalent of "bloody hell." By the time her husband arrived home, Rona was cooling her temper on the face of the Moon. Apparently, she put up quite a fight going, and sits with the uprooted trees she had in futility hoped would anchor her to earth.

In a Blackfoot story, the Moon was a loving wife to the creator Sun and the mother of the Big Dipper. Then one day, a snake came along to tempt the innocent woman. Sound familiar? Anyway, the Moon betrayed Creator Sun with the Snakeman by doing a lot more than eating an apple. It did not take long for the Sun to find out. He watched and followed the Moon to find out their meeting place and their signals. The next day, arriving at the meeting place before the Moon, the Sun gave the lovers' signal. The Snakeman came halfway out of his hole before he realized he had been summoned by the Creator Sun, his enemy. The Creator Sun killed the Snakeman. The Moon arrived as the Snakeman died. In witnessing her first death, the distraught Moon went berserk. In her craziness, she tried to kill her husband and sons, involving a chase scene to rival an Arnold Schwarzenegger movie. To defend himself and his sons, the Sun placed the Moon in the sky, where she chases them all still.

In a European story, there was one man who lived in town who was never friendly. He was a grudging neighbor and never wanted to join in the community activities. He didn't even try to get along. He had peculiar habits as well. For one thing, he was a sinner. He insisted on working on the Sabbath rather than sing in church with his neighbors. He like to collect briars by the fence as the church people passed by. (Those who know flower lore know the symbolism of briars is surliness.) One Sunday, the church emptied and no one saw the old man in his usual place. Not believing that reform was a possibility, they looked for what accident may have befallen him. Of course, many had predicted a fall would come of his sinfulness. They looked everywhere but no one could find the old man until night fell. They looked up and saw him scowling at them from the Moon, with his briar patch beside him.

In an African-American story, a slave named Sam lives on the Moon. This poor soul was happily married and working in the big house when his fate was changed by a jealous fellow slave. The jealous one turned the master against Sam. Convinced that Sam was plotting to kill him, the master sold Sam. Poor Sam was separated from his loving wife. The wretched creature went morose over his condition. His new master, trying to tease him back to work, promised to buy Sam's wife if he cleared enough new ground. The slave began working like crazy, even on Sunday. The Master couldn't stop him from violating the holy Sabbath. Many days passed. Sam's wife, alone on the plantation without Sam, wasted away. When his wife died, Sam saw her spirit pass. The angels carrying her were calling him too, but because he had worked on Sunday, he couldn't go to heaven. He didn't deserve hell either, however, so he sits on the Moon burning brush to light the sky, waiting for judgment day.

The Moon is a lonely place. That's why the Greek Moon goddess Selene hurried away at dawn to join the sleeping Endymion. Some say the grouchy old man on the Moon was soon joined by a woman caught churning butter on a Sabbath. Some say *Jack and Jill* is a story of two children who were kidnapped by the Moon and live on up there to foretell the weather. In other cultures the Moon was a predator.

According to an Aboriginal story, the fat, pale Moon was not considered an attractive suitor to the slim, black-skinned girls. The Moon sure liked them, though. One night he flirted with two girls who were half-amused with his banterings. When it was time to go home, the Moon asked for a ride across the lake to help speed his long journey to the sky. As the girls carried him on their backs, the Moon couldn't resist stroking their silky skin. They scolded the Moon, but he persisted. All at once, both girls flipped over, dumping the Moon into the water. Soon, they saw him trying to slip into the sky, but now, he had squeezed himself into a slender crescent. Don't worry, he'll get his wicked ways back and plump out again—until more girls show him the straight and narrow.

Sometimes, the Moon man, or woman, is the soul of goodness, especially in hot climates such as India, where the Sun can be blazing torment. It was one such afternoon when Sun, Moon, and Wind went to dinner at the home of their Uncle Thunder and Aunt Lightning. They left their mother, Distant Star, to wait at home alone. The feast was grand, with delicacies of all kinds imaginable. Sun and Wind ate greedily, wolfing down all that was put before them and asking for more. Moon, good daughter that she was, thought of her lonely mother and sneaked the best morsels into her lunar pockets. When the three children arrived home, Distant Star asked what they had brought her. Both Sun and Wind confessed to their greed and selfishness. Kind Moon got down a plate for her mother and served the feast anew. When Distant Star had eaten her fill, she turned to her children and cursed the selfish ones. Sun, she condemned to scorch the earth, so that few would see his midday brilliance. Wind, she condemned to blow hot and scour the earth so that all would run from him. But Moon she blessed with a cool, gentle light that all may look at and enjoy. In the cool evenings of a hot climate, the Moon's soft light is especially appreciated.

How Did the Moon Get in the Sky?

This question is as old as human speech. For a tribe in Mexico, it was a creation contest. The contending gods, Quezalcoatl (the good) and Tezcatlipoca (the black god) had tried to work together as Sun and Moon and had failed. For the fifth and final Sun, two new contenders arose, named Rich and Strong and Poor and Feeble. The gods lit the bonfire and invited Rich and Strong to jump into the flames so he could transform into the Sun. He balked. But Poor and Feeble jumped right in and sailed forth as the Sun. Rich and Strong followed when the embers began dying out and became the Moon, which is why his light is not as powerful. Isn't that like life? Those who are rich and strong have too much to lose and one who is already poor and feeble has much to gain from chance.

In Africa, the story is much simpler. The trickster spider figure Anansi had to solve a dispute between his six clever sons. These sons were always exhibiting their cleverness to get their father out of trouble. Anansi's job as the trickster is to make mistakes so people can learn from him, so essentially, trouble is his job. After one particularly harrowing rescue, Anansi found a beautiful silver ball of light. No one could decide who deserved the light the most, so the sons began to argue over it. To keep the peace, the sky god Nyamie decided to throw the light into the air. It's there still. Even the cleverest son can't figure out how to get it down.

By the way, the Moon is not made of green cheese. It simply looks like green cheese—not cheese dyed green, but cheese made fresh, before aging. Before pasteurization, etc., new cheese was pale and mottled, just like the Moon.

Moon Magic

Perhaps the most magical aspect of the Moon is its influence on lovers. The Greeks may have carried it a bit too far, however. In Ovid's account of a fertility celebration, the Full Moon was a co-conspirator in what turned out to be a drunken orgy. He describes the smiling, satisfied merrymakers not as staggering drunks, but as devotees who worshipped well.

One reason for the Moon's pull on romance is women's tendency to ovulate on the Full Moon. As feminine hormones surge to nature's call for procreation, a woman can usually persuade her partner to indulge in a romantic interlude, supervised by the full, round orb.

In spite of Juliet's doubts, what Byron said was true, "The night was made for loving...Yet, we'll go no more a-roving by the light of the Moon." Tennyson writes, "Woman...thy passions match'd with mine, are as moonlight unto sunlight, water unto wine." Milton, in one of his lighter moments, wrote, "I walk unseen on the dry smooth-shaven green, to behold the wandering Moon."

Ultimately, the Moon is inspiration: to scientists and physicians trying to decipher how this world works, to old wives with their thinly disguised lessons, to storytellers who weave mythical lives in the sky, and finally, to the poet in us all, who the Moon beckons to romance.

Business & Legal
How to Choose the Best Dates for Business & Legal Ventures
Business Decisions
Time & Tides: Lunar Financial Forecast for 1998

Business & Legal Ventures

How to Choose the Best Dates

When starting a new business or any type of new venture, check to make sure that the Moon is in the first or second quarter. This will help it get off to a better start. If there is a deadlock or anxiety, it will often be broken during the Full Moon.

You should also check the aspects of the Moon to the planet that rules the type of venture with which you are becoming involved. Look for positive aspects to the planet that rules the activity in the Lunar Aspectarian (pages 28–51), and avoid any dates marked Q or O, as you are sure to have trouble with the client or deal.

Planetary Business Rulerships

Listed below are the planets and the business activities that they rule. If you follow the guidelines given above and apply them to the occupations of activities listed for each planet, you should have excellent results in your new business ventures. Even if it is not a new venture, check the aspects to the ruler of the activity before making moves in your business.

Sun

Advertising, executive positions, banking, finance, government, jewelry, law, and public relations.

Mercury

Accounting, brokerage, clerical, disc jockey, doctor, editor, inspector, librarian, linguist, medical technician, scientist, teacher, writer, publishing, communication, and mass media.

Venus

Architect, art and artist, beautician, dancer, designer, fashion and marketing, musician, poet, and chiropractor.

Mars

Barber, butcher, carpenter, chemist, construction, dentist, metal worker, surgeon, and soldier.

Jupiter

Counseling, horse training, judge, lawyer, legislator, minister, pharmacist, psychologist, public analyst, social clubs, research, and self-improvement.

Saturn

Agronomy, math, mining, plumbing, real estate, repair person, printer, paper-making, and working with older people.

Uranus

Aeronautics, broadcasting, electrician, inventing, lecturing, radiology, and computers.

Neptune

Photography, investigator, institutions, shipping, pets, movies, wine merchant, health foods, resorts, travel by water, and welfare.

Pluto

Acrobatics, athletic manager, atomic energy, research, speculation, sports, stockbroker, and any purely personal endeavors.

Business Activities

Following are directions for choosing the best days to begin several business activites. Travel and air travel can be found in the Leisure & Recreation section.

Advertising, General

Write advertisements when it is a favorable day for your Sun sign and Mercury or Jupiter is conjunct, sextile, or trine the Moon. Mars and Saturn should not be aspecting the Moon by square, opposition, or conjunction. Advertising campaigns are best begun when the Moon is in Taurus, Cancer, Sagittarius, or Aquarius, and well aspected. Advertise to give away pets when the Moon is in Sagittarius or Pisces.

Adverstising, Newspaper

The Moon should be conjunct, sextile, or trine (C, X, or T) Mercury or Jupiter.

Advertising, Television, Radio, or Internet

The Moon should be in the first or second quarter in the signs of Gemini, Sagittarius, or Aquarius. The Moon should be conjunct, sextile or trine (C, X or T) Uranus, and Uranus should be sextile or trine (X or T) Jupiter.

Business, Education

When you begin training for an occupation, see that your lunar cycle is favorable that day and that the planet ruling your occupation is marked C or T.

Business, Opening

The Moon should be in Taurus, Virgo, or Capricorn and in the first or second quarter. It should also be sextile or trine (X or T) Jupiter or Saturn (both, if possible).

Business, Remodeling

The Moon should be conjunct, trine, or sextile (C, T, or X) Jupiter, and sextile (X) or trine (t) Saturn, and Pluto.

Business, Starting

In starting a business of your own, see that the Moon is free of afflictions and that the planet ruling the business is marked C or T.

Buying

Buy during the third quarter, when the Moon is in Taurus for quality, or in a mutable sign (Gemini, Virgo, Sagittarius, or Pisces) for savings. Good aspects from Venus or the Sun are desirable. If you are buying for yourself, it is good if the day is favorable to your Sun sign.

Buying Clothing

See that the Moon is sextile or trine to the Sun, and that the Moon is in the first or second quarters. When the Moon is in Taurus, buying clothes will bring pleasure and satisfaction. Do not buy clothing or jewelry or wear them for the first time when the Moon is in Scorpio or Aries. Buying clothes on a favorable day for your Sun sign and when Venus or Mercury are well aspected is best, but avoid aspects to Mars and Saturn.

Buying Furniture

Follow the rules for machinery and appliances but buy when the Moon is in Libra as well. Buy antique furniture when the Moon is in Cancer, Scorpio, or Capricorn.

Buying Machinery, Appliances, or Tools

Tools, machinery, and other implements should be bought on days when your lunar cycle is favorable and when Mars and Uranus are trine (T), sextile (X), or conjunct (C) the Moon. Any quarter of the Moon is suitable. When buying gas or electrical appliances, the Moon should be in Aquarius.

Buying Stock

The Moon should be in Taurus or Capricorn, and should be sextile or trine (X or T) Jupiter and Saturn.

Collections

Try to make collections on days when your Sun is well aspected. Avoid days during which Mars or Saturn are aspected. If possible, the Moon should be in a cardinal sign: Aries, Cancer, Libra, or Capricorn. It is more difficult to collect when the Moon is in Taurus or Scorpio.

Consultants, Work With

The Moon should be conjunct (C), sextile (X) or trine (T) Mercury or Jupiter.

Contracts

To make contracts, see that the Moon is in a fixed sign and sextile, trine, or conjunct Mercury.

Contracts, Bid On

The Moon should be in the sign of Libra, and either the Moon or Mercury should be conjunct, sextile or trine (C, X, or T) Jupiter.

Copyrights/Patents, Apply For

The Moon should be conjunct, trine, or sextile (C, T, or X) Mercury or Jupiter.

Electronics, Buying

When buying electronics, choose a day when the Moon is in an air sign (Gemini, Libra, or Aquarius) and well aspected by Mercury and/or Uranus.

Electronics, Repair

The Moon should be sextile or trine (X or T) Mars or Uranus, and be in one of the following signs: Taurus, Leo, Scorpio, or Aquarius.

Legal Matters

In general, a good aspect between the Moon and Jupiter is the best influence for a favorable decision. If you are starting a lawsuit to gain damages, begin during the increase of the Moon. If you are seeking to avoid payment, get a court date when the Moon is decreasing. A good Moon-Sun aspect strengthens your chance of success. In divorce cases, a favorable Moon-Venus aspect may produce a more amicable settlement. Moon in Cancer or Leo and well aspected by the Sun brings the best results in custody cases.

Loans

Moon in the first and second quarters favors the lender, in the third and fourth favors the borrower. Good aspects of Jupiter and Venus to the Moon are favorable to both, as is the Moon in Leo, Sagittarius, Aquarius, or Pisces.

Mailing

For best results, send mail on favorable days for your Sun sign. The Moon in Gemini is good, as are Virgo, Sagittarius, and Pisces.

Mining

Saturn rules drilling and mining. Begin this work on a day when Saturn is marked C, T, or X. If mining for gold, pick a day in which the Sun is also marked C, T, or X. Mercury rules quicksilver, Venus rules copper, Jupiter rules tin, Saturn rules lead and coal, Uranus rules radioactive elements, Neptune rules oil, and the Moon rules water. Choose a day when the planet ruling whatever is being drilled for is marked C, T, or X.

New Job, Beginning

When you take a new job, Jupiter and Venus should be sextile, trine, or conjunct the Moon.

News

The handling of news is related to Uranus, Mercury, and all of the air signs. When Uranus is aspected, there is always an increase in the spectacular side of the news. Collection of news is related to Saturn.

Photography, Radio, TV, Film, and Video

For all these activities it is best to have Neptune, Venus, and Mercury well aspected, that is trine (T), sextile (X), or conjunct (C) the Moon. The act of photographing is not dependent on any particular phase of the Moon, but Neptune rules photography, while Venus is related to beauty in line, form, and color.

Promotions

Choose a day when your Sun sign is favorable. Mercury should be marked C, T, or X. Avoid days when Mars or Saturn is aspected.

Selling or Canvassing

Contacts for these activities will be better during a day favorable to your Sun sign. Otherwise, make strong efforts to sell on days when Jupiter, Mercury, or Mars is trine, sextile, or conjunct the Moon. Avoid days when Saturn is square or opposite the Moon.

Signing Papers

Sign contracts or agreements when the Moon is increasing in a fruitful sign, and on a day when Moon-Mercury aspects are operating. Avoid days when Mars, Saturn, or Neptune are square or opposite the Moon.

Staff, Fire

The Moon should be in the third or fourth quarter, but not Full. There should be no squares (Q) to the Moon.

Staff, Hire

The Moon should be in the first or second quarter and should be conjunct, trine, or sextile (C, T, or X) Mercury or Jupiter.

Travel

See the travel listing in the Leisure & Recreation section.

Writing

Writing for pleasure or publication is best done when the Moon is in Gemini. Mercury should be direct. Favorable aspects to Mercury, Uranus, and Neptune promote ingenuity.

Business Decisions

By Bruce Scofield

Although most of what goes on in business and financial matters is routine, there are always crucial moments on which everything else hinges. Check aspects of the Moon and other planets for the date in question. Generally, you should avoid the quarters of the Moon (when the Sun and Moon are in square aspect) and avoid any squares between the planets. Events begun under squares have tension in them. Oppositions are preferable as they give power but also offer room for dealing and compromise. Trines and sextiles are easy aspects and you should make sure that some are in effect at the time you make a move.

The Moon's aspects are very important and they can help you plan an event to the hour. With the Moon you should look for trines and sextiles to the planets with the following effects: Mercury favors agreements, and is excellent for communication and transport matters. Venus favors peaceful negotiations and is good for buying luxury items. Mars is excellent for reaching goals quickly, success in competition, and mechanical or construction matters. Jupiter is favorable for risks, speculation, and good luck. Saturn ensures reliability and is good for the long haul.

The Moon void-of-course factor is important. Events planned and commitments made while the Moon is void (listed on page 55) will turn out differently than expected, and while this may not be bad, it will put you in a situation where you do not have much control.

Be aware of the three times each year when Mercury goes retrograde (see page 54). When Mercury is retrograde, attend to unfinished business, clean up messes, rewrite proposals, and reinvest in old stock. Do not move into uncharted or new territory—you'll be using your time inefficiently.

Aries

This is not the time to jump ahead and take big risks. Continue to work on your foundations and make long-term investments. Help and advice from friends will prove useful. This is also a good year for completions and closures.

Mercury's retrograde in Aries during March and April is an excellent time to attend to these matters. The later part of August and most of September is a good time to sell or promote something.

Taurus

Your finances are not as clean as you'd like them to be and you may feel pressured to organize your assets and bookkeeping this year. During March and April attend to debts and agreements affecting your finances. House or family expenses are likely during August and September, but these will not be unexpected. Make purchases during May, June, and July. Sell possessions or let go of entanglements during August, late October, and November.

Gemini

This is likely to be another growth year in financial and business matters. Your only real problem will be digesting all the growth. Try expanding in several areas at different times rather than all at once. Avoid impulsive or reckless spending during June, July to mid-August, and mid-October through early December. The most stable times for doing business are during January, March, and late August to early September.

Cancer

Business conditions and finances will gradually improve, and you may begin to reap returns on past investments. You'll need to rethink and maybe change your financial situation during March and April—but don't make major investments or purchases then. July is a good month for some risk-taking and so is early through mid-October. Settle differences with business partners in December.

Leo

You may be able to borrow more this year, but consider consulting with an advisor or good friend before spending it all. With a good plan and willingness to reorganize if necessary, you may be able to achieve goals you've been working toward for years. Move forward with your plans during March, June, and the later part of December. Be more conservative during April, August, and late October.

Virgo

Long-term investment opportunities that you should look into—carefully, of course—will develop this year. Although risk isn't your style, this year asks you to stretch to get more. Be cautious with your money during February, late May through early July, and especially during November, when real estate and legal matters are pressing. Good times for investing are during late April, May, the second half of July, and the second half of October.

Libra

This is the year to settle financial differences, change business partners, or simply start doing things differently in the money department. Consider being more creative with your money. Don't be afraid to make some unusual investments during January, May, June, and September. Periods to avoid potential financial trouble are April, July, and the second half of December.

Scorpio

This is a good year to sell something, or end a financial partnership or episode. Look for new opportunities in February and March, but don't wait until April to close a deal. May brings changes and adjustments. July and October are good months for business and money matters. August is not, however, and you should be careful then and through September.

Sagittarius

Real estate matters will be prominent this year. Be cautious; things may look better than they are. Take things slowly and be ready to do a lot of talking. Such opportunities may arise in February, July, and November. Better conditions, more balanced and realistic overall, may arise during January, March, late July through September, and late November and December.

Capricorn

Let go of unproductive entanglements this year. This is a year to clean up your finances and embrace the newer goals you've set for yourself during the past two years. Watch for financial or business chaos during Mercury's retrograde in April and also during late December. Good times for making important decisions are February, July into early August, and October.

Aquarius

Be realistic this year. Pay attention to practical things like cars (in March, April, and May) and real estate (in July and August). Purchases are best made during February, May, June, late November, and December. Go easy with your money in August and early September—be sure you know what you're doing, especially in partnerships.

Pisces

If you've set yourself up properly and invested intelligently, this could be a great year for business and financial matters. If not, it should be a good year anyway. First, finish paying off debts to friends during January. Then, in March and April, go over your books and see what you really have and what it's worth. Resist urges to spend during May and June. Make your big purchases or close deals in July.

Time & Tides

Financial Lunar Forecast for 1998

By Barbara Koval, D.F. Astrol.S.

In this second-to-the-last year of the millennium, we human beings look with hope for a new and brighter future and fill with anxiety at leaving the comforts and discomforts that we know. The Moon rules emotion and memory: personal, tribal, and global. It churns the unconscious and semi-conscious urges that drive our decisions, our loves, and our fears. With the approaching millennium comes end-of-the-world madness and alarm bells of doom and destruction. They are in our collective unconscious, in the Bible, and in ourselves. The millennium is the mirror of death, the vision of the dark side we prefer to forget. Through 1998 the planets still huddle in their trine in the sky to toss humankind's universal emotions high and low early and late in the year. We are creeping toward the new universal order, the Age of Aquarius.

The Economy

The economy always tightens as we near a Jupiter-Saturn conjunction, the lesser mutation that will occur in the year 2000. Look back every twenty years, and you will see the pattern clearly. 1980 capped a decade of inflation. 1960 ended the stagflation of the fifties. 1940 left the Great Depression in the dust. 1920 ended the spiraling indebtedness of World War I. The forties and fifties saw twenty years of sustained growth, both in the stock market and in the money supply. 1960 was the least difficult of the mutation turns. We, too, have witnessed almost twenty years of rising stock markets. Let's hope the twenty-first century will open as benignly as the sixties did.

Global Factors

All of the outer planets increase emotional intensity and unrealistic visions. All are now in their rising inflation cycles, which makes throwing money you don't have at every problem more and more risky. Each month the Moon illuminates and reinforces which of the universal factors a country or state will be forced to deal with. Pluto in Sagittarius in the First House of the U.S. chart brings emotional intensity, fear, and cries for reform. Taxes, education, law, and morals rub and chafe. Uranus and Neptune in Aquarius, wonderful for a rebirth of higher consciousness, transit the third house of the U.S. chart, increasing imports, and making incredible changes in communication and how we process our data. They create travel mania, and, not so pleasantly, a decaying travel infrastructure. Jupiter in Pisces is driven to excess, profligate borrowing from the future to get what it wants right now. This planet of morality and obliviousness in the sign of guilt and denial waves the right hand toward heaven, while the left hand dabbles in mud. Jupiter on the South Node hits bottom and forces us to reevaluate. In the fourth house of the U.S. chart, it bodes bumper crops, and rising real estate prices. The only counterbalance to this frenzied expansion, this fear and euphoria, is poor little Saturn in Aries, its weakest position. There is little discipline or order. Black and white succumb to rosy blurs. Believe half of what you hear and divide by two. Sell property this year. Don't buy. Don't go into debt. These planetary combinations bring record numbers of bankruptcies.

Those who see through the dark prosper in the bright

January

The year begins with Venus retrograde and the lunar tides at their most extreme. Both create a strong focus on money and security. The December 29 lunation occurred in the transiting

January 1998 Lunar Tide Table

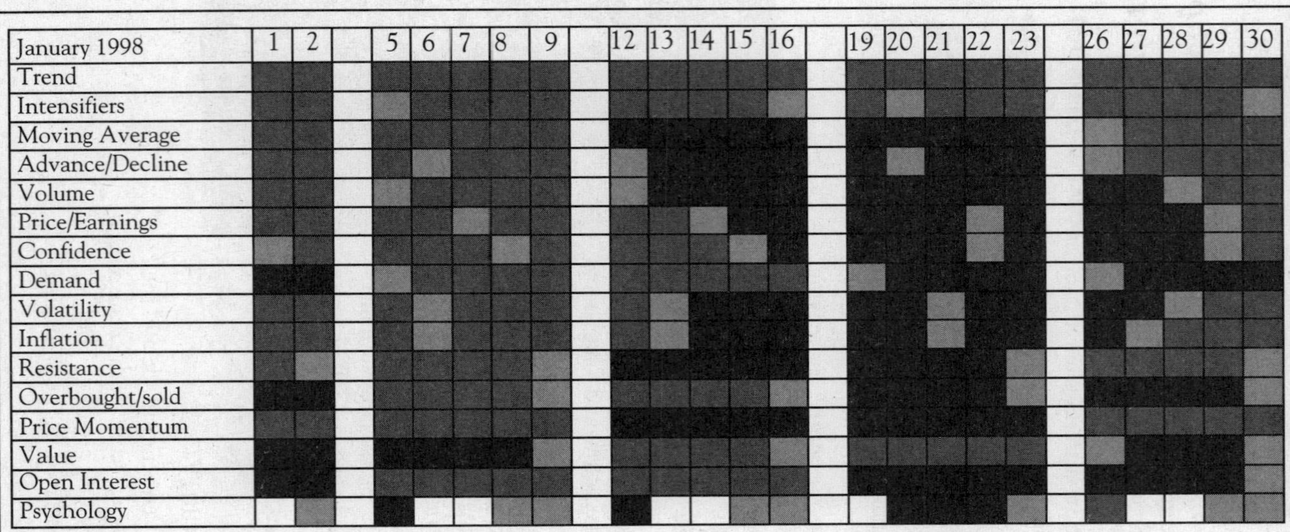

Light spaces indicate an "up" market, with rising price pressure. This is a tidal "heavy pressure" period.

Dark spaces indicate a "down" market, with falling price pressure. This is a tidal "light pressure" period.

Read chart down columns like a gauge. Missing dates are weekends, when the market is not open.

tenth house with Saturn rising. The somewhat gloomy focus is on government and the marketplace. People are nervous and complaining. Everybody is returning gifts they didn't want and buying things they did, or simply using the money for necessities. That particular New Moon was conjunct the Great Mutation, the 1842 conjunction of Jupiter and Saturn. We could be seeing a preview of economic and financial conditions to come. For the United States the transits mean record imports and tight budgets as Venus, Moon, Mars, Jupiter, and Uranus, all in Aquarius, travel the U.S. Third House. Neptune is getting ready to jump on board. Aquarius represents people in groups, acquaintances, customers, and the money pool. Though we may be awash in money as we start the year, the cost of living is likely to rise faster than income. Another important feature of 1998's opening planetary array is that all of the planets, except Saturn, are in south declination, the low trading range. All but Mercury are moving up, which means prices are rising from whatever lows they hit in the previous months. The Full Moon on January 12 keeps its focus on government, financial, and security matters. Full Moons often occur on or near the month's market high. The New Moon on January 28 is still in the Tenth House, but Saturn rises again. The mood turns sour as the check is paid. In the graph opposite, the light shading represents the increasing/rising price phase of the monthly lunar cycle. The dark shading represents the decreasing price phase. Vertical striping indicates days of high volatility and potential price reversals. All cycles rise to January 12 with a decided falling thereafter.

The Stock Market

The tides mid-month look strong for a turn in the stock market, most likely down. If we have been in a drastic decline, a significant bottom and turn up will occur in the final days.

February

The New Moon of January 28 puts the focus on domestic trade and balance of payments inequities. It has the same Ascendant as the Washington mutation, which gives it a stronger impact. Saturn square the United States Saturn indicates tight money and banking industry problems. The fight is on between more regulation and less. Exports slack off. Imports continue to rise, as does the cost of buying a home. Confidence lifts at the Full Moon on February 11. More money is available to spend and pay off holiday debts. Saturn in the Third House continues to limit exports

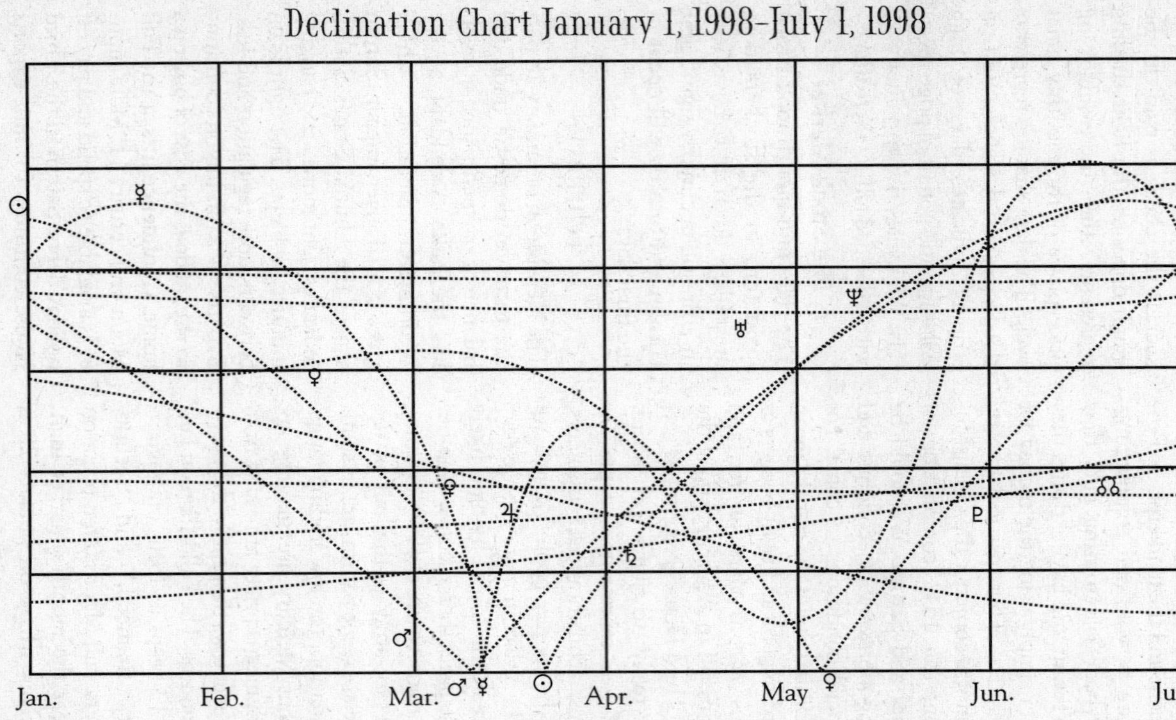

☉ Sun; ☽ Moon; ☿ Mercury; ♀ Venus; ♂ Mars; ♃ Jupiter; ♄ Saturn; ♅ Uranus; ♆ Neptune; ♇ Pluto; ☊ Node

and reduce domestic trade. Retail sales are sluggish. Though most everybody is feeling relief, there are still rising concerns about taxes and government cutbacks. Pluto in the Eleventh House decreases tax revenue as it increases demands for government funds (possibly the result of disaster relief) or it makes for cutbacks in outlay. Whichever way it goes, look for an increase in debt, both individual and public.

The Stock Market

The tides look positive to midmonth. The high should be reached by February 23, but the bigger moves may come early. Be cautioned; the South Node eclipse on February 26 could be a significant low. Venus retrograde is unlikely to take out her full decline until March 1. In other words, the high may only be higher than the low.

March

The New Moon on February 26 had a cluster of planets in or near the Ninth House and close to the Midheaven: government, the president, the courts, imports, and government regulation are affected. Significant decisions are likely to be made here, maybe even a new free trade, open market treaty. The Full Moon lunar eclipse on the North Node in Pisces on March 12 maintains its focus on the Fourth and Tenth House areas, with additional emphasis on the third. Full Moons are always revealing, but in Pisces they may exaggerate as well as expose the big lie. Pisces relates to pensions, retirement, and trust funds. Expect some revealing statistics about Social Security. Jupiter in Pisces means trust funds are healthy and growing. It also means greater expenditures due to fraud, and the growing number of retirees and claimants. The eclipse marks a mini-peak in inflation in the farming heartland, for land prices, fertilizers, feed, and machinery. In time the consumer will feel the pinch. The New Moon on March 27 still focuses on the Third and Fourth Houses, on the transit as well as on the U.S. chart. The lunation itself is in the Fifth House of speculation, recreation, and energy. Though we may hear news about energy shortages and rising costs, Jupiter in Pisces means the world is awash in oil.

The Stock Market

Investors may be shaken after the gyrations that usually accompany eclipses. The shorts are likely to have had a field day. While this could be a good time to get back in, better to wait till until the start of April. Though the effects of eclipses are impossible to predict, they do produce significant turns.

June 1998 Lunar Tide Table

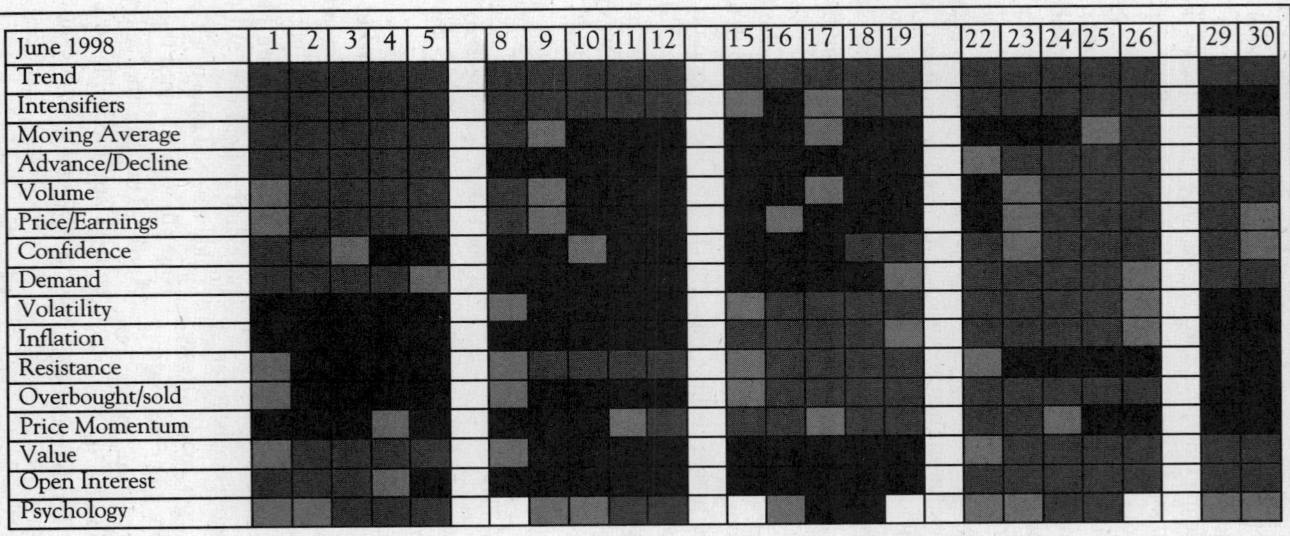

Light spaces indicate an "up" market, with rising price pressure. This is a tidal "heavy pressure" period.

Dark spaces indicate a "down" market, with falling price pressure. This is a tidal "light pressure" period.

Read chart down columns like a gauge. Missing dates are weekends, when the market is not open.

April

April opens in the midst of a significant declination reversal for the planet Mercury. After a very steep rise, which included a contraparallel with Jupiter, it turns sharply down and repeats the contraparallel as it forms declination aspects with both the Sun and Saturn, to produce a sharp downturn after April 10. The Full Moon on April 11 brings attacks from the loyal opposition and disagreements with our allies, competitors, and trading partners. Security needs are uppermost. Protectionist inclinations begin to make inroads on the free market policies of the last fifty years. Either imports will decline with Pluto in the Third House, or they will be taxed. The job market is growing. Retailers are still in pain. The New Moon on April 26 is back in the Twelfth House of bureaucracy, pensions, retirement, and prisons. Uranus in the Tenth House could mean extraordinary or lawbreaking action by the government, or a bounce out of office for the party in power. Since it's not election time, and Venus and Jupiter are both in the Eleventh House of how the government disposes of money, we could be looking at large off-budget and overbudget expenditures. Look for a raid on the trust funds. Prison costs stir the controversy. Pluto on the Seventh House cusp brings retaliation by allies, enemies, competitors, and trading partners, especially if tariffs or restrictions were enacted last month. We are not getting along well with others at this point. Let's hope the attacks are merely verbal. Protests are featured this month.

The Stock Market

While conditions in the middle of the month suggest falling prices, especially from April 11–22, we are in strongly positive longer term trends for a strong, or at least stable, market. Look for a turn down around April 18. Gradually the public mind is shifting toward investment rather than speculation. Corporations may start paying better dividends. Better dividends make for more comfortable and longer term investment.

May

The Full Moon on May 11 starts a sharp decline in stock prices after a strong rise. Venus in Aries is bad for money. The Sun, ruler of the Second House, conjunct Mars, is bad for money too. Though the Moon in Scorpio creates discomfort and insecurity, Venus' domination of the chart protects us from disaster. Safety is rapidly becoming more important than profit. The New Moon on April 25 occurs in the Eighth House, along with a slew of other planets. Indebtedness is back in the news, with the possibility of a tax shortfall as Venus, ruler of the Eighth House, conjuncts Saturn. Pluto in the Third House brings talk of a national sales tax. Uranus in the Fifth House reawakens the speculative urge. Jupiter in Pisces in the Sixth House increases jobs.

The Stock Market

Look for a sharp rise to May 12 and an equally sharp decline thereafter. Prices top again on May 29 before starting another slide.

June

As you can see on the monthly graph above, the lunar cycles have smoothed out, with the pressures fairly evenly divided throughout the month. The second week has a bit more down pressure; the fourth week a bit more up. Note the cluster of turn indicators on June 23 and 26. It is interesting that those on June 23 are primarily bottom indicators and those on June 26 are tops. We could see a short, fast rise and turn during that week. However, don't look for any major declines. Most planets are in North Declination, which tends to pull prices up. The Full Moon on June 9 is again across the Fourth and Tenth houses. Pluto conjunct the Tenth House changes government policy or puts the chief executive under the hammer. If nothing else, look for a battle royal with nasty tactics on both sides of the aisle. A sluggish consumer economy picks up as people start spending again. The New Moon on June 23 sits on the U.S. Jupiter, in the U.S. Eighth House, and moves through the transiting Fourth House to reinforce the bottom and rise potential of the tidal chart above. Taxation and debt issues, the cost of food, and rising real estate prices cause concern for some and joy for others. The domestic economy is looking good.

The Stock Market

Most likely the stock market will trade in a range. Look for the low of the month either the second week or at the New Moon on June 23.

July

Although the period from June to December is normally the downtrending portion of the year for the stock market, most planets remain in north declination into October. At the very least prices stay in a high-trading range. Sharp drops are likely to be followed by periods of recovery. Though the summer may be sluggish and occasionally volatile, the markets huff and puff right along. The differences in the tidal chart for July are negligible. The Full Moon on July 9 is once again across the Fourth and Tenth Houses of the transit chart. Government policy, the president, agriculture, and real estate are the concerns. Exports and retail sales are down. Imports are strong. Energy prices are dominated by cartels that create inflationary prices. Expect plenty of criticism and fighting words from both the White House and the House on the hill. With Mars about to hit the Tenth House of price, we could see a significant decline in the price of everything, including the dollar. The New Moon on July 23 is exactly at 0 degrees of Leo in the Eleventh House of corporations and customers. Either everybody is on vacation, or they are seriously reconsidering their involvement in the stock market and mutual funds. Venus conjunct Mars, ruler of the Third House, is positive for retail sales and exports, and unfavorable for imports. Jupiter in Pisces on the transiting Seventh House means a treaty or trade agreement or massive shipments of our produce overseas. It is more favorable for others than for ourselves.

The Stock Market

Markets are uncertain early in the month, as Mercury joins Venus and the Sun in the low price declination range. While this may have no great immediate impact, it sets the stage for a significant bottom when Mercury hits its lowest declination in mid-November, and Venus hits its lowest declination in mid-December.

August

In both August and September the tidal charts are evenly divided. The effect is to remove the day-to-day fluctuations from the price matrix. Without the Moon's buffer, prices can be wildly tossed by maverick storms. The lunar eclipse on August 7 is across the Fifth House of speculation and energy and the Eleventh House of corporations and buyers of stock. Two factors suggest a price high: The first is the recently completed Mars/Venus conjunction. The second is the euphoria/panic potential of the Moon in the Eleventh House in league with Uranus and Neptune. Uranus rules people in groups. Neptune represents emotional extremes. The Moon is the public. Speculation may well pay off as the potential for a strong rise is reinforced by Jupiter in a critical New York/Market degree. The solar eclipse on August 21 falls in the Fifth House, emphasizing speculation and energy. While it is vacation time, and the Fifth House is also recreation, this combination with Jupiter in Pisces makes for unrealistic expectations on the upside and down for the prices of stocks and bonds. Jupiter in Pisces also correlates with oil, so we could see an oversupply, or high

Top Wheel
Full Moon Chart
Aug 7, 1998
9:09:29 pm EST
New York, NY
Geocentric
Tropical
Koch

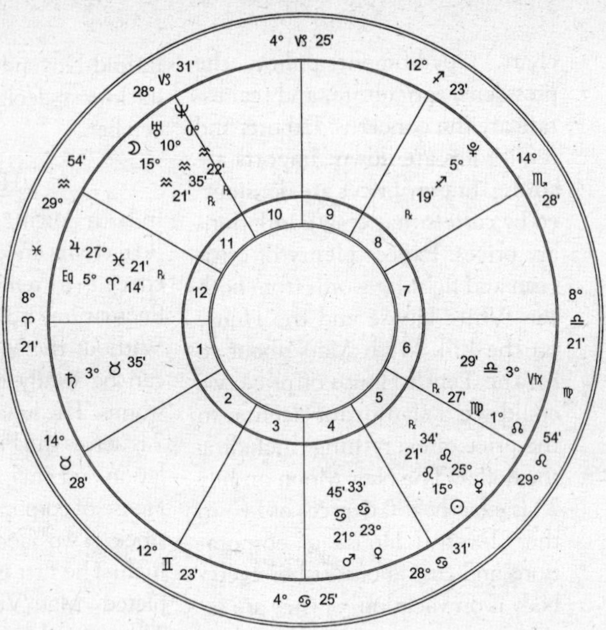

Bottom Wheel
New Moon Chart
Aug 21, 1998
9:02:50 pm EST
New York, NY
Geocentric
Tropical
Koch

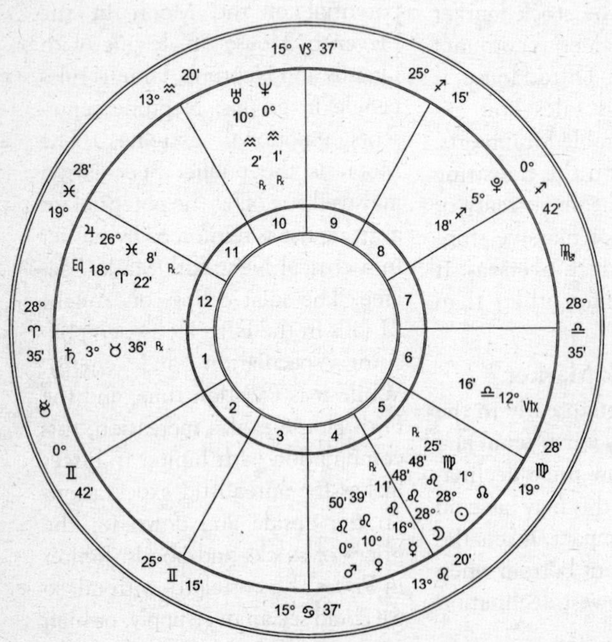

prices, or both. Saturn in the First House of the solar eclipse creates an undercurrent of anxiety, especially since it is within orbs of squares to both Uranus and Neptune. The eclipse occurs in the Fifth House of speculation and energy. Mars opposes Neptune to mark a high price for oil. The North Node eclipse in Leo marks a significant high price for gold.

The Stock Market

Although eclipses are difficult to predict with any degree of certainty, we could see the first high on or near August 7, a short decline, followed by another rise to August 21. It is also possible for the market to rise again after August 21, but be alert to potential reversals from whatever direction the trend is going. If oil prices are rising and/or repeating the trends of the seventies, a peak in oil is likely to mean a decline in stocks as more and more money is sucked out of stocks and mutual funds and into necessities. We could also see record gasoline usage as people travel here and abroad and abroad and here in a very travel-oriented year. Look for an oil high and a possible stock market low near the eclipse on August 21.

September

The Full Moon on August 6 finds Jupiter in the Seventh House, which brings foreign investors into our Stock and Bond markets. The United States makes another trading agreement that benefits competitors more than itself, most likely humanitarian aid or food exports. The speculative energy is high as Neptune and Uranus sit in the transiting Fifth House. The balance of trade continues negative. The New Moon on September 20 has a stellium in the Ninth House of imports. Both Uranus and Jupiter in the Third House suggest high retail sales, but most likely of foreign-made goods. Speculation declines with Saturn in the Fifth House, a likely hangover from months past. Oil costs are down, or oil is scarce. The Ninth House focus makes anything to do with global communication or advertising hot this month. It also means regulation and restrictive policies are on the rise. Mercury in north declination keeps the stock market up to the middle of the month.

The Stock Market

Look for a rise to mid-month, a decline, followed by another top near the end.

October

The Full Moon on the fifth day of the stock market's most dreaded month finds Pluto exactly conjunct the Tenth House. Jupiter in the Second House means big paper profits. Saturn in the Third House dulls all money exchange and dampens retail sales. This lunation could mark a significant top and turn. The New Moon on September 20 opposite Saturn is gloomy, but not gloomy enough for a crash. Prices may continue to hold up or rise for a couple more days before turning sharply down. Venus also tops out this month to start her Bear market on October 29.

The Stock Market

Prices are likely to trade in a high range all month, then drop drastically at the end.

November

If stock prices fell severely at the end of October, they are likely to keep falling right through to November 20 as the Lunar tides once again cluster to the downside in the middle two weeks. However, the Full Moon on November 4 finds the Nodes rising. The lunation itself lies right across the New York mutation ascendant. The combination suggests a limit up or a limit down. With the developing Venus/Sun superior conjunction, it will most likely be a top. Imports are down this month. The labor market is a mixture of layoffs and new, low-paying jobs. The New Moon on November 18 has a five-planet stellium in the Fourth House of land, products of the land, and supply in general. We see a number of difficult applying aspects on this chart: Mars square Mercury, Venus conjunct Pluto, Sun conjunct Pluto and the Nodes still hanging across the horizon line, all of which add up to a flash then a flood—more likely a waterfall. Actually it is difficult to say this far in advance whether we have been seeing a series of steps leading up to a precipice or steps down to the pits. A tremendous amount of energy is filling the marketplace with most of the planets in their low price positions.

The Stock Market

The market looks volatile as many cyclic factors signify turns. Most likely it will top near the Full Moon on November 4, fall to the New Moon on November 18, rise to November 29, and dive once again.

December

The last month of the year is the natural low of a year. Neptune is out of Capricorn and sitting on the Ascendant of the Full Moon on December. Jupiter in the Second House means money goes out as fast as it comes in, despite the potential for low retail sales with Saturn in the Third House. The latter is also bad for exports. The outlook is very positive for the banking industry, and even for real estate, though out of season. Venus has just emerged from behind the Sun to start her bear market in earnest. The month opens just past two strong indicators that usually coincide with a downturn for stocks. The lunation itself occurs across the Fifth House of speculation and the Eleventh House of corporations and money available for purchases. The combination suggests the number of people in the market has peaked, their profits have peaked, and they could take losses the next couple of weeks. The New Moon on December 18 finds most of the activity in the Sixth House of trouble and jobs. Either everybody is sick, sick at heart, or changing jobs as they are being soothed with reassuring words and statistics from the White House. Whatever the situation, Jupiter on the Midheaven is full of hope. Imports stay strong. Exports lag. Retail sales are down. On the bright side, the dollar has strengthened. The government inspires confidence. The United States is still seen as the land of opportunity and good luck.

The Stock Market

Look for a significant rise after the New Moon on December 18, which coincides with the strong upward pull of this month's lunar graph.

Overview

The striking factor in the lunation charts this year has been the heavy emphasis on the Fourth, Fifth, Tenth, and Eleventh Houses. As this is being written, we are in the middle of Indogate. Everybody is hanging on what action the special prosecutor will take relative to the president and first lady. If those matters were not put to rest in 1997, they may still dominate the news this year. Politically, expect a perpetual power struggle between the party in power and the party out. Economically, Jupiter in Pisces presages rising inflation, and rising real estate prices. While it also means the cost of farm land goes through the roof, it also gives bumper crops, especially those that do well under rainy conditions. This could lessen farm profits, even though consumer food prices rise. The Fifth House rules energy. For consumers, energy is gasoline and oil, for industry it is power no matter how it is generated, and for agriculture it means fertilizer. Watch oil prices very closely this year. In the seventies oil prices started their precipitous rise just as Jupiter finished the transit of Pisces. There are few indicators of deflation, falling prices, in this period. There is every reason to hope and to expect that the stock market will continue to ratchet back and forth in a high trading range. In other words, we have more to fear from inflation than deflation.

Saturn's movement into Taurus starts the decline toward the year 2000 and the lesser mutation. 1997 will be the last prosperous year. If it has not been prosperous, it will look prosperous in hindsight. Take your profits. Protect your assets. If you are thinking of moving, sell your house this year. Buy your new one in the next year or the year after that. Though the forecasts may appear gloomy, there are few indicators of insufferable economic hardship such as we saw in the thirties and seventies. The crucial factor remains government policy. If short-term measures are taken to support a sliding economy, e.g., artificially lowering the interest rates or giving up the annual shrinking of the federal budget deficit in hopes of stimulating investment and creating jobs, we could witness serious inflation. Watch the dollar. Watch oil. Save your pennies for the bargains up ahead. Conditions are rarely as good as we hope or as bad as we fear. Economies rarely collapse with a bang. Prosperity gets eaten away, bit by bit. The Moon casts light on the dark of the day. Those who see through the dark prosper in the light.

Farm, Garden, & Weather

- How to Choose the Best Dates for Farm, Garden, & Weather Activities
- Gardening by the Moon
- A Guide to Planting by Phase & Sign
- Gardening Dates
- Dates to Destroy Weeds & Pests
- Gestation Table & Egg Setting Dates
- Companion Planting
- Weather & Earthquake Predictions

The Moon & the Weather • Plan Your First Garden Patch • Water & the Moon • The Twilight Farmers • Vegetables of the Southwest • Moon Friendly Lawn Mowing • The Magic in Locally Grown Foods • Gardening as Cosmic Research • An Herbal Almanac

Farm, Garden, & Weather

How to Choose the Best Dates

Animals

Animals are easiest to handle when the Moon is in Taurus, Cancer, Libra, or Pisces. Avoid the Full Moon. Buy animals during the first quarter or New Moon in all signs except Scorpio or Pisces. Castrate animals in Gemini, Cancer, Capricorn, or Aquarius. Slaughter for food in the first three days after the Full Moon in any sign except Leo.

Animals, Breeding

Eggs should be set and animals mated so that the young will be born when the Moon is increasing and in Taurus, Cancer, Pisces, or Libra. Young born in these signs are generally healthier, mature faster and make better breeding stock. Those born during a semi-fruitful sign (Taurus and Capricorn) will generally mature quickly, but will produce leaner meat. The sign of Libra yields beautiful, graceful animals for showing and racing.

To determine the best date to mate animals or set eggs, subtract the number of days given for incubation or gestation from the fruitful dates given in the following tables. (Tables on pages 250–1.) For example, cats and dogs are mated sixty-three days previous to the desired birth date.

Companion Planting

See Companion Planting Tables on page 252.

Composting

Start compost when the Moon is in the fourth quarter in a water sign, especially Scorpio.

Cultivating

Cultivate when the Moon is in a barren sign and waning, ideally the fourth quarter in Aries, Gemini, Leo, Virgo, or Aquarius. The sign of Sagittarius and the third quarter also work.

Cutting Timber

Cut timber during the third and fourth quarters while the Moon is not in a water sign.

Drying Crops

Dry crops in the third quarter when the Moon is in a fire sign.

Fertilizing

Fertilize when the Moon is in a fruitful sign (Cancer, Scorpio,

Pisces). Organic fertilizers are best used when the Moon is in the third or fourth quarter. Chemical fertilizers are best used in the first or second quarter.

Grafting

Graft during first or second quarter Capricorn, Cancer, or Scorpio.

Harvesting

Harvest root crops when the Moon is in a dry sign (Aries, Leo, Sagittarius, Gemini, or Aquarius) and in the third or fourth quarter. Harvest root crops intended for seed during the Full Moon. Harvest grain for storage just after the Full Moon, avoiding the water signs (Cancer, Scorpio, Pisces). Fire signs are best for cutting down on water content. Harvest fruits in the third and fourth quarters in the dry signs.

Insect Control

See Dates to Destroy Weeds and Pests tables on page 248.

Irrigation

Irrigate when the Moon is in a water sign.

Lawn Mowing

Mow in the first and second quarters to increase growth and lushness, and in the third and fourth quarters to decrease growth.

Picking Mushrooms

Gather mushrooms at the Full Moon.

Planting

For complete instructions on planting by the phases and signs of the Moon, see Gardening by the Moon on page 228, A Guide to Planting by Sign and Phase on page 234, and Companion Planting on page 252.

Pruning

Prune during the third and fourth quarters in Scorpio to retard growth and to promote better fruit, and in Capricorn to promote better healing.

Spraying

Destroy pests and weeds during the fourth quarter when the Moon is in Aries, Gemini, Leo, Virgo, Sagittarius, or Aquarius.

Transplanting

Transplant when the Moon is increasing and preferably in Cancer, Scorpio, or Pisces.

Weather

For complete 1998 weather forecasts, see *1998 Weather Predictions* on page 255.

Weeding

See Dates to Destroy Weeds and Pests tables on page 248.

Gardening by the Moon

Today, we still find those who reject the notion of Moon gardening. The usual non-believer is not the scientist, but the city dweller who has never had any real contact with nature and no experience of natural rhythms.

Camille Flammarian, the French astronomer, testifies to Moon planting. "Cucumbers increase at Full Moon, as well as radishes, turnips, leeks, lilies, horseradish, and saffron; onions, on the contrary, are much larger and better nourished during the decline and old age of the Moon than at its increase, during its youth and fullness, which is the reason the Egyptians abstained from onions, on account of their antipathy to the Moon. Herbs gathered while the Moon increases are of great efficiency. If the vines are trimmed at night when the Moon is in the sign of the Lion, Sagittarius, the Scorpion, or the Bull, it will save them from field rats, moles, snails, flies, and other animals."

Dr. Clark Timmins is one of the few modern scientists to have conducted tests in Moon planting. The following is a summary of some of his experiments:

Beets: When sown with the Moon in Scorpio, the germination rate was 71 percent; when sown in Sagittarius, the germination rate was 58 percent.

Scotch marigold: When sown with the Moon in Cancer, the germination rate was 90 percent; when sown in Leo, the germination rate was 32 percent.

Carrots: When sown with the Moon in Scorpio, the germination rate was 64 percent; when sown in Sagittarius, the germination rate was 47 percent.

Tomatoes: When sown with the Moon in Cancer, the germination rate was 90 percent; when sown in Leo, the germination rate was 58 percent.

Two things should be emphasized. First, remember that this is only a summary of the results of the experiments; the experiments themselves were conducted in a scientific manner to eliminate any variation in soil, temperature, moisture, etc., so that only the Moon's sign varied. Second, note that these astonishing results were obtained without regard to the phase of the Moon—the other factor we use in Moon planting, and which presumably would have increased the differential in germination rates.

Further experiments by Dr. Timmins involved transplanting Cancer and Leo-planted tomato seedlings while the Moon was increasing and in Cancer. The result was 100 percent survival. When the transplanting was done with the Moon decreasing and in Sagittarius, there was 0 percent survival.

The results of Dr. Timmins' tests show that the Cancer-planted tomatoes had first blossoms twelve days earlier than those planted under Leo; the Cancer-planted tomatoes had an average height of twenty inches at the same age when the Leo plants were only fifteen inches high; the first ripe tomatoes were gathered from the Cancer plantings eleven days ahead of the Leo plantings; and finally, a count of the hanging fruit and comparison of size and weight shows an advantage to the Cancer plants over the Leo plants of 45 percent.

Dr. Timmins also observed that there have been similar tests that did not indicate results favorable to the Moon planting theory. As a scientist, he asked why one set of experiments indicated a positive verification of Moon planting, and others did not. He checked these other tests and found that the experimenters had not followed the geocentric system for determining the Moon sign positions, but the heliocentric. When the times used in these other tests were converted to the geocentric system, the dates chosen often were found to be in barren, rather than fertile, signs. Without going into the technical explanations, it is sufficient to point out that geocentric and heliocentric positions often vary by as much as four days. This is a large enough differential to place the Moon in Cancer, for example, in the heliocentric system, and at the same time in Leo by the geocentric system.

Most almanacs and calendars show the Moon's signs heliocentrically—and thus incorrectly for Moon planting—while the *Moon Sign Book* is calculated correctly for planting purposes, using the geocentric system.

Some readers are also confused because the *Moon Sign Book* talks of first, second, third, and fourth quarters, while some almanacs refer to these same divisions as New Moon, first quarter, Full Moon, and last quarter. Thus, the almanacs say first quarter when the *Moon Sign Book* says second quarter. (Refer to A Note About Almanacs, p. 10).

There is nothing complicated about using astrology in agriculture and horticulture in order to increase both pleasure and profit, but there is one very important rule that is often neglected—use common sense! Of course this is one rule that should be remembered in every activity we undertake, but in the case of gardening and farming by the Moon it is not always possible to use the best dates for planting or harvesting, and we must select the next best and just try to do the best we can.

This brings up the matter of the other factors to consider in your gardening work. The dates we give as best for a certain activity apply to the entire country (with slight time correction), but in your section of the country you may be buried under three feet of snow on a date we say is a good day to plant your flowers. So we have factors of weather, season, temperature and moisture variations, soil conditions, your own available time and opportunity, and so forth. Some astrologers like to think it is all a matter of science, but gardening is also an art. In art you develop an instinctive identification with your work so that you influence it with your feelings and visualization of what you want to accomplish.

The *Moon Sign Book* gives you the place of the Moon for every day of the year so that you can select the best times once you have become familiar with the rules and practices of lunar agriculture. We try to give you specific, easy-to-follow directions so that you can get right down to work.

We give you the best dates for planting, and also for various related activities, including cultivation, fertilizing, harvesting, irrigation, and getting rid of weeds and pests. But we cannot just tell you when it's good to plant at the time. Many of these rules were learned by observation and experience, but as our body of experience grew, we could see various patterns emerging that allowed us to make judgments about new things. Then we tested the new possible applications and learned still more. That's what you should do, too. After you have worked with lunar agriculture for a while and have gained a working background of knowledge, you will probably begin to try new things—and we hope you will share your experiments and findings with us. That's how the science grows.

Here's an example of what we mean. Years ago, Llewellyn George suggested that we try to combine our bits of knowledge about what to expect in planting under each of the Moon signs in order to benefit with several such lunar factors in one plant. From this came our rule for developing "thoroughbred seed." To develop thoroughbred seed, save the seed for three successive years from plants grown by the correct Moon sign and phase. You can plant in the first quarter phase and in the sign of Cancer for fruitfulness; the second year, plant seeds from the first year plants in Libra for beauty; and in the third year, plant the seeds from the second year plants in Taurus to produce hardiness. In a similar manner you can combine the fruitfulness of Cancer, the good root growth of Pisces, and the sturdiness and good vine growth of Scorpio. And don't forget the characteristics of Capricorn: hardy like Taurus, but drier and perhaps more resistant to drought and disease.

Unlike common almanacs, we consider both the Moon's phase and the Moon's sign in making our calculations for the proper timing of our work within nature's rhythm. It is perhaps a little easier to understand this if we remind you that we are all living in the center of a vast electromagnetic field that is the Earth and its environment in space. Everything that occurs within this electromagnetic field has an effect on everything else within the same field, but since we are living on the Earth we must relate these happenings and effects to our own health and happiness. The Moon and the Sun are the most important and dynamic of the rhythmically changing factors affecting the life of the Earth, and it is their relative positions to the Earth that we project for each day of the coming year.

Many people claim that not only do they achieve larger crops gardening by the Moon, but that their fruits and vegetables are much tastier and more healthful.

A number of organic gardeners have also become lunar gardeners using the natural growing methods within the natural rhythm of life forces that we experience through the relative movements of the Sun and Moon.

We provide a few basic rules and then give you month-by-month and day-by-day guidance for your farming and gardening work. You will be able to choose the best dates to meet your own needs and opportunities.

Planting by the Moon's Phases

During the increasing light (from New Moon to Full Moon), plant annuals that produce their yield above the ground. (An annual is a plant that completes its entire life cycle within one growing season and has to be seeded each year.)

During the decreasing light (from Full Moon to New Moon), plant biennials, perennials, bulb and root plants. (Biennials include crops that are planted one season to winter over and produce crops the next, such as winter wheat. Perennials and bulb and root plants include all plants that grow from the same root year after year.)

A simple, though less accurate, rule is to plant crops that produce above the ground during the increase of the Moon, and to plant crops that produce below the ground during the decrease of the Moon. This is the source of the old adage, "Plant potatoes during the dark of the Moon."

Llewellyn George went a step further and divided the lunar month into quarters. He called the first two from New Moon to Full Moon the first and second quarters, and the last two from Full Moon to New Moon the third and fourth quarters. Using these divisions, we can increase our accuracy in timing our efforts to coincide with natural forces.

First Quarter (Increasing)

Plant annuals producing their yield above the ground, which are generally of the leafy kind that produce their seed outside the fruit. Examples are asparagus, broccoli, Brussels sprouts, cabbage, cauliflower, celery, cress, endive, kohlrabi, lettuce, parsley, spinach, etc. Cucumbers are an exception, as they do best in the first quarter rather than the second, even though the seeds are inside the fruit. Also plant cereals and grains.

Second Quarter (Increasing)

Plant annuals producing their yield above the ground, which are generally of the viney kind that produce their seed inside the fruit. Examples include beans, eggplant, melons, peas, peppers, pumpkins, squash, tomatoes, etc. These are not hard and fast divisions. If you can't plant during the first quarter, plant during the second, and vice versa. There are many plants that seem to do equally well planted in either quarter, such as watermelon, hay, and cereals and grains.

Third Quarter (Decreasing)

Plant biennials, perennials, and bulb and root plants. Also plant trees, shrubs, berries, beets, carrots, onions, parsnips, peanuts, potatoes, radishes, rhubarb, rutabagas, strawberries, turnips, winter wheat, grapes, etc.

Fourth Quarter (Decreasing)

This is the best time to cultivate, turn sod, pull weeds, and destroy pests of all kinds, especially when the Moon is in the barren signs of Aries, Leo, Virgo, Gemini, Aquarius, and Sagittarius.

Planting by Moon Sign

Moon in Aries

Barren and dry, fiery and masculine. Used for destroying noxious growths, weeds, pests, etc., and for cultivating.

Moon in Taurus

Productive and moist, earthy and feminine. Used for planting many crops, particularly potatoes and root crops, and when hardiness is important. Also used for lettuce, cabbage, and similar leafy vegetables.

Moon in Gemini

Barren and dry, airy and masculine. Used for destroying noxious growths, weeds and pests, and for cultivation.

Moon in Cancer

Very fruitful and moist, watery and feminine. This is the most productive sign, used extensively for planting and irrigation.

Moon in Leo

Barren and dry, fiery and masculine. This is the most barren sign, used only for killing weeds and for cultivation.

Moon in Virgo

Barren and moist, earthy and feminine. Good for cultivation and destroying weeds and pests.

Moon in Libra

Semi-fruitful and moist, airy and masculine. Used for planting many crops and producing good pulp growth and roots. A very good sign for flowers and vines. Also used for seeding hay, corn fodder, etc.

Moon in Scorpio

Very fruitful and moist, watery and feminine. Nearly as productive as Cancer; used for the same purposes. Especially good for vine growth and sturdiness.

Moon in Sagittarius

Barren and dry, fiery and masculine. Used for planting onions, seeding hay, and for cultivation.

Moon in Capricorn

Productive and dry, earthy and feminine. Used for planting potatoes, tubers, etc.

Moon in Aquarius

Barren and dry, airy and masculine. Used for cultivation and destroying noxious growths, weeds, and pests.

Moon in Pisces

Very fruitful and moist, watery and feminine. Used along with Cancer and Scorpio, especially good for root growth.

A Guide to Planting

Using Phase & Sign Rulerships

Plant	Phase/Quarter	Sign
Annuals	1st or 2nd	
Apple trees	2nd or 3rd	Cancer, Pisces, Taurus, Virgo
Artichokes	1st	Cancer, Pisces,
Asparagus	1st	Cancer, Scorpio, Pisces
Asters	1st or 2nd	Virgo, Libra
Barley	1st or 2nd	Cancer, Pisces, Libra, Capricorn, Virgo
Beans (bush & pole)	2nd	Cancer, Taurus, Pisces, Libra
Beans (kidney, white, & navy)	1st or 2nd	Cancer, Pisces
Beech Trees	2nd or 3rd	Virgo, Taurus
Beets	3rd	Cancer, Capricorn, Pisces, Libra
Biennials	3rd or 4th	
Broccoli	1st	Cancer, Pisces, Libra, Scorpio
Brussels Sprouts	1st	Cancer, Scorpio, Pisces, Libra
Buckwheat	1st or 2nd	Capricorn
Bulbs	3rd	Cancer, Scorpio, Pisces
Bulbs for Seed	2nd or 3rd	
Cabbage	1st	Cancer, Scorpio, Pisces, Libra, Taurus

Plant	Phase/Quarter	Sign
Cactus		Taurus, Capricorn
Canes (raspberries, blackberries, and gooseberries)	2nd	Cancer, Scorpio, Pisces
Cantaloupes	1st or 2nd	Cancer, Scorpio, Pisces, Libra, Taurus
Carrots	3rd	Taurus, Cancer, Scorpio, Pisces, Libra
Cauliflower	1st	Cancer, Scorpio, Pisces, Libra
Celeriac	3rd	Cancer, Scorpio, Pisces
Celery	1st	Cancer, Scorpio, Pisces
Cereals	1st or 2nd	Cancer, Scorpio, Pisces, Libra
Chard	1st or 2nd	Cancer, Scorpio, Pisces
Chicory	2nd, 3rd	Cancer, Scorpio, Pisces
Chrysanthemums	1st or 2nd	Virgo
Clover	1st or 2nd	Cancer, Scorpio, Pisces
Corn	1st	Cancer, Scorpio, Pisces
Corn for Fodder	1st or 2nd	Libra
Coryopsis	2nd or 3rd	Libra
Cosmos	2nd or 3rd	Libra
Cress	1st	Cancer, Scorpio, Pisces
Crocus	1st or 2nd	Virgo
Cucumbers	1st	Cancer, Scorpio, Pisces

Plant	Phase/Quarter	Sign
Daffodils	1st or 2nd	Libra, Virgo
Dahlias	1st or 2nd	Libra, Virgo
Deciduous Trees	2nd or 3rd	Cancer, Scorpio, Pisces, Virgo, Taurus
Eggplant	2nd	Cancer, Scorpio, Pisces, Libra
Endive	1st	Cancer, Scorpio, Pisces, Libra
Flowers	1st	Libra, Cancer, Pisces, Virgo, Scorpio, Taurus
Garlic	3rd	Libra, Taurus, Pisces
Gladiola	1st or 2nd	Libra, Virgo
Gourds	1st or 2nd	Cancer, Scorpio, Pisces, Libra
Grapes	2nd or 3rd	Cancer, Scorpio, Pisces, Virgo
Hay	1st or 2nd	Cancer, Scorpio, Pisces, Libra, Taurus
Herbs	1st or 2nd	Cancer, Scorpio, Pisces
Honeysuckle	1st or 2nd	Scorpio, Virgo
Hops	1st or 2nd	Scorpio, Libra
Horseradish	1st or 2nd	Cancer, Scorpio, Pisces
House Plants	1st	Libra, Cancer, Scorpio, Pisces
Hyacinths	3rd	Cancer, Scorpio, Pisces
Iris	1st or 2nd	Cancer, Virgo
Kohlrabi	1st or 2nd	Cancer, Scorpio, Pisces, Libra

Plant	Phase/Quarter	Sign
Leeks	1st or 2nd	Cancer, Pisces
Lettuce	1st	Cancer, Scorpio, Pisces, Libra, Taurus
Lilies	1st or 2nd	Cancer, Scorpio, Pisces
Maple Trees	2nd or 3rd	Virgo, Taurus, Cancer, Pisces
Melons	2nd	Cancer, Scorpio, Pisces
Moon Vine	1st or 2nd	Virgo
Morning Glory	1st or 2nd	Cancer, Scorpio, Pisces, Virgo
Oak Trees	2nd or 3rd	Virgo, Taurus, Cancer, Pisces
Oats	1st or 2nd	Cancer, Scorpio, Pisces, Libra
Okra	1st	Cancer, Scorpio, Pisces, Libra
Onion Seeds	2nd	Scorpio, Cancer, Sagittarius
Onion Sets	3rd or 4th	Libra, Taurus, Pisces, Cancer
Pansies	1st or 2nd	Cancer, Scorpio, Pisces
Parsley	1st	Cancer, Scorpio, Pisces, Libra
Parsnips	3rd	Taurus, Capricorn, Cancer, Scorpio, Capricorn
Peach Trees	2nd or 3rd	Taurus, Libra, Virgo, Cancer
Peanuts	3rd	Cancer, Scorpio, Pisces
Pear Trees	2nd or 3rd	Taurus, Libra, Virgo, Cancer
Peas	2nd	Cancer, Scorpio, Pisces, Libra

Plant	Phase/Quarter	Sign
Peonies	1st or 2nd	Virgo
Peppers	2nd	Cancer, Pisces, Scorpio
Perennials	3rd	
Petunias	1st or 2nd	Libra, Virgo
Plum Trees	2nd or 3rd	Taurus, Virgo, Cancer, Pisces
Poppies	1st or 2nd	Virgo
Portulaca	1st or 2nd	Virgo
Potatoes	3rd	Cancer, Scorpio, Taurus, Libra, Capricorn
Privet	1st or 2nd	Taurus, Libra
Pumpkins	2nd	Cancer, Scorpio, Pisces, Libra
Quinces	1st or 2nd	Capricorn
Radishes	3rd	Cancer, Libra, Taurus, Pisces, Capricorn
Rhubarb	3rd	Cancer, Pisces
Rice	1st or 2nd	Scorpio
Roses	1st or 2nd	Cancer, Virgo, Roses
Rutabagas	3rd	Cancer, Scorpio, Pisces, Taurus
Saffron	1st or 2nd	Cancer, Scorpio, Pisces
Sage	3rd	Cancer, Scorpio, Pisces
Salsify	1st or 2nd	Cancer, Scorpio, Pisces

Plant	Phase/Quarter	Sign
Shallots	2nd	Scorpio
Spinach	1st	Cancer, Scorpio, Pisces
Squash	2nd	Cancer, Scorpio, Pisces, Libra
Strawberries	3rd	Cancer, Scorpio, Pisces
String Beans	1st or 2nd	Taurus
Sunflowers	1st or 2nd	Libra, Cancer
Sweet Peas	1st or 2nd	Cancer, Scorpio, Pisces
Tomatoes	2nd	Cancer, Scorpio, Pisces, Capricorn
Shade Trees	3rd	Taurus, Capricorn
Ornamental Trees	2nd	Libra, Taurus
Trumpet Vines	1st or 2nd	Cancer, Scorpio, Pisces
Tubers for Seed	3rd	Cancer, Scorpio, Pisces, Libra
Tulips	1st or 2nd	Libra, Virgo
Turnips	3rd	Cancer, Scorpio, Pisces, Taurus, Capricorn, Libra
Valerian	1st or 2nd	Virgo, Gemini
Watermelons	1st or 2nd	Cancer, Scorpio, Pisces, Libra
Wheat	1st or 2nd	Cancer, Scorpio, Pisces, Libra

1998 Gardening Dates

Dates	Qtr	Sign	Activity
Jan. 2, 4:56 am – Jan. 4, 7:44 am	1st	Pisces	Plant grains, leafy annuals. Fertilize (chemical). Graft or bud plants. Irrigate. Trim to increase growth
Jan. 6, 10:53 am – Jan. 8, 2:42 pm	2nd	Taurus	Plant annuals for hardiness. Trim to increase growth
Jan. 10, 7:43 pm – Jan. 12, 12:24 pm	2nd	Cancer	Plant grains, leafy annuals. Fertilize (chemical). Graft or bud plants. Irrigate. Trim to increase growth
Jan. 12, 12:24 pm – Jan. 13, 2:45 am	3rd	Cancer	Plant biennials, perennials, bulbs and roots. Prune. Irrigate. Fertilize (organic).
Jan. 13, 2:45 am – Jan. 15, 12:31 pm	3rd	Leo	Cultivate. Destroy weeds and pests. Harvest fruits and root crops for food. Trim to retard growth.
Jan. 15, 12:31 pm – Jan. 18, 12:45 am	3rd	Virgo	Cultivate, especially medicinal plants. Destroy weeds and pests. Trim to retard growth
Jan. 20, 1:35 pm – Jan. 20, 2:41 pm	3rd	Scorpio	Plant biennials, perennials, bulbs, and roots. Prune. Irrigate. Fertilize (organic).
Jan. 20, 2:41 pm – Jan. 23, 12:26 am	4th	Scorpio	Plant biennials, perennials, bulbs, and roots. Prune. Irrigate. Fertilize (organic).
Jan. 23, 12:26 am – Jan. 25, 7:40 am	4th	Sagittarius	Cultivate. Destroy weeds and pests. Harvest fruits and root crops for food. Trim to retard growth.
Jan. 25, 7:40 am – Jan. 27, 11:27 am	4th	Capricorn	Plant potatoes and tubers. Trim to retard growth.
Jan. 27, 11:27 am – Jan. 28, 1:01 am	4th	Aquarius	Cultivate. Destroy weeds and pests. Harvest fruits and root crops for food. Trim to retard growth.
Jan. 29, 1:09 pm – Jan. 31, 2:21 pm	1st	Pisces	Plant grains, leafy annuals. Fertilize (chemical). Graft or bud plants. Irrigate. Trim to increase growth.
Feb. 2, 4:25 pm – Feb. 3, 5:53 pm	1st	Taurus	Plant annuals for hardiness. Trim to increase growth.
Feb. 3, 5:53 pm – Feb. 4, 8:09 pm	2nd	Taurus	Plant annuals for hardiness. Trim to increase growth.
Feb. 7, 1:58 am – Feb. 9, 9:57 am	2nd	Cancer	Plant grains, leafy annuals. Fertilize (chemical). Graft or bud plants. Irrigate. Trim to increase growth.
Feb. 11, 5:23 am – Feb. 11, 8:10 pm	3rd	Leo	Cultivate. Destroy weeds and pests. Harvest fruits and root crops for food. Trim to retard growth.
Feb. 11, 8:10 pm – Feb. 14, 8:18 am	3rd	Virgo	Cultivate, especially medicinal plants. Destroy weeds and pests. Trim to retard growth.
Feb. 16, 9:14 pm – Feb. 19, 8:56 am	3rd	Scorpio	Plant biennials, perennials, bulbs and roots. Prune. Irrigate. Fertilize (organic).
Feb. 19, 8:56 am – Feb. 19, 10:27 am	3rd	Sagittarius	Cultivate. Destroy weeds and pests. Harvest fruits and root crops for food. Trim to retard growth.

1998 Gardening Dates

Dates	Qtr	Sign	Activity
Feb. 19, 10:27 am – Feb. 21, 5:30 pm	4th	Sagittarius	Cultivate. Destroy weeds and pests. Harvest fruits and root crops for food. Trim to retard growth.
Feb. 21, 5:30 pm – Feb. 23, 10:10 pm	4th	Capricorn	Plant potatoes and tubers. Trim to retard growth.
Feb. 23, 10:10 pm – Feb. 25, 11:42 pm	4th	Aquarius	Cultivate. Destroy weeds and pests. Harvest fruits and root crops for food. Trim to retard growth.
Feb. 25, 11:42 pm – Feb. 26, 12:26 pm	4th	Pisces	Plant biennials, perennials, bulbs, and roots. Prune. Irrigate. Fertilize (organic).
Feb. 26, 12:26 pm – Feb. 27, 11:42 pm	1st	Pisces	Plant grains, leafy annuals. Fertilize (chemical). Graft or bud plants. Irrigate. Trim to increase growth.
Mar. 2, 12:01 am – Mar. 4, 2:15 am	1st	Taurus	Plant annuals for hardiness. Trim to increase growth.
Mar. 6, 7:27 am – Mar. 8, 3:46 pm	2nd	Cancer	Plant grains, leafy annuals. Fertilize (chemical). Graft or bud plants. Irrigate. Trim to increase growth.
Mar. 12, 11:35 pm – Mar. 13, 2:59 pm	3rd	Virgo	Cultivate, especially medicinal plants. Destroy weeds and pests. Trim to retard growth.
Mar. 16, 3:51 am – Mar. 18, 3:56 pm	3rd	Scorpio	Plant biennials, perennials, bulbs, and roots. Prune. Irrigate. Fertilize (organic).
Mar. 18, 3:56 pm – Mar. 21, 1:43 am	3rd	Sagittarius	Cultivate. Destroy weeds and pests. Harvest fruits and root crops for food. Trim to retard growth.
Mar. 21, 1:43 am – Mar. 21, 2:38 am	3rd	Capricorn	Plant potatoes and tubers. Trim to retard growth.
Mar. 21, 2:38 am – Mar. 23, 8:02 am	4th	Capricorn	Plant potatoes and tubers. Trim to retard growth.
Mar. 23, 8:02 am – Mar. 25, 10:43 am	4th	Aquarius	Cultivate. Destroy weeds and pests. Harvest fruits and root crops for food. Trim to retard growth.
Mar. 25, 10:43 am – Mar. 27, 10:49 am	4th	Pisces	Plant biennials, perennials, bulbs and roots. Prune. Irrigate. Fertilize (organic).
Mar. 27, 10:49 am – Mar. 27, 10:14 pm	4th	Aries	Cultivate. Destroy weeds and pests. Harvest fruits and root crops for food. Trim to retard growth.
Mar. 29, 10:07 am – Mar. 31, 10:38 am	1st	Taurus	Plant annuals for hardiness. Trim to increase growth.
Apr. 2, 2:10 pm – Apr. 3, 3:19 pm	1st	Cancer	Plant grains, leafy annuals. Fertilize (chemical). Graft or bud plants. Irrigate. Trim to increase growth.
Apr. 3, 3:19 pm – Apr. 4, 9:36 pm	2nd	Cancer	Plant grains, leafy annuals. Fertilize (chemical). Graft or bud plants. Irrigate. Trim to increase growth.
Apr. 9, 9:05 pm – Apr. 11, 5:24 pm	2nd	Libra	Plant annuals for fragrance and beauty. Trim to increase growth.

1998 Gardening Dates

Dates	Qtr	Sign	Activity
Apr. 12, 9:55 am – Apr. 14, 9:52 pm	3rd	Scorpio	Plant biennials, perennials, bulbs, and roots. Prune. Irrigate. Fertilize (organic).
Apr. 14, 9:52 pm – Apr. 17, 8:05 am	3rd	Sagittarius	Cultivate. Destroy weeds and pests. Harvest fruits and root crops for food. Trim to retard growth.
Apr. 17, 8:05 am – Apr. 19, 2:53 pm	3rd	Capricorn	Plant potatoes and tubers. Trim to retard growth.
Apr. 19, 2:53 pm – Apr. 19, 3:42 pm	4th	Capricorn	Plant potatoes and tubers. Trim to retard growth.
Apr. 19, 3:42 pm – Apr. 21, 8:07 pm	4th	Aquarius	Cultivate. Destroy weeds and pests. Harvest fruits and root crops for food. Trim to retard growth.
Apr. 21, 8:07 pm – Apr. 23, 9:31 pm	4th	Pisces	Plant biennials, perennials, bulbs, and roots. Prune. Irrigate. Fertilize (organic).
Apr. 23, 9:31 pm – Apr. 25, 9:09 pm	4th	Aries	Cultivate. Destroy weeds and pests. Harvest fruits and root crops for food. Trim to retard growth.
Apr. 25, 9:09 pm – Apr. 26, 6:42 am	4th	Taurus	Plant potatoes and tubers. Trim to retard growth.
Apr. 26, 6:42 am – Apr. 27, 8:56 pm	1st	Taurus	Plant annuals for hardiness. Trim to increase growth.
Apr. 29, 10:57 pm – May 2, 4:49 am	1st	Cancer	Plant grains, leafy annuals. Fertilize (chemical). Graft or bud plants. Irrigate. Trim to increase growth.
May 7, 3:19 am – May 9, 4:10 pm	2nd	Libra	Plant annuals for fragrance and beauty. Trim to increase growth.
May 9, 4:10 pm – May 11, 9:30 am	2nd	Scorpio	Plant grains, leafy annuals. Fertilize (chemical). Graft or bud plants. Irrigate. Trim to increase growth.
May 11, 9:30 am – May 12, 3:48 am	3rd	Scorpio	Plant biennials, perennials, bulbs, and roots. Prune. Irrigate. Fertilize (organic).
May 12, 3:48 am – May 14, 1:40 pm	3rd	Sagittarius	Cultivate. Destroy weeds and pests. Harvest fruits and root crops for food. Trim to retard growth.
May 14, 1:40 pm – May 16, 9:31 pm	3rd	Capricorn	Plant potatoes and tubers. Trim to retard growth.
May 16, 9:31 pm – May 18, 11:36 pm	3rd	Aquarius	Cultivate. Destroy weeds and pests. Harvest fruits and root crops for food. Trim to retard growth.
May 18, 11:36 pm – May 19, 3:04 am	4th	Aquarius	Cultivate. Destroy weeds and pests. Harvest fruits and root crops for food. Trim to retard growth.
May 19, 3:04 am – May 21, 6:06 am	4th	Pisces	Plant biennials, perennials, bulbs, and roots. Prune. Irrigate. Fertilize (organic).
May 21, 6:06 am – May 23, 7:06 am	4th	Aries	Cultivate. Destroy weeds and pests. Harvest fruits and root crops for food. Trim to retard growth.

1998 Gardening Dates

Dates	Qtr	Sign	Activity
May 23, 7:06 am – May 25, 2:32 pm	4th	Taurus	Plant potatoes and tubers. Trim to retard growth.
May 25, 2:32 pm – May 25, 7:25 am	1st	Taurus	Plant annuals for hardiness. Trim to increase growth.
May 27, 8:58 am – May 29, 1:38 pm	1st	Cancer	Plant grains, leafy annuals. Fertilize (chemical). Graft or bud plants. Irrigate. Trim to increase growth.
Jun. 3, 10:17 am – Jun. 5, 11:06 pm	2nd	Libra	Plant annuals for fragrance and beauty. Trim to increase growth.
Jun. 5, 11:06 pm – Jun. 8, 10:35 am	2nd	Scorpio	Plant grains, leafy annuals. Fertilize (chemical). Graft or bud plants. Irrigate. Trim to increase growth.
Jun. 9, 11:19 pm – Jun. 10, 7:51 pm	3rd	Sagittarius	Cultivate. Destroy weeds and pests. Harvest fruits and root crops for food. Trim to retard growth.
Jun. 10, 7:51 pm – Jun. 13, 3:03 am	3rd	Capricorn	Plant potatoes and tubers. Trim to retard growth.
Jun. 13, 3:03 am – Jun. 15, 8:32 am	3rd	Aquarius	Cultivate. Destroy weeds and pests. Harvest fruits and root crops for food. Trim to retard growth.
Jun. 15, 8:32 am – Jun. 17, 5:38 am	3rd	Pisces	Plant biennials, perennials, bulbs, and roots. Prune. Irrigate. Fertilize (organic).
Jun. 17, 5:38 am – Jun. 17, 12:23 pm	4th	Pisces	Plant biennials, perennials, bulbs, and roots. Prune. Irrigate. Fertilize (organic).
Jun. 17, 12:23 pm – Jun. 19, 2:47 pm	4th	Aries	Cultivate. Destroy weeds and pests. Harvest fruits and root crops for food. Trim to retard growth.
Jun. 19, 2:47 pm – Jun. 21, 4:26 pm	4th	Taurus	Plant potatoes and tubers. Trim to retard growth.
Jun. 21, 4:26 pm – Jun. 23, 6:39 pm	4th	Gemini	Cultivate. Destroy weeds and pests. Harvest fruits and root crops for food. Trim to retard growth.
Jun. 23, 6:39 pm – Jun. 23, 10:50 pm	4th	Cancer	Plant biennials, perennials, bulbs, and roots. Prune. Irrigate. Fertilize (organic).
Jun. 23, 10:50 pm – Jun. 25, 11:04 pm	1st	Cancer	Plant grains, leafy annuals. Fertilize (chemical). Graft or bud plants. Irrigate. Trim to increase growth.
Jul. 30, 6:06 pm – Jul. 1, 1:44 pm	1st	Libra	Plant annuals for fragrance and beauty. Trim to increase growth.
Jul. 1, 1:44 pm – Jul. 3, 6:46 am	2nd	Libra	Plant annuals for fragrance and beauty. Trim to increase growth.
Jul. 3, 6:46 am – Jul. 5, 6:24 pm	2nd	Scorpio	Plant grains, leafy annuals. Fertilize (chemical). Graft or bud plants. Irrigate. Trim to increase growth.
Jul. 8, 3:28 am – Jul. 9, 11:01 am	2nd	Capricorn	Graft or bud plants. Trim to increase growth.

1998 Gardening Dates

Dates	Qtr	Sign	Activity
Jul. 9, 11:01 am – Jul. 10, 9:52 am	3rd	Capricorn	Plant potatoes and tubers. Trim to retard growth.
Jul. 10, 9:52 am – Jul. 12, 2:22 pm	3rd	Aquarius	Cultivate. Destroy weeds and pests. Harvest fruits and root crops for food. Trim to retard growth.
Jul. 12, 2:22 pm – Jul. 14, 5:45 pm	3rd	Pisces	Plant biennials, perennials, bulbs, and roots. Prune. Irrigate. Fertilize (organic).
Jul. 14, 5:45 pm – Jul. 16, 10:14 am	3rd	Aries	Cultivate. Destroy weeds and pests. Harvest fruits and root crops for food. Trim to retard growth.
Jul. 16, 10:14 am – Jul. 16, 8:33 pm	4th	Aries	Cultivate. Destroy weeds and pests. Harvest fruits and root crops for food. Trim to retard growth.
Jul. 16, 8:33 pm – Jul. 18, 11:18 pm	4th	Taurus	Plant potatoes and tubers. Trim to retard growth.
Jul. 18, 11:18 pm – Jul. 21, 2:43 am	4th	Gemini	Cultivate. Destroy weeds and pests. Harvest fruits and root crops for food. Trim to retard growth.
Jul. 21, 2:43 am – Jul. 23, 7:49 am	4th	Cancer	Plant biennials, perennials, bulbs, and roots. Prune. Irrigate. Fertilize (organic).
Jul. 23, 7:49 am – Jul. 23, 8:44 am	4th	Leo	Cultivate. Destroy weeds and pests. Harvest fruits and root crops for food. Trim to retard growth.
Jul. 28, 2:15 am – Jul. 30, 2:45 pm	1st	Libra	Plant annuals for fragrance and beauty. Trim to increase growth.
Jul. 30, 2:45 pm – Jul. 31, 7:05 am	1st	Scorpio	Plant grains, leafy annuals. Fertilize (chemical). Graft or bud plants. Irrigate. Trim to increase growth.
Jul. 31, 7:05 am – Aug. 2, 2:48 am	2nd	Scorpio	Plant grains, leafy annuals. Fertilize (chemical). Graft or bud plants. Irrigate. Trim to increase growth.
Aug. 4, 12:18 pm – Aug. 6, 6:31 pm	2nd	Capricorn	Graft or bud plants. Trim to increase growth.
Aug. 7, 9:10 pm – Aug. 8, 10:04 pm	3rd	Aquarius	Cultivate. Destroy weeds and pests. Harvest fruits and root crops for food. Trim to retard growth.
Aug. 8, 10:04 pm – Aug. 11, 12:11 am	3rd	Pisces	Plant biennials, perennials, bulbs, and roots. Prune. Irrigate. Fertilize (organic).
Aug. 11, 12:11 am – Aug. 13, 2:05 am	3rd	Aries	Cultivate. Destroy weeds and pests. Harvest fruits and root crops for food. Trim to retard growth.
Aug. 13, 2:05 am – Aug. 14, 2:49 pm	3rd	Taurus	Plant potatoes and tubers. Trim to retard growth.
Aug. 14, 2:49 pm – Aug. 15, 4:46 am	4th	Taurus	Plant potatoes and tubers. Trim to retard growth.
Aug. 15, 4:46 am – Aug. 17, 8:56 am	4th	Gemini	Cultivate. Destroy weeds and pests. Harvest fruits and root crops for food. Trim to retard growth.

1998 Gardening Dates

Dates	Qtr	Sign	Activity
Aug. 17, 8:56 am – Aug. 19, 3:01 pm	4th	Cancer	Plant biennials, perennials, bulbs, and roots. Prune. Irrigate. Fertilize (organic).
Aug. 19, 3:01 pm – Aug. 21, 9:03 pm	4th	Leo	Cultivate. Destroy weeds and pests. Harvest fruits and root crops for food. Trim to retard growth.
Aug. 24, 10:02 am – Aug. 26, 10:25 pm	1st	Libra	Plant annuals for fragrance and beauty. Trim to increase growth.
Aug. 26, 10:25 pm – Aug. 29, 10:55 am	1st	Scorpio	Plant grains, leafy annuals. Fertilize (chemical). Graft or bud plants. Irrigate. Trim to increase growth.
Aug. 31, 9:23 pm – Sep. 3, 4:21 am	2nd	Capricorn	Graft or bud plants. Trim to increase growth.
Sep. 5, 7:48 am – Sep. 6, 6:22 am	2nd	Pisces	Plant grains, leafy annuals. Fertilize (chemical). Graft or bud plants. Irrigate. Trim to increase growth.
Sep. 6, 6:22 am – Sep. 7, 8:53 am	3rd	Pisces	Plant biennials, perennials, bulbs and roots. Prune. Irrigate. Fertilize (organic).
Sep. 7, 8:53 am – Sep. 9, 9:17 am	3rd	Aries	Cultivate. Destroy weeds and pests. Harvest fruits and root crops for food. Trim to retard growth.
Sep. 9, 9:17 am – Sep. 11, 10:41 am	3rd	Taurus	Plant potatoes and tubers. Trim to retard growth.
Sep. 11, 10:41 am – Sep. 12, 8:58 pm	3rd	Gemini	Cultivate. Destroy weeds and pests. Harvest fruits and root crops for food. Trim to retard growth.
Sep. 12, 8:58 pm – Sep. 13, 2:20 pm	4th	Gemini	Cultivate. Destroy weeds and pests. Harvest fruits and root crops for food. Trim to retard growth.
Sep. 13, 2:20 pm – Sep. 15, 8:48 pm	4th	Cancer	Plant biennials, perennials, bulbs, and roots. Prune. Irrigate. Fertilize (organic).
Sep. 15, 8:48 pm – Sep. 18, 5:51 am	4th	Leo	Cultivate. Destroy weeds and pests. Harvest fruits and root crops for food. Trim to retard growth.
Sep. 18, 5:51 am – Sep. 20, 12:01 pm	4th	Virgo	Cultivate, especially medicinal plants. Destroy weeds and pests. Trim to retard growth
Sep. 20, 4:57 pm – Sep. 23, 5:22 am	1st	Libra	Plant annuals for fragrance and beauty. Trim to increase growth
Sep. 23, 5:22 am – Sep. 25, 6:05 pm	1st	Scorpio	Plant grains, leafy annuals. Fertilize (chemical). Graft or bud plants. Irrigate. Trim to increase growth.
Sep. 28, 5:31 am – Sep. 28, 4:12 pm	1st	Capricorn	Graft or bud plants. Trim to increase growth.
Sep. 28, 4:12 pm – Sep. 30, 1:54 pm	2nd	Capricorn	Graft or bud plants. Trim to increase growth.
Oct. 2, 6:24 pm – Oct. 4, 7:32 pm	2nd	Pisces	Plant grains, leafy annuals. Fertilize (chemical). Graft or bud plants. Irrigate. Trim to increase growth.

1998 Gardening Dates

Dates	Qtr	Sign	Activity
Oct. 5, 3:12 pm – Oct. 6, 6:58 pm	3rd	Aries	Cultivate. Destroy weeds and pests. Harvest fruits and root crops for food. Trim to retard growth.
Oct. 6, 6:58 pm – Oct. 8, 6:44 pm	3rd	Taurus	Plant potatoes and tubers. Trim to retard growth.
Oct. 8, 6:44 pm – Oct. 10, 8:48 pm	3rd	Gemini	Cultivate. Destroy weeds and pests. Harvest fruits and root crops for food. Trim to retard growth.
Oct. 10, 8:48 pm – Oct. 12, 6:11 am	3rd	Cancer	Plant biennials, perennials, bulbs, and roots. Prune. Irrigate. Fertilize (organic).
Oct. 12, 6:11 am – Oct. 13, 2:25 am	4th	Cancer	Plant biennials, perennials, bulbs, and roots. Prune. Irrigate. Fertilize (organic).
Oct. 13, 2:25 am – Oct. 15, 11:32 am	4th	Leo	Cultivate. Destroy weeds and pests. Harvest fruits and root crops for food. Trim to retard growth.
Oct. 15, 11:32 am – Oct. 17, 11:02 pm	4th	Virgo	Cultivate, especially medicinal plants. Destroy weeds and pests. Trim to retard growth.
Oct. 20, 5:10 am – Oct. 20, 11:37 am	1st	Libra	Plant annuals for fragrance and beauty. Trim to increase growth.
Oct. 20, 11:37 am – Oct. 23, 12:17 am	1st	Scorpio	Plant grains, leafy annuals. Fertilize (chemical). Graft or bud plants. Irrigate. Trim to increase growth.
Oct. 25, 12:05 pm – Oct. 27, 9:45 pm	1st	Capricorn	Graft or bud plants. Trim to increase growth.
Oct. 30, 3:58 am – Nov. 1, 6:27 am	2nd	Pisces	Plant grains, leafy annuals. Fertilize (chemical). Graft or bud plants. Irrigate. Trim to increase growth.
Nov. 3, 6:12 am – Nov. 4, 12:18 am	2nd	Taurus	Plant annuals for hardiness. Trim to increase growth.
Nov. 4, 12:18 am – Nov. 5, 5:11 am	3rd	Taurus	Plant potatoes and tubers. Trim to retard growth.
Nov. 5, 5:11 am – Nov. 7, 5:39 am	3rd	Gemini	Cultivate. Destroy weeds and pests. Harvest fruits and root crops for food. Trim to retard growth.
Nov. 7, 5:39 am – Nov. 9, 9:33 am	3rd	Cancer	Plant biennials, perennials, bulbs, and roots. Prune. Irrigate. Fertilize (organic).
Nov. 9, 9:33 am – Nov. 10, 7:29 pm	3rd	Leo	Cultivate. Destroy weeds and pests. Harvest fruits and root crops for food. Trim to retard growth.
Nov. 10, 7:29 pm – Nov. 11, 5:38 pm	4th	Leo	Cultivate. Destroy weeds and pests. Harvest fruits and root crops for food. Trim to retard growth.
Nov. 11, 5:38 pm – Nov. 14, 4:58 am	4th	Virgo	Cultivate, especially medicinal plants. Destroy weeds and pests. Trim to retard growth.
Nov. 16, 5:42 pm – Nov. 18, 11:27 pm	4th	Scorpio	Plant biennials, perennials, bulbs, and roots. Prune. Irrigate. Fertilize (organic).

1998 Gardening Dates

Dates	Qtr	Sign	Activity
Nov. 18, 11:27 pm – Nov. 19, 6:13 am	1st	Scorpio	Plant grains, leafy annuals. Fertilize (chemical). Graft or bud plants. Irrigate. Trim to increase growth.
Nov. 21, 5:46 pm – Nov. 24, 3:43 am	1st	Capricorn	Graft or bud plants. Trim to increase growth.
Nov. 26, 11:14 am – Nov. 26, 7:22 pm	1st	Pisces	Plant grains, leafy annuals. Fertilize (chemical). Graft or bud plants. Irrigate. Trim to increase growth.
Nov. 26, 7:22 pm – Nov. 28, 3:34 pm	2nd	Pisces	Plant grains, leafy annuals. Fertilize (chemical). Graft or bud plants. Irrigate. Trim to increase growth
Nov. 30, 4:52 pm – Dec. 2, 4:30 pm	2nd	Taurus	Plant annuals for hardiness. Trim to increase growth.
Dec. 3, 10:20 am – Dec. 4, 4:28 pm	3rd	Gemini	Cultivate. Destroy weeds and pests. Harvest fruits and root crops for food. Trim to retard growth.
Dec. 4, 4:28 pm – Dec. 6, 6:56 pm	3rd	Cancer	Plant biennials, perennials, bulbs, and roots. Prune. Irrigate. Fertilize (organic).
Dec. 6, 6:56 pm – Dec. 9, 1:22 am	3rd	Leo	Cultivate. Destroy weeds and pests. Harvest fruits and root crops for food. Trim to retard growth.
Dec. 9, 1:22 am – Dec. 10, 12:54 pm	3rd	Virgo	Cultivate, especially medicinal plants. Destroy weeds and pests. Trim to retard growth.
Dec. 10, 12:54 pm – Dec. 11, 11:44 am	4th	Virgo	Cultivate, especially medicinal plants. Destroy weeds and pests. Trim to retard growth.
Dec. 14, 12:17 am – Dec. 16, 12:47 pm	4th	Scorpio	Plant biennials, perennials, bulbs, and roots. Prune. Irrigate. Fertilize (organic).
Dec. 16, 12:47 pm – Dec. 18, 5:42 pm	4th	Sagittarius	Cultivate. Destroy weeds and pests. Harvest fruits and root crops for food. Trim to retard growth.
Dec. 18, 11:55 pm – Dec. 21, 9:17 am	1st	Capricorn	Graft or bud plants. Trim to increase growth.
Dec. 23, 4:45 pm – Dec. 25, 10:04 pm	1st	Pisces	Plant grains, leafy annuals. Fertilize (chemical). Graft or bud plants. Irrigate. Trim to increase growth.
Dec. 28, 1:05 am – Dec. 30, 2:22 am	2nd	Taurus	Plant annuals for hardiness. Trim to increase growth.

Dates to Destroy Weeds & Pests

From		To		Sign	Quarter
Jan. 13	2:45 am	Jan. 15	12:31 pm	Leo	3rd
Jan. 15	12:31 pm	Jan. 18	12:45 am	Virgo	3rd
Jan. 23	12:26 am	Jan. 25	7:40 am	Sagittarius	4th
Jan. 27	11:27 am	Jan. 28	1:01 am	Aquarius	4th
Feb. 11	5:23 am	Feb. 11	8:10 pm	Leo	3rd
Feb. 11	8:10 pm	Feb. 14	8:18 am	Virgo	3rd
Feb. 19	8:56 am	Feb. 19	8:56 am	Sagittarius	3rd
Feb. 19	10:27 am	Feb. 21	5:30 pm	Sagittarius	4th
Feb. 23	10:10 pm	Feb. 25	11:42 pm	Aquarius	4th
Mar. 12	11:35 pm	Mar. 13	2:59 pm	Virgo	3rd
Mar. 18	3:56 pm	Mar. 21	1:43 am	Sagittarius	3rd
Mar. 23	8:02 am	Mar. 25	10:43 am	Aquarius	4th
Mar. 27	10:49 am	Mar. 27	10:14 pm	Aries	4th
Apr. 14	9:52 pm	Apr. 17	8:05 am	Sagittarius	3rd
Apr. 19	3:42 pm	Apr. 21	8:07 pm	Aquarius	4th
Apr. 23	9:31 pm	Apr. 25	9:09 pm	Aries	4th
May 12	3:48 am	May 14	1:40 pm	Sagittarius	3rd
May 16	9:31 pm	May 18	11:36 pm	Aquarius	3rd
May 18	11:36 pm	May 19	3:04 am	Aquarius	4th
May 21	6:06 am	May 23	7:06 am	Aries	4th
Jun. 9	11:19 pm	Jun. 10	7:51 pm	Sagittarius	3rd
Jun. 13	3:03 am	Jun. 15	8:32 am	Aquarius	3rd
Jun. 17	12:23 pm	Jun. 19	2:47 pm	Aries	4th
Jun. 21	4:26 pm	Jun. 23	6:39 pm	Gemini	4th
Jul. 10	9:52 am	Jul. 12	2:22 pm	Aquarius	3rd
Jul. 14	5:45 pm	Jul. 16	10:14 am	Aries	3rd
Jul. 16	10:14 am	Jul. 16	8:33 pm	Aries	4th

Dates to Destroy Weeds & Pests

From		To		Sign	Quarter
Jul. 18	11:18 pm	Jul. 21	2:43 am	Gemini	4th
Jul. 23	7:49 am	Jul. 23	8:44 am	Leo	4th
Aug. 7	9:10 pm	Aug. 8	10:04 pm	Aquarius	3rd
Aug. 11	12:11 am	Aug. 13	2:05 am	Aries	3rd
Aug. 15	4:46 am	Aug. 17	8:56 am	Gemini	4th
Aug. 19	3:01 pm	Aug. 21	9:03 pm	Leo	4th
Sep. 7	8:53 am	Sep. 9	9:17 am	Aries	3rd
Sep. 11	10:41 am	Sep. 12	8:58 pm	Gemini	3rd
Sep. 12	8:58 pm	Sep. 13	2:20 pm	Gemini	4th
Sep. 15	8:48 pm	Sep. 18	5:51 am	Leo	4th
Sep. 18	5:51 am	Sep. 20	12:01 pm	Virgo	4th
Oct. 5	3:12 pm	Oct. 6	6:58 pm	Aries	3rd
Oct. 8	6:44 pm	Oct. 10	8:48 pm	Gemini	3rd
Oct. 13	2:25 am	Oct. 15	11:32 am	Leo	4th
Oct. 15	11:32 am	Oct. 17	11:02 pm	Virgo	4th
Nov. 5	5:11 am	Nov. 7	5:39 am	Gemini	3rd
Nov. 9	9:33 am	Nov. 10	7:29 pm	Leo	3rd
Nov. 10	7:29 pm	Nov. 11	5:38 pm	Leo	4th
Nov. 11	5:38 pm	Nov. 14	4:58 am	Virgo	4th
Dec. 3	10:20 am	Dec. 4	4:28 pm	Gemini	3rd
Dec. 6	6:56 pm	Dec. 9	1:22 am	Leo	3rd
Dec. 9	1:22 am	Dec. 10	12:54 pm	Virgo	3rd
Dec. 10	12:54 pm	Dec. 11	11:44 am	Virgo	4th
Dec. 16	12:47 pm	Dec. 18	5:42 pm	Sagittarius	4th

Editor's note: See Gardening by the Moon *(beginning on page 228) for more information.*

Gestation & Incubation

Animal	Young/Eggs	Gestation/Incubation
Horse	1	346 days
Cow	1	283 days
Monkey	1	164 days
Goat	1-2	151 days
Sheep	1-2	150 days
Pig	10	112 days
Chinchilla	2	110 days
Fox	5-8	63 days
Dog	6-8	63 days
Cat	4-6	63 days
Guinea Pig	2-6	62 days
Ferret	6-9	40 days
Rabbit	4-8	30 days
Rat	10	22 days
Mouse	10	22 days
Turkey	12-15	26-30 days
Guinea	15-18	25-26 days
Pea Hen	10	28-30 days
Duck	9-12	25-32 days
Goose	15-18	27-33 days
Hen	12-15	19-24 days
Pigeon	2	16-20 days
Canary	3-4	13-14 days

Dates to be Born	Sign	Qtr.	Set Eggs
Jan. 2, 4:56 am–Jan. 4, 7:44 am	Pisces	1st	Dec. 12, 14, 1997
Jan. 6, 10:53 am–Jan. 8, 2:42 pm	Taurus	2nd	Dec.16, 18, 1997
Jan. 10, 7:43 pm–Jan. 12, 12:24 pm	Cancer	2nd	Dec. 20, 22, 1997
Jan. 29, 1:09 pm–Jan. 31, 2:21 pm	Pisces	1st	Jan. 8, 10
Feb. 2, 4:25 pm–Feb. 3, 5:53 pm	Taurus	1st	Jan. 12, 13
Feb. 7, 1:58 am–Feb. 9, 9:57 am	Cancer	2nd	Jan. 17, 19
Feb. 26, 12:26 pm–Feb. 27, 11:42 pm	Pisces	1st	Feb. 5, 7
Mar. 2, 12:01 am–Mar. 4, 2:15 am	Taurus	1st	Feb. 9, 11
Mar. 6, 7:27 am–Mar. 8, 3:46 pm	Cancer	2nd	Feb. 13, 15
Mar. 29, 10:07 am–Mar. 31, 10:38 am	Taurus	1st	Mar. 8, 10
Apr. 2, 2:10 pm–Apr. 3, 3:19 pm	Cancer	1st	Mar. 12, 13
Apr. 9, 9:05 pm–Apr. 11, 5:24 pm	Libra	2nd	Mar. 19, 21
Apr. 26, 6:42 am–Apr. 27, 8:56 pm	Taurus	1st	Apr. 5, 6
Apr. 29, 10:57 pm–May 2, 4:49 am	Cancer	1st	Apr. 8, 11
May 7, 3:19 am–May 9, 4:10 pm	Libra	2nd	Apr. 16, 18
May 25, 2:32 pm–May 25, 7:25 am	Taurus	1st	May 4
May 27, 8:58 am–May 29, 1:38 pm	Cancer	1st	May 6, 8
Jun. 3, 10:17 am–Jun. 5, 11:06 pm	Libra	2nd	May 13, 15
Jun. 23, 10:50 pm–Jun. 25, 11:04 pm	Cancer	1st	June 2, 4
Jun. 30, 6:06 pm–Jul. 1, 1:44 pm	Libra	1st	Jun 9, 10
Jul. 28, 2:15 am–Jul. 30, 2:45 pm	Libra	1st	Jul 7, 10
Aug. 24, 10:02 am–Aug. 26, 10:25 pm	Libra	1st	Aug. 3, 5
Sep. 5, 7:48 am–Sep. 6, 6:22 am	Pisces	2nd	Aug. 15, 16
Sep. 20, 4:57 pm–Sep. 23, 5:22 am	Libra	1st	Aug. 30, 31, Sep. 1, 2
Oct. 2, 6:24 pm–Oct. 4, 7:32 pm	Pisces	2nd	Sep. 11,13
Oct. 20, 5:10 am–Oct. 20, 11:37 am	Libra	1st	Sep. 29
Oct. 30, 3:58 am–Nov. 1, 6:27 am	Pisces	2nd	Oct. 9, 11
Nov. 3, 6:12 am–Nov. 4, 12:18 am	Taurus	2nd	Oct. 13, 14
Nov. 26, 11:14 am–Nov. 26, 7:22 pm	Pisces	1st	Nov. 5
Nov. 30, 4:52 pm–Dec. 2, 4:30 pm	Taurus	2nd	Nov. 9, 11
Dec. 23, 4:45 pm–Dec. 25, 10:04 pm	Pisces	1st	Dec. 2, 4
Dec. 28, 1:05 am–Dec. 30, 2:22 am	Taurus	2nd	Dec. 7, 9

Companion Planting

Plant Helpers and Hinderers

Plant	Helped By	Hindered By
Asparagus	Tomatoes, Parsley, Basil	
Beans	Carrots, Cucumbers, Cabbage, Beets, Corn	Onions, Gladiola
Bush Beans	Cucumbers, Cabbage, Strawberries	Fennel, Onions
Beets	Onions, Cabbage, Lettuce	Pale Beans
Cabbage	Beets, Potatoes, Onions, Celery	Strawberries, Tomatoes
Carrots	Peas, Lettuce, Chives, Radishes, Leeks, Onions	Dill
Celery	Leeks, Bush Beans	
Chives	Beans	
Corn	Potatoes, Beans, Peas, Melons, Squash, Pumpkins, Cucumbers	
Cucumbers	Beans, Cabbage, Radishes, Sunflowers, Lettuce	Potatoes, Aromatic Herbs
Eggplant	Beans	
Lettuce	Strawberries, Carrots	
Melons	Morning glories	
Onions, Leeks	Beets, Chamomile, Carrots, Lettuce	Peas, Beans
Garlic	Summer Savory	
Peas	Radishes, Carrots, Corn, Cucumbers, Beans, Turnips	Onions
Potatoes	Beans, Corn, Peas, Cabbage, Hemp, Cucumbers	Sunflowers

Plant	Helped By	Hindered By
Radishes	Peas, Lettuce, Nasturtium, Cucumbers	Hyssop
Spinach	Strawberries	
Squash, Pumpkins	Nasturtium, Corn	Potatoes
Tomatoes	Asparagus, Parsley, Chives, Onions, Carrots, Marigold, Nasturtium	Dill, Cabbage, Fennel
Turnips	Peas, Beans	

Plant Companions and Uses

Plant	Companions and Uses
Anise	Coriander
Basil	Tomatoes; dislikes rue; repels flies and mosquitos
Borage	Tomatoes and squash
Buttercup	Clover; hinders delphiniums, peonies, monkshood, columbines
Chamomile	Helps peppermint, wheat, onions and cabbage; large amounts destructive
Catnip	Repels flea beetles
Chervil	Radishes
Chives	Carrots; prone to apple scab and powdery mildew
Coriander	Hinders seed formation in fennel
Cosmos	Repels corn earworm
Dill	Cabbage; hinders carrots and tomatoes
Fennel	Disliked by all garden plants
Garlic	Aids vetch and roses; hinders peas and beans
Hemp	Beneficial as a neighbor to most plants
Horseradish	Repels potato bugs

Plant	Companions and Uses
Horsetail	Makes fungicide spray
Hyssop	Attracts cabbage fly away from cabbages; harmful to radishes
Lovage	Improves hardiness and flavor of neighbor plants
Marigold	Pest repellent; use against Mexican bean beetles and nematodes
Mint	Repels ants, flea beetles and cabbage worm butterflies
Morning glory	Corn; helps melon germination
Nasturtium	Cabbage, cucumbers; deters aphids, squash bugs and pumpkin beetles
Nettles	Increase oil content in neighbors
Parsley	Tomatoes, asparagus
Purslane	Good ground cover
Rosemary	Repels cabbage moths, bean beetles, and carrot flies
Sage	Repels cabbage moths and carrot flies
Savory	Deters bean beetles
Sunflower	Hinders potatoes; improves soil
Tansy	Deters Japanese beetles, striped cucumber beetles, and squash bugs
Thyme	Repels cabbage worm
Yarrow	Increases essential oils of neighbors

Editor's note: Companion planting, or placing plants that "help" each other together, can greatly enhance your garden when used in conjunction with organic gardening methods. This table is a general guide to companion planting, and is not meant to be comprehensive.

Place
First Class
Stamp
Here

Llewellyn Worldwide
P.O. Box 64383, Dept. SK-933
St. Paul, MN 55164-0383

Get 15% Off Your Next Purchase!

WE WANT TO KNOW ABOUT YOU! Knowing about our audience helps Llewellyn to keep developing quality products with YOU in mind. Please fill out this survey and send it in to receive a catalog and coupon for 15% off your next purchase of Llewellyn products.

Name: ______________________________

Address: ______________________________

City: __________________ State: ______ Zip: ____________

Please check the boxes that apply:

Gender: ☐ Male ☐ Female

Age: ☐ Under 18 yrs old ☐ 18-26 ☐ 27-36
☐ 37-54 ☐ 55-65 ☐ 65+

Marital Status: ☐ Single ☐ Married
☐ Divorced ☐ Other

Do you have children? ☐ Yes ☐ No

Income: ☐ less than $15,000 ☐ $15,000-20,000
☐ $20,000-30,000 ☐ $30,000-40,000
☐ $40,000-50,000 ☐ $50,000+

Where did you purchase this product? ☐ Independent bookstore
☐ Chain bookstore ☐ Newsstand
☐ Mail order ☐ Other______________

What attracted you to this product? (choose all that apply):
☐ Interested in subject/content ☐ Artwork
☐ Friend's recommendation ☐ Gift for someone
☐ Received as a gift ☐ Buy it every year
☐ First time purchased ☐ Book review

How many books do you purchase a year? ________

What subject matter would you like to see more of?______________

We welcome your suggestions and content ideas. Write to: Attn: Annuals Editor, Llewellyn Worldwide, P.O. Box 64383, St Paul, MN 55164-0383

1998 Weather Predictions

By Nancy Soller

Winter on the East Coast will be dry, with below-normal temperatures in the extreme south and normal lows in other areas. Between the Appalachians and the Mississippi there will be dry weather east and normal precipitation in other areas. Temperatures will be seasonable. Areas west of the Mississippi should be wet with normal lows. Watch for seasonable precipitation and seasonable lows in the Rockies. The West Coast will have the most severe weather of the winter. Watch for very low temperatures and more snow north than there has been in a very long time. Excess precipitation is due south, too. The Alaskan Panhandle will be cold, dry, and windy, but central Alaska will have dry weather with above-normal temperatures. Seasonable weather is predicted for Hawaii.

Cold, wet weather is forecast for the East Coast in the spring. Areas west of the Appalachians will also have wet weather, but areas near the Mississippi will not be quite as chill. Most of the Plains, however, will see much precipitation and very low temperatures. Areas near the Rockies will be drier and warmer, with most locations in the Rockies having unseasonably warm weather and little precipitation. The West Coast may be slightly cool and dry, and the Alaskan Panhandle warm and dry. Central Alaska will be cold and wet, and Hawaii will have unusually large amounts of precipitation.

A wet summer is predicted for northern portions of zone one; areas in the extreme south will be dry. Temperatures should be within the normal range. Dry weather is predicted in zone two; however, near the Mississippi it will be very wet. Summer will bring very wet weather to the Eastern Plains, but in the west near the Rockies it will be very dry. Temperatures will be seasonable east, but in western dry areas it will be slightly cooler than normal. The Eastern Rockies will have a cool, dry summer. To the west it will be extremely cool and damp with much precipitation. Warm, dry weather is forecast for the West Coast. Look for dry weather with above-normal

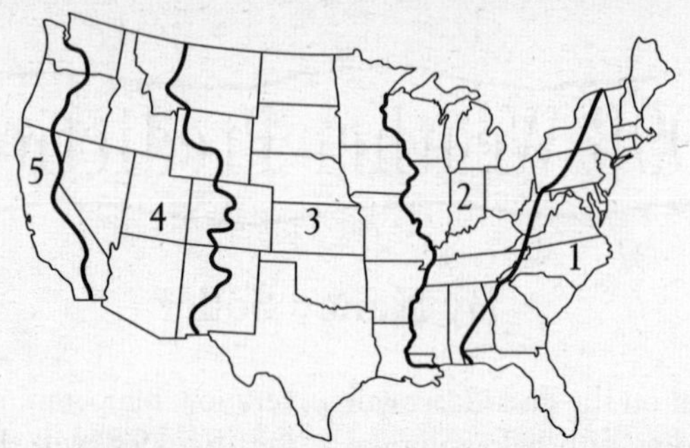

Map of Weather Zones

temperatures in Eastern Alaska. Farther west it will be wet with seasonable temperatures. Hawaii will see normal weather patterns.

A cool, wet fall may be experienced on the East Coast north; areas south will see seasonable weather. Cool, dry weather is forecast for areas between the Appalachians and the Mississippi. Wet weather with seasonable temperatures is forecast for the Plains in the fall. Watch for dry weather with temperatures a little above normal in the Rockies in the fall. The West Coast will see dry weather with above-normal temperatures. Watch for chill, dry weather on the Alaskan Panhandle and wet weather in the central part of the state.

In the Dates to Watch sections italics indicate strong winds.

November 1997

Zone 1: Chill, wet weather is predicted for this zone in November. Watch for very heavy precipitation November 7, November 14 south, and November 23. Winds are due November 2, 10, November 14 south, November 16, 23, and 27. Precipitation on other dates will be common. November weather patterns extend well into December.

Zone 2: Seasonable weather is forecast for this zone in November. Dates most likely to result in heavy precipitation include November 7, 14, and 23. Winds are due November 2, 4, 10, 14, 16, 23, and 27. Precipitation will be common on other dates as well. Seasonable weather patterns should extend into December.

Zone 3: Seasonable weather is forecast for most of this zone in November, but from Fort Dodge west the forecast is for dry, chill, and windy weather. Dates likely for precipitation include November 4, 5, 14, 17, 21, and 22. Winds are forecast November 4, 10, 14, 16, 27, and November 17 west.

Zone 4: Chill, windy weather is forecast east, but most of this zone will have above-normal temperatures. Dry weather is forecast for the entire zone. Best chances for precipitation come November 4, 5, 14, 17, 19, 21, and 22. Winds are likely November 4, 10, 16, 17, 19, and 27. Dry weather should extend into the month of December.

Zone 5: Mild temperatures and dry weather are forecast for this zone in November. Precipitation will be most likely November 4, 5, 14, 19, 20, 22, 23, 27, and 29. Some of these dates may only see overcast skies. Winds are likely November 4, 5, 17, and 19. Dry weather patterns should extend into December.

Zone 6: Mild, dry weather is predicted for most of Alaska, but some areas east will have excessive precipitation. Hawaii may have a slightly dry month. Precipitation is likely November 4, 5, 7, 14, 19, 20–23, 27, and possibly 29. Watch for winds November 2, 4, 5, 10, 19, 23, and 27. November's weather patterns extend into December.

Dates to Watch

Watch for rain November 4, 5, 10, 14, and 15.

Watch for snow November 17, 19, 20, 21, 23, 27, and 30.

Watch for winds November 2, 4, 5, *11*, *16*, *17*, *19*, *23*, and *27*.

December 1997

Zone 1: Most of this zone will see plenty of precipitation this month along with very chill temperatures. Watch for snow north and rain south December 5, 8, 14, and 16; also December 21, 22, and 23 north, 25, and 29. Winds are likely December 8, 12, 16, 21 south, 22 and 23 north; also 25, 26, and 29. Note that a white Christmas with winds is very likely in northern portions of this zone.

Zone 2: Seasonable temperatures and normal amounts of precipitation are forecast for this zone in December. Watch for snowfall December 5, 7 west, 8, 16, 21, 22, and 25. Winds are likely December 8, 16, 21, 22, 25, 26, and 29. Notice that both wind and snow are forecast north for Christmas Day.

Zone 3: Seasonable weather is forecast for most of this zone in December, but areas 100 degrees west and to the west of that will have very dry, chill, and windy weather. Watch for snowfall December 5 east, December 7, 8, 22, 25, and 29. Watch for winds December 8, 16, 22, 25, and 26 west. Note that Christmas may be white and windy.

Zone 4: Chill weather is forecast east, but most portions of this zone will have temperatures above normal and there will be little precipitation anywhere in the zone.

Watch for snowfall December 7, 8, 22, and possibly 25 east. Watch for winds December 8, 22, and 26. The mild, dry weather in effect in this zone this month should extend west to the coast.

Zone 5: A very mild, dry month is forecast for the West Coast in December, but precipitation could result on December 8, 19, and 22. Winds will be likely on December 8, 12, 16, 17, 19, 21, 22, and 26. Relatively warm weather is also forecast for British Colombia, but January should bring much colder weather to the entire area.

Zone 6: Temperatures will be relatively mild in Alaska and most of the state will be dry, but the panhandle and some other areas east may see excessive moisture. Hawaii will likely have a slightly dry month. Precipitation will be most likely December 5, 8, 16, 19, 21, 22, 23, 25, and 29. Winds will be frequent. A chill January will follow east.

Dates to Watch

Watch for snow December 5, 7, 8, 14, 16, 19, 21, 22, 23, 25, and 29.

Watch for winds December 8, 12, 16, 17, 22, 23, 25, 26, 27, and 29.

January 1998

Zone 1: Northern areas in this zone will have a mild, dry month. In southern portions of this zone it will be colder than normal and possibly very wet. Watch for precipitation January 4, 13, 16, and 23. Watch for winds January 4, 6, 23, 26, and 27. Weather patterns in effect this month should continue into February and possibly into the month of March.

Zone 2: This zone could be very cold this month. Precipitation dates may be few, but precipitation, when it comes, should be generous. Watch for precipitation January 4, 13, 16, 19, 23, and 28. Watch for winds January 4, 6, 26, and 27. Weather patterns established this month should continue into February and the first three weeks of March.

Zone 3: Very cold weather is possible in January in this zone, especially in the extreme west. Precipitation dates include January 4, 12, 16, 19, and 28. Wind is likely January 4, 6, and 21. Weather patterns in effect this month should continue into the month of February and possibly throughout the first three weeks of March. Spring should see overcast skies and frequent tornadoes.

Zone 4: Western portions of this zone will have a severe winter with much snow and very low temperatures. Watch for very heavy snows January 14 and 19. Watch for winds January 6, 9, 14, and 21. Weather patterns established this month should continue throughout February and well into the month of March. Spring will see dry weather in this zone.

Zone 5: A severe winter is predicted for most areas in this zone. There will be much snow and below-normal temperatures north; much rain and below-normal temperatures south. Watch for precipitation January 5, 10, 14, 20, 21, 23, 27, and 28. Watch for winds January 9, 14, 20, 23, 27, and 28. January's weather should continue well into the month of February.

Zone 6: Cold, dry weather is predicted for the Alaskan Panhandle this month; the rest of the state should see dry weather with above-normal temperatures. Hawaii should see a relatively dry month with seasonable temperatures. Watch for precipitation January 5, 10, 14, 20, 21, 23, 27, and 28 east; watch for precipitation elsewhere in this zone January 4, 13, 16, and 23.

Dates to Watch

Watch for snow January 4, 5, 10, 13, 14, 16, 19–21, 23, 27, and 28.

Watch for winds January 4, 6, 9, *14*, *20*, *21*, *23*, *26*, *27*, and *28*.

February 1998

Zone 1: Dry weather with above-normal temperatures is forecast for northern portions of this zone; cold weather with more precipitation is forecast south. Watch for snowfall February 7, 8, 12, 16, 19, and 26. Watch for winds February 3, 7, 8, 12, 16, and 25. Weather patterns in effect this month in this zone should continue well into the month of March.

Zone 2: Very cold weather is forecast east; areas near the Mississippi will have temperatures well above normal. Precipitation should be normal for the season. Watch for snowfall north and rain south February 3, 7, 8, 12, 16, and 25. Watch for winds February 3, 7, 8, 12, 16, and 25. February's weather patterns should continue well into the month of March.

Zone 3: Seasonable temperatures and much snowfall are predicted for this zone for the month of February. Snow is due February 3, 4, 7, 8, 12, and 26; also February 16 east. Watch for winds February 3, 7, 11, 12, and 24; also February 25 east. February's weather patterns should continue into the month of March and be followed by a chill spring.

Zone 4: There will be seasonable weather in eastern portions of this zone this month, but there will be very cold weather with much snowfall in the western portions of this zone. Watch for very heavy snowfall February 4, 7, and 12. Watch for winds February 3, 7, 11, and 24. March should continue

February's weather patterns for several weeks and then be followed by a warm-up west.

Zone 5: A severe winter is forecast in this zone with very low temperatures and much precipitation. Very heavy snowfall is due north and generous rainfall south February 2, 4, 7, 16, and 19. Watch for winds February 2, 3, 16, 22, 23, 24, and 26. This severe weather will continue into the month of March, but more normal weather will follow after the spring equinox.

Zone 6: Cold, dry weather is forecast for the Alaskan Panhandle and Eastern Alaska; dry weather with above-normal temperatures are due in the central and western parts of the state. Seasonable weather is forecast for Hawaii. Watch for snowfall east February 2, 4, 7, 16, and 19; watch for snowfall west February 7, 8, 12, 16, and 25. Winds will be frequent in Alaska all month.

Dates to Watch

Watch for snow February 2, 3, 4, 7, 8, 12, 16, 19, and 26.

Watch for winds February 2, 3, 7, 8, 11, 16, 22, 23, 24, 25, and 26.

March 1998

Zone 1: Dry weather with above-average temperatures is predicted north; in the extreme south dry weather with cooler-than-normal temperatures is predicted. However, the last week of the month may see some extremely wet weather in the entire zone. Watch for precipitation March 4, 8, 11, 13, 14, 22, 26, and 28. Winds are due March 4, 7, 8, 11, 12, 14, 19, 26, and 28.

Zone 2: Dry, warmer-than-normal weather is predicted east; very wet weather is predicted near the Mississippi. The last week of the month, however, should be wet in the entire zone. Watch for precipitation March 4 and 6 east, March 8, 11, 13, 14, 26, and 28. Watch for winds March 6, 8, 9, 11, 14, and 28.

Zone 3: Extremely wet weather is forecast for this zone for most of the month of March. Temperatures will be seasonable. The last week of the month, however, may be very dry in all portions of this zone. Watch for precipitation March 4, 6, 8, and 12 east; also March 14 and 28. Watch for winds March 4, 6, 8, 9, 12, 14, 19, and 28.

Zone 4: Eastern portions of this zone could see weather normal for the month, but a very cold and wet month is predicted for western portions of this zone. Watch for very heavy precipitation March 8, 14, and 28. Watch for winds March 8, 9, 14, 19, and 28. The last week of the month may see some extremely cold weather throughout the entire zone.

Zone 5: A very cold month with much precipitation is forecast for this zone in March. Watch for precipitation March 5, 6, 11, 18, 21, 23, and 27. Watch for winds March 6, 8, 10, 11, 14, 18, and 23; also March 31. While a very cold March is predicted for most of the month, more seasonable temperatures are likely at the month's end.

Zone 6: Cold, dry weather is forecast for the Alaskan Panhandle and eastern portions of the state, but central Alaska will be dry and warmer than usual. Hawaii should have seasonable weather. Watch for precipitation east March 5, 6, 11, 18, 21, 23, and 27. Watch for precipitation west March 4, 6, 8, 11, 14, 22, 26, and 28. Winds will be frequent all month.

Dates to Watch

Watch for snow March 4, 5, 6, 8, 11, and 14.

Watch for rain March 18, 21, 22, 23, 26, 27, and 28.

Watch for winds March 4, 6, 7, 8, 9, *10*, 11, 12, *14*, *18*, 19, *23*, *26*, *28*, and 29.

April 1998

Zone 1: Cold, wet weather is forecast for this zone in April. Watch for rainfall April 3, 10, 12, 13, 21, and 22. Watch for winds April 6, 9, 10, 12, 13, and 28. The wet, cold, and dreary weather in effect this month should be repeated in May and again in the first part of June. Summer should be wet north and dry south.

Zone 2: Wet weather is predicted for this zone in April. Temperatures will be below normal east and seasonable west. Heavy rainfall is due April 5, 6, 10, 12, 13, 21, and 22. Watch for winds April 5, 6, 10, 12, 13, and 28. April weather patterns should extend into March in this zone. Summer should see dry weather east and wet weather west.

Zone 3: Cold, wet weather near the Mississippi and dry weather west is the forecast for this zone in April. Temperatures west should be seasonable. Watch for rainfall April 5, 6, 10, April 11 east, April 13, 15, 22, and 26. Watch for winds April 5, 6, 10, 12, 13, and 28. April weather patterns should continue into the months of May and June.

Zone 4: There will be cold, wet weather east, but most portions of this zone will see hot, dry weather this month. Rainfall is predicted for April 5, 6, 10, 13, 22 east, and 26. Watch for winds April 1, 5, 10, 13, 15, and 28. April's weather patterns should continue throughout May and most of June. A very cool summer is predicted.

Zone 5: Seasonable temperatures and normal amounts of precipitation are forecast for this zone in

April. Watch for rainfall April 2, 10, 15, 19, and 22. Watch for winds April 1, 2, 10, 15, 28, and 29. April weather patterns are likely to continue throughout May and into the month of June. A very dry summer is forecast for most areas in this zone.

Zone 6: Dry weather is forecast for the Alaskan Panhandle and eastern portions of the state. Seasonable weather is forecast west. Hawaii should have an unusually wet month. Watch for precipitation April 1, 2, 10, 15, 28, and 29 in Eastern Alaska. Other parts of the state should see rainfall April 3, 10, 12, 13, 21, and 22. Winds will be frequent all of the month.

Dates to Watch

Watch for rain April 2, 3, 6, 10, 12, 13, 19, 21, 22, and 26.

Watch for winds April 1, 2, 5, 6, 9, *10*, 12, *13*, *15*, 28, and *29*.

May 1998

Zone 1: Wet weather is forecast for this zone in May. Temperatures will be below normal. Watch for precipitation May 3, 12, 14, 23, 26, and 28. Watch for winds May 12, 13, 14, 16, 22, 26, and 29. May weather patterns should continue well into the month of June. Extremely wet weather north and dry weather in the extreme south is the summer forecast.

Zone 2: Wet, cool weather is forecast east; western portions of this zone should see wet weather with seasonable temperatures. Precipitation is due May 3, 10, 12, 14, 18, 23, 26, 28, and 30. Watch for winds May 12, 13, 14, 16, 22, 26, 28, and 29. Summer will be dry east and very, very wet near the Mississippi.

Zone 3: A cool, wet month is predicted east; dry weather with seasonable temperatures is predicted west. Rainfall is due May 3, 5, May 9 west, May 10, 12, 14, May 18 east, and May 23, 26, 28, and 30. Winds are likely May 9 west, May 12, 13, 14, 22, 26, 28, and 29. May's weather patterns should extend well into the month of June.

Zone 4: Dry weather is forecast for this zone in May. Temperatures in most parts of this zone will be above normal. Watch for rainfall May 5, 9, 12, 25, 26, 28, and 30. Watch for winds May 3, 9, 12, 26, and 29. May weather conditions will extend into June. Summer should be cool with dry weather east and wet weather in the extreme west.

Zone 5: Seasonable temperatures and normal amounts of precipitation are forecast for this zone in May. Watch for rainfall May 5, 25, 26, 28, and 30. Watch for winds May 3, 9, 12, 26, and 29. May weather conditions should extend well into the month of June. Summer should bring dry weather, which should continue the entire summer long.

Zone 6: Dry weather east and normal precipitation west are forecast for Alaska in May. Temperatures should be seasonable. Hawaii should have a wet month with normal temperatures. Watch for rainfall in Eastern Alaska May 5, 25, 26, 28, and 30. Watch for rainfall in other parts of the state May 3, 12, 14, 23, 26, and 28. Winds will be frequent most of the month.

Dates to Watch

Watch for rain May 3, 5, 9, 11, 12, 14, 16, 18, 23, 26, 28, and 30.

Watch for winds May *3*, 9, *12*, *13*, *14*, *16*, *22*, 26, *28*, and 29.

June 1998

Zone 1: Wet, cool weather is forecast for this zone in June, but temperatures should rise the last week of the month. Watch for rainfall June 2 in the extreme north. Watch for rainfall June 9, 15, 17, 21, 24, and 25. Winds are due June 2 in the extreme north, and June 3, 5, 10, 13, 15, 25, and 29. There will be a wet summer north.

Zone 2: Wet, cool weather is forecast for this zone in June. Temperatures will be cool east, but more seasonable temperatures are forecast for western portions of this zone. Much rainfall is due June 9, 15, 17, 21, and 25. Winds are likely June 3, 5, 13, 15, 25, and 29. Dry weather is likely to follow in the summer in most portions of this zone.

Zone 3: Wet weather east and dry weather west is the forecast for this zone in June. Temperatures should be seasonable. Generous rainfall is due June 15, 17, 21, 22, and 25. Watch for winds June 2, 3, 4, 10, 13, 15, 20, 25, and 29. Very wet weather may come in the last week of the month and continue throughout the summer.

Zone 4: Dry weather is forecast for this zone in June, but areas in the extreme east may see very, cool wet weather. Watch for rainfall June 1, 2, 9, 25, and 29. Watch for winds June 2, 5, 7, 9, 10, 20, 25, 26, and 29. The last week of the month may see dry weather east and wet, cool weather west. Summer should echo this last week's pattern.

Zone 5: Seasonable temperatures and normal amounts of precipitation are forecast for this zone in June. Precipitation is due June 1, 2, 9, 25, and 29. Winds are likely June 2, 5, 7, 9, 10, 20, 25, 26, and 29. The last week of the month should be very hot and dry, and dry, hot weather is forecast for the rest of the summer.

Zone 6: Dry weather east and normal precipitation patterns with seasonable temperatures west is the forecast for Alaska this month. Hawaii will have a wet month.

Watch for rainfall east June 1, 2, 9, 25, and 29. Watch for rainfall west June 9, 15, 17, 21, 24, and 25. Dry weather east and wet weather west is the summer forecast.

Dates to Watch

Watch for rain June 1, 2, 9, 10, 15, 17, 21, 22, 25, and 29.

Watch for winds June 2, 3, 4, 5, *7, 9, 10, 13,* 15, *20, 21,* 25, 26, and *29.*

July 1998

Zone 1: Wet weather north and very dry weather south is the forecast for this zone in July. Temperatures should be seasonable. Watch for precipitation July 2, 4, 9, 16, 25, 26, and 31. Watch for winds July 2, 4, 25, and 28. Weather patterns established this month should continue through August and well into September. Fall should be pleasant.

Zone 2: Dry weather east and wet weather west is the forecast for this zone. Temperatures should be within the normal range. Watch for precipitation July 2, 4, 9, 16, 25, 26, and 31. Watch for winds July 2, 4, 25, and 28. July weather patterns should continue throughout August. Late September should bring cool, dry weather to the zone.

Zone 3: Very wet weather is predicted for this zone this month. Heavy precipitation is due July 1, 2, and 4 east, and July 9, 22, 26, and 31. Winds are likely July 1, 2, 4, 9, and 28. August should continue July's soggy weather patterns in most of this zone, but some areas in the extreme northwest should see cool, dry weather. A wet fall is likely.

Zone 4: Dry weather is forecast east; very wet, cool weather is forecast in western portions of this zone. Watch for rainfall July 1, 9, 22, 26, and 31. Watch for winds July 1, 2, and 9. July weather patterns should continue throughout August and well into September. A wet fall should follow in the extreme east, but most of this zone will be very dry in the fall.

Zone 5: Dry, pleasant weather is forecast for northern portions of this zone, but it could be dry and very hot south. The best chances of rain come July 4, 11, 17, 22, 23, and 25. Winds are likely July 4, 8, 9, 25, and 28. July weather patterns should be repeated in August and the first part of September. A very dry, warm fall is predicted.

Zone 6: Warm, dry weather east and wet weather west is the forecast for Alaska in July. Hawaii will be wet east and dry and cool west. Watch for rainfall east July 4, 11, 17, 22, 23, and 25. Watch for rainfall west July 2, 4, 9, 16, 25, 26, and 31. Winds will be frequent in Alaska this month. Watch for July's weather patterns to be repeated through August.

Dates to Watch

Watch for rain July 1, 2, 4, 9, 10, 11, 16, 17, 22, 23, 25, 26, and 31.

Watch for winds July 1, 2, 4, 8, 9, 25, and 28.

August 1998

Zone 1: The forecast is for wet weather north and dry weather in the extreme south in August in this zone. Precipitation will be most likely August 4, 10, 13, 14, 16, 17, 20, 21, 26, and 30. Winds are due August 4, 13, 14, 15, 17, 20, 21, 26, and 28. August's weather patterns should continue into the month of September.

Zone 2: Dry weather east and wet weather west is the forecast for this zone in August. Watch for precipitation August 4, 10, 13, 14, 16, 17, 20, 21, 26, and 30. Winds are likely August 4, 13, 14, 15, 17, 20, 21, 26, and 28. Dry weather east and wet weather west should continue into the month of September.

Zone 3: Wet weather is predicted for most of this zone this month, but areas in the extreme west may be dry. Temperatures should be normal, but dry areas may see temperatures a little above normal. Watch for heavy precipitation August 10, 16, 26, and 30. Watch for winds August 15, 20, and 28. Watch for August weather to repeat itself in September.

Zone 4: There should be dry, cool weather east and wet, cool weather west in this zone in August. There may be some record lows in this zone this month. Dates most likely to result in rain include August 10, 16, 26, and 30. Winds are likely August 15, 20, and 28. August weather patterns should continue throughout most of September. Fall should bring wet weather east and dry weather west.

Zone 5: Dry weather with seasonable temperatures is forecast for this zone in August. Best dates for precipitation include August 8, 10, 14, and 26. Winds are likely August 3, 15, 20, and 28. August weather patterns should continue well into the month of September, but very wet, chill weather should come in the end of that month and continue throughout the fall.

Zone 6: Dry, hot weather is forecast for Eastern Alaska this month. Western Alaska will be wet. Most of Hawaii will be wet too. Watch for precipitation east August 8, 10, 14, and 26. Watch for rainfall west August 4, 10, 13, 14, 16, 17, 20, 21, 26, and 30. Winds will be frequent in Alaska all month. August weather should extend into the month of September.

Dates to Watch

Watch for rain August 4, 8, 10, 13, 14, 16, 17, 20, 21, 26, and 30.

Watch for winds August *3*, *4*, *13*, *14*, 15, *17*, *20*, *21*, *26*, and *28*.

September 1998

Zone 1: Wet north and dry in the extreme south is the forecast for this zone in September. The last week of the month, however, may see more normal weather setting the pattern for both October and November. Watch for rainfall September 9, 12, 22, 23, 28, and 30. Winds are likely September 9, 12, 20, 23, 27, 28, 29, and 30.

Zone 2: Dry east and wet west is the forecast for this zone in September. Temperatures should be seasonable. Rainfall is due September 1, 9, 12, and 20; also September 22, 23, 28, and 30. Winds are likely September 1, 9, 12, 20, 27, 28, 29, and 30. The last week of the month should bring dry, cool weather to this zone.

Zone 3: Very wet east and very dry in the extreme west is the prediction for this zone in September. Temperatures will be seasonable east and slightly chill near the Rockies. Rainfall is likely September 1, 6, 9, 11, 12, 20, 24, and 30. Winds are likely September 1, 9, 11, and 27. Very wet weather is forecast for the last week of the month, setting a pattern for the fall.

Zone 4: Cool, dry weather is forecast for this zone in September. Precipitation is likely September 6, 9, 11, 20, 24, and 30. Winds can be expected September 6, 9, 11, 27, and 30. The last week of the month may see some very wet weather east. Dry weather with temperatures markedly above normal is forecast for most of this zone in the fall.

Zone 5: Warm, dry weather is forecast for this zone this month. Weather patterns established this month should intensify in the fall. Temperatures should be markedly above normal in September, October and November, and it should be very dry. Best chances for rain come on September 11, 12, 22, 23, and 28. Watch for winds September 23, 25, 28, and 29.

Zone 6: Dry weather east and wet weather west is the forecast for Alaska this month. This forecast should extend into the fall with chill, dry weather on the Alaskan Panhandle and seasonable temperatures where there is precipitation. Hawaii will have a normal month. Watch for rainfall east on September 11, 12, 22, 23, and 28. Rainfall is due west on September 9, 12, 22, 23, 28, and 30. Winds will be frequent.

Dates to Watch

Watch for rain September 1, 7, 9, 11, 12, 20, 22, 23, 24, 28, and 30.

Watch for winds September *1*, *4*, 9, *11*, *12*, *20*, 23, *25*, 27, *28*, and 29.

October 1998

Zone 1: Seasonable temperatures and normal amounts of precipitation are forecast for this zone in October. Watch for rainfall October 11, 12, 13, 20, 23, and 29. Watch for winds October 2, 11, 14, 17, 23, 24, 25, and 26. October weather patterns should repeat themselves in November and the first part of December.

Zone 2: Very dry, cool weather is forecast for this zone in October. Best dates for rain include October 11, 12, 13, 20, 23, and 29. Winds are likely October 2, 11, 14, 17, 23, 24, 25, and 26. October's weather patterns should continue throughout November and into the first three weeks of December.

Zone 3: Dry, cool weather is predicted for areas near the Mississippi River, but most portions of this zone will have very wet weather with seasonable temperatures. Precipitation is most likely October 7, 9, 11 east, 12, 13, 20, 24, 25, 26, and 28. Winds are due October 12, 13, 17, 18, 24, and 26.

Zone 4: Wet weather east and dry, warmer-than-normal weather west is the forecast for this zone in October. Best dates for rain include October 7, 9, 12, 13, 20, 24, 25, 26, and 28. Winds are likely October 2, 7, 9, 12, 13, 20, 24, 25, and 26.

Zone 5: Dry weather with temperatures markedly above normal is forecast for this zone in October. Precipitation would be most likely on October 5, 7, 22, 25, and 31. Winds are due October 2, 5, 7, 9, 14, 17, 18, 23, 25, and 31. October's weather patterns should continue throughout November and well into the month of December.

Zone 6: Dry and cool east and south and very wet west and in the central part of state is the forecast for Alaska in October. Hawaii will have seasonable temperatures and normal precipitation. Watch for precipitation east and south October 5, 7, 22–25, and 31. Precipitation is likely west October 11, 12, 13, and 20.

Dates to Watch

Watch for rain October 5, 6, 7, 9, 11–13, 20, 22, 23, 24, 25, 26, 28, 29, and 31.

Watch for winds October 2, 5, 7, 9, *11*, *12*, 14, *17*, *18*, 23, 24, *25*, 26, and 31.

November 1998

Zone 1: Seasonable temperatures and normal precipitation are forecast for this zone in November. Watch for precipitation November 7, 8, 9, 13, 17, 18, 21, 25, 27, and 28. Winds are likely November 9, 13, 15, 25, 27, and 28. November weather patterns should continue into December.

Zone 2: Dry, cold weather is forecast for this zone in November, but many days could result in small amounts of precipitation, including November 7–9, 13, 17, 18, 21, 25, 27, and 28. Winds are due November 9, 13, 15, 25, 27, and 28. Very cold temperatures before Thanksgiving could bring snow.

Zone 3: Dry, chill weather is forecast for areas near the Mississippi; wet weather, however, is forecast for most of this zone. Temperatures should be seasonable. Watch for precipitation November 4, 10, 17, 21, 22, 23, 26, and 27. Winds are likely November 1, 7, 8, 15, 23, and 27. December should come in wet over most of this zone.

Zone 4: Wet weather in the extreme east and dry weather for most of this zone is predicted. Temperatures should be above normal. Best chances for precipitation come November 4, 10, 17, 21, 22, 23, 26, and 27. Winds are due November 22, 23, 26, and 27.

Zone 5: Dry weather with temperatures well above normal is the forecast for this zone in November. Best chances for precipitation should come on November 9, 10, 25, 26, and 27. Winds are likely November 6, 9, 25, 27, 29, and 30. Wind and snow are possible north the day before Thanksgiving.

Zone 6: The Alaskan Panhandle will be cold and dry, but central parts of the state will be wet with seasonable temperatures. Hawaii will have normal precipitation and temperatures. Watch for precipitation east November 9, 10, 25, 26, and 27. Precipitation is due west November 7–9, 13, 17, 18, 21, 25, 27, and 28.

Dates to Watch

Watch for rain November 5, 7, 8, 9, and 13.

Watch for snow November 17, 18, 21, 22, 23, 25, 26, 27, and 28.

Watch for winds November 1, 6, 7, 8, 9, 13, 15, 17, 23, 25, 27, 28, 29, and 30.

December 1998

Zone 1: Seasonable temperatures and normal amounts of precipitation are forecast for this zone in December. Snowfall is most likely north December 2, 3, 9, 18, 25, 26, 28, and 31. Rainfall is likely south December 1, 3, 5, 12, 15, 23, 27, 28, and 31. Notice that a white Christmas is possible north.

Zone 2: Dry, very cold weather is forecast for this zone in December. The best chances for snow or rain in this zone will come on December 4, 18, 26, 28, and 31. Winds are likely December 1, 2, 3, 5, 12, 15, 23, 27, 28, and 31. Notice that snow is likely north New Year's Eve, but a white Christmas is unlikely.

Zone 3: Dry weather is possible near the Mississippi, but most of this zone will have some extremely wet weather. Temperatures should be normal. Look for snow north and rain south December 2, 3, 9, 18, 21, 22, 25, and 31. Winds are likely December 2, 15, 16, 21, 23, 28, and 31.

Zone 4: The most eastern portions of this zone may see moisture, but dry weather with above-normal temperatures is forecast most of this zone in December. Dates that could result in precipitation include December 2, 3, 9, 18, 21, 22, 25, and 31. Watch for winds December 15, 16, 21, 28, and 31. Notice that snow is possible north on the holidays.

Zone 5: Very dry weather with above-normal temperatures is forecast for this zone in December. Best chances for precipitation come on December 2, 3, 18, 22, and 25. Winds are likely December 1, 3, 5, 6, 12, 21, 22, and 23. Snow is possible north for Christmas, but New Year's Eve will probably not see precipitation.

Zone 6: Cold, dry weather is forecast for the Alaskan Panhandle, but most of the state will see much precipitation. Hawaii should have above-normal rainfall and seasonable temperatures. Watch for snow in Eastern Alaska December 2, 3, 18, 22, and 25. Watch for snow in most other parts of the state December 2–4, 9, 18, 25, 26, 28, and 31. Winds will be frequent all month.

Dates to Watch

Watch for snow December 2, 3, 4, 9, 18, 21, 22, 25, 26, 28, and 31.

Watch for winds December *1*, 2, 3, 5, 6, 12, 15, *16*, *21*, 22, 23, *27*, 28, and *31*.

Earthquake Predictions

By Nancy Soller

Ann E. Parker of Skokie, Illinois, has devised a way to predict the dates and locations of large, destructive earthquakes. Ann watches recent and near-future solar and lunar eclipse points as Mars forms hard aspects to them. The large, destructive quakes occur on the dates that Mars forms these aspects, which include the conjunction, square, opposition, semisquare, and sesquiquadrate. The aspects may be made either geocentrically or heliocentrically. Location is determined by watching the degree and sign of the eclipse. This is found to conjunct the geodetic midheaven, the geodetic ascendant or the geodetic vertex.

Each eclipse results in several possible locations and several possible high-risk dates. Persons living in these high-risk locations should be watching for precursors of quakes before the high-risk dates. Small movements along a fault and sudden changes in the water level of wells are two precursors.

The September 27, 1996, lunar eclipse at 4 degrees of Aries could result in a large, destructive quake in 1998. High risk areas would include the U.S. midwest, Indonesia, Sumatra, Algeria, Nicaragua, Honduras, and El Salvador. High risk dates include January 11 and 12, February 21 and 22, March 10 and 11, May 8–10, July 12 and 13, August 2 and 3, September 20 and 21, November 8 and 9, and December 5 and 6.

The October 12, 1996, solar eclipse at 20 degrees of Libra could result in a large, disastrous quake in 1998. Areas in danger include the Aleutian Islands, central Alaska, New Brunswick, Indonesia, Japan, Bolivia, China, and Saint Vincent's Island. Danger dates include January 6 and 7, February 1 and 2, March 19 and 20, March 30 and 31, June 1 and 2, June 6 and 7, August 5 and 6, September 5 and 6, October 16 and 17, and December 15 and 16.

The March 9, 1997, solar eclipse at 19 degrees of Pisces could result in a large, destructive quake in 1998. Areas in danger include Oklahoma, Kansas, Nebraska, and the Caroline Islands and Mexico. Dangerous dates include

January 28 and 29, February 18 and 19, April 11 and 12, April 18 and 19, June 20 and 21, July 3 and 4, August 27 and 28, October 6 and 7, and November 8 and 9.

The March 24, 1997, lunar eclipse at 4 degrees of Libra could result in a large, disastrous earthquake in 1998. Areas that could be affected include the American Midwest, Sumatra, the Dominican Republic, Nicaragua, Honduras, and El Salvador. Danger dates include February 21 and 22, March 10 and 11, May 8–10, July 12 and 13, August 3 and 4, September 20 and 21, November 9 and 10, and December 5 and 6.

The September 1, 1997, solar eclipse at 9 degrees of Virgo could result in a large, destructive quake in 1998. Areas that could be affected include Texas, Nevada, Montana, and California; also the Solomon Islands. Critical dates include January 12 and 13, February 6 and 7, March 26 and 27, April 5 and 6, June 6 and 7, June 14 and 15, August 12 and 13, September 14 and 15, October 22 and 23, and December 24 and 25.

The September 16, 1997, lunar eclipse at 24 degrees of Pisces could result in a large, destructive quake in 1998. Danger areas include points on the American plains, Malaysia, Kenya, Northern Ireland, Morocco, Guatemala, and Mexico City. Critical dates include February 5 and 6, February 25 and 26, April 20 and 21, April 25 and 26, June 28 and 29, July 13 and 14, September 4 and 5, October 17 and 18, and November 17 and 18.

The February 26, 1998, solar eclipse at 8 degrees of Pisces could result in a large, disastrous earthquake in 1998. The American West could be affected, as well as the Azores. Dates that could result in a quake include January 11 and 12, February 5 and 6, March 24 and 25, April 4 and 5, June 4 and 5, June 12 and 13, August 10 and 11, September 12 and 13, October 21 and 22, and December 22 and 23.

The August 22, 1998, solar eclipse at 29 degrees of Leo could result in a destructive quake in 1998. Areas in danger include Hawaii, California, Oregon, Washington, Guam, Iran, Moscow, and the Marshall Islands. Critical dates include January 24 and 25, March 9 and 10, March 24 and 25, May 23 and 24, May 26 and 27, July 27 and 28, August 23 and 24, October 5 and 6, December 1 and 2, and December 24 and 25. Volcanic activity in Hawaii or at Mt. St. Helens are also possibilities on those dates.

The February 16, 1999, solar eclipse at 27 degrees of Aquarius could result in a big, destructive quake in 1998. Areas in danger include Utah, Arizona, Southern and Baja California, and also Brazil. Danger dates include January 21 and 22, March 6 and 7, March 20 and 21, May 20–23, July 24 and 25, August 19 and 20, October 3 and 4, November 27 and 28, and December 20 and 21.

The July 28, 1999, lunar eclipse at 5 degrees of Aquarius could result in a large, destructive earthquake in 1998. Areas in danger include California, Washington and Oregon, Newfoundland, Paraguay, and Brazil. Danger dates include January 30 and 31, February 20 and 21, April 13 and 14, April 20 and 21, June 22 and 23, July 5 and 6, August 29 and 30, October 8 and 9, and November 10 and 11.

The August 11, 1999, solar eclipse at 18 degrees of Leo could result in a large, disastrous earthquake in 1998. This eclipse will be a total eclipse and will form the fourth arm of a giant earth-centered cross in the sky. The eclipse and Uranus will be on opposite sides of the earth with Mars and Saturn opposite each other and at right angles to the eclipse-Uranus axis. Areas in special danger include southeastern Alaska, Japan, Indonesia, the Caroline Islands, Baghdad, and Turkey. Dates that could bring danger include January 11, February 20, March 9, May 6–8, July 11 and 12, July 31 and August 1, September 19, November 6 and 7, and December 3 and 4. This eclipse will be visible over central Europe.

The January 21, 2000, lunar eclipse at 0 degrees of Leo could result in a large, destructive quake in 1998. Areas in special danger include Alaska and the Aleutian Islands, Manila, Shanghai, Kenya, Athens, Belgrade, and points in Italy. Danger dates include January 22 and 23, February 14, April 5 and 14, June 15 and 26, August 21, September 22, and November 2.

The February 5, 2000, solar eclipse at 16 degrees of Aquarius could result in a large, destructive earthquake in 1998. Areas in danger include points in California, Nevada, Utah, Brazil, and India. Dates when such a quake could occur include January 9, February 17, March 6, May 3–6, July 27 and 28, September 15 and 16, November 2 and 3, November 30 and December 1, and December 23 and 24.

Weather Sayings

By Verna Gates

Rain

- When ditch and pond offend the nose, go straight home and windows close.
- When chickweed blossoms open wide and free, then rain can't come before hours three.
- The farther the sight, the nearer the rain.
- Sound traveling far and wide, a stormy day will decide.
- Curls that kink, straight hair links, look for rain in a blink.
- If ants build high, look for rain in the sky.
- A fly on your nose, you swat and it goes. If it comes back again, it will bring a good rain.
- When snails on the road you see, rain tomorrow it will be.
- Spiders do their webs expand when rainy weather is at hand.
- Sunshine shower won't last half an hour.
- Point a finger, there lightning will linger.
- When cocks crow and take a drink, thunder and lightning are on the brink.

Winter

- Year of snow, fruit will grow.
- A bad winter is betide if hair grows thick on the bear's hide.
- When the buffalo hide is thick, the winter will be very cold.
- Onion skins very thin, mild winter coming in. Onion skins hard and tough, winter's coming cold and rough.
- If on the trees the leaves still hold, the coming winter will be cold.
- Thick husks on the corn and large crops of acorns predict a long winter ahead.

Spring

- April showers bring May flowers.
- Spring has come when you can put your foot on three daisies.
- Warm Christmas, cold Easter.
- When March roars in like a lion, it goes out like a lamb.
- To point at a rainbow brings bad luck.

The Moon & the Weather

By Bruce Scofield

Throughout history people have noticed correlations between the Moon and the weather. We've all heard the old saying "a ring around the Moon means rain, the smaller the ring the sooner the rain." A practical farmer and a skeptical scientist would both agree that there is truth to this saying. The farmer knows it from experience and the scientist has an explanation for it in the high levels of moisture in the atmosphere that cause the ring, and later the rain.

Another lunar observation that goes back to ancient times has links with the weather. A day or two after the New Moon (its conjunction with the Sun), the Moon is first seen as a narrow crescent standing just above the western horizon at sunset. The horns of the Moon, that is the points of this sharp lunar crescent, have long been thought to be an indicator of dryness, winds, rains, cold, and heat in the coming quarter—or even month. In general, when the horns of the Moon are turned upright, the weather lore says that it won't rain for the next quarter. The crescent in this position was seen as a container that holds the rainwater. When the horns are turned down, the water is said to run out in the form of rain. Visibly sharp lunar horns were said to threaten windy weather and squalls. If the New Moon is to the north, the weather will be cold; to the south, warm.

Sailors have long used the Moon, planets, and stars as guides to the weather. Being out at sea and at the mercy of the weather, one would expect these people to have an excellent knowledge of the weather and how to predict it. Also, a more perfect place to observe the skies could not be asked for. The sea has no horizon obstructions. One observation that sailors have made is that the presence of a large star or planet near the Moon means that wild weather is coming. They said that the planet near the Moon was "dogging" it.

The alignment of the Moon with a planet is a cornerstone of lunar weather forecasting. Almanacs from the late Middle Ages to the present use the Moon to make predictions about the coming weather. Today most almanacs simply make weather forecasts and don't tell the reader how it was done. In earlier times, however, some almanacs let their users do it by themselves. These early almanacs would list the lunar aspects for the year and the reader would have to turn to a list of prognostications for each of the aspects in another part of the almanac to determine the weather. Let's look at how this was done in an almanac from 550 years ago.

The alignment of the Moon with a planet is a cornerstone of lunar weather forecasting

Leonard Digges, the father of the astronomer Thomas Digges, was an English writer of almanacs who combined astrology and astronomy in his publications. His 1556 almanac titled *A Prognostication Everlasting of Right Good Effect* contains plenty of information on weather forecasting that could be used year after year, providing one knows what the current lunar and planetary aspects are. After introducing the astrological symbols at the beginning of his almanac, Digges lists the correspondences between the aspects and the weather. He uses only the conjunction, square, and opposition aspects, which are listed in the tables at the beginning of this year's *Moon Sign Book,* pages 28–51. Using the tables and the delineations below, you may be able to make your own weather forecasts based on the Moon.

The section in Digges' almanac that we are concerned with is titled *A Declaration of Weather by the Aspects of the Moon and the Planets*, a portion of which is printed below. I've changed the spelling of many words from the "olde" English to a more modern form. Also, notice that in places the signs are referred to as "moist" or "hot." An old classification of signs, and one that reveals the strong linkage of astrology to weather, uses the terms hot, cold, moist, and dry—which is different from fire, earth, air, and water. The hot signs are all the fire and air signs. The cold signs are the earth and water signs, especially Capricorn and Cancer. The moist signs are the water and air signs, the dry signs the fire and earth signs.

Here's what Digges has to say about the Moon's aspects to the planets. It was made for the weather in England, but it does seem to work well in other parts of the world where frequent weather variations are the norm.

Moon conjunct, square, and opposition Saturn: in moist signs, it brings a cloudy day or cold air according to the nature of the sign. If the Moon is moving from Saturn to the Sun, harder weather will ensue.

Moon conjunct, square, and opposition Jupiter: brings fair weather with white clouds, especially if Jupiter is in Aries or Scorpio.

Moon conjunct, square, and opposition Mars: in water signs it brings rain; in fire signs colorful red clouds; in summer, thunder.

Moon conjunct, square, and opposition Sun: in moist signs rainy weather, more so if the Moon is moving from the Sun to Saturn.

Moon conjunct, square, and opposition Venus: in moist signs, rain.

Moon conjunct, square, and opposition Mercury: in moist signs it brings rain and winds, more so when the Moon is moving from Mercury to Jupiter.

In the seventeenth century, John Goad, one of history's greatest writers on astro-meteorology, noted that the planet the Moon moves toward immediately after the New or Full Moon has much to say about the weather. If the Moon moves toward Saturn, especially in the water signs, there will be rain. If toward Jupiter, there will be fine weather. Toward Mars, rain will follow, unless Mars is in a fire sign or in aspect to Jupiter. When the Moon moves toward Venus, rain is sure to follow, unless Jupiter is also nearby. When Venus is in aspect to Saturn, there will be cold rain or snow. When the Moon moves toward Mercury when it is retrograde, there will be rain. If Mercury is in aspect to Mars or Jupiter, warm or dry weather will follow.

Goad was a tireless observer of nature, and left us with numerous insights into the Moon and the weather. He labored for years making daily weather observations and reading those of Johannes Kepler, the great astrologer/astronomer. What these told him was that there were not only patterns that occur when the Moon was near a planet, as the sailors knew, but that there were underlying patterns that involved just the phases of the Moon. His astute observation that heavy rains tend to occur more frequently about four to five days after New Moon and Full Moon has been demonstrated to be true in scientific studies. Goad's years of weather observations also demonstrated that the first half of the Sun/Moon cycle, from New Moon to Full Moon, was generally more rainy than the second half.

Weather forecasts have long been made by observing exactly when and where in the zodiac the quarters of the Moon occur. Serious astro-meteorologists often cast a chart for each phase of the Moon for the location they wish to study. The exact minute that the New Moon, Full Moon, or quarter occurs is used as the basis of the chart. The planetary alignments within the chart provide clues as to what the weather will be like over the next week. Traditionally, it is said that the lunation closest to the equinoxes or solstices is very significant and can be used to forecast the weather over the next season.

Perhaps the most famous almanac today, and one that has outlasted the many that flourished in this country's early history, is the *Farmer's Almanac*. For years readers have speculated as to how this almanac's writers were able to predict the weather so well and so far in advance. The publishers say that their weather forecasts are based on a combination of factors including projections of solar activity and a table created for them 160 years ago by a Dr. Herschell. It is this table that is of interest to lunar weather forecasters.

Dr. Herschell's table correlates the time of day that a lunation (New Moon, Full Moon, or quarter) occurs with the weather in summer and in winter. For example, let's take the Full Moon of January 12, 1998. According to the astronomical ephemeris, this Full Moon occurs at 12:25 pm Eastern Standard Time. Dr. Herschell's table says that a lunation that occurs between Noon and 2:00 pm (in winter) brings snow or rain. In Central Standard Time this Full Moon occurs at 11:25 and, according to Dr. Herschell, a lunation between 10:00 am and Noon (in winter) indicates cold with high winds. As to how well this one particular lunation works—we shall see.

Plan Your First Garden Patch

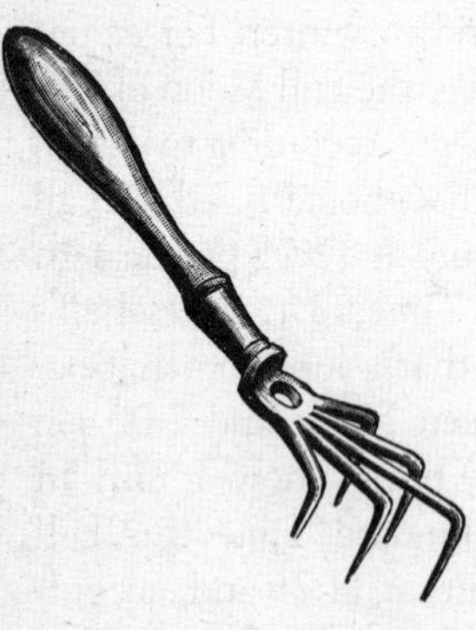

By Penny Kelly

If you dream about tomatoes with flavor, cucumbers that last two weeks in the refrigerator, or sweet corn and carrots that transcend all former taste sensations, it's time to plant your first garden. Don't worry about finding the perfect location, getting it tilled, or where to get a soil test. Instead, look out the window and see those dreamed-of vegetables in your mind's eye. Forget about fertilizers, tools, and techniques. All of that can be learned as you go along. Instead, let yourself daydream about the magical garden that lives in your heart and nurtures a sense of connection between you and nature. Be pleased, and be aware that your health, your consciousness, and your sense of who you are and what you are capable of is basically incomplete without this connection.

Seeds and Seedlings

Once inside the garden that grows in your heart, begin thinking about seeds and the bedding plants you will buy. Seeds can be found in many places—from grocery to discount to hardware stores. You can also order from one of the many seed companies that send out catalogs every winter, but beware! Once you start ordering, word gets around and you'll be swamped with seed catalogs every January. Of course, garden catalogs are the doorway to that mythical Garden of Eden that lives inside your mind, and once you step inside, you will be hooked forever. You will become like the rest of us—the more garden catalogs the better!

Other than the need to buy plants that will grow in your weather zone, there aren't many rules when it comes to choosing seeds and plants, but do order or buy early. If you see something that strikes you as delectable in a seed display in February, don't wait until late

April or early May to go back and look for it. You may find that the seeds you wanted most are all sold out. Follow your heart and choose what looks good to you, what you think you would be interested in growing and eating. Try growing a few perennial items like asparagus and strawberries or blueberries, but keep one eye on your pocketbook. While we're on the subject of pocketbooks, consider heirloom seeds.

Heirloom seeds are those that grow reliably, produce wonderful, flavorful, nutrient-rich fruits and vegetables, and generate seeds that can be saved to reproduce another delightful crop the next year. Hybrid seeds have been cross-bred, usually for uniformity; for their tendency to ripen all at once; for tougher skins and fibers that will withstand cross-country marketing; for good looks instead of good taste or super-nutrient capabilities; and with the recognition that they will not reproduce!

If seed companies can get everyone to start using a limited selection of hybrid seeds that do not reproduce themselves, gradually they can force people to buy new seeds every year. If you want anything outside their limited selection, you'll pay exorbitant prices, and they know that if you're like most gardeners you'll want to try one or two new things each year.

Prices and Paybacks

Even if you are an absolute beginner as far as gardening is concerned, you are probably going to be shocked at the cost of your first seeds and bedding plants. Thirty-five years ago you could plant a seventy-five by one hundred-foot garden for twenty dollars, and that included a large variety of annual seeds, your strawberry plants, seed potatoes, fertilizer, onion sets, corn, and a flat or two of seedling tomatoes, cabbage, broccoli, and

Daydream about the magical garden that lives in your heart

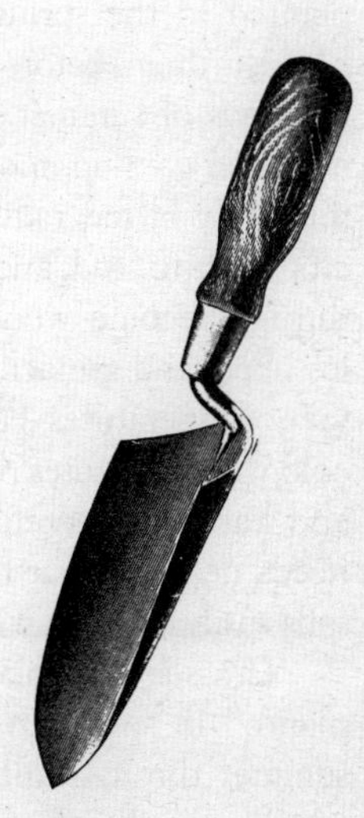

cauliflower. Today that same garden can easily cost two hundred dollars. Whatever you spend, the rule of thumb is that you will get back approximately four times your initial investment. If you spend one hundred dollars the first year, you will probably reap about four hundred dollars' worth of delicious produce.

Seasonal Considerations

Once you have your seeds and you know which vegetables you are going to buy as "bedding plants," divide your crops into cool weather, hot weather, and cross-season plants. A beautiful, excellent, and inspiring garden reference with this information can be found in *The Natural Food Garden* by Patrick Lima.

Cool-weather plants do best if planted in the spring so that you harvest them before the ungodly hot days of summer. As the thermometer goes up, most greens turn miserably bitter, radishes and kale crops bolt to seed, and kohlrabi and turnips become woody and tasteless. Peas and spinach regularly survive temperatures below freezing, cold weather causes parsnips, chard and kale to sweeten, while garlic needs nearly a year to mature and sails easily through winter.

Cross-season plants are often planted in spring, harvested from summer through fall, and do reasonably well throughout. Hot weather plants should only be planted after all danger of frost is past. They thrive on long summer days, need warm summer nights in order to ripen at all, and collapse at the first hint of cold.

How Much to Plant

With some idea of what to plant and when, get out a piece of paper and a pencil and decide what you are going to do with each vegetable. A partial list might look something like the following.

Sugar snap peas: Six pints frozen peas; eat the rest fresh.

Parsley: One pint dried parsley for me, one pint for Mom.

Carrots: Six pints frozen carrots; some for salads and steaming.

Tomatoes: Twelve quarts of juice; six pints of salsa; some fresh.

Sweet Corn: Ten quarts frozen corn; two dozen for family reunion; eat the rest fresh.

When your garden begins to produce and you are drowning in vegetables, you won't be overwhelmed or find yourself trying to decide what to do with all those zucchini or tomatoes. If you're going to can, freeze, or dry something, you'll have time to get yourself a canning/freezing book and look up the necessary equipment and processes so you're ready when the time comes. You'll also be much better able to evaluate how many of each vegetable you need to plant and whether you can actually take care of that size garden. *The Ball Blue Book Guide to Home Canning and Freezing* has a garden planning guide that estimates how many pounds of produce you can expect to average from a hundred-foot row of a given vegetable. For example, a hundred-foot row of winter squash will yield four hundred pounds of squash. The average squash weighs three to four pounds. Therefore, a hundred-foot row of squash will produce between one hundred and one hundred thirty squash. If you want to have squash at least once a week from November through the end of April, you need twenty-six weeks x one meal = approximately twenty-six squash. Thus you know that a hundred-foot row is way too much. You will have all you need with a twenty-five-foot row and this will help you gauge how much land area you need to prepare in order to accommodate the vegetables you want to enjoy. You're not so likely to till up more soil than you need, and you're less likely to run out of room as well.

The Paper Garden

Once you have decided what and how much you're going to plant, do a rough layout of your garden on paper before committing seeds to soil. Keep to some kind of scale so you get a fair idea of how it will actually work out. Using a quarter inch to equal a foot on an ordinary piece of typing paper, you can lay out a garden roughly thirty-four by forty-four feet. Then start drawing your vegetables in rows on the paper. Seed packets and catalogs will tell you how far apart to plant the seeds, how far apart to plant the rows, and how deep the various seeds can go and still find their way to the sun before using up the stored food in the seed. If you plant things too close together you may end up with plants that cannot get enough nutrients to produce healthy vegetables. Plant them too far apart and you end up with too many weeds in all that open space.

If you have a Troy-type garden tiller, you may not want to bother with weed barriers or mulch and will want to be able to get down the rows when plants are at full size. Remember, a full-grown tomato plant is easily four feet tall and three feet in diameter—and that's if you make an effort to contain it in a tomato cage!

If you're using a hoe for most of your tilling and cultivating, you will be able to put things somewhat closer together, but be sure you save room to walk here and there or you won't be able to move through every section of the garden. This is essential if you want to keep your eye on what's happening and to pick your vegetables at their peak.

If your garden ends up being large, say fifty feet deep and a hundred feet wide, consider a lane every twenty-five feet that will allow you to move a wheelbarrow, garden cart, or wagon up and down the rows to haul compost, remove weeds, or carry tools and vegetables. If it is fifty feet wide and one hundred feet deep, don't plant hundred-foot rows. Break the rows at fifty feet, creating a lane that allows easy access across the rows. This, combined with one center lane running the entire length of the rows, will make weeding, tilling and fertilizing much less daunting. Also, if you want to train your pole beans, cucumbers, peas, squash, or tomatoes up, fencing comes in fifty to one hundred-foot rolls, which means you are all set up with the right dimensions.

If you plan to harvest cool weather goodies in spring, hot weather veggies in summer, and go on to plant more cool weather bounty in fall, you might want to plant your garden in seasonal sections. Maybe you want to have a nice balance of vegetables, herbs and small fruits, dividing the garden into sections that will accommodate these three kinds of produce. Maybe you want a perennial section and an annual section. Perhaps you just want to interplant everything and see what happens. Whatever you decide, explore the possibilities on paper first, think about the maintenance each arrangement will require, and then follow your heart.

Location

An Unused Field

Once you've got a picture of the size and what you'd like to have in your garden, go outside, walk your land or your yard, and survey the possible locations for your garden patch.

Perfectly flat land is not the perfect choice. If you have a bit of acreage, choose an area with a slight slope. Water will not sit on it, and if it slopes to the south, the effect is sort of like the land "raising its face to the Sun." Plants love this, their roots will stay warm, and they will flourish. If your chosen location is currently a field of wild grasses, keep reading until you get to the section on back yards and grasses.

If the location you decide on is now a weed field, turn the soil over or till it "as early as the soil can be worked." Understanding the meaning of this phrase is fairly important. In autumn the earth and her soils begin to shrink and become quite compact. Over the winter it is a tight, wet, heavy, sometimes frozen mass. When spring comes, the earth expands, and the soil begins to loosen and dry out a bit. Over the summer, healthy soil lofts itself into a loose, moist assembly of crumbs. The soil is ready to be worked when it passes the following test. Reach down and scoop up a handful of soil, then close your hand and squeeze the dirt with medium pressure. First, it should definitely not be so wet that it oozes water through your fingers. Second, when you release your fingers and open your hand wide, the dirt should not be so dry that it tends to fall apart like sand. Soil that is ready for tilling or turning will be just moist enough to sort of hang together in the palm of your hand, but dry enough to separate into several "chunks" of compressed soil with small crumbs falling away here and there. If you till the soil when it is too dry, you will suffer a small dust storm and a lot of your good topsoil will blow away in the wind. If you till the soil when it is too wet, you end up interfering with the lofting process and your soil will not have a good structure of loose, moist crumbs. Instead it will be full of hard chunks whose edges seem to glaze like pottery. Working in this stuff is about as comfortable as working in broken glass.

The Back or Front Yard

If the gardening space you have available is a small, flat yard with wall-to-wall grass and a few shade trees, there are different things to consider. You could put the garden behind a garage or shed, but if you do you won't be able to enjoy just looking at it—which is a considerable pleasure. Also, out of sight is out of mind, and you will not be nearly as likely to keep up with it if you have to go out of your way or into some isolated corner to see what's happening with your plants.

You will want to put your garden where it gets at least six hours of direct Sun a day during the spring and summer months. If this means you have to put it where grass or sod are presently flourishing, there are several choices to make.

One, you can dig out the grass or sod and then turn the remaining soil under with a shovel or some kind of tiller, removing as many roots as possible. Twice more, at three-to-four week intervals, repeat this turning or tilling and you will then be ready to plant this year's vegetables.

If digging out the sod seems like too much work for you, and if you are the patient, "plan ahead" type, you can simply turn the sod under, breaking it up as much as possible with your shovel or tiller. Repeat this turning or tilling at least two more times, at one-month intervals, pulling out as many roots as possible and leaving the grass to compost itself. Depending on when you begin, this method may mean you have to wait until next year to plant any vegetables.

If you think you can't wait and you go ahead and plant seeds or seedlings among the remains of sod that's been freshly tilled, it's likely you will have one of your first serious gardening lessons—that of "preparation of the seed bed." The grass will re-root itself and come up in spotty clumps, seeming to prefer exactly the same places where leaf lettuce is putting out its first pale green leaves, where tomato and green pepper seedlings are clinging bravely to the soil, and microscopic carrots can't even be seen. Worse, when you pull on an innocent piece of dried-looking root that was once part of a large clump of grass, you discover to your horror that it still is part of a large clump of grass that just happened to be upside down at the moment. You end up with a clod of dirt ten inches wide, dangling at the end of that dried-looking root. Embedded in the clod are two of your pepper plants or a good-sized section of your carrot row.

Let's say you decide to leave the returning grass alone until all your seeds are up and a little stronger, more deeply rooted. This is usually worse. By then the grass has a terrific head start and is impossible to get under control. It ends up choking two-thirds of the garden, maybe even all of it, and you give up in despair and disillusionment. Rather than think "It can't be done" or "Good God, this is too much work," simply realize that it would have been best to have waited for another tilling or two. My rule of thumb for gardening in grass fields is that tilling for a year before planting is not too much, and a cover crop of dwarf white clover may be necessary during that time to compete with grass.

If there is just no decent area of your yard that is suitable for turning into a vegetable garden, you still have a couple more options. If you already have flower beds around your house, try interspersing some vegetables in with the flowers. Don't plant more than, say, 30 percent to 40 percent of your flower beds into vegetables. Otherwise, when the vegetables are done for the year, your flower garden will look devastated. As a last resort, if you're really determined to have a garden, look into a "community garden," commonly called a CSA—for community supported agriculture. They are popping up in many places and serve to bring people, plants and good food together in wonderful ways.

Compost?

Once you choose your location, examine the soil. If you think you need to add something to the soil, your best bet is going to be compost, but be aware! If you're going to the local franchised garden or hardware center to buy compost, read the fine print. I have found some compost for sale that was marked "sterilized." Horrors! The reason for putting compost on in the first place is to replace the micro-organisms that live in the soil, that eat and digest things like old leaves and garbage, that excrete their wastes into that soil, and that end up creating humus, which becomes humic acid. The humic acid helps the plant dissolve minerals that are present in the soil, and these minerals are essential to a plant's ability to build a nourishing strawberry or cauliflower. The absence of these minerals in most grocery store food is the reason it's so tasteless and rots so quickly.

If you're putting your garden in a location that has never been used to grow vegetables before, chances are you can get away without any soil amendments the first year, unless your soil is very sandy or nearly all clay. In either of these cases, compost becomes a necessity, both to improve the manageability of the soil and to feed your plants.

One last word about deciding on a location and preparing the soil: Don't wait until the weather has warmed up too much before you get out there to turn over the soil and dig out the sod, or you will find yourself dripping with sweat and wanting to take off clothing that is needed for protection from cuts, bumps, and Sun. In the South you can probably start working the soil in February; in the North and Midwest it is best to have the preparation done by mid-April.

If you have been toying with the idea of creating a vegetable garden but aren't really sure if, or where, or how to begin, be aware that this same aura of uncertainty will probably be present at the start of every garden year for the rest of your gardening life. Even with forty years of actual hands-on experience, every time I buy seeds for some new and unusual vegetable or flower I still feel that same sense of vague anxiety. "What if it doesn't grow? What if I ruin the seeds? How will I tell the seedlings from the weeds?"

These questions and other deep uncertainties are an important and necessary part of the magic that surrounds gardening. Planting a garden is a ritual of trust placed in a seed. First you put the seed in the ground, then you water it. Performing this simple ritual is the magic that results in the wonder of incredibly delicious food that grows at your feet and your fingertips. There, waiting for you to indulge yourself, are an array of vegetables to feed you for weeks, and when you have to go back to grocery store food, you can't help wondering how you ate such dry, rubbery, tasteless stuff all your life and never noticed how awful it was.

Water & the Moon

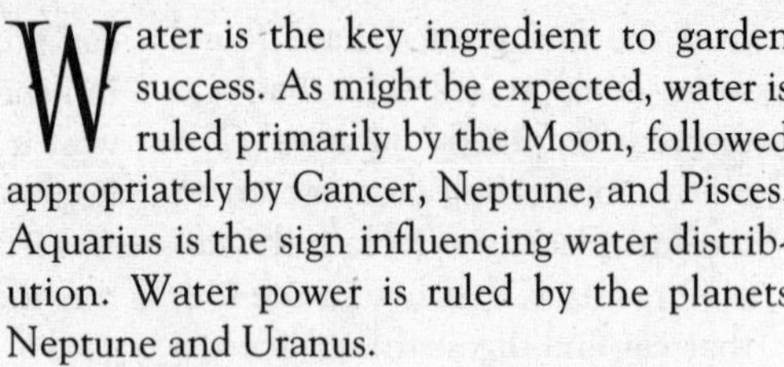

Water is the key ingredient to garden success. As might be expected, water is ruled primarily by the Moon, followed appropriately by Cancer, Neptune, and Pisces. Aquarius is the sign influencing water distribution. Water power is ruled by the planets Neptune and Uranus.

Extending the Garden Season

When that hot summer sun starts bearing down we may begin to feel as wilted as our gardens—but if we want to keep at least a portion of our gardens producing, we must take action. For many years I have practiced rotation, using a different part of the garden each year to plant my "hot weather" vegetables in adjacent rows—tomatoes, peppers, eggplant, and okra are usually still producing long after the cool-weather veggies have been harvested.

While the warm-weather vegetables may be slowing down a bit during July and August, they are still worth saving. Indeed, with care and ample moisture, okra plants will often produce at their best up until late fall in southern states. To get them to do this it is important to keep the seed pods picked, and never let them get dry and hard. Plants, picked regularly, will keep going longer because it is plant nature to keep trying to produce seed and reproduce themselves.

Eggplants and peppers, too, seem to take a new lease on life in the fall, and often produce heavily. You must keep them alive during the hot summer with ample water.

How to Water

By Louise Riotte

Of course, we practicing Moon signers know that for best results water should be given in a water sign: Cancer, Scorpio, or Pisces. For those who must garden and irrigate on weekends, it is good to know that Libra and Taurus may also be used. Always remember that a deep, thorough watering is better than several "sprinkles."

The main factors affecting plant growth are the soil, water, and Sun. The gardener can do little about the latter except to provide for full exposure or shade as needed. Even when it comes to rain at the right time, we gardeners are almost as much "at the mercy of the weather" as our grandparents. Soil and water conditions can be greatly improved, however.

Water is ruled primarily by the Moon, followed appropriately by Cancer, Neptune, and Pisces

No question about it, rain water is best. It is often full of vitamins and minerals. Even lightning can act as a fertilizer. If rain does not arrive when it is most needed, there are a number of ways to overcome this handicap. Again, we must remember that all growth-inducing factors must be at the highest levels for maximum yields, and water is one of the most important. There is another factor: we can control the time of watering—whether morning or evening is best in our particular area—and our astrological knowledge aids us also. We know that it is best to water under the moist signs of Cancer, Scorpio, and Pisces, or Taurus and Libra if better suited to our gardening time. The Gardening Dates section in the *Moon Sign Book* makes it easy for us to know the right time and date to irrigate.

Sprinklers

In early spring, when I have just seeded my garden, before the plants emerge and for a period afterward while they are still small, I prefer overhead watering.

This seems to suit the cool-season crops very well. For this purpose, I use an oscillating-type sprinkler attached to my garden hose, being sure to use a large diameter hose, for this determines the number of gallons that will be put out in an hour.

With overhead watering you need only to place your rainmaker where it can cover the vegetables, and the gentle falling drops will wet the soil slowly and thoroughly, without washing the seeds from the rows where they have been planted. I try to water early in the morning, usually before 9:00 am, because later the wind comes up and much water is lost through evaporation before it reaches the ground. For those who work, it is convenient to use a timer. If I am leaving the house I set the timer for an hour, after which it automatically cuts off.

If you like using overhead watering, there is a useful tip that you may find helpful if your garden area is small. Set your oscillating sprinkler where you intend to make your garden—before you plow and plant—and turn it on and watch to see just how large an area it will wet down; then plan to make your garden exactly that size. Set markers and proceed to plow and plant as usual. For the small-space gardener this will save moving the sprinkler several times.

Surface Watering

As the season advances, however, I consider overhead watering wasteful and inefficient in my own hot, dry, windy climate. Too much water is lost by evaporation caused by Sun and wind, and does not even reach the ground. This is the time to turn to surface watering. With shallow trenches between your garden rows, well filled with mulch such as hay, straw, leaves, or grass clippings, etc., you can do a pretty good job of watering just by laying the hose in alternate rows, reversing the procedure a week or so later.

By planting my summer vegetables adjacent to each other I can water the plants as a group, often digging shallow trenches between the rows in which to lay the hose or the soil soaker, so just as little water as possible is lost by evaporation. Grass clippings placed in the trench will rise to the top and sink back down again, providing a mulch to hold the moisture longer.

Mulching the plants with leaves or grass clippings will not only help to prevent evaporation, but will also result in a more even temperature for the plant, giving it a better growth environment. Put grass clippings on a thin layer at a time.

Mulch tomatoes when they start blooming. They need the Sun on their roots until that time.

Tomatoes that have water evenly and at regular intervals are less apt to crack or get "blossom end rot." Cracking occurs when plants are allowed to dry out for too long and are then given too much water at one time.

If you cannot dig trenches, so-called "soaker" hoses will help you do the job. Since these are relatively inexpensive, I sometimes use several, covering them with mulch and just leaving them in the row, attaching the service hose as needed. This method of watering gets moisture to the roots of your plants where it will do the most good, and the mulch prevents rapid evaporation.

Drip Irrigation

As water supplies become increasingly expensive and even limited for many, new systems are appearing on the market to give the root systems—and only the root systems—the water they need for growth. The principle of making less water go further is something we all may have to do in the near future.

Home gardeners may be a little late in getting in on this technique (which commercial gardeners have been using for a long time), but they are rapidly catching up, as a variety of these systems are available.

Certainly such systems are not foolproof, but equipment manufacturers are constantly testing and modifying parts as experience shows which systems are the most practical, and some very definite advances have been made.

The basic idea of drip irrigation (which is said to have originated in Israel, where water and rainfall is very scarce and where it has proven to be of great value) is to water every day but not too much, replacing only the moisture that the plant uses each day. By confining the moistened area to the plant's root zone, not only is there a dramatic saving of water, but also weed growth is discouraged, and nutrients are not so readily depleted from the soil. Weeds, when they appear, are best kept under control if pulled in the dry signs of Aries, Leo, and Sagittarius during the third and fourth quarters.

There is still another advantage: since the area is not wet to the point of saturation, the ground temperature is increased, further stimulating plant growth. This is less important as a factor in my own area than it is in localities of limited sunshine. In summers of extreme heat and drought, we should endeavor to keep the soil temperature even by increased use of mulch.

When Should You Water?

As mentioned previously, it is always best to water under the moist signs of Cancer, Scorpio, and Pisces, or the secondary signs of

Taurus and Libra, for plants take up water best and derive the most benefit from the water under these signs. There is also the question of the best time of day, however. The answer to this may depend on the geographical area where you live. Just about all the books I have ever read that gave rules for watering say it should be done so plants will dry off before nightfall. This holds true for many areas and will help to prevent mildew.

I don't think any of the authors of those books lived in my own hot, dry climate, however. In the intense heat and often drought of our southern Oklahoma summers, I often water twice a day. Early morning watering helps my plants go through the blistering heat of hundred-degree (and often hotter) temperatures, giving them much-needed moisture to enable them to resist wilting from the Sun and wind. It has been my practice for many years to water late in the evening, and even after dark in the heat of summer. For one thing, the practice is easier on me, for another, late in the afternoon the Sun's heat is less intense and less evaporation takes place. Strong, hardy plants like corn greatly benefit from watering after nightfall.

However, if you do decide to water late in the evening or at night, you should be careful not to wet the foliage of your plants, for therein lies the danger as the moisture, clinging to the leaves, may cause mildew.

How Long Should You Water?

This is something we generally have to "play by ear." Working your soil, you will soon learn what type you have and will water according to its composition, whether it is clay, light, and sandy, or that gardener's dream, well drained, rich, sandy loam.

Probably the very best way to solve the problem of water management is to work toward preparing a garden soil that can't be overwatered. This is best done by adding plenty of organic material. Plant roots need both moisture and air to grow well. That is, they need a growing medium that air can move through, bringing oxygen for their growth and removing the carbon dioxide they respire.

Where Will You Obtain Water?

For most of us there is a simple, but possibly expensive answer—you will simply obtain your water from the supply system of the city where you live.

However, even for a city lot there is the possibility of drilling a water well, and a good supply of water usable for irrigation (though possibly not for drinking) may often be obtained in this way. My husband and I, when we were young, agile, and full of energy, actually dug our first water well ourselves, casing it as we went along. We struck a good supply of water for irrigating our garden at twenty-two feet. The digging, however, was not without adventure. This being Oklahoma, when we were down about twenty feet we struck a gas pocket—it scared us so much we almost knocked each other down getting up the ladder. Nothing happened and we went on down until water became evident. With care we had sufficient water all during the hot, dry summer, when water rationing was in effect.

Another possibility for a small acreage is to build a "sky pond," impounding water simply by rainfall, if there is no nearby spring to feed the pond. A small pond, well kept, also may add to the beauty of your home site. It can also provide a place for ducks to swim, and if large enough you may wish to stock it with fish.

A further advantage to having a pond nearby is its cooling qualities in summer, and it will also make your home warmer in winter.

The Twilight Farmers

Beginning a Worm Farm

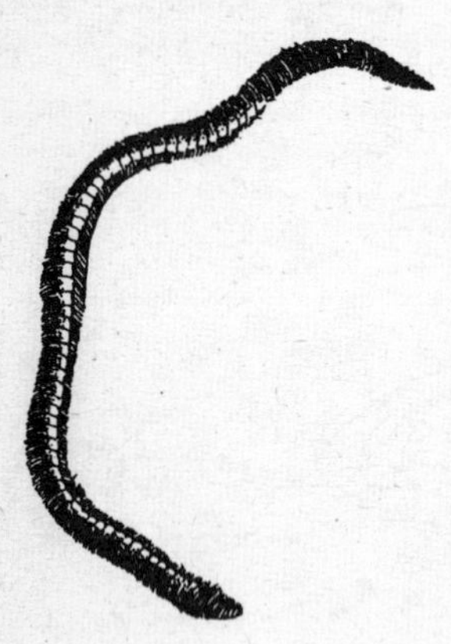

By Carly Wall

When the Moon rises over the horizon, it is a signal that the creatures of the night can take over the landscape. There are many night creatures that live by lunar light, but there is one that lives a low-profile life—the nightcrawler. Night is the best time for the worms to appear. After all, they make a tasty treat for birds, moles, shrews, and other animals because they are a rich source of protein. Usually they come up to the surface to find food (leaves and other plant material), mate, or to seek other places to live. When dawn rises they disappear back into the ground. Gardeners have a special place in their hearts for worms because these slimy creatures hold the living world in their "hands." It is because of them that plants can grow, that the soil is "alive."

They aren't much to look at, but nightcrawlers and other worms may just be the most important creatures of the night in terms of a healthy, functioning mother earth. The worms serve as underground farmers. Their main job is tunneling underground like plows, creating spaces for air and water to reach the roots of plants. They also loosen the soil and mix the layers, bringing up important soil and minerals from below for plants and animals to use in the never-ending cycle of life.

One acre of good land can have from fifty thousand to a million worms living within the top eighteen inches of soil. The worms living within one acre of ground will turn over forty tons of soil a year.

Worms are extremely sensitive to weedkillers and poisons. Spraying a garden or yard will destroy these sensitive but hard working gardeners. When the worms are destroyed, that means the soil has become dead. A dead soil is very hard to work with. It becomes hard and compacted. Vital minerals are soon leached out, and plants cannot grow without them. That is why organic farmers in the know understand that by enriching their gardens with mulches, shredded leaves, and composted manure, they are giving worms a food source and inviting them to live in their gardens, thereby giving themselves an extra boost in crop yields. The worms constantly return nutrients to the soil; what they eat is digested and expelled as castings. These castings are rich in minerals, and as the worms plow the ground, they put the minerals back into the soil in a form the plants can easily absorb during their growing season.

Worms may just be the most important creatures of the night in terms of a healthy, functioning mother earth

Vermicomposting: The Wave of Future Gardening

The exciting thing is that small-time organic gardeners are discovering that not only can they use worms to help increase garden yields—they can also use them to recycle their kitchen wastes, and, as an added bonus, they get rich soil for potting houseplants or adding to flowerbeds, as well as adding to the garden. Worm farming is the answer.

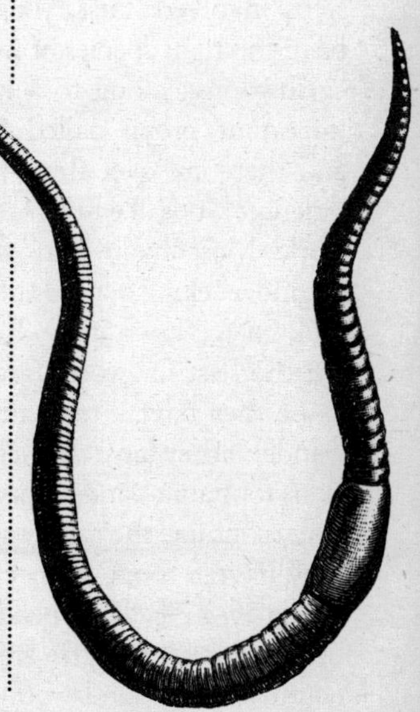

Not all of us garden in a big way. Most of us live in the 'burbs, in the city with small lots, or in apartments. Not to worry, you too can benefit from worm farming. Many people are finding that they can grow part of their own food source wherever they live. You can grow magnificent tomatoes on a patio, a gorgeous herb garden in a windowsill planter, and with the french intensive method of growing, a small plot tucked into a corner lot can yield surprising numbers of beans. It's fun to see how creative you can be, and worms help out tremendously, for now you can get rid of your household waste and turn it into free potting soil! Talk about recycling and becoming more independent—within less than six weeks your old lettuce salad and newspapers will turn into rich, black compost.

Getting started is the hardest part. You have to have a proper container, get the right type of worm (which can be ordered through mail order), and learn the basics of worm care. All this is easily accomplished by reading books on composting and organic gardening. There's one book out there you may want to purchase or check out at the library called *Worms Eat My Garbage*, by Mary Appelhof. She tells you how easy worm maintenance can be.

Here's a brief outline of the steps involved. First, you have to have the right species of worm. All earthworms belong to a large and important group called annelids, and there are over three thousand different kinds of earthworms in the world. Most live in burrows underground, peeking out only at night to look for food or a mate. Redworms are the best for worm farming because they have a tendency not to wander if they have the right conditions for habitat and plenty of food. They consume the most waste when they have a room temperature between 55–77°F. Their bedding must be kept moist. In warm areas of the country, year-round worm farming can be done outside in a garage, on a patio, or in an outside shallow shaded pit. In the northern areas, or where temperatures fall low, the worm container can be kept inside anywhere: basement, utility room, or even under the kitchen sink. Because the worms act quickly to turn the waste to soil, there isn't a problem with odors.

Worm bins or holders should be eight to twelve inches deep with a loose top so air can flow. They should have drainage holes, as well as two and three-quarter-inch legs with a drip pan, so that excess moisture can escape (you don't want the worms to drown—also this compost tea is a great treat for plants). You can make your own box or you can order a ready-made bin. Some garden supply places and mail-order companies sell the set-up all ready to go. One place to get the worms and bin is Nichols Garden Nursery, (541) 928-9280.

The best beddings are light and airy, but the bedding must be non-toxic, as the worms will eat it eventually. A mixture of shredded cardboard, newspaper with black print, and leaves makes a good bedding. Moisten this mixture down (not soggy, just wet). Add several handfuls of soil and a few tablespoons of powdered agricultural lime.

Now you are ready to add the worms. About a thousand should do. To feed them, you will need to make a small garbage pail with a lid to keep handy in the kitchen. There's a gallon-size plastic bucket that ice cream comes in. I recycled one of these and it is perfect, as it has a nice plastic lid and wire handle to make carrying easy. Every bit of vegetable waste goes in, as well as shredded newspaper, coffee grounds, and the filter too. Here's a partial list of things you can put in the bin, but anything that decomposes can be added: potato peelings, citrus rinds, old leftovers, moldy cheese, tea bags, egg shells, apple cores, old lettuce leaves, and vegetable bits and ends made when making salads. Meat products can be added to outdoor bins, but you may want to forego it indoors as meat takes a while to decompose and can cause odors.

Don't put cat litter box stuff in (dangerous organisms can be transmitted from soil to humans by handling this way). Bones can only be added if they are ground up (the white bones are irritating to pick out of the soil as they take a long time to decompose), and at all costs avoid adding anything that will not decompose, such as plastic, bottle caps, rubber bands, tin foil, or glass.

When your bucket is half full or so, take it to your worm box, dig a hole, dump, and cover it up. Next time, dig a hole in the spot next to that and go around the box thusly. By the time you get back to the first spot, the waste will have magically disappeared.

As time goes on, you will see the bedding becoming darker and will spot individual worm casts. The bedding will vanish eventually. Now you have to renew your box by harvesting your "soil" compost, and returning the worms to the box with fresh bedding. There are simple methods to doing this. One method suggests adding fresh bedding on top and upending the bin into a larger box. The fresh bedding is now on the bottom. Do this in a sunny area, and the worms will move down. Now the top "soil" compost can be removed into another container to be used later, and the worms and leftover bedding returned to the original bin. More bedding can be added and this wetted down to begin the cycle again. Excess worms can be released outdoors, given to friends, or even sold as fishing bait. You'll only have to renew the bin in this way every four months or so. Basically, that's about it.

You can see that this "lowly" creature of the night is ready to help you reduce the amount of trash you create and turn it into valuable compost to feed your garden and in the end, you and your family itself. By working with the cycles of nature, we can't go wrong.

Vegetables of the Southwest

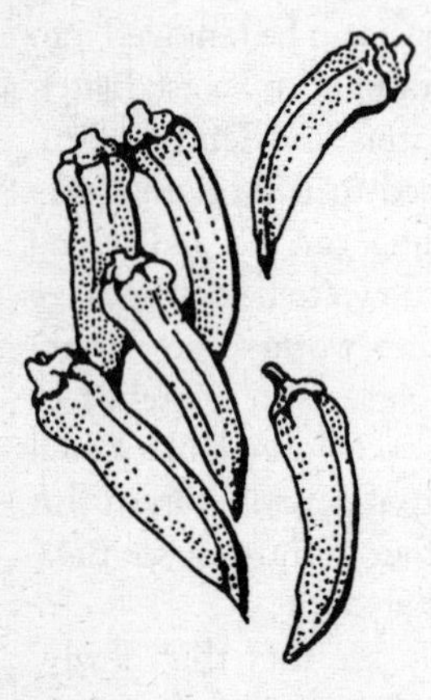

By Louise Riotte

In early days, Mexican fruits and vegetables were not widely known outside the Southwest. The areas that bordered on or were part of Mexico enjoyed many of Mexico's fresh fruits and vegetables. These areas are famous for their outdoor markets, filled with lush and plentiful produce such as avocados, tomatoes, chocolate, vanilla, and chiles. The Spaniards are credited with introducing new and unusual fruits into Mexico, such as peaches, cherries, apples, and plums, as well as nuts, figs, dates, and pomegranates.

Vanilla

One of our most widely used flavorings, vanilla, apparently originated in Mexico as a wild vine. Vanilla, according to *The World Book Encyclopedia*, is the name of a group of climbing orchids. The true vanilla, used to flavor chocolate, ice cream, pastry, and candy, comes from these plants.

The vanilla vine has been cultivated in Mexico for hundreds of years. Once almost exclusively a Mexican plant, it has been introduced into other tropical areas. Madagascar and the Comoro and Reunion Islands now produce over three-fourths of the world's supply. The beans are the part of the plant used. The cultivated plant lives for about ten years, producing its first crop at the end of three years. Vanilla is Sun-ruled.

Chocolate

Another of our favorite foods, chocolate, was more widely distributed in the early days than many of us realize. The early-day peoples of the Americas held fairs and traded fruits and vegetables along with other products. The American Indians liked chocolate just as we do now.

Cacao is an evergreen tree whose seeds or beans are used to make chocolate and cocoa. The cacao tree may grow up to twenty-five feet high. Its fruit is a melon-like pod that may be twelve inches long. The cacao seeds, embedded in the pod, are about the size of lima beans. They range in color from light brown to purple. The beans supply not only chocolate and cocoa, but also cocoa butter, used in candies and medicines.

We can better understand Mexican-American food if we first come to grips with the chile or, as it is often called, the chile-pepper

Jicama

While we may not be able to grow vanilla vines and cacao trees in our own gardens, there are lots of vegetables native to North, South, and Central America that we can grow. One of these is the jicama, described by Gurney's seed catalog as a "crisp, sweet snack, best peeled, sliced, and eaten raw, that has a water chestnut flavor. It does best in a warm, sunny spot and stores well if kept warm and dry." Among its other desirable qualities, it will keep for two weeks if refrigerated, and peeled jicama does not turn brown. The first year I grew jicama, I got a real surprise—nobody said anything about the beautiful clusters of purple, sweet pea-like flowers on the plants. I could not bring myself to cut them, but later found out that I should have, for the edible root will not produce well if the energy of the plant goes into the blossoms. So steel yourself and cut. Jicama is ruled by Saturn.

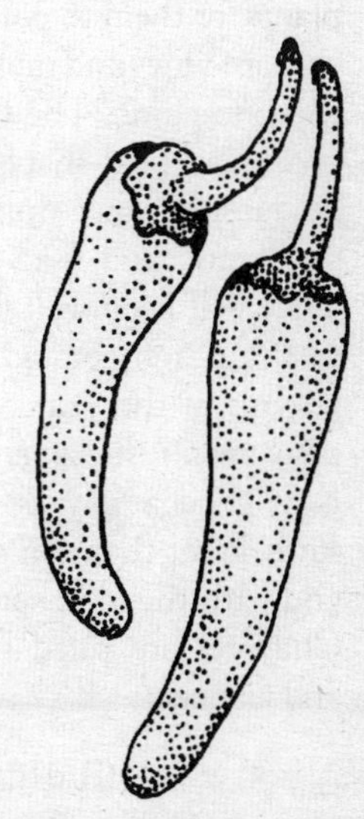

Tomatillo

If you are a salsa aficionado you will want to grow the tomatillo. Plants of the Southwest is one of the companies that sells tomatillo seeds. Direct sow the seeds one-fourth to one-half inch deep and thin the seedlings to stand about twelve to eighteen inches apart. Plant away from tomatoes. This interesting vegetable is called *tomate verde* in Mexico, and is an essential ingredient of salsa verde. It bears green, berry-like fruits enclosed in a papery husk, and is also called the husk tomato or ground cherry. Tomatillos are easy to grow and prolific, but give them full Sun. Tomatillos have a taste between a lemon and a tomato that is dynamite in stews. Plant them in Cancer, Scorpio, and Pisces. They are ruled by Jupiter, Neptune, and Mars.

Chayotes

I have also had good luck growing chayotes, which are delicious cooked or eaten raw in salads. Chayotes come in male and female plants, and you must have several plants for them to pollinate. Chayotes are vines and must have something to climb. The fruits are pale green and pear-shaped. They may be mashed and stuffed, or even sweetened and used as a dessert. They will keep well for about two weeks if refrigerated. At certain seasons of the year, you may find chayotes in the supermarket. This is as good a way as any to get a start. Plant them on a slant so the end with the vine sprout is above. Chayotes are ruled by the Moon and Cancer.

Nopales

Nopales (cactus pads) are also beginning to show up in the supermarkets. Flavorful and succulent, they are somewhat similar in taste to green beans. In her book *Cuisine of the Southwest*, Anne Lindsay Greer tells us that we should remove all "eyes" from the nopales before preparation, using a knife or a potato peeler. Nopales may be used in egg dishes, vegetable casseroles, or cold in salads. To prepare nopales, wash them, cut them in squares, and cook them in salted water. In selecting your nopales, choose unbruised cactus; smaller leaves are generally more tender. Nopales need refrigeration, and are ruled by Mars.

Beans

Probably no bean is more popular or widely used in Mexican and Native American cookery than the pinto bean. A very early, high yielder with excellent flavor, *Frijol en Seco*, a variety of bush bean, will tolerate both drought and poor soil.

There are many other delicious beans that are not so well known. Generally speaking, the dry beans usually grown in the Southwest require similar care to the pinto bean. Sow them when danger of frost has passed and the soil is warm. Plant them one to two inches deep and two to three inches apart in rows eighteen to twenty-four inches apart. Thin the plants to six inches apart. Cultivate frequently to control weeds until blossoms appear. Stop watering after the beans form. When the leaves drop and pods are dry, pull the plant by the roots. Beans thresh easily. If you like, you can put them in cloth bags and invite the neighbor kids over to jump up and down on them! Dry bean varieties are also delicious string beans when picked young. Plant beans in the second quarter under Cancer, Scorpio, Pisces, Libra, and Taurus. If beans are to be grown for dry beans, plant under Leo.

The Anasazi bean, whose name in Navajo translates as "the ancient ones," is a baking bean with a sweet flavor and a meaty texture. This bean is one of the few cultivated crops grown by this ancient cliff-dwelling people (the Anasazi).

The appaloosa bean is a beautiful white bean with maroon and black mottling, like the rump of an Appaloosa. It sends off short runners requiring no staking.

The scarlet runner Aztec bean is not only a delicious black and red speckled bean, but a beautiful ornamental line as well with lovely red, pea-like blossoms. Young pods may be used as snap beans—if sliced French style, the beans are more tender. Beans may be dried on the plant for shell beans.

Chiles

The Aztec *dhilli* or the Spanish *chile* is known to have existed as early as 700 BCE. We can better understand Mexican-American food if we first come to grips with the chile or, as it is often called, the "chile-pepper." More chiles are consumed than any other seasoning in the world. All chiles have an element of unpredictability: climate, season, etc., affecting their degree of "hotness" or lack of it. Peppers are best grown in the second quarter under Scorpio or Sagittarius. Pepper plants are ruled by the Sun and Mars. It is not true that all chiles are hot. The hotness of each chile pepper depends on the climate in which it is grown. Chiles can be direct seeded after the last frost in long, warm-season areas. Sow a quarter inch deep, twelve to fourteen inches apart in the rows, in rows twenty-four to thirty inches apart.

The chile pepper we are probably most familiar with is the jalapeño. Plants of the Southwest seed company offers the jalapeño "M" chile, a three-inch dark green, almost black, chile with thick, meaty walls. They are large, dark, and hot, and good for pickling, or if you are brave, eating fresh.

The Anaheim chile is an eight-inch long tapering pepper, which can be used green for chiles rellenos and green chile sauce, or dry for red enchilada sauce. It is medium-hot and bears well.

Roasted chiles are a southwestern favorite. The object is to blister the skin of the chile, which lets you pull it away from the delectable fleshy part. Blister them over an open fire or the hot surface of a stove, or under a broiler. Rotate the chiles. To make them easier to peel after blistering, plunge them under cold water, steam in a damp towel, or put them in the freezer and peel later.

If your green chile is to be used for stew or salsa, remove the stems, seeds, and veins. If you like your stew extra hot, leave the seeds and veins. For chiles relleños, keep the chile intact, stuff with cheese, dip in flour/egg batter and deep-fry.

Corn

Sweet corn as we know it today was unknown to the Native Americans, but they enjoyed a wide variety of dry corn, including Indian popping corn, which has beautiful miniature ears with yellow and red kernels.

The Native Americans used corn for food, and it also played an important part in their religious ceremonies. Squash and beans are good companions for corn. Corn should be planted in the first quarter under Cancer, Scorpio, or Pisces for best results. Corn is ruled by the Sun, Mercury, Taurus, and Uranus.

Blue corn, used by the Alamo-Navajo, has large, full ears of dark blue-purple to almost black. Papago corn has small, slender cream-colored ears and is very drought-tolerant, and posole corn has large, plump ears on vigorous drought-tolerant plants. It is the traditional variety of dry dent corn used for making *posole*, one of the finest dishes of southwest cuisine. It is the hominy of the southwest.

To make posole, dissolve ½ cup of slaked lime in two quarts of water. Add 1 quart of dry, white posole kernels and boil thirty minutes or until hulls loosen. Let the mixture stand for thirty minutes, then wash the posole well in cold water, rubbing the kernels until the dark tips are removed. Rinse again until the water is clear. This prepared posole is now ready for your recipes. With another three hours of cooking, it is an excellent addition to soups and stews, especially in combination with pork and chile.

Rainbow corn is very popular, and you often find it in the supermarkets around Thanksgiving. You can grow your own. The full-sized ears of this decorative dry corn have every possible color combination. Pull the husks back when they are still green and braid, knot, or tie the husks together for corn "braids." Use as a table centerpiece or a wall decoration.

Squash

Most of the varieties of squash used by the Indians were winter squashes with good keeping qualities. Green stripe Hopi squash is dark green, almost black, with golden flecks. It averages fifteen pounds and more, with a thick, straight neck. It has light yellow flesh, and is very smooth, thick, and solid, with a sweet, nutty taste.

Santo Domingo squash is large and dark green, reaching about twelve pounds. It is drought-tolerant, sweet with pale yellow flesh. To store, keep in a cool, dry place. When cutting squash for storage leave several inches of stem. This squash, when picked young, can be eaten like a summer squash.

The Tarahumara squash can be traced back to the Tarahumara Indians in Mexico. It may be eaten young like zucchini, or left on the vine until the rind is hard and warty for winter squash. The flesh is mild and sweet, good steamed or for pies and baking.

Pine Nuts

Pine nuts, variously known as piñon or pignolas, are the seeds of large pine cones from trees grown throughout Arizona and New Mexico. I have bought them in the shops there. They are ruled by Saturn, Capricorn, and Mars.

Pumpkin Seeds

Pumpkin seeds, available shelled, either unsalted or lightly salted, are a favorite snack. They are also used ground for sauces. They are ruled by the Moon and Cancer.

Garlic

Garlic, ruled by Mars and Aries, is widely used in Mexican dishes, but the Mexican garlic most often used has heads of bluish purple, and a sharper taste than white garlic. You may find these bulbs sometimes in the supermarket. You can separate the cloves and plant them.

Melons

The Native Americans also had melons. Spanish melon is dark green and wrinkled on the outside, sweet green-gold inside. The fruits average eight to twelve pounds each, with four to five fruits to a vine. It is very sweet, even when harvested as immature fruits. If kept cool and dry, it is an excellent keeper, up to four or five months.

The Hopi watermelon was and is highly prized. It is small and round (averaging three to four pounds), with exceptionally sweet, full-flavored, yellow flesh. Crushed watermelon seeds are used to grease the stone on which the traditional Indian bread, piki, is baked.

Avocado

The green, buttery avocado is now widely found in supermarkets, and is available year-round. It is used as a garnish, in salads, or as an accompaniment. It can be grown in California and parts of other southern states. The seeds will grow as an ornamental house plant in northern and eastern states, and grown like this, the leaves make an interesting seasoning. Avocado is ruled by the Sun.

Mexican Fruits

Limes, lemons, and oranges are very popular in Mexican drinks and cookery, being used in *sangria* and *ceviche*. Fresh fruit is essential. Ruled by Sun and Leo.

Pineapple, used in salads or as a fresh fruit for dessert, is a very popular fruit. Desserts in the Southwest, says Anne Lindsay Greer, "are more than just the finale of a meal; they serve a salutary purpose. The sweetness present in a dessert has a tempering and neutralizing effect on the tongue, disarming the aftermath of hot chiles and spicy foods. It goes without saying that Southwestern desserts are colorful and delicious."

Pecans

The pecan is a tree of the Southwest and Southern states. It will grow in the North and make a beautiful tree as well, but may not produce as often. Pecans are widely used in pralines and desserts—especially famous is pecan pie. Here is a recipe, originated by my sister-in-law, Emile von Helbach, as given in my book, *Sleeping with a Sunflower*. Pecans are ruled by the planet Venus.

Oklahoma Pecan Pie

- 1 (9") deep-dish pie shell, unbaked
- 3 eggs, slightly beaten
- ½ cup sugar
- 1 cup corn syrup (half light, half dark)
- 1 teaspoon vanilla
- ⅛ teaspoon salt
- 2 tablespoons melted butter or margarine
- 1 cup pecans, chopped (makes cutting easier)
- Whipped cream or vanilla ice cream for topping (optional)

Preheat oven to 375°F. Perforate pie shell. Mix all remaining ingredients except ice cream in order given, making sure pecans are well coated, as this gives them an attractive glossy appearance. Spoon pecan mixture into crust. Place pie on a cookie sheet in oven. Bake 40 minutes or until firm. Cool and cover with topping, if desired, just before serving. Makes one nine-inch pie.

Herbs and Greens

Fresh herbs often used in Southwest cooking include cilantro, which is the leaf of fresh coriander, sometimes called Chinese parsley. The taste complements hot chiles. It is best used fresh and is easily grown. Cilantro is preferred to parsley.

Epazote is a green that grows in my own garden and in our region is popularly known as "lamb's quarters." It is a welcome weed that springs up all over the place, and I mix it with spinach and other greens, or use it alone if nothing else is handy. It is an especially good seasoning for beans, and is supposed to reduce the bloating caused by beans.

Wild mint is commonly used for flavoring soups, sauces, and for garnish. The Parks and Burpee catalogs have several mints to choose from.

Tomato soups and tomato dishes are very popular in the Southwest, and basil is widely used to flavor them. It combines well with other fresh herbs such as oregano, and dried spices like cumin.

The favored dried herb in the Southwest is *azafran* (saffron), but the Mexican saffron is not the same as the very expensive true saffron. Either may be used to flavor rice.

Bibliography

Bills Rex. *The Rulership Book*. Richmond, VA: Macoy Publishing Company and Masonic Supply House, 1971.

Chalmers, Irene, and Milton Glaser. *Great American Food Almanac*. New York: Harper & Row, 1986.

Creasy, Rosalind. *Edible Landscaping*. *San Francisco*, CA: Sierra Club, 1982.

Firth, Grace. A *Natural Year*. New York: Simon & Schuster, 1972.

Greer, Anne Lindsay. *Cuisine of the American Southwest*. New York: Harper & Row, 1983.

Lehner, Ernst and Johannna. *Food and Medicinal Plants*. New York: Tudor Publishing Company, 1962.

Natural Magic. New York: Black Watch, 1974.

Riotte, Louise. *Sleeping with a Sunflower*. Pownal, VT: Storey Communications, Inc., 1995.

World Book Encyclopedia. Chicago, IL: Field Enterprises Educational Corp., 1963.

Moon Friendly Lawn Mowing

By Louise Riotte

That light spring rain that barely wet the soil in your garden produced a minor miracle on your lawn. Let's face it—another season of lawn mowing is about to begin, and you are the star of the show!

Don't you wish there was a way to slow down the growth of the grass, or at least lengthen the time between cuttings? Well, there is. You can retard the growth of your lawn (and well-maintained lawns are ruled by Venus) by taking care to mow it in the third or fourth quarter when the Moon is in the signs of Leo, Virgo, or Gemini.

On the other hand, if you take great pride in the appearance of your lawn, even enjoy mowing it and consider this healthful exercise, you may want to promote lush growth. In this case, mow it in the first or second quarter under Cancer, Scorpio, or Pisces. Grass in general is under the rulership of Venus and Virgo.

In *Time*, May 16, 1988, Joan Quigley emphasized the fact that we astrologers are eminently practical people by saying: "An astrologer just picks the best possible time to do something that someone has already planned to do... It is like being in the ocean; you should go with the waves, not against them."

Watering Lawns

In a mild climate, an inch of water a week is usually sufficient to keep the grass green and attractive. Cancer, Scorpio, and Pisces are considered the best signs for watering, but Libra or Taurus may also be used. It is time to water when you can see footprints on the lawn or when the surface soil appears dry.

To keep lawn watering to a minimum, sow seed (in Cancer, Scorpio, or Pisces) on a well-prepared garden loam, choosing a grass adapted to your area, and keep the lawn well fed and free of weeds. Arno and Irene Nehrling, writing in *Easy Gardening with Drought-Resistant Plants*, tell us that this will encourage deep, healthy roots—and a lawn is as good as its roots. Such a lawn will survive summer dryness and heat.

Another season of lawn mowing is about to begin, and you are the star of the show

Give your new lawn constant care until it achieves a heavy turf. Dry, windy, warm spring days can kill off young tender grass. If these conditions occur apply a light, misty spray daily using a mist nozzle.

It is best to maintain a mowing height of at least two inches during the hot months of July and August. Lawns cut short with shallow roots dry out quickly and suffer if moisture is not given by natural rainfall and the growth of crabgrass is encouraged. Taller cut, two-inch grass provides a mulch and shade to conserve the soil water.

It is better to omit frequent light sprinklings as they cause more harm than good—a good, deep soaking is required in hot weather. Anything that causes roots to grow deeper and thus draw on water reserves is helpful during dry periods.

Most homeowners are very concerned about the appearance of their lawns. Bluegrass, especially, will go partly dormant and turn brown in summer heat and drought. Don't be too upset, because cooler weather and fall moisture will stimulate new green growth.

It may be expensive, but you may find it worthwhile to install an underground irrigation system, equipped with risers containing pop-up sprinkler heads spaced to distribute water without wasteful overlap. There is also an innovation that involves underground low-pressure or micro-watering that keeps the soil moist from below. With this system, little or no water is lost through evaporation. These systems work best where the soil is not filled with rock, land is level, and the landscape design is open—without large trees, whose roots may fill the soil, or flowers and shrubs scattered over the lawn.

Easy-Care Grasses and Ground Covers

Yes, a well-maintained lawn does require care, but even so, a lawn may be something you just do not want to give up. Popular lawn grasses, such as Kentucky bluegrass, bent grass, ryegrass, and fescue need more water than any other type of grass, and require more water then any other type of garden plant.

However, John M. O'Keefe, in *Water-Conserving Gardens and Landscapes*, suggests that drought-tolerant grasses, which require less water, can be used.

These drought-tolerant turf grasses will lie dormant in the winter and are likely to turn brown. If you find this brownness unappealing and live in a mild climate, you can seed a lawn in the fall for a winter lawn with a cool season annual grass, which requires much less water. I seed my southern Oklahoma lawn with winter wheat, which can be mowed down in the spring. This will keep down dust and prevent erosion.

Drought-tolerant grasses include Bermuda grass (*Cynodon dactylon*), Centipede grass (*Fremochlos ophiuroides*), St. Augustine grass (*Stenotaphrum secundatum*), Zoysia Grass (*Zoysia spp*), Buffalo Grass (*Buchloe dactyloides*), Blue Gramma (*Boutelons gracilia*), Smooth Brome (*Bromus inermus*), and Tall Fescue (*Festuca arundinaces*).

Drought-tolerant ornamental grasses also have possibilities as ground cover plants, and have some advantages over turf plants. They have lower water demands, prevent erosion, and weeds are reduced by denying them light. These grasses also cool the garden and evaporation of water from the soil is lessened. The landscape is enriched by their texture, form, and color. Some of these species are apt to become quite tall and wide-spreading, so they are most useful if you have large garden spaces. These grasses include: Big Bluestem (*Andropogon gerardii*), which is seven feet high; Blue Fescue (*Festuca ovina var. glauca*), which is twelve inches high; Eulalia Grass (*Miscanthus sinensis*), which is slow-growing and four to ten feet high; Fountain Grass (*Pennisetum setaceum*), which grows in dense clumps four feet high; Giant Reed (*Arondo donax*), eight to twenty feet high; Pampas Grass (*Cortaderis selloana*), twenty feet high with beautiful plumes; and Plume Grass (*Erianthus ravennae*), which is a perennial in the South and an annual in the North. It resembles Pampas Grass, but grows only five to twelve feet tall. It is hardier than Pampas Grass, though.

Easy Care Chamomile and Wildflowers

Where you live and what type of grass you will grow has a lot to do with actually mowing the lawn. Certain grasses are better suited to certain areas than others. Average rainfall is important. In a dry, windy climate it's hard to keep a good-looking lawn going—possibly even any lawn going! Ruled by the Sun and Leo, chamomile is a good substitute for grass in a dry climate. Furhermore, it is delightfully fragrant when walked on. Growing only about a foot tall, it may even be used in certain areas where mowing is not necessary at all.

The true chamomile (*Anthemis nobilis*) is a perennial herbaceous plant, and has fine, fern-like leaves and small, white, daisy-like flowers. It has a history of many uses, including a rinse that gives golden highlights to hair. The flower heads were once in great demand for medicinal use in the treatment of fevers. In times past, if you had a headache, you drank a cup of chamomile tea much as we take an aspirin today.

You can easily raise chamomile from seeds sown in early spring in the first or second quarters. You can also propagate from established plants. Chamomile does well in a warm, well-drained, light soil in a sunny location. However, it has one drawback. It will not stand heavy traffic as grass will, so it is good to remember this and use it in areas where it will not be heavily walked on.

Let us suppose you have a steep, sunny bank where mowing is impractical. Wildflowers, ruled by Mercury, may be an attractive solution. Butterfly weed (*Asclepias tuberosa*) will thrive and spread in these conditions. So will black-eyed susan (*Rudbeckia hirta*), purple coneflower (*Echinacea purpurea*), blanket flower (*Gaillardia*), Queen Anne's lace (*Daucus carota*), oxeye daisy (*Chrysanthemum leucanthemum*), mistflower (*Eupatorium coelestinum*), Indian paintbrush (*Castilleja*), and goldenrod (*Solidago*). Transplants may be set out in the spring. Many catalogs now offer wildflower seeds.

The Lawn Machinery

That machine you mow the lawn with is ruled by Mercury, he of the winged heels, and if you do the pushing your machine is known as "hand-operated." Machinery in general is ruled first by Uranus and secondly by Mars. You can make the mowing job easier by a little forethought. In my book, *Astrological*

Gardening, I suggest that you lightly coat your power mower (or even the old battered hand one) with a no-stick cooking spray. Less grass will adhere to the mower and it will make for easier cutting.

Eventually there comes a day when you've had it with the old mower and you decide to treat yourself to a new one. Plan to buy machinery, tools, and other implements on days marked favorable for your Sun sign (consult pages 28–51 to find this), and on days when Mars and Uranus are well aspected also, if possible.

If you plan to order a new mower by mail, try to send your order as near to your Lunar Cycle high (see pages 28–51) as possible. Moon in Gemini, Virgo, Sagittarius, and Pisces are possibilities for getting a good buy and a machine free of troubles.

Finally, cool days approach and the lawn-mowing season begins to wind down. Yes, I know, you would like nothing better than pushing the mower into a dark corner and forgetting it. Don't! There's always next year and caring for your machine will pay off. The Lawn Institute recommends cleaning (Moon ruled), and if you heed their advice you'll be glad you did, for conditioning the mower now will give you a trouble-free machine in the spring.

First, they recommend disconnecting the spark-plug wire to prevent any mishaps. Remove and clean the plug and, if needed, replace it. Next clean the mower inside and out, washing and scraping away all the caked clippings. If your mower is a rotary type, remove the blade and have it sharpened. Sharpening is ruled by Mars. Reel models should have the bed knife and reel sharpened and adjusted. Check wheels to make sure they turn smoothly and that wheel bearings are in good condition. Make a muffler check, and if it is rusted through, replace it. Clean the air filter, or get a new one if it's worn out. Change the oil. Now, reassemble everything. If you number the pieces as you remove them the job will be easier. Fill the gas tank and run the engine a few minutes before storing it away. Put the machine away, hopefully in a dust-free area.

Now, you can heave a sigh of relief and go back and finish that book you were reading before lawn mowing interrupted you.

Are You Allergic to Pollen?

Pollen (ruled by Jupiter) is probably one of the worst problems encountered by the mower of lawns. Grass pollen can be reduced by cutting the grass. That is, some types of grass.

It is the bloom of the grass that releases the allergy-aggravating pollen. Most lawn grasses can't bloom if they are kept clipped. There are two exceptions—annual bluegrass and Bermuda grass. These will bloom even when cut. However, if you keep your grass trimmed (remembering to cut in the proper sign and quarter to slow down growth), and minimize watering, you can keep pollen levels low. It is also fortunate that a healthy lawn does not need pollination.

Unfortunately, for many southern areas, Bermuda grass is just about the only grass that will grow. So, for those who must mow Bermuda, another measure can be taken. A Saturn-ruled mask will help, and you will be less subject to so much discomfort from all the pollen and molds that mowing kicks up. Best to get the mouth-and-nose type used by home renovators to keep from breathing dust as they work. Do not get the painter's type, which may have larger openings. Hardware stores and home centers usually keep masks, which are inexpensive. Try on the mask for a tight fit. Don't be tempted to reuse it. The inside may be contaminated with pollen the instant you take it off.

Peak pollen times can be avoided by mowing after a rain, when pollen levels are low. In rural areas, pollen counts have been shown to peak around 3:00 pm when the temperature is high, the sun is shining, the wind is strong, and the humidity is low.

Personal care after mowing can also help. Shower, shampoo your hair (which acts like a giant filter holding lots of wind-blown pollen), and change your clothing.

Bibliography

Bills, Rex. *The Rulership Book*. Richmond, VA: Macoy Publishing & Masonic Supply Co., Inc., 1976.

Cornell, H. L., M.D. *Encyclopedia of Medical Astrology*. St. Paul: Llewellyn Publications, 1972.

Creasy, Rosalind. *Edible Landscaping*. San Francisco: Sierra Club Books, 1982.

Nehrling, Arno and Irene. *Easy Gardening with Drought-Resistant Plants*. New York: Dover Publications, Inc., 1988.

O'Keefe, John M. *Water-Conserving Gardens and Landscapes*. Pownal, VT: Storey Communications, Inc., 1992.

Quigley, Joan. *Time Magazine*. May 16, 1988.

Riotte, Louise. *Astrological Gardening*. Pownal, VT: Storey Communications, Inc., 1989.

Rose, Jeanne. *The Aromatherapy Book*. Berkeley, CA: North Atlantic Books, 1992.

The Magic in Locally Grown Foods

By Penny Kelly, N.D.

It was an odd piece of advice: "You should eat organic, locally grown fruits and vegetables." It popped up from time to time, always simply stated, never with any further explanation as to why. I couldn't remember who may have first said it or where I might have read it, but I clearly remember thinking, "Organic, sure. But why locally grown? What difference could it possibly make? Food is food." Many times while enjoying grapes from Chile in January, lettuce and tomatoes from California in March, or bananas from across the ocean all year round, I would tell myself these things were good for me, even necessary, because I needed fresh fruits and vegetables regularly. Then one day a couple of unusual factors came together to provide me with the understanding I had been looking for.

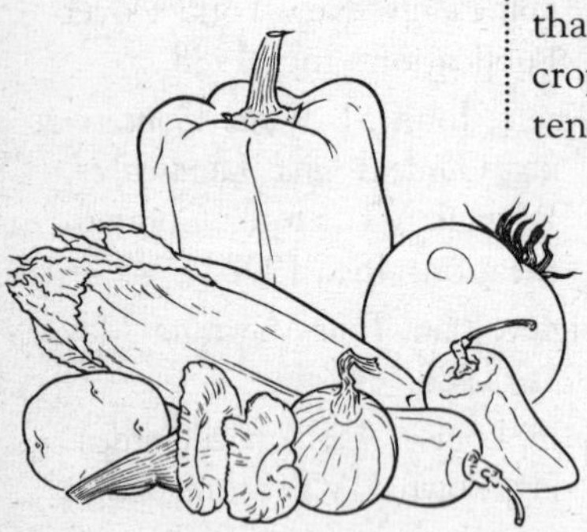

The first had to do with the soil. Having bought a fifty-seven-acre farm and become the owners of two small Concord grape vineyards, my husband and I were shocked to discover that in order to end up with a salable grape crop each year, we had to institute an "every-ten-days" spray program in the vineyards. As weather and soil conditions changed over the growing season, we cycled from herbicides to fungicides to pesticides back to herbicides then more fungicides and pesticides as the season continued. These sprays cost between four and six thousand dollars each year, which was almost half of the total income potential.

At first we sprayed without questioning. We wanted that income regardless of cost. Gradually we began reading about the soil, hoping to improve our chances of a good grape crop, and to our surprise we discovered that soil was supposed to be full of living organisms of all sorts. The most important organisms were actinomycetes, but also necessary were fungi like penicillium, and bacteria like staphylococcus and streptococcus.

About the same time that we began pursuing better soil and healthy vines for our grapes, the second factor came into play—I decided to take up the study of naturopathic healing. I had always been interested in health, and since I was experiencing a steadily increasing pain in all my joints, I was looking for ways to heal my whole self—mind and body—from the ugly deformities and overall degeneration of arthritis that I had witnessed in my mother's side of the family.

One day, about halfway through a course in nutritional theory and techniques of healing, I came across the work of Dr. Paavo Airola, Ph.D., who noted the existence of pacifarins in foods, describing them as an "antibiotic resistance factor that increased man's natural resistance to disease." In a flash I understood that this was the answer to the curious advice to eat organic, locally grown fruits and vegetables.

Having learned through my studies of healthy soil that streptococcus and staphylococcus bacteria live naturally in the soil, and that the penicillium fungus lives right there with it, and having learned in a high school science class—and many times since—that organisms will quickly mutate to protect themselves from other organisms, it was clear that in a healthy, well-balanced soil, the penicillium fungi had mutated to exactly neutralize, balance, and thus control the staph and strep present in their environment.

Since we humans also live in the same general environment of soil, air, and water, we are vulnerable to the same staph and strep

The advice to eat organic, locally grown foods isn't just one of those biased or superstitious tales that has no basis in reality

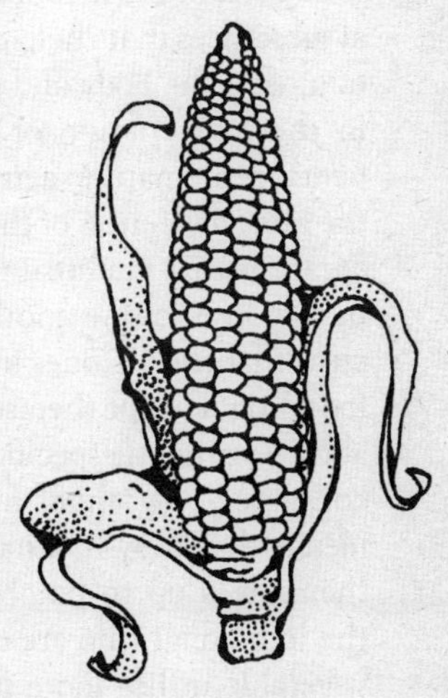

bacteria as our resident penicillium fungus. By eating food grown in our own local area, we are getting the benefit of the wisdom and experience of our local penicillium fungi, who not only develop their own resistance to the local staph and strep bacteria, but they confer that resistance to the food grown in that soil, and from there to the people who live in that area and eat that food.

Eating grapes from Chile in January confers added immunity to the unique bacteria living in South America, but it does not do much for the immunity needed to thrive in southwest Michigan.

Dr. Airola also describes another helpful factor, this time present in the pacifarins themselves, called auxones. Auxones are natural substances that "help produce vitamins in the body and play a part in the rejuvenation of cells, preventing premature aging." Using the same awareness of the ability of organisms to mutate intelligently in response to one another, it was clear that the auxones in a specific food would adapt themselves to be able to utilize the specific nutrients contained in that food. This meant that they had naturally set themselves up to be able to help the individual who ate the fruit or vegetable utilize more fully whatever nutrients were contained in that fruit or veggie, like a built-in expert assistant. Since each person has a fairly unique metabolism, by assisting the body to produce its own vitamins, auxones would help a person get the most out of whatever food was eaten, thus having a good supply of the very high quality building blocks that were necessary to continuously repair and rebuild the human body.

Of course, spraying the soil with pesticides, fungicides, herbicides, and other poisons kills most, if not all, of the organisms living in the soil, and thus there are no intelligent fungi left to counterbalance the staphylococcus or streptococcus bacteria. Worse, all but the most virulent strains of staph and strep are killed, leaving us open to amputation of limbs and even death if we happen to cut or scratch ourselves in a fall and pick up an infection by one of these virulent, fast-growing strains of staph or strep bacteria. To say such an infection is unlikely is naive. This is what happened to Jim Henson, the creator of the Muppets, and also to a close friend of my mother. Even my husband spent six days in a hospital hooked up to some of the most powerful antibiotics we have in an effort to stop an infection. This infection started as a tiny scratch on his knee at 2:00 in the afternoon and took him to the emergency room by 10:00 that evening with a leg swollen as big as an elephant.

The advice to eat organic, locally grown foods isn't just one of those biased or superstitious tales that has no basis in reality. We live enmeshed in a universe of soil and stars, subtle energies, and hidden truths. In exploring the many individual paths to health, it could pay handsomely to explore not only some of the old advice, but to make the commitment to finding and eating organic, locally grown produce. It isn't impossible to do, and in our family we don't even consider it difficult anymore—just different. There is no one thing that will guarantee absolute health for anyone, but the more you can bring into alignment some of the subtle factors that affect you in positive ways, the better off you'll be. Finding a local farmer or gardener willing to sell his or her organic produce and striking up a relationship may be the best medicine yet!

Reference

Airola, Dr. Paavo. *How to Get Well*. Sherwood, OR: Health Plus Publishers.

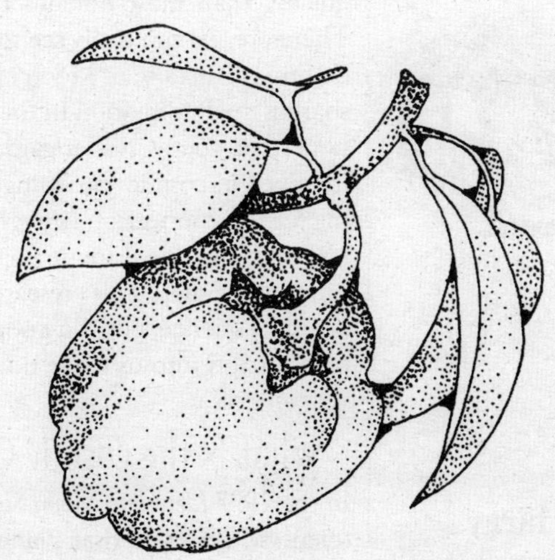

Gardening As Cosmic Research

By Harry MacCormack

As Sunbow Farm begins its twenty-fifth season, we've learned a lot about gardening with organic methods. At our farm in Oregon we learned that microorganisms, their life cycles, and their interactions with minerals and other nutrients must be given the best environment possible if soils are to be supportive homes for plants. That means that as growers we spend a lot of time and attention on soil building and health. We've learned to look for and pay attention to patterns of the life-producing process, surges in fertility, periodic repressive conditions, or any apparent cycle that allows us predictability.

Behind all the biology, chemistry, harvesting, and marketing of produce, there remains another level of drama that gives our gardening practices excitement. For over twenty years, we at Sunbow Farm have studied the cosmic mysteries as they are manifest in gardening practices and products. Plants go through life cycles more quickly than most humans or other animals. Therefore, we can easily see the effects of galactic, interplanetary, or Moon cycles on them. By sharing the information in the following pages I hope that you as reader/gardener will become involved in cosmic gardening research, searching for the connection between cosmic mysteries and gardening. I invite you to share your results with me. This research is unpopular practical science, but you know what? It is what puts passion into us as we do gardening chores year after year.

What Is the Cosmic Connection?

In the *1997 Llewellyn Moon Sign Book* I wrote of scientific evidence that planetary cycles influence Earth life processes. We live in field energies, some of which are electromagnetic. We and all lifeforms are resonant beings. We are transmitter/receivers. As Dr. Robert Becker shows in his research, "On earth, all entities formed within the ten-hertz discharge—and all of their descendants—would resonate at the same frequency or show extreme sensitivity to it, even after the original power source had been disconnected. The ten-hertz band would remain supremely important for most life forms, as indeed it has" (Becker, 1985).

Astrologers see lunar and planetary influences on specific vegetables, fruits, and grains

As we become familiar with the background magnetosphere pulsations of other planets and moons, and understand that they exist in relationship to each other, we have a basis for understanding that more intensively transmitted energies can influence less intense receivers. Data show that Jupiter, Mars, Saturn, Uranus, and Neptune all vibrate at higher, faster, and more violently interactive rates than Earth. Depending on their proximity to Earth, it is at least reasonable to believe that the other solar bodies cause changes in Earth life processes.

A scientist named Maurice Cotterell, in his book *Astrogenetics*, makes a strong case that solar cycles affect all Earth life, and that many of these effects correspond to the astrological zodiacal signs, which reflect a thirty-day cycle. Astrology is the "language" that we use to discuss the effects of the Sun, Moon, and planets on life on Earth.

Tropical vs. Sidereal Astrology

In *Llewellyn's 1993 Lunar Organic Gardener* I wrote that lunar organic garden managers recognize and use both astrological (tropical) and astronomic/constellational (sidereal) calendars to determine planting, harvest and other important timing for garden activities. There is a difference between these two types of calendars. The zodiac is an imaginary belt extending 8 degrees each side of the ecliptic, or apparent pathway of the Sun, in relationship to Earth. Within that pathway move Earth's Moon and the other planets, all in relation to our Sun. In astrology, influences of planets are calculated by the relationship of the location of the Sun, Moon, and planets, to the zodiacal signs, and to each other.

Tropical astrologers divide the zodiac using a system in which each sign consists of 30 degrees of arc. In other words, if the zodiac belt is a 360-degree circle-belt around the earth, each of the twelve signs corresponds to a section of 30 degrees. This is how the sky looked in 220 CE when the system was created. Because of natural planetary shifts, the placement of planets in the tropical system is more than 26 degrees different from where the planets are located in the sky today. Sidereal astrologers work with the celestial bodies where they are located now, in relation to the constellations, whereas tropical astrologers work with the system developed around 220 CE. So, a primary question arises about cosmic influence on earth life: Do either of these human systems of interpretation called astrology allow us to see and predict differences in growth processes? Remember this question. It is the basis for basic cosmic research in your own garden.

The Rulerships

Astrologers see lunar and planetary influences on specific vegetables, fruits, and grains. One most often used method is assigning rulerships to specific plants. When we say that a plant is "ruled" by a certain planet, we are saying that the energy of that planet has an affinity with and an effect on the plant. For an exhaustive list of these rulerships see Rex Bills' *The Rulership Book*, the classic in the field. In that book you learn that tomatoes are ruled by Jupiter, Neptune, and Mars. Beans are ruled by Venus, Taurus, and Scorpio. How these rulerships came to be is not often a topic of discussion, but the notion of rulerships guides astrological gardening books like *Astrological Gardening* by Louise Riotte, the calendar in this *Moon Sign Book*, the *Farmer's Almanac*, Jim Maynard's *Celestial Influences*, and *Stella Natura*, the Biodynamic Gardening calendar. The qualities associated with a planet and superimposed within a zodiacal sign, and the Moon's relationship with those combinations, set a cosmic condition for Earthly beings. I have argued that rulerships function much like images, sounds, and motions, giving humans a sense of meaning.

Rulerships are astrologically important because certain planets and their associated qualities are believed to have potent (or less potent) impacts on certain zodiacal signs. As the Moon moves through each of these signs during the month, it stimulates the energy of the signs and their ruling planets. The Moon always moves through these signs in the same order, and takes roughly twenty-eight days to do so, forming a cosmic pattern. What is implied is that there is a level of predictability to the effects of the Moon's movement on living things on Earth.

Maurice Cotterell's astrogenetic work and my research based on space probes sent by the U.S.A. and Russia to the planets indicates that electromagnetic influences from other planetary fields on Earth's field, hence earth life, are more than symbolic reality. As you do your own cosmic garden research, keep in mind the distinction between symbolic, projected, zodiacal/astrological realities and resonant, wave energy influences resulting from cosmic body interactions. The first is a meaningful system of culturally accepted characters, the second is measurable energy impacting cellular life.

The Elements

Another very important astrological claim is that four principal elements are reflected in the twelve zodiacal signs. These elements and their signs are: earth—Taurus, Virgo, and Capricorn; water—Cancer, Scorpio, and Pisces; air—Gemini, Libra, and Aquarius; and fire—Aries, Leo, and Sagittarius.

The element stimulated when the Moon moves into one of its signs informs us when to do certain gardening tasks. As an example, when the Moon moves into the sign of Cancer, Scorpio, or Pisces, it has moved into a water sign. Most planting is best done in the fertile signs associated with the elements earth and water. (There are exceptions.) Most retardation practices and harvesting for storage are done in fire signs. Maurice Cotterell finds that there are four different types of solar equatorial magnetic fields that reflect this sign/element relationship, which is so critical for astrological understanding. Cotterell suggests that four elements are indeed stimulated in recognizable cycles, but that it is solar radiation that is causing the effects we perceive as an astrological Moon/sign relationship.

Phases

Astrologers claim that Moon phases inform us of lunar push/pull forces. The phases of the Moon are first quarter, beginning at the New Moon; second quarter, beginning halfway between the New Moon and the Full Moon; third quarter, which begins at the Full Moon, and fourth quarter, which begins halfway between the Full Moon and the New Moon. During the first and second quarters, the Moon appears to be getting bigger in the sky, hence this period is called the waxing Moon. During the third and fourth quarters the Moon appears to be getting smaller, and so this period is called the waning Moon. The forces symbolized by the phases of the Moon are thought to stimulate above-ground growth and edible plant parts when the Moon is waxing, getting larger. Below-ground plant parts, rooting, etc. are stimulated as the Moon wanes, gets visibly smaller. However, the phase of the Moon isn't the only thing a gardener should take into account because these lunar motions happen in conjunction with lunar movement within the zodiacal signs. So, knowing which element is stimulated by a sign (the Moon in Cancer stimulates the element of water, for example) and knowing Mercury, which is the "ruler" of Carrots, is well aspected in the zodiac (check the Lunar Aspectarian, pages 28–51), you could break the "rules" and plant carrots against the Moon, instead of with the Moon. That is, you could plant a root crop (i.e. carrots), that is usually planted during the third quarter (the Moon's waning period), during the first or second quarter instead because the beneficial influence of Mercury will offset planting in the "wrong" phase. More importantly, you could feel good about your planting, particularly if all other gardening elements were optimum. So, a primary question for your research is, what role do Moon phases play in gardening?

Which System?

Rulerships, elements, and phases are a few basic astrological/astronomical concepts that are considered by researchers who find that lunar/zodiacal cycles indeed allow us predictability in the practice of gardening/farming. There exists much disagreement about these claims. The work of Dr. Clark Timmins has been noted in the *Moon Sign Book*. Dr. Timmins used the tropical system. Following the tropical astrological planting dates, interesting results occur (see page 226). Dr. Timmins got these results without reference to lunar phase, although temperature variation, soil and moisture were all controlled. Note two things: one, planting date is what Dr. Timmins is testing, and two, that we do not know the solar position relative to Earth—that is, the month in which these plantings took place. To replicate this study we would need to know these things. Presumably these experiments took place under lab/greenhouse conditions. The controls listed are a clue to that.

Sherry Wildfeuer's work, which follows researcher Maria Thun's incredible work based on sidereal astrology, seems to contradict Dr. Timmins'. Wildfeuer states that "during the planting period (when the arc of the Moon is descending) it is always possible to sow seed according to the part of the plant we want to encourage." This is also true for transplanting. Thun notes four aspects of the plant: root, leaf, flower, and fruit. Using rulership correspondences (to determine the best planting times based on which time will encourage growth in which part of the plant), the Biodynamic calendar *Stella Natura* suggests that planting times are based on other than lunar phase (Wildfeuer, 1997).

Meanwhile, replicated research conducted for eight years by Hartmut Speiss at the Biodynamic Research Center in Germany found no significant data to support the specific day/sign planting theories that are the basis of both tropical and sidereal calendars (Speiss, 1990). What he did find was response to synodic rhythm, which is planting and harvesting during optimum quarters of the Moon. Speiss found that maximum emergence of sprouts occurred as a result of seeding in the second quarter before the Full Moon, or in the third quarter. He saw relationships between crude protein levels in rye and the synodic Moon cycle. The quality and size of radish root also responded to lunar planting date. In this case the researcher found significant evidence for "planting by the Moon." Astrological and planetary influences were considered non-significant. Again, it is interesting to note that the Sun's radiation has a "monthly" fluctuation of twenty-eight Earth days. According to Cotterell's calculations, molecules within a living cell exposed to ionizing radiations are subject to chemical change, and such changes occur very quickly in the genetic material DNA after energy absorption. Could this be why all gardening research looking at astrological/cosmological impacts focuses on planting times? Is it in the delicate germination period that the Sun cycles mirror the Moon/sign cycle? Are cellular/molecular growth properties set at whatever time a seed actually germinates, usually some period after planting? Is this why both tropical and sidereal calendars have supporters in labs and out in the field?

Be Your Own Researcher

Our years of astrological/lunar plantings at Sunbow Farm have shown us that both tropical and sidereal calendars can aid us in timing our sowing, caretaking, harvesting, and marketing chores. We keep records on both our tropical and sidereal calendars. What we do is look for what we call "hot spots," periods of apparently prime fertility. We first ask, where is the Sun in relation to Earth? Are the solar angles such that soils are cold? Are light levels low? Is the Sun waxing or waning? Our market gardening situation, the Northwest Coast microclimate, and our findings about the influence of the above solar factors alert us to having to start seeds under artificial conditions, providing heat, water, and light. It is the status of solar conditions in relation to earth conditions that has us transplanting a great deal of our field produce.

Another primary set of questions has to do with Moon sign placement. Many of our major plantings for seasonal transplant occur in February and March. So, for a large tomato planting I look at where the Full Moons lie in those two months. For 1997, the Full Moon is Feburary 23. So I would aim at planting in the second quarter, a week ahead of this Full Moon. I look to the tropical calendar and find the Moon in the fertile sign Cancer for two plus days from February 18. I look to the sidereal calendar (*Stella Natura*) and find that the Moon is in Cancer for only a little over one day, and that is on February 19. According to Maria Thun's work, that is a day that stimulates leaf. When I look at the *Llewellyn Astrological Calendar* the aspects do not look particularly good. I want/need to plant tomatoes during this period, however. So I look back, closer to the first quarter Moon. The best I can do is planting in Taurus, but according to the sidereal calendar I will be stimulating root growth, not fruit. If I skip this planting, my next best planting dates are not until mid-March. I could plant against the Moon, in the third quarter, and pick up fertile planting times that are fruitful around the first of March. As all these times will be used under conditions of controlled heat/light and water sources, we will be able to watch the results of our decision. We decide to go for it, do a smaller planting, keep the plants carefully labeled, and do another planting in Scorpio, against the Moon.

Accurate record keeping is essential to give meaning to these kinds of decisions. We tag trays of plants with all astrological/cosmological information. We add to these tags during transplantings. They go with the plants into whatever location (greenhouse or field) the plant is moving and are there for comparison work at harvest. Documenting years of this kind of data (which isn't all that complicated) gives you a sense of how plants interact with your best guess-cosmic management practices. Successive plantings of crops during one season allow you to see that there is much more going on than lunar phase plantings. As solar angles change and seasons warm, fertility levels differ radically, even under intense controls. I am convinced that our Sun affects both Moon and Earth magnetically. I am sure that we human garden managers and the plants we cultivate receive this information at a cellular level. Learning to work with this information, and utilizing astrological language makes our lives more meaningful and gives us living proof that we are indeed cyclic beings in a cosmic sea of resonance.

Bibliography

Becker, Robert and Gary Welden. *The Body Electric*. New York: William Morrow, 1985.

Bills, Rex. *The Rulership Book*. Macoy Publishing and Masonic Supply Co., 1971.

Bio-dynamic Farming and Gardening Organization. *Stella Nautura Agricultural Calendar*. Kimberton, PA, 1997.

Cotterell, M. M. *Astrogenetics*. England: Brooks Hill Robinson Co., 1988.

"Gardening by the Moon." *The Moon Sign Book*. St. Paul, MN: Llewellyn Publications, 1997.

Gilbert and Cotterell. *Mayan Prophecies*. Dorset, England: Element, 1995.

MacCormack, Harry. "Lunar Organic Management." *Lunar Organic Gardener*. St. Paul, MN: Llewellyn Publications, 1993.

Maynard, Jim. *Celestial Influences*. Ashland, OR: Quicksilver Productions, 1997.

Speiss, Hartmut. "Chronological Investigations of Crops Grown under Biodynamic Management: Experiments with Seeding Dates to Ascertain the Effects of Lunar Rhythms on the Growth of Winter Rye." *Biological Agriculture and Horticulture*. Volume 7, Great Britain.

Riotte, Louise. *Astrological Gardening*. Pownal, VT : Storey Garden Way Publishing, 1990.

Wildfeuer, Sherry. "How Do Cosmic Influences Affect Plant Growth?" *Stella Natura*. Kimberton, PA: Bio-dynamic Farming and Gardening Association, 1997.

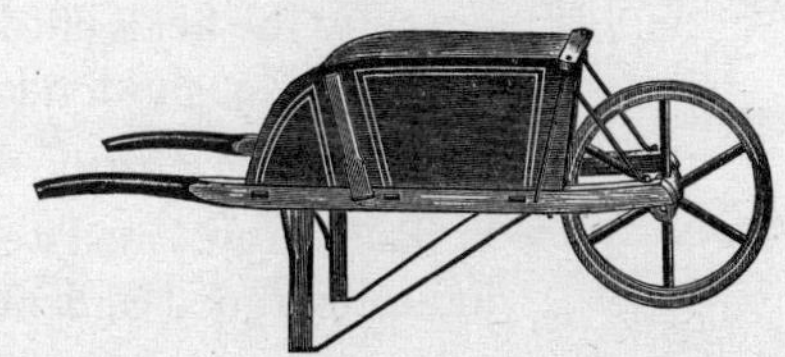

An Herbal Almanac

By Caroline Moss

January

January is the month of the Wolf Moon when wolves are hungry and roam in feared packs, searching for sparse pickings in the mid winter. Protect your house with wolf's bane (*Aconitum napellus*).

- Clear the last of any dead growth—things lost in the frosts and leaves—to give yourself a neat canvas for the spring.
- Dig ground if weather permits, especially around evergreens.
- Check that anything in need of protection is covered, depending on your temperature zone (e.g. young bays and rosemary).
- Get mower serviced.
- Enjoy warming homemade soups with lots of herbs for flavor and food value. Many herbs are packed with vitamins and minerals, notably sorrel and parsley.
- Don't be tempted to plant seeds too early unless you have very controlled conditions (light as well as heat), although seed trays may be warmed indoors or in a heated greenhouse when there are not enough hours of daylight yet to ensure success.

Special days

6 Epiphany, when the Three Kings arrived in Bethlehem.

7 St. Distaff's Day, when women traditionally returned to their spinning work after the Christmas break. Men did not have to return to the fields until the following Monday, Plough Monday.

21 St. Agnes' Day, patron saint of young girls.

25 St. Paul's Day. Good weather on this day indicates a good gardening year.

February

February is the month of the Snow Moon when the worst storms and blizzards are liable to strike.

- Wash and disinfect plant pots and trays.
- Start seeds under controlled conditions. Hold off most things if you have no artificial light and heat, although parsley should be okay indoors.
- Plant garlic outside if you didn't do it in fall.
- Draw up herb garden plans on paper with list of plants to buy, grow from seed, take cuttings of, purloin from friends, etc.

Special Days

1 St. Brigit's Day, symbol of fertility depicted with a white cow.

2 Candlemas, the end of the Christmas season in the church calendar.

14 St. Valentine's Day. Use the romantic herbs of rose, lavender, and artemisias.

29 St. Job's Day. Wear a sprig of rue as protection against ill luck.

March

March is the month of the Worm Moon when the thaw starts and the soil's precious earthworms can once again come to the surface. Wear artemisia in honor of the Moon goddess. It is also the month of the Sap Moon, with sap rising in the trees.

- Get going on seeds in trays. Don't be tempted to plant outdoors yet.
- Trim evergreen herbs into shape.
- Take indoor cuttings, such as scented geraniums and lemon verbena. Cut off a one-foot piece just below a leaf joint, discard all

March is the month of the Worm Moon when the thaw starts and the soil's precious earthworms can once again come to the surface

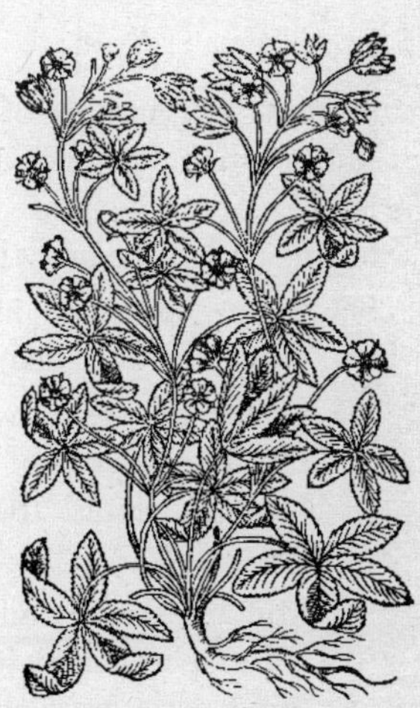

but the top leaves, dip the cut end in rooting powder, put it into a pot filled with proprietary cutting mix or 50/50 sand and peat (a five-inch pot will hold five cuttings), water lightly, and remove any buds that form before root has taken. Geraniums don't need covering, but lemon verbena, rosemary, and fuchsias like to be covered with a clear plastic bag until they "take."

Special Days

17 St. Patrick's Day, patron of Ireland, whose symbol is the green shamrock.

24 St. Gabriel's Day, patron of messengers, who should place mugwort in their shoes to prevent fatigue.

April

April is the month of the Pink Moon when flowers covered the land, or Sprouting Grass Moon, referring to the new growth of spring.

- Many herbs are in vigorous growth now, so take cuttings.
- Check on positions of things that may get out of hand. Cut back and move them now if necessary.
- Mulch prize and delicate plants, particularly heavy flowering varieties such as roses, fuchsias, etc.
- Harden off potted herbs by taking them outside during the day.
- Finish preparing beds and patches of soil for new cuttings and seeds.
- Divide plants where necessary to strengthen and expand stocks, e.g. chives. Dig in a little compost when replanting.
- Dead head daffodils when they are done blooming to prevent them from putting their strength into producing seed heads rather then sending the strength back into their bulbs. Feed with virtually any liquid plant food for about six weeks after flowering. Leave foliage on until it has died down.

Special Days

13 Thomas Jefferson's birthday. Jefferson was a keen and learned gardener and farmer at his estate in Monticello, Virginia.

26 Shakespeare's birthday.

May

May is the month of the Corn Planting Moon, whose name is self explanatory. May was probably named after Maia, the Roman Goddess of growth and increase.

- After last fear of frost, plant seeds of fennel, coriander, and dill. Plant basil indoors in early

May (it's probably okay in late April, but basil disappoints if temperatures aren't up).

- Plant out seedlings. Protect from wind until firmly established, using cardboard screens.
- Keep on top of weeds with a vengeance.
- Although soil won't be parched make sure real moisture lovers (like mint) and new plantings have plenty of water. Growth will be vigorous by now so enjoy picking your herbs to encourage more sprouting.

Special Days

1 May Day. Celebrate by making a batch of traditional German *Mei Wein* (May Wine). Infuse a few sprigs of dried or wilted sweet woodruff in a bottle of sweet white wine for twenty-four hours. You can "water" it down with lemonade and/or float strawberries in it.

June

June is the month of the Strawberry Moon, when wild strawberries were abundant. June was named after Juno, the goddess of beauty and marriage.

- Traditionally the month for brides. Make sure their bouquets include rosemary for remembrance, sage for domestic bliss and long life, myrtle for love, lavender for luck, and pale pink rose buds for love.
- Feed and fertilize regularly with your favorite brand of fertilizer, or water in which comfrey and nettles have been soaking.
- Propagate some herbs by ground layering (pin branch to soil with a stone), try thyme, lavender, and sage.
- Decide whether you want to be forever cutting, pulling out, and primping your herbs for a formal look, or whether, like me, you go for the more blowsy approach and let things run their course.
- On warm days enjoy an iced lemon verbena and mint tea while brushing past your fragrant herbs. Frost the glasses first by dipping rims into lightly beaten egg white and then in castor sugar. Repeat for thicker rim and let dry before use. Children enjoy coloring the sugar first.
- Make ice cubes from lemon balm tea.

Special Days

5 Traditional day for sheep shearing.

11 St. Barnabas' Day, when homes were hung with sweet woodruff and roses.

22 Midsummer's Eve, a day of feasting and festival.

July

Month of the Thunder Moon when violent storms can erupt unexpectedly.

- Start cuttings of herbs for indoor winter pots.
- Gather herbs to dry for arrangements, potpourri, and culinary use now that plants are at their peak.
- Make wreaths from herbs that can dry after crafting, such as sage (green and purple), Sweet Annie (*Artemisia annua*), tansy, and rosemary.
- Make flower-scented vinegars as hair rinses. Steep one measure of petals to two measures of white wine vinegar for six to eight weeks. Strain and rebottle. Try lavender, rose, pinks, lemon verbena, or scented geranium.
- Make a batch of pesto.
- Collect perfect rose petals and make scented beads. These were originally made for rosaries, and are lovely for a bride or bridesmaids. Simply collect as many petals as possible, put them in a saucepan with very little water, bring to a boil, turn off the stove and leave for twenty-four hours. Then bring the mixture to a boil again, and simmer very gently until a thick paste is formed. Add a couple of drops of attar of rose (essential oil) if desired. Cool and mold mixture into small beads. Thread onto waxed cotton (dental floss is ideal).

Special Days

26 Feast of St. Anne, patron saint of housewives.

August

Month of the Sturgeon Moon, when fish go up river.

- Gather seeds from annual herbs. Cover the seed heads with a paper bag, fastened with an elastic band, to catch seeds before they drop.
- Pinch out basil flowers to prolong leaf growth.
- Sow flower seeds for next summer—foxglove and hollyhock.
- Make cat toys by drying catnip and stuffing felt cutouts.
- Make lavender wands and tie with lots of pastel ribbons. Save droppings for potpourri.
- Experiment with edible flowers to add a conversation point to your salads and puddings. Chive flowers, calendula, heart's ease, nasturtium (these can be stuffed with an herby cream cheese), rose petals, courgette blossoms (try deep-frying in a light batter), and violets are often used.

Special Days

1 Lammas Day, festival of the beginning of harvest.

10 St. Lawrence / San Lorenzo's Day, patron of cooks and wine makers.

September

Month of the Corn Moon when the harvest can start.

- Start clearing annuals, being careful to catch and keep seeds.
- Sow bulbs and seeds of hardy annuals.
- Press leaves and flowers for winter crafts. If pictures seem too ambitious, try making gift tags for Christmas out of a single herb leaf or sprig.
- Think about bringing in tender herbs.
- Harvest garlic dry with stems on and braid them.
- Make pantry gifts such as herb jelly (try rose geranium or mint in an apple jelly base), and vinegars (basils, tarragon, or chilli pepper).
- Make a large batch of potpourri with your dried herbs and flowers. If you want it for Christmas gifts, mix bulk materials now and leave essential oils and fixative until later in the year so that you've done most of the work prior to the holiday rush.

Special Days

26 Johnny Appleseed's birthday.

29 Michaelmas goose is the traditional dinner today.

Varies, Native American Day.

October

Month of the Hunter's Moon when elk, deer, and bear were sought for winter food and warmth.

- Check for frosts, and bring in delicates at first threat (lemon verbena, scented geraniums, pineapple sage, young bays).
- Cloche hardy but sensitive herbs (young rosemary, balm of Gilead, fancy sages).
- Root out annuals.
- Mulch roots where added protection is needed. This is especially useful when spring comes and snow melts but freezes again at night. Don't forget to mulch strawberries.
- Cut artemisias for Christmas wreaths (one of the best for this is Silver King). If you have no artemisias, honeysuckle and ivy twine into lovely wreaths.
- Make and freeze herb breads with the last of the annuals—basil, chervil, etc.

Special Days

28 St. Jude's Day. Who can resist St. Jude, the patron saint of lost causes!

November

Month of the Beaver Moon when trapping to ensure winter stores was begun in earnest.

- Plant garlic. It benefits greatly from winter frosts.
- To keep warm and brighten a dull November day, drink lovage cordial with brandy. To make this, steep lovage seeds in sugar and brandy to taste.
- Have bird food ready now that cold is setting in.
- Make your herb jellies, vinegars, and oils if not done already, to ensure supply of Christmas gifts.
- Dig over soil and dig in compost in new areas to give ideal preparation for next year.
- Have pots of fennel and dill seed on hand to chew as digestives after heavy winter meals.

Special Days

1 All Saints' Day.

25 St. Catherine's Day, patron saint of spinsters.

December

Month of the Cold Moon—no explanation necessary!

- For dingy winter skin, try a herbal steam using any mixture of sage, mint, chamomile flowers, calendula petals, lavender, nettle, fennel, or yarrow.
- Decorate a potted rosemary bush with tiny ribbons, gingerbread shapes, and the like for an herbal Christmas tree.
- Decorate a "normal" Christmas tree with tiny posies of herbs, wreaths of thyme (just wrap long springs around three fingers and tuck in), and scented fir cones for a fragrant tree. Scent melted wax with essential oils and dip pine cones in it. These can also be used for fragrant firelighters.
- Put a handful of cinnamon bark, cloves, bay leaves, orange peel, star anise, rosemary, and lavender (whatever combination you fancy and have on hand) in a small saucepan. Add water and simmer to scent the whole house.
- Make a dream pillow to take to bed on Christmas Eve. Include hops, rose, and lavender.
- Give little potted fresh, fragrant herbs to those who do not have gardens.

Special Days

6 St. Nicholas' Day (the original Santa Claus).

13 St. Lucia honored throughout Scandinavia.

16 The Boston Tea Party. Drink herb teas to commemorate the uprising against unfairly taxed imported tea.

Personal Lunar Forecasts

By Gloria Star

About the Author

Gloria Star has been a professional astrologer for over twenty years. She has written the *Sun Sign Book* forecasts for Llewellyn since 1990, and has been a contributing author of the *Moon Sign Book* since 1995. She is the author of *Optimum Child: Developing Your Child's Fullest Potential through Astrology*, and has contributed to two anthologies—*Houses: Power Places in the Horoscope* (Llewellyn 1990), and *How to Manage the Astrology of Crisis* (Llewellyn 1993). Her most recently completed work has been as creator, editor, and contributing writer for Llewellyn's new astrological anthology *Astrology for Women: Roles and Relationships* (1997).

Gloria has served on the faculty of the United Astrology Congress (UAC) since its inception in 1986, and has lectured for groups and conferences throughout the U.S.A. and abroad. She is a member of the Advisory Board for the National Council for Geocosmic Research (NCGR), has served on the Steering Committee for the Association for Astrological Networking (AFAN) and was editor of the AFAN Newsletter from 1992–1997. She also writes a column for *The Mountain Astrologer Magazine*.

Understanding Your Personal Moon Sign

By Gloria Star

You are familiar with the Moon. You see her shining brightly and may casually observe the reflections of her many faces through the course of her ever-changing cycle. Musings about the Moon and her influences are scattered over time and throughout the literature of human history. Do you know that you have your personal Moon? It is one of the many features of your astrological chart.

When calculating your horoscope, an astrologer charts the positions of the Moon, Sun, and planets at the time of your birth. The detailed portrait presented by the picture of your astrological chart symbolizes the multiple levels of energy that are part of your whole being. You probably know about your Sun sign, which describes the ways you express your ego, something easy to see. Your Moon tells a more intimate story, since it describes your subconscious nature, and is much more internalized than the energy of the Sun. You *feel* your Moon.

Refer to the detailed directions on page 62 of this book if you want to determine your personal Moon sign. This is a close approximation of your Moon's sign, but if you want to know the exact degree and placement of your Moon you'll need to obtain your astrological chart. To do this you can visit a competent astrologer or order your chart calculations from Llewellyn Chart Services by using the form in the back of this book.

Even though you may not be familiar with your Moon sign, you are very well acquainted with this energy. Whenever you tune into your basic feelings about anything, you're connecting through the Moon. You express the qualities of the Moon through your attitudes and habits. Think of your Moon as a highly impressionable internal recording device that collects, stores, and assimilates everything you experience. Some of your recorded messages operate automatically, but you can add more information at any time and you can also make alterations. However, since you hold these impressions at a very deep level, it's not always easy to change or erase an old internal message!

The astrological sign of your natal Moon gives you insights into the filter through which you absorb your impressions and life experiences. It shows your inner strength, but is also the key to your deepest vulnerabilities. Here you experience your feeling of "home," and as you learn more about yourself and your needs through experiencing life, you may find that by concentrating on the nature of your needs as illustrated by your Moon sign you can create an environment that provides comfortable security and safety. Once you're in the flow of the energy of your Moon, you carry that sense of home everywhere you go.

When you express nurturance and support you're sharing your lunar energy, and your Moon sign indicates the manner in which you express these qualities toward others and yourself. Whether you're male or female, your Moon shows how you "mother" others. Psychologically, Moon depicts the archetypal feminine quality and represents your relationship with your mother, with women, and with the feminine part of your own psyche.

When you probe more deeply into the mystery of your Moon, you find your soul. At this level, your Moon is the repository of all that you have been, and therefore influences all that you can become. Shining forth from deep within your eyes, the light of your Moon reflects the inner aspects of yourself. Your Moon represents your most dominant emotional tendencies and needs; it is the part of yourself that has flown to the pinnacle of ecstasy and that also remembers the true emptiness of despair.

This part of the *Moon Sign Book* is designed to help you understand the basic cycles throughout 1998 that will affect you at an emotional level. Transits to your Moon stimulate change, and you may discover that some of the cycles help you transform your life. Astrology can show you the cycles, but you are the one who determines the outcome through your responses. By opening to your own needs and responding to the planetary energies in a way that allows you to fulfill these needs, you can experience a renewed sense of hope and self-confirmation.

Aries Moon

To be secure you must first feel that you are free. With the Moon in Aries you're always ready to move ahead, and are driven by a desire to experience life on your own terms. Sometimes the best way to find yourself is to face a challenge. If you are leading the way as the champion of a cause, the gratification you feel when you know you've had an influence on others can be completely invigorating. You have the courage to face change, and may frequently be the initiator of new situations.

Relationships are important to you, although you are not comfortable in relationships that infringe on your need for independent action and thinking. You may even appreciate a connection that fosters mutual autonomy, and can also be the inspiration for others to become more self-sufficient. You dislike getting stuck in a rut and enjoy the sweet taste of excitement. Waiting around for things to get better is definitely not your style. You'll either bring problems out into the open or head off into new territory.

The beckoning call of new frontiers brings out the best in you, and your playful spirit of adventure can be highly attractive. You may be an incurable flirt, and sometimes just like playing that teasing game without feeling a need to take it anywhere "permanent." In fact, starting things may always be easier than seeing them through. Feeling passionate about your life and loves keeps you ever-young. Since your internal psyche can be crisis-oriented, it's a good idea to find something to do in the world that allows you to be in the midst of crisis in a positive way—like the medical profession, crisis counseling or military service. Your courage and capability to rise to the occasion are invaluable when others are paralyzed by fear, since you're the one who can step into action and lead the charge!

The Year at a Glance for Aries Moon

Saturn completes its cycle in Aries this year and the heavy energy you feel is a result of pressing needs and responsibilities taking their toll. The weight depends on how clearly you've embraced your deepest needs and whether or not you've been honest about your feelings about your career and your relationships. If this sounds familiar, well, it is. Saturn takes a while to move through a sign and when it's near your Moon you're definitely aware of time.

This can be a period of great accomplishment, and marks a time of well-defined clarification about what you need to become whole. It's time to consolidate, complete, and step onto a stronger platform of personal security that is based on greater self-reliance. This cycle is especially powerful if your Moon is from15–29 degrees of Aries.

From Jupiter you're experiencing the stimulation to open more fully to your inner voice. The landscape of your dreams plays an important role now, and if you're listening more carefully to your intuitive voice you may find that your consciousness is connected to a place of greater self-assurance. Although you may not feel the powerful burst of confidence that spurred you toward new directions last year, you are experiencing a strong level of optimism and now need to find a way to weave your renewed hope into your everyday life experience. Merging your spiritual awareness and practice into your daily life can make a significant difference.

The outer planets, Uranus, Neptune, and Pluto, are also stimulating different facets of your psyche, challenging you to open your heart and soul to new possibilities. If your Moon is from 0–15 degrees Aries you're at the peak of change, breaking out of outworn situations and attitudes through the influence of the outer planetary energies.

All Aries Moons are experiencing a burst of new confidence. You may feel frustrated with the slow pace of manifesting change, since you may have a very clear idea about where you want to go and how you want to alter your life. Let your imagination and creativity lead the way, allowing your priorities and responsibilities to form the framework for personal rejuvenation.

Affirmation for the Year

"I am clear and focused on the best ways to fulfill my needs."

January

This is a high-energy month, although there are a few storms possible in your love life. It's easier to express your emotional needs and talk openly about your feelings from January 1–10, but if you've been holding back or hiding from yourself you may face a crisis during the Full Moon on January 12. Although it's tempting to point your finger at someone else as the culprit, this is the time that requires you to face the results of your own expressions and attitudes. Others may play a part, but fitting them into the picture correctly means that you have to be honest about what they really need from you. The New Moon on January 28 stimulates hope and reassurance, even if you are still having second thoughts about a close relationship. Adopting an open-minded attitude can actually confirm your faith in yourself.

February

An undercurrent of frustration seems to follow you, but you can handle it if you'll direct that energy somewhere. Make a decision about the things that are creating worry or concern. Talk with a friend over coffee or lunch and let your mutual support for one another work its magic. Your life needs a special edge now and if you'll concentrate your energy on becoming the creator of your life during the Full Moon on February 11 you may be thoroughly delighted with the outcome. It's not like you to wait for results, anyway! Impatience can be a source of agitation, particularly if everybody else seems to be wandering around in a fog. Turn on your awareness during the solar eclipse on February 26 by listening more carefully to your intuitive voice. Try a moving meditation, like yoga or mild exercise, to get in touch with your total being. This is one of those periods during which logic alone may not be sufficient.

March

You're raring to go, and definitely need a challenge. In your enthusiasm to get things moving you can create a bit of havoc that may require mending or adjustment before the lunar eclipse on March 12. Think of the early part of the month as your chance to get yourself and your life into shape and to experiment with something different. You may even feel like changing your routine or trying that new restaurant in town. It's important to add ingredients to the mix that invigorate and inspire you. Your time of renewal arrives with the Aries New Moon on March 27, marking an important cycle centered on greater clarity about your needs and desires. However, you may still have some old business to complete before you have a clear path to try something completely new. Go ahead and get it out of the way. Just think how much better you'll feel!

April

The month gets off to an interesting start, especially if you're faced with the challenge of satisfying requirements you really don't like. However, this is the perfect time to marshal your courage, bite the bullet, and take on significant responsibility. If you're doing something only because someone else thinks it's important, that situation could blow up in your face during the Full Moon on April 11. It's also the time when you'll hear about the things you're not doing to satisfy someone else. Since you're probably thinking, "I can't win," stop for a moment and really look at your relationships. If you're not being fair-minded, it's time to start. To begin on the right track, look in the mirror and remind yourself that you are important and that you deserve to have your needs fulfilled. Be honest about your feelings. You may not be able to change what someone else wants, but you can deal with it!

May

You're experiencing a positive period of inner strength and can take actions now that will confirm your sense of self-worth. With Venus transiting over your Moon you're ready to open to the experience of loving more fully, and may even attract someone special into your life. This is a great time to indulge yourself a little. During the Full Moon on May 11 you may feel more vulnerable, particularly if you've been open about your feelings and have not experienced reciprocity. Before you close the door, take a realistic approach to the situation and decide exactly how far you're ready to go! Do something at home that brings your nest to life after the New Moon on May 25. Throw a party, or get together with people you enjoy and light up the night with mirth and laughter. Life is supposed to be fun, at least part of the time!

June

An easygoing style sets the pace this month, and you may feel more like playful adventure than everyday doldrums. Wonderful! Plan something festive for the Full Moon on June 9, and consider getting away from the daily grind or changing your routine enough to keep the light in your eyes. Watch your promises, because you can easily get in over your head by underestimating a situation. Whether you're spending more time or money, you might resent feeling stretched too far. As long as you leave a little room for the excess you'll be okay, but pushing yourself against the wall will cost on several levels. Expressing what you feel can seem complicated after June 14, especially if you feel that someone else does not really hear what you're trying to say. Just remember that communication is a two-way street, and you may have to make room for someone else's needs, too.

July

You may be highly demonstrative of your feelings and needs during July, finding it easier to share your thoughts and desires. However, there is some friction, and it is likely to begin at home or with family issues, escalating to a peak during the Full Moon on July 9. Selfish manipulation will not go over very well, whether you're the perpetuator or the victim! If you fall into the trap of pushing too hard or fast, try to pull back just a little. Impatience can get you into trouble, adding unnecessary tension to your life mid-month. Knowing your limits makes the difference between contentment and agitation, whether at work or in your love life. Take an emotional inventory during the New Moon on July 23 and initiate a new plan of action centered on your desire to have greater autonomy.

August

Sometimes what you want and what you need are not the same thing, and that very dilemma can be the source of your discontent right now. In many respects you're experiencing a period of objectivity and increased awareness, but it can come at the cost of breaking away from some attachments that are standing in the way of your growth. During the lunar eclipse on August 7 you are capable of stepping away from conflict or frustration long enough to identify the problems. Be careful because you may take actions that are like shooting yourself in the foot, so think first. After August 14, listen to that small voice that may be urging you to embrace a more playful attitude (as long as you don't regress to acting too much like a child!). By the time of the solar eclipse on August 21 you're ready to let go of old habits and try something completely different.

September

Yes, there is another lunar eclipse. It occurs on September 6, stimulating further illumination concerning the link between mind, spirit, and body, and you may discover that by integrating these different levels of need and experience, your life will change. Some of the anxiety you're feeling can be a result of trying to push some of your needs away, or you may be experiencing uncomfortable difficulties in a relationship because both parties are not feeling equally supported. Subtle changes can help—you don't have to move a mountain. If the problem is at work, ask yourself what you want to change. If the answer is "everything," then you may want to think about the reasons you're still there! After the New Moon on September 20 you may feel more inclined to shift your attitudes and allow yourself the luxury of accepting some assistance from others. Don't you deserve it?

October

Your need for acceptance may prompt you to make a more concerted effort in your personal relationships, especially if you feel you haven't been doing enough to maintain the balance of power. Don't ignore your deeper motivations, since the Full Moon in Aries on October 5 amplifies your true feelings and underscores your need for personal satisfaction. Relationship issues definitely reach a critical point and if you've been denying your feelings or hoping that things will change, you're quickly realizing that you hold the power of transformation within your responses and attitudes. Any relationship, even those at work, improves through open communication from October 1–12, although there are power struggles from October 11–21. Work out agreements during the New Moon on October 20, but watch for the possibilities of deception, since once again you might ignore some important issues that could undermine your stability.

November

On the surface everything may seem to be okay, but you can feel an undercurrent of agitation resulting from unfulfilled expectations. This escalates near the Full Moon on November 4, continuing to be problematic unless you pay attention to the root causes of your discontent. Although it's not like you to sit on the fence, you may feel uncertain about the best choices. Start by listening to your deeper feelings, and then find a way to objectify your situation. Write in a journal or talk over your concerns with a friend or counselor. Consider different options after the New Moon on November 18, when your emotional attachments may actually decrease, allowing you to leave outworn situations behind and move forward with your life. Even though there may be some unfinished business, you can see the path ahead, and just knowing that you're on your way makes all the difference in your self-confidence.

December

You're experiencing a strong level of self-assertiveness and may take action too quickly, especially if you're feeling impatient (well, when are you *not* impatient?). But try to think about the consequences of your words and actions, and be aware of the impact you have on the people around you. You're feeling hopeful during the Full Moon on December 3 when there are ample energies to help confirm your sense of personal power. Utilize your own strengths to make a difference in your life circumstances, and take advantage of this period to undo some misunderstandings and clear the way for greater satisfaction. Give yourself ample opportunities to laugh. You need something to do with your nervous energy after the New Moon on December 18, but try to stay out of situations for which you are not well-suited, since you're rarely happy with egg on your face!

Taurus Moon

Through your Taurus Moon you hold a solid footing in the midst of life's storms and struggles. Your heart is filled when you focus on serenity, beauty, and peace, and those you love are comforted by your calm stability. You love to be around the things and people that make you feel at home and may also be soothed when you feel close to energy of the earth. Your conservative nature attracts situations that will support the foundation you are carefully creating.

Commitment is an important quality in your life, and once you've made a promise—whether to an idea, an environment, or a person—you do not like to change. You understand how costly it is to start over, and prefer to make changes that can accommodate what you have already put into place. After all, you're interested in creating a solid foundation, and it does not really move very easily! During the times when changes occur beyond your control you may get stuck in a stubborn, blinding energy that seems to inhibit your ability to move. It is fear that blinds your ability to realize that you can direct many of the varying circumstances of life by maintaining the strength that will help you accommodate these new situations.

In your personal relationships you can be possessive, because when you love you bring another into that deep space in your heart. Letting go is not easy for you when a relationship ends. Your unwavering support is usually appreciated by your friends, children, and lovers, who count on you to be there for them, but you may sometimes have to let them make their own mistakes! You understand that, in most instances, growth is a slow process, and you can patiently wait.

The Year at a Glance for Taurus Moon

You're entering a period of stability during 1998, and may have a long list of plans centered on broadening your horizons and increasing your options. Before you reach that stable place, though, you may have to face some disruptions and integrate some new people, situations, and attitudes into your life. It may take some time to get used to things that are completely out of your everyday familiarity, but you're ready for something different and may welcome a few disruptions.

Saturn moves into Taurus this year, and until the end of this century will continue its transit in the sign of your Moon. However, you only get a glimpse of this cycle from June to October, so plan to use these months to take a careful look at the areas in your life that need some assessment. There are other factors that will make it difficult to firm up the basic structures of your life this year, but you can certainly get your plans in order and let your imagination and creativity stir the process. If your Moon is in the fist 10 degrees of Taurus you're experiencing the most sweeping personal revolution you've felt for a long time. Even if your Moon is in later degrees of Taurus you're starting to see the signs of change, and instead of getting into a panic, look around for the things that you've outgrown. All Taurean Moons have a grand opportunity to use the cycles of '98 to expand their inner strength.

You may even want to alter your home environment (dare we say consider moving?) to give yourself more room. Jupiter is transiting in sextile to your Moon, stimulating a desire for more of everything, including space. This year marks an excellent period of discovery. New friends, exciting information, and alterations that trim away the heaviness from your life are all part of the renewal.

If others are challenging you to explore things you don't really want to do, listen to the source of your resistance before you walk away in a huff. You're definitely leaving some old patterns behind as you move toward the challenge of creating security on your own terms, and you may actually surprise a few people who have allowed their expectations of you to get stuck in the mud. This process of continual personal growth and broadening awareness are the driving forces you're feeling at an emotional level. Enjoy the progress you're making, and remember to show your gratitude for your good fortune.

Affirmation for the Year

"My life is filled with abundance enough to share."

January

The feeling of agitation that sweeps through your innermost being can be the result of disappointment. Whether your expectations for yourself or another are shattered, try to be more forgiving. Open the lines of communication during the Full Moon on January 12 and pour out your feelings to someone you trust. You may be having second thoughts about your choices or decisions, and instead of tearing yourself apart or lashing out unnecessarily, listen to your dreams and desires. Sometimes life contrasts drastically with what you think you deserve, but when you get to the core of it you may realize that you are the one who has sabotaged your happiness. Let go of the past and suspend your tendency to judge yourself so harshly. Concentrate instead on peaceful solutions. Even if you're ending your association you can part on good terms, unless you're still feeling competitive!

February

Renewed hope brightens your life, especially if you see ways to put your plans and dreams into action. You may be struggling against unusual odds very early in the month, but can quickly get to the bottom of any problems. The stress you feel during the Full Moon on February 11 may rest in your attempts to satisfy your obligations to work or family, and it's tempting to close away from those who would comfort or encourage you just because you don't want to take on any unspoken promises. Try the approach of using direct communication, which works exceedingly well just before, during, and after the solar eclipse on February 26. In many respects this period is like getting a fresh perspective on what you really want and need from your life. Tune in to your inner feelings and finally let go of those old situations that no longer fit the picture of your current life pattern.

March

Although you may feel more like taking some time away from the pressures of your life until just after the lunar eclipse on March 12, this can be a productive period of emotional growth. Allow ample time for reflection early in the month, and try to become more aware of your inner dialogue. You may discover some hidden messages that are no longer valid, and this is also an excellent time to let go of some old outworn or destructive habits. A meeting or minor altercation with someone or something you just don't like can dampen your spirits from March 14–18, although later reflection may reveal to you that you were jumping to a conclusion before you had a chance to fully understand or review the situation. Consider trying something unusual or out of the ordinary after the New Moon on March 27, even if it's as simple as adding a new ingredient to your salad for lunch. You're ready for a bit of a change!

April

You're most comfortable in familiar surroundings or returning to a situation with which you have some prior experience from April 1 until after the Full Moon on April 11. Jumping into something completely different can seem far too threatening, unless you feel you're well-prepared or accompanied by someone you trust explicitly. After April 14 you're feeling a bit more experimental, and can at least entertain the idea of indulging in the fantasy of something (or someone!) you crave. The time to put the wheels in motion is during or after the New Moon in Taurus on April 26 when you may feel more secure. If you still have reservations, focus your energy creatively since you need to express yourself with greater abandon. Surround yourself with beauty—beautiful people, the bounty of nature, and the things you dearly appreciate. Indulge your sensuality.

May

The emotional bond you feel with those you love grows stronger, although you can be a bit too pushy if you want something. If your actions or attitudes are problematic you'll definitely find out about it during the Full Moon on May 11, when there's little guesswork about anything. You may also lose your patience if you've reached the end of your rope. This is a wonderful time to break out of situations that work against your best interests, and you may even surprise yourself with your boldness about taking a stand. There's rarely a doubt about how you feel, but now you're putting more energy behind your convictions. You can be quite convincing. The pressure eases after the New Moon on May 25, but your desire to have what you want does not diminish one iota!

June

You may feel that the realization of your dreams is just an arm's length away, but somehow your reach may not quite accomplish what you hope to achieve. Look at the sources of tension in your life. You may be holding yourself back due to emotional stress or anxiety, particularly near the Full Moon on June 9 when you may want to enjoy a calm atmosphere, when instead there's frustration around you. The pressure may coax you into denial, but that's not your best option! By the middle of the month everything begins to fall into place and you can take advantage of the ease of flow while Venus transits over your Moon. Let yourself indulge in your favorite pastimes after June 21, and try something out of the ordinary during the New Moon on June 23, when you fully appreciate the value of variety.

July

Even though you may run into a few misunderstandings, mostly due to problems with semantics, you're feeling more alive and confident. Be aware of the manner in which you're taking responsibility for your own feelings, since this is an excellent time of increased inner focus. Do something that underscores your sense of stability during the Full Moon on July 9, and take actions that illustrate your true sentiments. This is no time to be sitting on the fence, particularly if you want to know where you stand with someone else! Even in career situations you need to clarify what you expect and require. Romantic experiences can be especially memorable from July 19–22, but you may be disappointed during the New Moon on July 23 if obligations such as work get in the way of your plans. Take a rain check for early next month.

August

You may feel like you're leading a double life. There's the "you" operating with some people showing love, affection, and tenderness, then there's the other "you" struggling to keep everything in line—especially those situations that involve your responsibilities. Look at your deeper feelings during the lunar eclipse on August 7 and try to compare what you do and do not like about your life. Even though you may not be able to change everything, you can begin to shift your focus and allow your creative self a little more leeway. The solar eclipse on August 21 heralds a challenge to release things from your past that no longer fit into your life. You may also run into old friends in new places, and the contrast gives you a chance to reach closure with any unfinished business. Watch your temper after August 21. Even though you may be in control it's a good idea to express your anger somewhere. Repressed emotion is dead weight.

September

After a crazy start from September 1–5 when unpredictable is the order of the day, energy shifts during the lunar eclipse on September 6, encouraging you to regroup, let go, and forgive so you can move forward. All the disruptions may succeed in helping you develop a different perspective about your deeper needs. By structuring your time according to your current needs you'll create a better flow in your life. This is important since you're eager to accomplish the realization of something you hold dear. Engage the assistance of others after September 8 by inviting them to employ their talents and abilities, creating a situation that is more cooperative and supportive. You'll still accomplish your aims, and may even make a few friends in the process. Talk over your dreams and plans with someone you trust during the New Moon on September 20. Try to avoid overindulging yourself after that day, when it's just hard to say "No!"

October

It's time to do some clearing and cleaning—getting rid of the clutter in your life and relationships. You might start by getting to the bottom of that stack on your desk or rearranging your closet. In the process you may discover something you've forgotten that holds special importance. The Full Moon on October 5 may not mark an especially significant event, but it's a great time to bring issues to the forefront. You need to feel that you've accomplished something after October 8, and are likely to stay rather busy. However, there's a bump in the road from October 13–20 when you may encounter a power play that just leaves you cold. Even if you have to stand your ground you're still not likely to sink to the level of nasty games, but watch your back anyway! Relationships can be testy from October 23–26, particularly if you're not happy. Before you start packing or pushing someone out the door make sure that's what you want. Your actions will definitely be taken seriously.

November

You can be rather demanding, or may get involved in a situation that allows you to see the cost of personal selfishness by observing someone else. Objectivity lessons are not always fun, and during the Full Moon in Taurus on November 4 you have a good one. This could be the time to clarify exactly what you want, where you stand and what you will not accept—but you have to be sure of yourself. There's a difference between stubborn opposition that arises from hurt feelings and steadfast conviction. Now, everything is not at a loss. It's just that there are so many expectations flying about and demands on your time coming from all directions and you may not actually know what you want. Nothing looks good. Everything seems complicated. Before you're washed away in the tidal wave of discontent that may just be a result of your list of wants getting too long, stop and center yourself. Then, during the New Moon on November 18, start again.

December

If what you're seeking looks like it's just going to cost more than you're willing to pay (and I don't mean just money!), then give it some time. Everything is a bit inflated from December 1–6 (especially near the Full Moon on December 3). After December 12, practicality takes over and you're much more content with your options. Listen to your inner voice, and try to be aware of the reasons for your actions and attitudes. If you're being driven by your desire to please someone else, at least be honest about it, and really find out what they want instead of putting your own values at the top of the list. If you just want to express yourself, then let your creativity open fully. There's nothing like the satisfaction of seeing your ideas come to life—whether those desires relate to people, places, or things. After December 23, that kind of magic is happening, and you are creating it!

Gemini Moon

There simply may not be enough time in one life to explore everything you would like to experience. With your Gemini Moon driving your deepest needs, you have an insatiable appetite for mental stimulation. Whether you're exploring ordinary people, situations, or ideas, or taking an adventurous journey into the unknown, your yearning to know helps you maintain an open mind and keeps you ever young. You like change, too, and sometimes just need to try completely different places, people, or careers to keep your spirit alive. In many ways, you are the eternal child, and may be distracted from your focus. Before you know it, you can be up to your ears with so many activities or possibilities that you have difficulty keeping up with yourself. That burning desire to know somehow gets lost in the shuffle, especially if the people who are telling you the answers are out of date or boring—then it's so hard to listen.

Despite all the fast-paced changes, you're capable of keeping your wits about you, especially in trying or painful moments. It's then that your clear objectivity rises to the occasion, a trait others value, too. You're happiest when everything makes sense, but unfortunately life is frequently illogical, especially when it concerns matters of the heart. You need plenty of space to express your independence in relationships, and will adore friends and partners who give you room to breathe. Your lighthearted soul secretly desires to be revered for your wisdom and intelligence, and you may ultimately become a truly wise teacher. As you travel through the years of your life you discover that your sense of home can go anywhere. Even settling into one place can work, if you feel free. As long as your mind is free, you are free.

The Year at a Glance for Gemini Moon

There are plenty of reasons to try something new this year, although you need to keep your personal limitations in clear focus—since it's easy to keep that proverbial fire filled with way too many hot irons! The expansive energy of Jupiter strengthens your confidence, but during 1998 you can be overly confident, particularly if you have not done your homework. If you're using personal discipline and responsibility to help stabilize your life then you may be able to push those limits a little, but you will not enjoy the feeling if you have to put on the brakes just when you were getting up to speed. Your intuitive sensibilities are heightened now, so you already know when you've gone too far. All you have to do is listen!

Since exploring different ideas or opening new avenues of creativity is always an option, this year can be exceptionally exciting. Your awareness is also expanding, and you may feel more inclined to get rid of the things, people, and situations that inhibit your need to reach beyond the ordinary into the extraordinary. You may think that just because you need to make room to grow that you can just wipe the slate clean and start again, but life is not quite that simple. Pluto continues its long cycle in opposition to your Moon sign, and you need to dig deeper into your psyche and discover your motivations while you're releasing the past. If your Moon is in the first 12 degrees of Gemini you're making more sweeping changes in consciousness and in everyday experience. Regardless of the degree of your Gemini Moon, you're opening your mind to possibilities that will allow you to alter your attitudes and attachments while you create open avenues for change. Transformation at these levels takes patience and self-love if you are to emerge as the person you truly want to become. Let your gentility have a free reign, and use tools like affirmations and positive self-talk to help you stay in touch with the new you while you let go of your outworn self.

Becoming reborn is almost like your physical birth. You feel vulnerable and a little confused with your new surroundings and way of existence, but after a while you're raring to go. It's that clumsy period when everything seems bigger than you that is most disconcerting. The difference now is that you have knowledge of the ways to navigate through life. All you have to do is use it!

Affirmation for the Year

"*My life is filled with golden opportunities each and every moment.*"

January

Your enthusiasm and joy add to your feeling of confidence, and if there's something important you really want to do, then this is a wonderful time to take the leap and go for it! You may feel most self-assured from January 1–9, but you're likely to start second-guessing yourself during the Full Moon on January 12. Before you completely undermine your plans, listen to your deepest needs. It's likely that you're responding to the concerns or fears of others, which is okay as long as you're not using them as convenient excuses to avoid feeling happy. Making too many promises can get you into trouble from January 12–24, but by the time of the New Moon on January 28 you'll be able to regroup and start on a different path. A bit of anxiety creeps into your emotions after January 26, when you're also more easily hurt by others who discount your needs or feelings.

February

You've heard that phrase, "rude awakening?" Well, if you've been ignoring power issues or feelings of frustration they rise to the surface in explosive ways from February 1–6. Clear the air before the Full Moon on February 11 by communicating your thoughts and feelings. Sometimes just talking over your concerns with a good friend works like magic, but you may need to have a serious heart to heart with your lover or partner if there are things you're ready to change. You may feel some frustration building, and if there are crises at home or at work they can reach a peak during the solar eclipse on February 26. There may be more problems happening around you that can have an effect on your life, but more indirectly than directly. What you have to deal with is the manner in which you respond and the way you draw the line. If it doesn't concern you, bow out gracefully.

March

A feeling of buoyancy and joy carries you smoothly over the bumps in the road of life this month. You can get into a bit of trouble by overstepping your bounds from March 1–13, and you'll feel the pressure brewing during the lunar eclipse on March 12. Sometimes you have to get involved whether you want to or not; just be aware of the times when you may serve yourself and someone else better by saying "No." Your objectivity and resilience are in fine form after March 14, and your sense of self-worth is enhanced. If you love something or someone, find the best way to show your feelings. Let your inventiveness work to your advantage—do something clever! Think about the modifications you'd like to make, consider your options, and create clearly defined goals for yourself. Then, on or after the New Moon on March 27, set out on the path that encourages your dreams to become reality.

April

As long as you keep your mind on your primary needs you'll stay on track. But there are so many things to distract you—the kinds of things that spark your imagination in a big way. Your focus is best from April 1–5, and near the Full Moon on April 11 you're feeling reasonably self-assured. Something (or more likely, someone) tempts you to pursue a different interest or path, and before you know it, you can get in over your head or feel overwhelmed, or you may simply get tired of juggling everything you're trying to do. Your ingenuity can get you out of a jam, but it's best not to back yourself into that tight spot in the first place. On the home front, you may decide you need a little more room. Sometimes rearranging the furniture is much simpler than moving, so consider your options before you start packing! Emotionally, you also need a little space. Release old hurts, clarify what you honestly need now and change your life accordingly.

May

Those wheels inside your head are turning furiously as you consider the opportunities in your path. You'll be most successful when you integrate a few practical options with your inventive ideas. Unfinished emotional business—you know, the kind of experience that you never dealt with completely because you didn't have the time—raises its head during the Full Moon on May 11. As a result, you may need to reconsider some of your choices. It's time for you to get a new lease on life, and that starts by knowing what you want. Get in touch with your feelings and needs during the Gemini New Moon on May 25 and take action that will open the doors to your imagination and creativity.

June

You're likely to take the lead in most situations now, and that's just fine with you, since you have little patience for someone else who may be dragging his or her heels. You can stir up a hornet's nest if you try to force someone else to do what you want early in the month, so watch your actions *and* your words, because what you say can be just as inflammatory as anything you might do! Emotions run high during the Full Moon on June 9, particularly in the realm of relationships, but you can also bump into a few issues on the social scene. Try to listen and observe before you take sides. If you need to take a stand, do it, since sitting on the fence can be devastating on many levels. After all, you still have to live with yourself, regardless of what someone else might think or say. Look for healthy ways to release anger. Maybe it's time to dust off your bicycle or get into that fitness class.

July

Life seems to be running a bit more smoothly, although the first week is rather busy and you may feel like you're scattered to the four winds. Fun is the key word, and you're ready to play. You may even find a new delightful playmate. It could be only a flirtation, and that might feel quite comfortable for you. But the other person may want something more, so try to read the signals if you're just in it for the game. It's certainly okay to enjoy yourself, as long as it's not at another's expense. From the July 11–17 you may feel a little disappointed if your expectations are not met, especially those you have for yourself. If you're feeling low, try to avoid the temptation to do something that will set you back—like pulling out those charge cards and shopping when you can't afford it! Indulge yourself in an experience that inspires you and adds potency to your life. After the New Moon on July 23 you're more centered, although you may not feel energetic.

August

The lunar eclipse on August 7 draws your attention to your needs for independence. You're seeking the best ways to achieve true freedom without compromising your security and stability. Talk over your ideas with a close friend, or spend more time in reflective activities like meditation, journal writing, or using tools like tarot or astrology to give you objective confirmation about your decisions. Excessive emotionality (or what seems excessive to you!) can complicate the process from August 1–14. After August 14 you're more self-assured, and may even feel newly inspired. The solar eclipse on August 21 emphasizes your desire to transcend the ordinary and experience something out of this world. That feeling starts with forgiveness and continues to grow as you extend unconditional love from within to the world around you.

September

Off to an exciting start from September 1 through the lunar eclipse on September 6, you're eager to put a fabulous idea into action. Your self-confidence is high, and you may feel that you can take advantage of an unusual situation that will allow you to show the best of your abilities. After September 7 you have to get down to the practical side of whatever you're doing, including the practicality of your personal life. If having fun is getting in the way of your obligations, redirect your energy so you can enjoy your responsibilities. They will not go away, especially now, and if you cannot integrate them into the flow of your life then you may feel buried by their weight. There may be others in your life whose ideas, talents, or insights can give you a hand, but keep the situation equitable and show some appreciation unless you want to ruin your reputation!

October

It's easier to talk about your feelings and needs now, and if you want to let someone know how you feel, pour out those feelings at the depth of your heart near the time of the Full Moon on October 5. Your mental ingenuity gives you an edge in all sorts of situations, even in your love life, from October 1–10. There's a little power struggle brewing that can escalate from October 12–19. Sticking your head in the sand will only leave you in the lurch, so open your eyes, listen to what's being said, and use your good judgment to take action that will lead to a resolution. You can successfully put your plan into full force during the New Moon on October 20, but it's okay to drop a few hints beforehand just to give you room to make necessary alterations. Conservative (or stubborn) thinkers can throw a monkey wrench into your plans after October 24.

November

You may have the best intentions, but working cooperatively with others can simply be a nightmare unless you're on the same wavelength. Make a strong effort to accomplish real communication. That means everyone listens and everyone puts their two cents into the pot. You may discover that it all comes down to a matter of finances during the Full Moon on November 4, when dividing the profits or assigning jobs gets pretty complex. Step back for a moment and redefine your priorities. Decide why you're involved and what you need from the experience, and try again. Expectations are high from November 1–14, and that's okay as long as you use the energy to stimulate realistic optimism. Be careful: you can easily underestimate the time, money, or energy necessary and end up feeling completely frustrated. Make sure that others are doing their part, too!

December

This is a high-energy month, filled with a positive sense of anticipation and ample opportunities to share your generosity. Of course, the holiday season gives you an excellent chance to extend a helping hand, but there's more to it. During the Gemini Full Moon on December 3 you're ready to move beyond old limitations and explore life from a sense of renewed hope and joy. You may even have a unique opportunity to experience something truly magical from December 11–18. Open your eyes during the New Moon on December 18 and allow yourself to see yourself and your life from a new perspective. If you've been unhappy with someone else, maybe it's just a reflection of something you don't like about yourself. It's much easier to fix your own inner discontent than to try to change another person. You have to be willing to admit your true feelings. Come on, it's not that bad—it's only *you* in there!

Cancer Moon

With your Moon in Cancer you have a special sense of the ebb and flow of life. You feel the natural rhythms of change and can easily connect to the vibration of your intuitive self. Your life centers on creating a home, and you radiate an energy that reflects your deep yearning. As a result, others may be naturally drawn to you when they need comfort or support. Extending this sensibility, you are strongly connected to family, and once someone has become a part of your life it seems only natural that you consider them to be part of your family.

The haven you create for yourself is more than a place, and once you've developed your own sense of security you may enjoy reaching into the lives of others. Those who are in need of help may spring back to life through your nurturant understanding and support. You may be reluctant to allow others to strike out on their own until *you're* ready! This is especially troublesome if you've failed to establish reasonable emotional boundaries, resulting in your feeling their pain, loss, or fear as though it were your own. Watch your own fear of abandonment. If you've created nurturant support and not stifled growth, then the link you've established will extend far beyond time and space.

Intimate relationships will endure if your partner shares a similar need for home and family ties. You'll prosper most fully in an environment of trust and respect, and this will grow most easily when you allow ample time for your own interests while encouraging your partner. By celebrating the progressive stages of life you fall back into that rhythm that rocks your soul into contentment and affirms your connection to your soul. Give yourself time to enjoy it and drink in the feeling of peace. From that space, you are whole.

The Year at a Glance for Cancer Moon

You're feeling more confident about yourself and your choices this year. Although you may still be tested by your responsibilities and obligations, you have more resources available for meeting them. There are partings alongside new introductions as you move toward the future and strike out into a changing world. Your hopes are high, but you can also keep your feet on the ground long enough to maintain your orientation!

Making adjustments can keep your life in a state of flux, and that's okay as long as you're in surroundings that seem familiar. You may be in foreign territory, however—either a new place, with different people, in unusual family circumstances, or shifting circumstances in your job—and your ability to be flexible in your attitudes will go a long way toward helping you feel safe. The one thing that can carry you through any challenge is your sense of faith, which is riding high while Jupiter transits in trine to your Moon.

Because Saturn is continuing its cycle in square aspect to your Moon sign you may feel that you're facing life alone—or not as supported as you want to be. This energy draws you into yourself, and even when you need help you can find it difficult to ask. The real test centers on your need to establish stronger personal priorities and to find a way to let go of the emotional attachments that are standing in the way of your personal progress and growth. If you're dealing with increased responsibilities, it is crucial that you allow ample time to recharge your batteries. Use the energy that flows through the quality of Jupiter to sustain you when you are challenged—pray, meditate, travel, or read and reflect on ideas that send your spirit into a space of peace.

The world around you continues in its ever-changing evolution, and some of those changes may require a few adjustments before they feel natural to you. This is the time to try something different. Create new supports by developing your sense of gratitude and trusting the law of abundance.

Affirmation for the Year

"My heart is filled with hope, my life is filled with grace."

January

You may feel that you're on a dizzying merry-go-round, since there are things to do at every turn with little time to catch your breath. Try to reach the perspective of letting life flow around you like the currents of a great river. During the Cancer Full Moon on January 12 it's easy to feel vulnerable, and unless you're with people or in a situation you trust you may not be particularly open. You may be testing your partnership, or feel tested by it, and if you have questions about your feelings try to draw a distinction between the issues that are currently a high priority and those that are only vague memories. Your dreams are an excellent key to the core of your deeper feelings and issues, and by becoming more attentive to their messages you'll feel more sure of your choices. If you're uncertain or confused, look to a trusted counselor who can help you become more objective.

February

Even though February begins with a few days of strange occurrences, life seems to return to a more normal pace as the month progresses. Unsettling information can lead to a series of discoveries near the time of the Full Moon on February 11. By setting clear priorities within personal relationships and at work you're accomplishing a greater sense of fulfillment, even though you may have to let go of something in the process. Put some energy into manifesting your hopes after February 6, and determine a plan of action that will help you make room for the things you want. Your heart is open to new possibilities as the solar eclipse on February 26 nears, and if you've left no room for them then you may be disappointed. It's time for you to experience a truly uplifting quality of love and joy, and you're eager to share it with the world.

March

The early part of the month is most productive, and through the time of the lunar eclipse on March 12 you may be amazed at the high levels of creativity that inspire you. You're starting to lose your patience with situations and people standing in the way of your progress, but you'll probably try to be cooperative unless you sense that you're being used. Although it is uncharacteristic, you'll be happier if you confront problems and deal with them when they arise, since going around them will only succeed in creating a feeling of frustration. You can be easily hurt now, and you're most vulnerable if you allow someone to take advantage of you. Find healthy ways to release your anger, particularly after March 25 when the pressure of unresolved anger can lead to physical discomfort. If your stomach hurts, pay attention! The cause may not be associated with dinner after all.

April

There's a bit of friction over unfinished business from April 1 until just after the Full Moon on April 11. Whether you're grappling with some long-standing problems or dealing with the results of past actions or experiences, your emotional responses are centered on old memories and feelings in addition to what you're experiencing now. If this sounds complicated, it certainly can be, especially if you're trying to move forward. Sometimes you simply have to put the past to rest before you can move on, and this is one of those periods. Renewed hope emerges after April 18, when much of the confusion lifts as the pressures diminish. Although you may feel like you're ready to start with a clean slate, make certain you're clear about your responsibilities before you make commitments during and after the New Moon on April 26.

May

Taking a conservative approach makes a great deal of sense to you now, and you'll prefer to have a feeling of control both at work and in your personal life. You may feel that others have priorities that are very different from your own, yet you can bridge the gap by clarifying the desired outcome. If you're working toward similar or mutual goals, it makes sense to get personal issues out of the way in favor of something larger. Joining forces really can bring greater rewards. Combined efforts during the Full Moon on May 11 can be highly productive. If you simply cannot agree, this is also the time for a parting of the ways, and you may feel that it's easier to sort through things on your own after May 20—that is if family, spouse or your job will let you! It's time to say good-bye to the things and people you no longer need. Look carefully at your personal attachments. You may be holding onto something useless!

June

You need confirmation and results, and they should be forthcoming. First, try to have a little more fun. The Full Moon on June 9 stimulates a playful energy—an excellent time to let your hair down a little. Maybe you'll just take a walk around the park before you start the day, feed the ducks, try a sample of that interesting looking food they're giving away in the supermarket—you just need a bit of a change. Resisting change will actually be costly, because you may end up paying with regret. While you're getting things in order and making the space for greater joy, reflect on your deeper needs. Listen to your heart, and allow yourself to dream a little about the way you want life to be. Then, during the New Moon in Cancer on June 23, make a solid commitment to yourself that you'll honor those needs—with joy!

July

With the self-confirming energies of the Sun and Mars transiting in Cancer, you can be much more assertive about getting what you want. Just make sure you avoid excessively manipulative options, since you really don't want your plans to backfire. Just as important, try to stay clear of others who have their personal agenda way ahead of your own. Relationships take a high priority during the Full Moon on July 9 when mutual support strengthens your trust. Venus moves into Cancer on July 19, adding a high degree of sentimentality to your impressionable soul. This ingredient stimulates your desire to share your feelings, especially if you've been holding back. You'd also appreciate a little special indulgence or two from your sweetheart, but your sweetheart may never know unless you say something (or drop a large hint!).

August

Use your imagination. It's working just fine right now! This is the time to let your creative ideas and expressive nature work to your benefit, especially in the realm of romance and intimate relationships. You may feel that you're a stranger in a strange land during the lunar eclipse on August 7 if you've jumped into something unprepared. Sometimes, these experiences lead to a more profound awareness of yourself, so try to be open. You may simply need a little time to adapt. The potential to be misled or to fall into the trap of self-deception is strong from August 13–17, and again from August 20–26, and you may not be kind to yourself if it happens. Try to remember that you're only human. Does this sound like a month filled with weird occurrences? The energy of the solar eclipse on August 20 prompts deep self-exploration, and sometimes you just run into some pretty unusual shadows within yourself.

September

There is yet another eclipse of the Moon on September 6, and this one ushers in a more kind and gentle quality. Heaven knows you're ready for it, and although the circumstances of your life may not be drastically altered, your manner of dealing with your everyday happenings can be different. Look for or create opportunities to enjoy working cooperatively with others, since sharing the joy of accomplishment may seem much sweeter than celebrating alone. You're feeling most optimistic in situations that are goal directed, and if you don't have definite plans, then make some. Set your strategies into motion during and after the New Moon on September 20, when there's plenty of room for expansion if you're starting on a solid foundation. Even though you may have to make a few adjustments later, at least you're getting started.

October

A high activity month, you may feel like you'd just prefer to be a spectator some of the time. That's okay, too, and it's a good idea to listen to your intuitive voice when you hear, "Slow down a little." Until after the Full Moon on October 5 you may feel that much of your time is encumbered by demands from others. Although your calendar may still be rather full, at least you seem to be calling the shots more frequently after October 12. You're much more comfortable setting limits and working from a schedule, since a completely unpredictable life might feel strangely insecure and unstable. Choose activities that leave you feeling that you've created something worthwhile at the end of the day. Make sure to leave enough time to unleash your sensuality. That's good news for your partner, but you're likely to enjoy it even more!

November

You're filled with anticipation and high levels of self-confidence. This is a great time to schedule activities that can lead to a meaningful alteration of your life—like an important meeting or presentation, a special celebration with your sweetheart, or a significant family gathering. During the Full Moon on November 4 you may be inspired to make changes in your home environment or showcase your creative efforts. If you're not quite ready, wait until the New Moon on November 18. Personally satisfying experiences are high on your priority list, and you expect a lot from yourself. Just try to remember to be kind with your expectations of yourself and others, since there's nothing quite so painful as a fall from the pinnacle of shattered anticipation. If you've been listening to your intuitive sensibilities while observing the responses from the people around you, you're likely to gauge your hopes more carefully.

December

If you're feeling a bit short-tempered this month don't be surprised. You're more sensitive to criticism, too. It sounds like you might need a little time to yourself just to escape from the pressures around you. This is most frustrating in the middle of the month, when you may feel like you're running on fumes. If everyone else seems to have abandoned you it could be that they're also stressed out. Create a haven from the hassles by taking time out for little breaks on December 5, 6, 15, 24, and 25. These are the times when you need to feel wanted and appreciated, and you might even feel better if you have a chance to show others how much you care for them. There's no need to overextend yourself, though. A totally exhausted version of you is not nearly as much fun to be around.

Leo Moon

Something about you engages the attention of others. Your Leo Moon can be radiant in the gleam of the spotlight. The warm glow that fills your soul when someone you admire or care for shows their respect and appreciation keeps you going, and your lively energy can inspire others, too. You can be big-hearted and possess a playful nature that nurtures your ever-present inner child.

You need to know that those you love will be loyal. When friends, lovers, and family are on the receiving end of your unforgettable hugs and protective grace they learn to understand the true power of the love you feel for them. Despite your generosity, you can be selfish, possessive, and willful when you're feeling insecure, and if you've been betrayed or abandoned you can feel completely devastated. When you're stuck in a jag of self-absorption you may have great difficulty establishing objectivity, and it is then that your selfishness can wreck a relationship. You need to find options for exercising your creativity and imagination that will help you reach outside yourself and stay in touch with the rest of the world. Then, you'll also become more adaptable when you're faced with the challenge of change or disruption. Sometimes, your mind and heart are uplifted by change, yet when you must respond to those changes that seem to come from outside, you can be stubborn.

Your soul is on fire with creativity. When you share your expressiveness with the world, you're shining with the power of love. It is this feeling that allows you to embrace yourself and develop your link with universal power. This stimulates a release from self-absorption and you become more self-expressive. After all, the world is your stage and you are the ultimate performer. Just remember that you are always adored, even if you cannot hear the applause.

The Year at a Glance for Leo Moon

Some of your old attachments are loosening this year and you're breaking free of attitudes that have blocked your ability to fully experience a new level of awakening. After a year of expansive opportunity during 1997, you're making some adjustments that will strengthen your stability while you move into new areas of personal growth during 1998. Your ability to direct the course of your life is strengthened, but you must stay connected with your inner self.

The eclipse cycles have a significant impact in your life during 1998, and it is during the next two years that you have an exceptional opportunity to get in touch with your feelings. You'll run into problems if you try to hide from your real feelings, but if you embrace them you may discover something about yourself that sparks a renewed sense of vitality. Saturn continues its transit in trine to your Moon, but you're also feeling some restraint from Saturn's travels as this energy moves into a square aspect to your Moon. You get a little preview of the emotionally stressful areas of your life during the summer months when Saturn moves into Taurus for a brief period. Listen to yourself during this time, and look around you for the areas in your life that need revision and resolution.

The slower moving outer planets—Uranus, Neptune, and Pluto—all present their own special challenges and dawnings. If your Moon is from 0–14 degrees Leo, you're experiencing the impact of these cycles in a more profound way during this year. The very foundations of your life may seem to be disrupted as you look toward a future that holds a freer sense of yourself. If your Moon is in later degrees of Leo you're feeling more stabilized, but may perceive that you're at the tip of the iceberg of change. You're right!

Even though the temptation to think that life is only what you sense on the physical plane—the things you can touch, taste and feel for "real"—there are other planes of reality that are just as powerful. It is your connection to these other realms that will allow you to manifest what you most need and desire. Change begins on the inside and extends into the world around you.

Affirmation for the Year

"When I release my will to the Source I become the magical creator of change and opportunity!"

January

It is through self-expression and inspired action that you manifest the realization of long-held dreams this month. Even though this can be a lucky period, your best fortune comes from the results of extending yourself to others and allowing the love and warmth to return to you as naturally as the rays of the Sun illuminate the day. Practical considerations may require you to make a few adjustments in your plans near the Full Moon on January 12, but you're ready to make tracks from January 12–24. The major problem resides in trying to do too much or attempting to force a situation that may not be quite ready. Be alert to the signals that tell you where you stand. Generate enthusiasm and garner support during this time, and then set your course for action during and after the New Moon on January 28, when the support you feel from others galvanizes your confidence.

February

From February 1 until the Full Moon in Leo on February 11 your passion for life inspires a need to reach out. This can be a truly productive period, but you may have to share the limelight with someone else. In fact, you may not fully enjoy your successes unless those you love are there with you. This can also be a critical period in relationships, and if you're dissatisfied or frustrated or feel the same from your partner you'll do yourself a favor by finding out what's wrong. You may just need to bring your love back to life and get out of those stale routines. Outside the realm of relationships, you're ready to make a few adjustments in your routine or to let go of habits that are costing you precious energy and time. Keep your expectations in line with realistic possibility, and look beneath the surface if you really want to make a difference in your life. The solar eclipse on February 26 emphasizes the importance of your intuitive voice. Listen to it.

March

During the early part of the month you're in a reflective mood and may feel a bit withdrawn. The lunar eclipse on March 12 marks an important period of reflection and inner awareness, which can be especially helpful if you've just made a significant change. Your dreams speak volumes from March 4–13 and may be the source of valuable information about an emerging new direction. This awareness empowers you with the confidence to let go of the past and to move into fresh territory through your creativity and personal expression. By surrounding yourself with situations and people who inspire your imagination you may surprise yourself with the emerging realizations you're experiencing after March 9. Take advantage of the energy of the New Moon on March 27 to stabilize a significant plan or project.

April

The conservative flavor of energy until after the Full Moon on April 11 can actually be quite useful if you're trying to get to the bottom of a situation. Be sure your actions and words are in harmony with one another, since sending double messages now will only get you into hot water. You're vulnerable from Arpil 15–30, when you may only see what you want to see about someone or something. This can be especially bothersome if you're trying to make a long-term decision or questioning a commitment. Unless you feel confident and clear, use this time to investigate your deeper desires and feelings. You may want something so desperately that you'll settle for a person or situation that almost fits the bill, but you deserve more. Before you sell out, be honest with yourself. If you know you're compromising, you're less likely to be angry with yourself if you later discover you've sabotaged yourself.

May

Greater clarity ushers in the month, although you may still be feeling frustrated with the status quo. Sometimes the need to change overwhelms your ability to decide in which direction to go first, and since you can see yourself and your needs more clearly now at least you have a better perspective on the best place to start. Stressful circumstances escalate near the Full Moon on May 11, when the demands and needs of others can overwhelm your own. By May 17 you're in a better position to negotiate, but watch your temper, because if you're angry with the options it will definitely alter the outcome of your agreement. Straightforward interactions are more the order of the day after the New Moon on May 25. Use the time prior to get rid of unnecessary baggage. You need an entertaining escape from May 29–31, but keep it simple.

June

Your feelings about someone or something you once enjoyed can suddenly change prior to the Full Moon on June 9, and if you're wondering why you have only to realize that you've been undergoing an awakening and those old things just don't fit with your new reality. This energy stimulates a breakthrough and can be self-confirming. You may realize that you've been emotionally tied to someone despite your best efforts to conceal if from yourself, and if you need to break away, then this is a good time. You may also need to open a door, and if that's the case, then look carefully at the illusions you cherish before you turn the key. There's nothing like staring your dream in the face only to discover that it wasn't what you wanted after all.

July

Heightened awareness results from open communication of your needs this month. You may experience a ground-breaking opportunity that alters your attitudes about your connections to others from July 1–7. New friends emerge and different circumstances prompt you to employ your most inventive ideas and expressions. Inspired by the challenge, you may feel that you're capable of altering the course of your life—and you are. Your old security needs beckon during the Full Moon on July 9, but they may be just a test of your ability to break through the blocks into a different reality. Initiate the changes you wish to make just after the New Moon on July 23, but be clear about where you're going, since it's easy to head off into a fog and feel confused. Get your bearings, move carefully, and then forge ahead. Watch for a few pitfalls on July 31, otherwise, it's pretty clear sailing.

August

The eclipses this month are significant indicators of brewing crisis. Changes are reaching their peak, and you're ready to experience a feeling of rebirth. During the lunar eclipse on August 7, explore what you need from your relationships. Look at yourself and the way you've been responding as a partner. What can you alter that will provide a more fulfilling experience of love? You may decide you're ready for a complete change, and that's okay, too. Just be sure to reach closure or you'll carry the same issues into your next relationship. The solar eclipse in Leo on August 21 marks a powerful time of renewal, but also challenges you to abandon purely selfish motivations in favor of actions and attitudes that empower all concerned. You don't have to give up self-control, but may have to relinquish control over a situation that is not yours to direct.

September

You may feel that most of the barriers are out of the way, and have every opportunity to clarify your intentions and move forward until the lunar eclipse on September 6. Then it's time to examine your motivations and make room for the new discoveries you've just encountered. With Mars influencing your Moon you may be too intense, so watch for signals that tell you when it's time to back away just a little. Your drive to fulfill your needs is very powerful, and if you're frustrated or feeling blocked you may become more demanding or competitive. With so many details complicating the picture it's critical that you remain organized. An easier flow of energy emerges after September 25, but your drive does not diminish. This is an excellent time to make repairs—at home or in a relationship. It's difficult to know how far to go when you're tearing down walls!

October

Your eye for elegance is searching for that which is beautiful, and you can express those elements of yourself that qualify as bedazzling. Take advantage of situations that give you a chance to shine during the Full Moon on October 5. Allow yourself to be open to unusual or innovative opportunities from October 1–15, when incorporating advances into your creative endeavors can be invigorating. Personal relationships can also be more rewarding, especially if you're enjoying the energy of your partner. Despite a positive turn of events during the New Moon on October 20, complex situations are likely to emerge by October 25. You may simply need to allow room for the idiosyncrasies of another, but you can also feel offended or assaulted if you're confronted with someone whose sensibilities are completely foreign to your own. You don't have to like it, but before you turn away, ask yourself if you were at all interested.

November

After a bumpy start during the Full Moon on November 4 you're ready to explore the best ways to mend fences so you can move on. Inspired by new places, unusual people or special interests, you're expanding your options and may be more confident. Try to avoid the temptation to fulfill expectations from others that don't really fit, and watch your own tendency to anticipate the actions or support of another. Although you have a right to expect certain things, your expectations can be out of line with possibility. Give yourself a chance to experience the reality of your situation before you jump to any conclusions! After November 23, despite the fact that Mercury is in retrograde, your optimism seems to be well founded. Don't start anything that will completely alter your life until you've considered everything. Minimal knowledge will only lead to trouble.

December

Surround yourself with inspiring possibilities during the Full Moon on December 3. You may feel ready to begin a new project or to incorporate changes into your life, and this is an excellent time of clarity. Continuing with the things that have been successful in the past is your best option until after December 11, and then you're in a good position to make some adjustments, bring something important to a close, and prepare for the new year. Take advantage of the high energy of the New Moon on December 18 to initiate significant alterations in your life. If you're feeling resistance it could be that you're a little ahead of the game. It's still good to lay the groundwork, but you're likely to be eager to get moving. If you can't take major steps, do something that underscores the fact that you're on your way.

Virgo Moon

Somewhere in the back of your mind is a long list of preferences that rarely go unnoticed by your subconscious self. Through your Virgo Moon you're drawn into a world of fine detail. It is those fine points that titillate your interest and add to your sense of perfection. You're much more sensitive than others think you are, and may even be more sensitive than you realize.

You love it when you've had a good day—one of those times when you've produced something that meets with your high standards. Your mind is continually busy analyzing everything, and if you're without a positive focus you can waste your energy worrying about trivia. Developing the patience and deliberate focus required to filter your thoughts and slow down your ever-spinning mind is your best avenue for creating inner peace. If you're seeking self-improvement, this may be the most important place for you to start!

Your eyes shine when you have a chance to give of yourself and realize positive results of your service. Whether you're teaching what you know, concentrating on improving something, or building a foundation of greater knowledge—it is the process of personal development that will ultimately allow you to accept yourself and gain a true sense of individual worth and power. If you're feeling inadequate all the time you may fall into the trap of becoming a victim or martyr.

Since very little escapes your critical sensibilities, you need to find a reasonable outlet for their expression. Striking a few requirements from your unwritten list of expectations for yourself will lead to more fulfilling life experiences, including better relationships. Training your keen awareness so that you are more tolerant of the diversity of life can be just as exciting as uncovering the problems you see with such clarity. When you're faced with those mistakes you find so frustrating, try to remember that you are, after all, still human.

The Year at a Glance for Virgo Moon

While this can be an especially productive and rewarding year, you're also facing the challenge of uncovering the inner aspects of your psyche. This is not an overnight process, so relax, you have plenty of time. But there's a quality of impatience driving your need to "get it right," and that makes it difficult to enjoy the fun you could be having along the way! 1998 is a great year to laugh more and play more often, discovering the key to developing true joy.

This year, the eclipses complete their cycle in the Virgo-Pisces axis, and as a result you may feel a little more vulnerable. You can no longer ignore the areas in your life that are the sore points—it's time to be clear about your feelings and to make the changes necessary that will allow you to feel more whole. You have a little help from the energy of Saturn that makes its entry into a trine aspect to your Moon, adding a sense of stability and focus.

Jupiter is transiting in opposition to your Moon this year, adding high expectations to your list of feelings. This cycle can be a wonderful confidence builder if you have a strong foundation. If you're trying to boost your confidence based on false security, however, you're likely to overcompensate by indulging in things that are not really good for you.

The slower-moving outer planets—Uranus, Neptune, and Pluto—are stimulating their own challenges. First and foremost, realize that you're ready for change and that everything may not be perfectly in place before those changes are happening. If your Moon is in the first 15 degrees of Virgo, these changes may be more immediate. Take a deep breath and keep your eyes open. You don't want to miss anything! If your Moon is from 15–29 degrees of Virgo, you're making a series of adjustments this year. Those adjustments can range from simple things like rearranging the furniture to larger changes, like moving or changing jobs. The crux of what's happening centers on preparation for a period of greater stability. After all, you are quite flexible and capable of adapting and making the most of whatever situation you're in!

Affirmation for the Year

"My life is filled with true abundance and my heart sings with joy!"

January

The distractions you're experiencing early in the month can leave you feeling too scattered, and you may simply require a period of retreat near the time of the Full Moon on January 12 to regroup and refocus your energy. It's easy to be irritated by people whose motives are purely selfish and situations that remain in crisis when there are perfectly workable solutions. As a result, you may break away from the action and shift your priorities to your own needs. Allow more time for experiences that bring you a sense of peace, since there are plenty of reasons to feel stressed. Nonproductive circumstances can become conflict ridden simply out of frustration, but relationships that inspire your sense of beauty and expression of love can prosper.

February

The intense tension from Mars and Pluto to your Moon from February 1 until the Full Moon on February 11 can leave you feeling like you're in a pressure cooker. You can direct these energies positively by cleaning out clutter, eliminating useless or outworn things and ridding yourself of unnecessary frustration. Expectation can be a problem if you're being unrealistic about yourself or others, or if you allow someone to expect things of you that are impossible. This is a period of strong objectivity lessons, and if you're having trouble seeing yourself or your options clearly, talk over your concerns with a trusted counselor. The solar eclipse on February 26 can bring any relationship issues to a crisis point, and you may be scrambling to respond to the actions or attitudes of your partner or a social situation. Maintaining your emotional center can be a real trial.

March

You may feel especially vulnerable near the time of the Virgo lunar eclipse on March 12. There's no more fence-sitting on important issues. In fact, you may feel like the fence has just collapsed and you're left with a pile of debris if you've put off standing up for yourself and your needs. If you've been too shortsighted and holding onto ideas or feelings out of fear, those foundations are rather shaky now, too. Old beliefs that no longer stand up to your awareness of truth are vulnerable—including the things you've allowed yourself to hang onto despite your better judgment. It may take a while to get used to the changes you're making, but there's always a period of adjustment while you struggle against your old way of thinking. Remind yourself of your priorities frequently, and affirm your needs by honoring your deepest feelings and carefully considering the needs of others.

April

Hard work or attention to projects that require more fastidious detail takes much of your time until after the Full Moon on April 11. You may be especially tense—emotionally and physically—during this period, and can benefit by remaining aware of the things that create tension in your life. You may be the one causing the problems through your subconscious responses, and by shifting your attitudes you can develop a more profound sense of self-control and control over your environment and life. Smooth over the rough spots in your love life by giving your partner a little extra attention after April 12, and find ways to praise and support your family and friends that are meaningful to them. You can turn over a new leaf during and following the New Moon on April 26 by concentrating on ways to have fun while employing your creativity.

May

Your security base and emotional foundations can grow stronger, leading to a feeling of safety and self-assurance. From May 1 through the Full Moon on May 11 you're experiencing a firm confirmation of yourself through higher levels of productivity, and you may be much more confident about asserting yourself where it really matters. Personal relationships improve through shared vision and by taking time out to enjoy the best qualities of those you love. Getting back to nature can be thoroughly invigorating for you now, so let yourself enjoy spending time in your garden, walking through the park or woods, or enjoying a weekend in natural surroundings. Intellectual pursuits stimulate innovative change or unusual directions after the New Moon on May 25, but watch a tendency to over-commit your time. Maybe losing a little sleep is okay, but exhausting yourself will only leave you feeling grumpy.

June

There's excitement in the air, and you're ready to enjoy the more playful side of life. You can also feel that your energy is dissipated by too many activities or demands on your time, and if you'd rather do something else you may rebel during the Full Moon on June 9. Sometimes you just have to reach that boiling point before you finally let go, but be aware of the manner in which you're shifting gears if you want to avoid alienating someone you love. It's that part of you that doesn't want to miss anything important that can drive you nuts, so ask yourself if that's a well-founded fear or just a desire to escape before you give it much credibility. After the New Moon on June 23 you're feeling more centered, although your list of "wants" continues to grow longer. It's probably a good idea to keep your expenditures to a minimum unless you really need something.

July

Your imagination is working overtime early in the month, although practical considerations, like getting all your "work" done may stand in the way of enjoying the benefits of your imaginative reverie. Is it possible to make working more playful? Now, that may sound contradictory, but when you get in touch with your feelings during the Full Moon on July 9, you may discover that you really need to enjoy everything you're doing. Try this exercise: Each time you pass a mirror, stop and smile. Before you know it, you'll be smiling more often, laughing more easily and allowing your jovial side to emerge without such trouble. It's just that there have been a few tests and trials lately, and your worrisome side may have left your childlike innocence somewhere in the dust. Make a resolution to recover that part of yourself by the New Moon on July 23.

August

Even though you may be surrounded by a series of changes during the lunar eclipse on August 7, you're finding practical ways to assimilate them into your life. Those who share your life are very important now, and if you seek out excellent methods of showing your appreciation you can turn around a situation that may have grown difficult. Since you're more comfortable expressing your feelings and asserting your needs in a positive manner from August 1–21, you may be the one who initiates some of the changes. The solar eclipse on August 21 marks a period of release, and although you may not feel completely satisfied with everything, you can strengthen those areas in your life that are working. After all, if everything was already perfect, what would you have to do?

September

Others around you may be going through a period of trial or testing near the lunar eclipse on September 6, and the manner in which you express your care and support will make a difference in the quality of your relationship to them. Even though you may want to just take charge of a situation, it could be more productive if you keep the door open by taking on the role of teacher, guide, or counselor instead of just doing everything yourself. With the help of the energies of Mercury and Venus transiting over your Moon this month you're in a great position to express your best attributes and share your deepest feelings. So, if you've been waiting for the right time to tell someone how you feel, watch for the signals, listen to your heart, and confess its yearnings. The Virgo New Moon on September 20 is an excellent time to open the door to love.

October

Although you may be spending a little more time on personal matters through the Full Moon on October 5, you're feeling an increased drive after October 7 when Mars enters Virgo. This can be a period of strong productivity, but you can also be more critical and less sensitive, since your focus is on getting the job done. Patience is not easy to come by under this influence, which will extend into next month, so pace yourself and remember that impatience is a form of tension! The overall flow of your life improves after October 16, although you may not feel that you're free of some of the things that cause you worry or concern until after October 24. It's just easier to let go of the controls a little, but remember that the part of you that wants to keep everything running smoothly is working overtime.

November

If you're involved in a large project, extended travel, or situations that have you juggling your time, you can feel way too much emotional stress early in the month. Use the power of the Full Moon on November 4 to release your anxieties and relinquish your attachment to the things that are really unnecessary. You need to open the doors of emotion just a bit and take a few more deep sighs, but just as important, you need to make room for positive growth and expansion. If you're hanging onto old hurts, issues, or feelings that have their roots in the past, it is now time to tell them good-bye so you can make room for greater joy. There's nothing frivolous about this, it's just common sense. If your coffers are full of old junk, where are you going to place the treasure you've just found?

December

A few extra obligations on your time emerge during the Full Moon on December 3, but you might actually enjoy yourself by letting your hair down for a while. The changes around you can deflect your attention from the things that are at the top of your priority list, so think before you agree to be somewhere, do something or give up your resources. Otherwise, you may end up stuck in a situation you simply do not enjoy. Choices are easier after December 12, although there are still a few pressures around until just after the New Moon on December 18. From December 23 until the end of the month you are more focused on your values and need a chance to illustrate your feelings to those you dearly love. It's a good thing there's a holiday period, because you can really make the most of it this year by doing something you do well for those who touch your heart.

Libra Moon

Feeling connected to someone is not just a whim for you, it's a deep need driven by your Moon in Libra. Your connections range from lighthearted social contacts to intimate partnerships, and in each of them you may strive for a level of perfect harmony. Beautiful places, gorgeous people, and wondrous delights all fill your soul, and if you could live in a peaceful world where everyone is in rapport, you would be in paradise. You are actually fascinated by the imperfections, and as you mature you discover that the most wondrous parts of your life tapestry may be the texture and interest created by a few flaws. However, you do prefer that which is refined, and most enjoy being around people who have good taste!

One of your talents resides in your ability to maintain an inner balance, and others seek out your objective point of view. You can actually blend the elements of paradox because you can accept the beauty of divergent qualities. Finding the right life partner can be rather difficult, and the internal conflict you experience in the process can result from your need to have it all. You want the thrill that arises from a little conflict or chase, but don't want to be overtaken in the process.

Your approach to decision-making can drive some people crazy because you have your own complex set of deliberations that must be completed before you can make choices. Even when you do decide you may be filled with regret for what you did not choose. Once you've taken a stand for your needs, though, you can be passionate about maintaining your position. Sometimes, the price you pay is the awful pain of shattering the peace, and you walk away feeling very fragile. In the end, you discover that you must become your own perfect partner. What an amazing thought—you cannot have the "other" partner until you've found the one inside yourself!

The Year at a Glance for Libra Moon

You begin the year with strong confidence and enthusiasm, although you do have some challenges ahead. First and foremost you must make a determination about your primary needs and stick with your priorities once you've set them. There is room for alteration. In fact, you need to leave a little room in your life for the unexpected this year.

Saturn almost completes its cycle in opposition to your Moon this year, so it may take you a little beyond the end of 1998 until you feel this energy lifting. This is a period of personal testing, and what you're testing most stringently are your primary needs. If you've been avoiding coming to grips with the way you really feel about your life, your relationships, and yourself, then this is the time you'll face the music. You may also discover that it's time to reach closure with any unfinished emotional business so you can move on. The true reckoning occurs within yourself, and if you're making decisions that will open the way for growth, then the smile others see will be genuine.

Jupiter's transit presents a dilemma of too many choices, and learning to say "No" when necessary will serve you well. If you agree to every opportunity, you may end up being stretched beyond your personal limits, especially the limits of your tolerance! The outer planets—Uranus, Neptune, and Pluto—bring innovation and rejuvenation into your life this year. Your intuitive sensibilities are enhanced, and when they are coupled with your powerful logical thought you may be the instigator of ingenious alterations. This is especially true if your Moon is in the first 10 degrees of Libra, since the impact of evolutionary change and healing can be felt in most levels that relate to your home, security, and inner strength. If your Moon is in later degrees of Libra, you're likely to perceive that there are some emotional attachments loosening, but you may not be ready to let go just yet!

Affirmation for the Year

"By sharing joy and love I bring greater hope and harmony into the world."

January

You're feeling optimistic about the prospects ahead, and the actions you take now to assure that your needs are met can have a long-term impact. There is a little friction during the Full Moon on January 12 when you may run into conflict about whose needs are most important, and if, instead of trying to win, your energy is directed toward reaching a mutual understanding everyone can come out ahead of the game. You may be having second thoughts about promises you've made, including those in a relationship. It's necessary to re-examine your choices since you're continually growing, and some of the reasons you had before may not be important any longer. Make a few adjustments, then step forward onto a more fulfilling path with conviction and confidence during the New Moon on January 28.

February

Your attitudes may be positive, but you may have your doubts about your feelings in a love relationship, especially if your needs are unanswered. Before you give up, make an effort to change the way you're expressing what you want and need. A sweet, indirect approach may just result in a ho-hum response, but if you'll take the time to honestly express your feelings about the situation you're likely to see better results. At least you'll know where you stand, and that helps a lot when you're trying to decide what to do! The Full Moon on February 11 heightens your senses and marks a wonderful time to indulge your passions. The solar eclipse on February 26 can underscore a period of vague anxiety concerning home and family. Instead of worrying, try to get to the bottom of your concerns by staying in touch with your loved ones.

March

Your ability to assert yourself is stronger—you may even be painfully direct with those who are used to your agreeable air and expect you to try to please! If you're trying to catch the eye of someone special, your flirtation skills rise to the occasion from March 4–20. During the Moon's eclipse on March 12 you may prefer quiet time for reflection and creative contemplation, especially if you're tempted to jump into something unfamiliar. It's important to sharpen your priority list after

March 21, since you can be too easily pressured by others and their demands through the remainder of the month. If you're clear about your own feelings and needs, then you'll be able to say "No" when necessary, and can be cooperative and supportive when it will really work for you. An old love can resurface near the time of the New Moon on March 27, but this time, you're in a different frame of mind.

April

The pressures you feel until after the Full Moon in Libra on April 11 may be the result of trying to cram too much into too little time or space. There's a lot going on that falls into the category of "leftover business," so it's difficult to get new things started. That's fine, since if you are scattering your energy you'll only be extremely frustrated. You need to focus and may even feel that you're forced into some things you'd rather not do, but that fall under the category of "responsibility." It's okay not to like everything, but if you're obligated you still have to fulfill those promises. The internal pressures may be the result of wanting what you can't have, or craving what you do not need. Instead of making yourself miserable, bite the bullet and finish what you started. That's "Saturn talk"—it's about dealing with reality as it exists. If you want to change it, you first have to accept it!

May

You can see the light at the end of the tunnel, but you may feel that there is a lot resting on your shoulders right now. Take time out during the Full Moon on May 11 to release old emotional baggage and surrender worn-out expectations. Look for healthy ways to engage the support of others, especially if you feel you're carrying burdens that you need not carry alone; there are ample rewards to be gained from giving others a chance to show their talents. However, you may feel a little vulnerable if you start comparing yourself with others, so use your inner voice to remind yourself of your strengths. If an old relationship or unfinished feelings are plaguing you, be honest about what you need right now. Imaginative and fun-loving communication turns the tide with the New Moon on May 25. Enjoy yourself!

June

Practical considerations take a high priority, but you're feeling much more energetic and need to let your creativity emerge as a primary force. The Full Moon on May 9 stimulates an optimistic and hopeful viewpoint, and you'll enjoy experiences that allow you to be inspired and uplifted. The same old routine is not what you're after at all, and even if you only take a break for the afternoon or try a new place for lunch, you need a fresh perspective on life. You may be the initiator of change this month, but watch out, because you can be too convincing from May 12–16, when you could end up getting in over your head! Emotionally charged situations emerge during the New Moon on May 23, when you may have to juggle your priorities if you're going to satisfy all your obligations.

July

You may really want to have a peaceful, enjoyable time, but there are conflicts brewing. Look for the areas in your life where battle lines are being drawn and determine whether or not you really need to get involved in the fray. Otherwise, you could be pulled into uncomfortable situations during the Full Moon on July 9 that wreck your focus and cost you precious time. Use your sense of humor to diffuse a crisis, and focus your energy on creative and entertaining activities. The New Moon on July 23 stirs your imagination and ushers in a time of renewed hope, although there may still be some stick in the mud whose stubborn resistance could spoil a good time—if you let it! Keep your emotional boundaries intact and you'll be just fine.

August

Differences in opinion or priorities can put a damper on your plans from August 1–13, although there is hope of reaching an understanding. If you're trying to please everyone, just wait a while. There are other issues that need to be addressed, and once they're settled you can proceed. During the lunar eclipse on August 7 your imaginative ideas are a hit, and social activities or special interests can be very enjoyable. It's as though the clouds lift during the solar eclipse on August 21, when your creative sensibilities and need for peace and harmony are met with positive avenues for realization. There's even an element of surprise that can lead to opportunities you had not even considered. Personal relationships get a boost from breaking out of routine and doing something that sets a new precedent.

September

Find dramatic ways to express yourself from September 1–7, but be aware of the sensitivities of others during the lunar eclipse on September 6. There may be an emotional crisis, and if someone needs your support you may have regrets if you're not there for them. You're ready for change, and even if you just make a few minor alterations you'll feel more alive. Your risk-taking is more balanced early in the month, but for a few days before and after the New Moon on September 20 you can go overboard. Before you make promises try to be aware of their implications. Your clarity is better after September 23, when you're also more connected to your emotional center and can make decisions that fit your needs more comfortably. If you're considering making changes in your personal environment, wait until this time.

October

The social scene and your personal life get a positive boost from the energy of Venus transiting over your Moon this month. It's easier to express yourself and to feel that you're gaining the right kind of attention from others, too. Although you may be a little competitive during the Full Moon on October 5, you can have fun with that drive if you decide to be aware of what you're really doing. You may also be more accepting of extraordinary situations, people, or ideas, and since you need a little boost, this could be just what you're seeking to pull you out of the rut of predictability. Social activities like parties, community gatherings, or even a special lunch or dinner with good friends or family can initiate the forging of important bonds from October 18 until just after the New Moon in Libra on October 20.

November

Although there may be a bit of emotional tension in the air from November 1 through the Full Moon on November 4, you're the perfect person to break the ice and start things moving in a different direction. After all, you hate getting caught in those sticky situations where everyone is miserable. Just be sure you're not trapped by unrealistic expectations about the outcome of a situation, or that you don't get trampled because someone had the wrong expectations of you. You're seeing the true colors of those who've been pushing their own agendas out of greed or a need for power, and by November 22 you're breaking away from situations that fail to provide what you need. It's crucial that you complete your obligations, though, because you don't want to leave anything hanging over your head. You need to feel free.

December

Everything accelerates this month, thanks to the fiery energy of Mars igniting excitement and action. During the Full Moon on December 3 you're eager to explore something that will inspire your sense of adventure (without being too treacherous), and this is a good time to express your passion. Conflicts can arise from December 13–21, but if you are attentive to their origins you can actually be the peacemaker. This is a hopeful and joy-filled period, with ample energy behind your emotional self-expression. If there's something you want to say, or a connection you'd really like to make, take a deep breath and go for it during the New Moon on December 18. Maintaining your emotional center may be difficult if you're yielding to demands of others that don't feel good for you, but if you know what you want, you're not likely to be thrown off balance.

Scorpio Moon

There's no such thing as halfway for you when it comes to emotions—you've probed the depths and risen to the heights. Some can get away with scratching the surface of life, but your soul yearns to embrace the total experience of feeling. Your penetrating gaze conveys your awareness of what's happening beneath the surface to those who look into your eyes. You're driven by a need to experience the mysteries that "polite" society considers taboo: death, sex, pain, birth, power, or anything else easily denied. All these elements of life that require transformation fascinate you.

Although you're not particularly keen about anyone knowing your secrets, you do prefer relationships that allow you to experience a deep bond. Whether family member, friend, or lover, if someone wants to be close to you, they must be honest, since if they're not, you'll never trust them. Sometimes, your feelings become too intense even for you, and if you're not ready to deal with them, you can just stuff them into that vault that contains all your shame, guilt, and self-doubt. To avoid being found out, you're capable of erecting barriers that keep everyone else out of your inner sanctum. Although this protects your vulnerability, it can be the source of monumental frustration when you do want to let someone get close to you.

Phenomenal changes have accompanied you all your life, and will continue. You're always transforming, always in the process of rebirth. Peeling away the layers of life, you discover yourself and the hidden truths at every turn. Throughout this process, you have amazing experiences. It's just that some of them are too personal to include anyone but you.

The Year at a Glance for Scorpio Moon

In many respects, 1998 is an inspiring and optimistic year for you. You do have some tests, but you may feel better equipped to deal with them. You're ready to experience a period of reward and opportunity that will allow you to expand your security base and trust your emotions more fully. To take advantage of these changes, you may have to let go of some of your old habitual responses.

The most advantageous cycle for you during 1998 is the result of Jupiter transiting in trine aspect to your Moon. During this cycle you're ready to take more risks, particularly if they could result in growth or expansion. Emotionally, you're more confident about fulfilling your needs. It's necessary to remain aware of your personal boundaries and to honor your responsibilities and limitations during this period.

If your Moon is in the very early degrees of Scorpio you may feel more frustrated, since Saturn is moving into an opposition to your Moon while Neptune is squaring your Moon. These two influences can leave you with a sense of self-doubt, particularly if you've trusted the wrong people. If you're aware that you need to establish a firm foundation that will support your dreams, then you'll make better choices.

If your Moon is about 10 degrees Scorpio (plus or minus 3 degrees) you're feeling some agitation from the energy of Uranus. It's difficult during this cycle to feel centered or in control, since life is more unpredictable. Getting settled may seem impossible, but trying to hold on to what you no longer need won't help a bit. Flowing with this cycle requires that you admit to yourself that you're ready for greater independence and freedom of expression. If your Moon is in the last 15 degrees of Scorpio you're making adjustments that will lead to greater stability as you face the changes ahead during the next two years. Your self-assurance is strong now and will function like a beacon.

This is a powerful year of healing for all individuals with Scorpio Moon, and a time filled with penetrating vision. You'll be amazed at the results if you develop your inner sensibilities more fully and trust your power to create life on your own terms.

Affirmation for the Year

"My heart is filled with perfect peace as I open to new levels of personal prosperity."

January

Although you may look calm, you can feel rather agitated—especially if you're waiting for something you really want. You're filled with high hopes. Use the energy of the Full Moon on January 12 to open the doors of your heart and allow yourself to receive positive rewards for your efforts and self-expression. Take care of all the contacts, meetings, plans, and details, and allow extra time for unanticipated interruptions this month, but plan for fast-paced changes after January 17. The New Moon on January 28 marks a significant period of innovation and change in your life, and if you'll be a little flexible, you can take advantage of an opening that will allow you to further your aims. If there's something you've been hoping to do, a contact you've wanted to make, or new paths you've hoped to pursue, get ready to take the leap on January 29.

February

You're more effective in getting what you've wanted, especially in your personal life. During the Full Moon on February 11 you may run into some outside distractions, but you're still in a wonderful position to open up just a little. If you're not quite certain of how far you should go or whether you can trust someone, this is a good time to test the water. Make a few adjustments from February 12–14, and then move into position on February 17. You can sense big changes in the atmosphere, and as the time of the solar eclipse on February 26 grows closer you can use your imagination and creativity to alter the course of events so that your needs are met in a more advantageous fashion. You're definitely capable of getting right into the flow, and those currents can help carry you into ecstasy.

March

You're feeling hopeful, although there are a few problems resulting from different styles. Discovering that your favorite thing ranks low on the list of favorites for your sweetheart can be one of those issues. On an internal level, you're in pretty good shape, however. The lunar eclipse on March 12 helps you release some of your expectations and is a wonderful time to tune into your higher consciousness. From this perspective, you're okay with all these silly little diversions, since you can see that you will be getting back on track. So don't panic. Stop for a moment and go inside yourself; let go of the small stuff. The everyday hassles may be irritating, and if you have your mind on the larger goal, they will be less problematic.

April

You may feel like you're surrounded by control freaks. You don't have to play their game (besides that, you're probably better at it than they are anyway). There are just a few delays, reruns, and repetitions that add a pinch of anxiety to your life until after the Full Moon on April 11. Then the flow begins to shift again because some of the details have been worked out carefully enough to please all concerned. Your close relationships need a little fine-tuning, and some of the tiny frustrations you've been stuffing in that closet of yours are likely to emerge after April 12. Use conflict to initiate growth, and deal with anger when it arises. You'll be amazed at how much better you feel, not carrying all those explosive emotions around! If you're not getting what you want from your relationship, you're likely to be very clear about it during the New Moon. The cards are on the table. Your deal.

May

The process of re-shaping your life begins when you experience a deeper awareness of yourself and your needs. During the Scorpio Full Moon on May 11 everything seems more intense, but you're also very clearly aware of your feelings. If you're overwhelmed, spend a little time breaking down the situations and responsibilities that seem to be bombarding you. Release your attachment to particular outcomes, special situations, and things you know you don't need any longer. Forgive yourself for being merely human, and then surrender to your power—the power that connects you with the source. From this perspective, you can accomplish anything, including overcoming any insurmountable pressures. You're getting lighter and more self-confident, and even situations beyond your control can be incorporated into your life. Find your magic, and use it!

June

You know how irritating a mosquito can be—well, there are a few mosquitos in the shape of people and situations that can be really pesky. You can make yourself crazy dealing with them, you can make a few changes, or you can zap them. Now, squashing everyone who bothers you could leave a pretty messy situation, so you might want to find a more creative option—nonviolent zapping, or better yet, metaphysical repellent! Basically, you just have to make a few adjustments. You'll identify the areas requiring alteration during the Full Moon on June 9. After June 16, it's easier to find better support for your needs and wants. Then during the New Moon on June 23 you're in a great position to stabilize your life again.

July

Blocks in communication from July 1–3 may make you wonder if you're going to get through the month, but you're extra sensitive during this time. Give yourself a rest, and then you'll be ready to make your point with grace and ease during the Full Moon on July 9. Watch out for distractions that can take your focus away from the things you really want to be doing from July 12–18, because you'll resent yourself if you fall into those traps. By July 20 your clarity and concentration improve, and you're more comfortable with your choices. However, you may need to change your routine or shift your priorities just after the New Moon on July 23 due to situations that are beyond your control.

August

The eclipses mark a time of enhanced focus or awareness, and you're challenged to draw the line between what you want for yourself and what you're doing to satisfy someone else. It's okay to alter your life or your needs to include the needs of others as long as you feel good about it. If you've felt resentful, then the situation could be ready to explode during the lunar eclipse on August 7, or you can reach the end of your rope by the time of the solar eclipse on August 21. From August 1–13 you're in a good position to find creative solutions to the problems you perceive, and your talents and imagination give you what you need to illustrate your deeper feelings in a positive manner. Try to keep a low profile if you want to stay out of somebody else's issues or problems for the last few days of the month.

September

You're entering a more productive and easygoing cycle during September, and can reach a positive solution to problems or issues during the lunar eclipse on September 6. It is important to be attentive to things others need from you—even if that just includes a card, e-mail, or phone call—since your actions now can cement relationships with lovers, partners, friends, or family in a very positive way. After Septebmer 7 you're experiencing strong support for your aims and desires, and this is a great time to take action that will boost your self-esteem. Watch out for a few surprises during the month, particularly in the realm of family matters, and if you've done something that disturbs the balance, seek out ways to bring peace during the New Moon on September 20.

October

Change is in the wind, and you are its catalyst. Early on, until the Full Moon on October 5, you may feel that everything around you takes precedence over your priorities and needs—or at least that the power seems to be more "outside." That's really an illusion. You are preparing yourself for a period of profound personal empowerment by becoming more aware of the flow between internal and external energy. It's just that the external seems to be more intense in the beginning. By October 14, there's a shift in the balance of power, and your awareness yields to your intuitive flow and psychic attunement. Listen to it. You hear within you the stirring of alchemical renewal, healing, and transformation. If you want to change something, clarify it during the New Moon on October 20, let it gestate until October 25, and then put it into motion.

November

Subtle alterations in your environment, like moving furniture, hanging a wind chime in the doorway, draping a scarf in the corner of the room—all act to change the feng shui of your living space. You're interested in making the energy flow more powerfully and positively through your life, and you have a pure sensibility about the best ways to do this in your home environment during the Full Moon on November 4. Your heart is filled with love this month, and there are ample outlets for that expression—from relationships, to your work, to your quiet, creative moments. Do something that adds color and texture to your life. Change the way you look. Let your power emerge more freely. The Scorpio New Moon on November 18 is a time of renewal for you. Use it to your best advantage by expressions that strengthen your sense of personal power.

December

If someone does not fully understand the new you that has emerged, help them out by listening to their concerns. You don't have to be a chameleon for anyone—but you may want to know the effects you've had and decide if you like it or not. The Full Moon on December 3 marks a strongly opinionated cycle, when philosophical ideologies can create havoc. This includes your own, so watch the things that flip your emotional switches. If you prefer to respond differently, you can control that. After December 12 you're feeling more self-assured and are less likely to question whether you've done the right thing. Then on December 20 you're opening more to the needs to let your love and caring smooth the way for an easier understanding. Touch the people you love, and let them touch you.

Sagittarius Moon

Most content when you're on the move, your soul yearns to feel free. You think in terms of boundless possibilities. Through your Sagittarius Moon you're fascinated by the grand adventure of life, and whether you're traveling or taking trips in your mind, you're continually seeking answers to a never-ending barrage of questions. The quest for wisdom and truth keeps you on the move, emotionally, and often physically! Wide open spaces are much more to your liking in every part of your life—from environment to career to philosophical ideologies.

Relationships can be a strain in your life, especially if you've not found a fellow adventurer who understands your occasional bouts of wanderlust. Since everyone may not be so eager to hit the road in search of adventure, you can appear to be less loving than you really are. You are passionate and can be very demonstrative. When you're given ample independence it's easier for you to share the secrets of your heart. If you're smothered or inhibited, your spirit withers and you can become bitter.

Your approach to establishing a home is more like finding the right quest than it is finding a particular place. You may be quite capable of living in a variety of environments, and as long as you're learning and can maintain a sense of harmony between your spirit and your heart, you can be at home almost anywhere. Wherever you're nesting, you'll adore being surrounded by an environment that inspires you. In your heart, your mind, and your soul, you will forever be journeying, questioning, and wondering about the vast possibilities and reasons—ever continuing your search for the grail of truth.

The Year at a Glance for Sagittarius Moon

The energies for 1998 provide a strong balance between flexible change and stabilizing growth. Everything happens with increased intensity, and that will be the story for the next ten years while Pluto is transiting in Sagittarius, influencing your innermost needs. There are special cycles that will be influential through this year, indicating that you're experiencing a positive sense of renewal and hope.

The stability you're feeling is due to your connection with the realities of life. Saturn's cycle provides a sense of focus and self-discipline that can be very helpful if you're trying to get your life in order or if you're ready to settle into a routine for a while. However, it's unlikely that you'll be satisfied with too many restraints, so you can also utilize this influence to help you eliminate inhibitions or restrictions.

Jupiter's cycle provides distractions, and you may find that you're continually promising too much or obligating yourself to situations that end up taking more time and energy than you had anticipated. However, you're also feeling very confident and optimistic, and that's part of the problem: you may be too optimistic when you actually need to consider your choices more carefully. This is a wonderful time for study or travel, even though you may find it hard to stick with one subject or interest for very long.

If your Moon is from 0–10 degrees of Sagittarius you're feeling an exceptional sense of transformation and evolution. You may even experience changes you had not considered possible, and your response to situations that are beyond your direction will determine how successfully you assimilate these alterations into your life. It's time for you to let go of the people, attitudes, and situations that stand in the way of your personal growth—but you need to watch a tendency to escape too quickly before you've said all your good-byes. If your Moon is in later degrees of Sagittarius, use this time to get your life and your goals in order.

For all Sagittarius Moons, the next few years will be filled with a series of changes and challenges, opening to new vistas in your quest for truth. If you have your feet on the ground you'll handle them with greater ease.

Affirmation for the Year

"I am confident and filled with joy!"

January

You begin the year with strong vision and a powerful, optimistic attitude. Feeling more self-assured from January 1–12, you're ready to take a few risks on the personal level and tell someone how you feel. This is a great time to have a heart-to-heart talk with your partner or best friend, although you're a bit more vulnerable during the Full Moon on January 12 and might prefer to keep your thoughts to yourself. Take a look at your personal environment and clear away clutter and things that leave you feeling cramped. You might enjoy time away from home for a while this month, when travel, study, or business can invigorate and inspire you. From January 23–24 you're experiencing a strong desire to break out of routine and change your habits, and during the New Moon on January 28 you're ready for a change of scenery. New friends instill a fascination with innovative possibilities.

February

Don't be surprised if you're more short-tempered than usual, especially if you're hoping for things to go one way and discovering that you're in a totally different circumstance. Staying focused is difficult if you're in too much of a rush, so when you feel that life is getting away from you, try to slow yourself down and take a deep breath. The Full Moon on February 11 brings excitement and hope, and you're filled with anticipation about your plans. You may sense that there's impending doom. Relax—it's just the pressure arising from the solar eclipse on February 26 that can bring a brewing conflict to a climax. You'd prefer a resolution to all the tension, anyway, so try to avoid the knee-jerk reaction of running away and deal with the problems as they arise, particularly in the realm of family matters. Take a careful look at your habitual responses and find ways to alter those that rob you of the joy you deserve.

March

After a bumpy start, most of the emotional intensity dies down following the lunar eclipse on March 12. Feeling more optimistic by March 4, your imagination is stirred and your spirits lifted through the experience of unconditional love and acceptance. You're finding it more rewarding to focus on the spiritual elements of your life, and the efforts you're putting into merging your spirituality with your everyday life are paying off through a clear awareness of the difference between your wants and your needs. Staying busy and active keeps you alive and free, and you may derive an especially positive benefit from travel, teaching or writing (although you may not feel you have much time to elaborate on your busy life!). Make the contacts that will open doors of opportunity and future growth from March 14–26, and then take bold steps to strengthen the relationships and situations that are your highest priorities after the New Moon on March 27.

April

If you can keep your focus on your highest priorities through the Full Moon on April 11, you'll be amazed at your progress! You'll have the best success when you listen to the prompting of your intuitive voice, although you may be tempted to let some of the apparent "facts" lead you astray. Blending your intuitive sensibilities with the facts of a situation is your best bet, but if your feelings tell you something is not right, listen. Look carefully before you decide to follow the guidance of others or before you make major alterations in your life, since you're vulnerable to seeing only the the facade from April 13–19, and can make choices that you later regret. You may feel trapped by the expectations of others, wanting to please or satisfy them, but feeling that you want or need something different. Let your heart provide the guiding light.

May

Your passion for life is powerful, and you're prompted more by a desire to fill your life with joy. This quality can shift your focus toward more satisfying experiences in your personal relationships, although you may run into a sticky situation during the Full Moon on May 11. This is more trouble if you've failed to make your feelings or needs clear, so use crisis to get everything out into the open. You don't really like any situation that backs you into a corner, and unless you're certain that you want to keep a connection going, you're ready to find the first way out. Playful, humorous activities lift your spirits this month, and even though you may be surrounded by a few sticks in the mud, you can at least see the humor in your circumstance!

Make room for the needs of others during the New Moon on May 25, when smiles on their faces can be just the ticket for turning your life around.

June

You're feeling playful and footloose, and during the Sagittarius Full Moon on June 9 you're ready to pull out the stops and do something fabulously enjoyable. If your feelings about a relationship or your career are shifting, listen to them. It may be time to pursue a different direction or to incorporate features into your life that more clearly suit your needs. What others see as competitive you may intend to be fun, so watch out for responses and alter your actions and words if you've stirred a hornets' nest—that is, unless you intended to stir it up, then you need to have your shield up and ready! Sending mixed messages can also be a problem, particularly if you're not paying attention to the responses of others. This is not a time to trust your first impression when making major decisions, since you're really not in the mood to dig deeply, and you could be stuck in a trap if you leap too quickly.

July

Since you can usually talk your way out of trouble, you may have to use those skills from July 1–7. Whether you're defending yourself or the actions of another, your ability to dazzle others long enough to get the door open serves you well, except during the Full Moon on July 9 when you may be asked to produce proof of your claims! Emotionally complex circumstances can slow you down a bit after July 8, and if you're willing to sort through the issues, you may be able to reach a resolution before the New Moon on July 23. Be watchful for a tendency to take on more than you can carry or to want more than you actually need from July 12–20, when your overextended reach can leave you holding a very heavy bag of obligations. Even though you may not like what you've created, you can make a few adjustments and enjoy this period. It's like learning to like broccoli without cheese sauce.

August

After a few days of emotional intensity, you see a way beyond inconvenient issues during the lunar eclipse on August 7. The perspective you achieve during this cycle is enhanced if you're dealing with problems as they arise instead of thinking that things will get better by themselves. As you work your way through the maze you may even discover some unfinished emotional business that's been haunting your dreams and standing in the way of your happiness. After the solar eclipse on August 21 you're poised to lay out a fresh path, and may be inspired to redirect your energy into areas that bring substantial results. Loving relationships provide the support you crave, and there are different avenues to explore through an introduction to someone whose ideas provoke you to pursue a more fulfilling life direction.

September

The strength of your ideals carries you into a new realm of possibilities from September 1–5, but you may have to scale back on your plans after the lunar eclipse on September 6. It's those pesky practical matters that take so much of your time—you know, like balancing the checkbook, keeping track of your belongings, remembering to stop and eat dinner—all the things that slow your pace a little. You can actually enjoy the experience of settling into a routine if the things you're doing stir your spirituality and intellect. You'll have plenty of time next month to indulge your fantasies, so deal with your obligations now. Your drive to continue moving forward is powerful throughout the month, and after September 24 you'll feel less inhibited. Plan to break free and take a little trip or retreat from September 25–27.

October

It's easier to talk about your feelings, and if you've been wanting to clarify what's really going on in your close relationships the Full Moon on October 5 will prompt you to get into the essence of your situation. Despite the fact that you may like most things about your life, there's a little discontent brewing that feels like an undercurrent of agitation after October 7. This becomes more bothersome if someone is goading you into doing something you really don't want to do, and you're likely to lose your patience with the situation (or person) if it goes too far. Your saturation point is most intense from October

16 until just after the New Moon on October 20, when you're feeling more temperamental. Take the edge off by indulging yourself a little from October 13–15 and then on October 23 and 24, but cover your responsibilities unless you want to repeat some of the lessons you're learning.

November

If you're involved in a situation at work or in your personal life where others are pressing their personal agendas at the cost of progress, you're likely to call them on it. You have little patience for manipulation, especially in circumstances that could affect the success of something you hold dear. Selfish attitudes may seem to run rampant during the Full Moon on November 4, and unless you want to make things worse, be sure you're not one of those whose personal interests are compromising the higher good. If you can't reach resolutions, look for creative distractions that allow you to dissipate some of your own frustration. Watch what you say (particularly after November 18) because this is prime time for putting your foot in your mouth! You have a chance to pursue a special interest after November 23, and can be in a situation to wield powerful influence. Choose wisely.

December

Although the pathway seems much less rocky you can still overstep your boundaries during the Full Moon on Decebmer 3, especially in the realm of social activities or partnerships. If you do step on somebody's toes you may actually find a gracious way to deal with it. Flowers are nice. Martial your courage and take a stand on something important if your position is compromised or threatened. You can be a formidable force now, and may also find it easier to surround yourself with others whose influence and support provide just the platform you need. The New Moon in Sagittarius on December 18 stimulates a period of adventure and generosity, and your actions and attitudes can actually alter the course of events that have become stale or routine. This is one of those times when you can have things *your* way!

Capricorn Moon

Thriving on a steady diet of challenges, you love the sweetness of success. Your Capricorn Moon drives you to accomplish your aims, and you feel most alive when you're making your way toward your goals. You take your responsibilities seriously, and appreciate others who have the self-respect to honor their own. Even when you reach the top you're likely to look for another peak to conquer, especially if it will afford you a sense of greater security.

You're cautious, and sometimes appear to be too somber, but once a job is done, you can let your hair down and do love to play. Your dry sense of humor is always operating, and in a tough situation you may be the one who finds a way to laugh through the pain. Producing tangible results brings deeper meaning to your life, and you'll feel most at peace when you've done a job well. Wasted time and effort simply do not make sense to you. Trouble can arise when control issues emerge: you really don't like someone else telling you what to do or how to do it. Sometimes it's hard to remember to put the shoe on the other foot, though!

Creating a home and family may be highly important, and once you make a commitment in a relationship you intend to honor it fully. To have the stable and fulfilling life you need you'll require a partner who appreciates your practical needs and understands your priorities. Learning to express your feelings may be difficult for you since you don't really like excessive displays of emotion. Once you've overcome your inhibitions, you may discover that you gain strength by letting others know what's in your heart.

The Year at a Glance for Capricorn Moon

Steady focus on your priorities and goals pays off during 1998. Although the pace of progress can be a little slow, it is definitely noticeable, and the confirmation you feel as a result can be quite satisfying. Your self-confidence expands, making it easier to accomplish your aims. There are some challenges, but nothing beyond your capabilities!

Jupiter's cycle in sextile aspect to your Moon brings true opportunity your way, and marks an excellent time to expand your personal space. If you want to move, it's easier now, although you may have to settle a few obligations first. You might also want to create a feeling of space by getting rid of clutter and making room for the things you really want. You may decide to travel, get involved in educational pursuits, or extend your influence in some way, and this is the perfect cycle to reach beyond your current situation and make improvements.

If your Moon is from 0–10 degrees of Capricorn, you're breaking through the barriers that have held you back and are now revolutionizing your life. The influence of Uranus, Neptune, and Pluto stirs powerful emotional changes that help you release your attachment to the past and look toward the future with greater hope. You're even more self-assured if your Moon is between 0–4 degrees of Capricorn, since Saturn is transiting in trine aspect to your Moon, bringing stability and self-awareness.

However, if your Moon is from 10–29 degrees of Capricorn you may feel that you're being tested while Saturn completes its square to your Moon. If you're feeling depressed or discouraged, try to look at your life situation from the viewpoint of what you really need. This cycle tests your ability to let go of the things that interfere with your growth, and marks a time when you learn better ways to satisfy your needs.

All Capricorn Moon individuals are experiencing a more profound awareness of new possibilities, allowing you to direct your practicality toward avenues that can free you of heavy obligations and give you more time to enjoy the fruits of your labor.

Affirmation for the Year

"*My life is filled with abundant opportunities for self-fulfillment.*"

January

There are a few distractions that may make it a little difficult to stay on track, but after making adjustments for the things you really must add to your busy schedule you can accomplish many of your aims. From January 1 until the Full Moon on January 12 you may have to answer to the demands of others more than you usually do, and this can lead to a period of reviewing your emotional entanglements. If you're unhappy with a relationship, look first at what you're giving to it. You may have been too busy with work or other obligations, but this is the perfect time to rearrange your priorities a little and give more of yourself. Since you're putting love to the test, clarify how you feel about yourself in the process and remind yourself that you deserve love that is truly fulfilling and supportive. It's okay to test your situation, just don't give up on your needs!

February

Incorporating change into your daily life is a little easier, and you'll enjoy those innovations that give you more time to explore your creativity. It's easier to be assertive, and you may even have to take charge in a situation that has gotten out of hand due to undermining power struggles from February 1–7. Love relationships require you to be open about your true feelings, and if you're holding back you may only be hurting yourself. By the time of the solar eclipse on February 26 you've had a chance to explore many of your doubts and questions. The opportunity to move forward with your aims in the world also adds a feeling of confidence to your emotional commitments. Celebrate your good fortune with those you love; a party or gathering after February 21 can be a truly memorable experience.

March

Early in the month you feel much more calm and self-assured. Surround yourself with people who echo your values, and demonstrate your trust and good faith in those who deserve it. Life gets hectic after March 5, although there's a little break for reflection during the lunar eclipse on March 12, when you may want to take time out to deal with personal business. Competitive situations can leave you feeling on edge after March 14, though, so look for the best ways to solidify your position while still staying in the game. Trying to take charge when it's not really your responsibility will get you into trouble, and may even put a definite block in your path. When you do have responsibilities, you can't shirk them either. The choice is to carry burdens that belong to you and to set limits and be strong when necessary. There's no waffling here—if there are guidelines and promises, honor them.

April

Friction with others may be the order of the day until after the Full Moon on April 11. You may even decide to break away from a situation that has become intolerable, but you can't say good-bye until your part of the bargain is fulfilled. Even though you can't control the way someone else is acting or responding, you can alter the outcome for yourself by maintaining an honest desire to reach closure. It's easier to forgive and move on after April 14, when you have better things to do than trying to revive a lifeless situation. Acts of generosity strengthen your self-worth after April 17, and if there is something you really want to do that will set a precedent for your "new" life, put it into action after the New Moon on April 26. Productive emotional situations are more the order of the day from April 17–30, when a stable home life provides the perfect anchor for the challenges you're facing.

May

There can be a little conflict between what you need and what you want, particularly if you're feeling pressured by someone else. Although you may have to put another's needs or priorities above your own for a while, you can still fulfill your primary needs, and during the Full Moon on May 11 can be rather creative about balancing the two. Watch what you say and do, though, because your actions and attitudes are likely to reflect your real feelings, and if you're trying to disguise your feelings and are just going through the motions, someone will see your insincerity. This could create a bit of a problem from May 10–16, and again near the time of the New Moon on May 25. It's okay not to like something (or someone, for that matter), but if harmony is necessary to get the job done, this is the test of whether you can buckle down and deal with the job and hand and then move on. Why drag it out with unnecessary conflicts?

June

Do you know how to juggle? Well, you can use that talent from June 1–15, when there are plenty of things to keep going at once! The Full Moon on June 9 can bring up situations that seem like the last straw, but with Saturn moving into Taurus, you may see a way to make it all work. It's a good thing you're adept at utilizing the talents of others, because now more than ever you'll benefit from drawing on their resources. This is also a time when you may be able to let go of old resentments and move toward more cooperative endeavors. The New Moon on June 23 marks a time when social obligations can actually prove to be beneficial, and you'll enjoy a party or festive family gathering on June 28 or 29.

July

Your priorities and the things others want from you don't really jibe very well from July 1–10, and since the Full Moon is in Capricorn on July 9 you may even be easily hurt if you feel that your needs always seem to come last. Before you get too down in the dumps identify the things about your life that are working, and put more energy into them. It's easier to focus your energy outward than inward, and consequently it's tempting to think that someone or something else is the cause of your discontent. Angry feelings can explode after July 15 unless you're releasing your frustrations and breaking away from situations that need to be changed. Relationships can be rewarding, but only if they're working for both of you. A one-way reward leaves somebody in a lurch!

August

Joining forces with someone you admire and trust can be especially satisfying, and for that reason your relationships can improve if you're actively participating in the process. If not, you may simply be on the receiving end of your partner's discontent. Watch your automatic responses to others during the lunar eclipse on August 7 and listen to your own internal dialogue. The illumination you gain in the process opens the way for fresh possibilities. Trying to contain your feelings works against you during the solar eclipse on August 21, when demonstrating your emotional needs and responses can turn the tide at a critical time. Your discontent may be a signal to shift your focus onto something else, although new options may not open up until after August 24. Even then, there's a conservative climate and you'll prefer to move slowly,

September

After a brief period of adjustment you're feeling more safe and secure. By the time of the lunar eclipse on September 6 your feet are on the ground and you have your bearings. Expressing your feelings and satisfying your needs is much easier, and everything may not arise from an intimate relationship. Your work can be exceptionally rewarding after September 7, and by using your abilities and talents to your best advantage you'll create a wonderful platform for long-term growth. Getting back to nature may be your best source of rejuvenation. If you can't take the time for a grand adventure, at least take a long walk in the park, around the lake, or through the woods. This is a period for your needs to take root and grow, and your choices can result in deeper levels of contentment. The New Moon on September 20 marks a positive time to establish yourself within a career, relationship, or life choice.

October

The frustrations you're experiencing until a few days after the Full Moon on October 5 are a direct result of tying up a few loose ends with too many interruptions in the process. Your confidence and courage are stronger after October 8, but there's a period of confusion from October 7–12 that results from a lack of communication or a breakdown in your routine. Your focus returns on October 13 and may catapult you into some heavy responsibilities. Before you pick up burdens that don't belong to you, make sure that someone really needs your help. Your life is back on track after October 24 when you're also willing to pay the price necessary for eliminating habits that undermine your needs and psychological well-being. Self-discipline and focus are powerful from October 24–27, marking an excellent time to modify your diet and routine and to re-evaluate your nutritional needs.

November

You need to feel productive this month, and can attract the support and help you need to accomplish your aims. You may also want to put your creativity to the test, and since you feel less vulnerable, this is a good time to do it! Allowing ample time to enjoy the people you love makes a huge difference in your sense of accomplishment and feelings of contentment. During the Full Moon on November 4 you're feeling very sensual, and if you're involved in a trusting relationship will enjoy indulging your needs to be close. Splurge a little and do something special. Make improvements at home, move, redecorate, or make repairs from November 1–23 when everything will go more smoothly. After the New Moon on November 18 you're eager to put your life in order, and if you're not satisfied by November 27 you'll feel pretty grumpy.

December

From December 1–11 you're easily agitated, especially if everything seems to be blown out of proportion during the Full Moon on December 3. Try to avoid the temptation to take charge of everything. Focus instead on the things that really need your energy and put everything else on the back burner. After December 12 Venus moves into Capricorn, adding a softness to your mood, and allowing you to be more expressive—if you will! But there's a little friction between Venus and Mars until after the New Moon on December 18 that can indicate a bit of difficulty in personal relationships, especially if you really want or need something and don't know how to ask for it (or don't have a good avenue to satisfy those needs). It's easier to focus on your emotional priorities after the winter solstice on December 21 when your inner self gets a bit of a boost. After then, allow more time to do things that fill your soul with true contentment. Forget about all those demands that take you away from the things you love for just a while.

Aquarius Moon

Even though you don't always admit it openly, you really like being different. Your Aquarius Moon generates a strong desire to break away from the ordinary, and it's the part of yourself that is truly extraordinary. Following a singular path toward personal fulfillment is crucial to your individual development. Your clear connection to the humanitarian spirit cries for liberation from prejudice and ignorance, and you may even lead the charge for revolutionary changes in the world around you.

Fascinated by unusual ideas, people, and circumstances, you admire that which is different, but may prefer to be the trendsetter. Factions that require you to adhere to values or ideals that compete with your high principles trigger your sense of rebellion. You're highly intuitive, and although you may strive to be purely logical, you frequently hear the whisper of your intuitive voice urging you to explore or include other possibilities. Through blending your logical and intuitive sensibilities you have the potential of developing a quality of genius. Your need to associate with others is powerful, and you can love your friends unconditionally. You're a bit difficult to tether, however, and prefer relationships without restraints.

It may surprise others to learn that you can be quite conservative, although anyone who has tried to get close to you will attest to your emotional walls. The detachment you project can feel cold to someone who wants your embrace. It's rarely been your intention to break hearts, but you sometimes do—just because you must follow that eternal urging to be, feel, and experience that which is beyond ordinary reality.

The Year Ahead for Aquarius Moon

You're ready to bring your life back into focus and build upon the opportunities you've encountered. 1998 can be a year of crystallization and stabilization for you, and although the pace slows down just a bit, you may welcome a break from the intensive growth. You're ready to acknowledge a more profound level of personal needs.

Jupiter leaves its conjunction to your Moon in February, but as this energy moves into the next sign you may feel a sense of peace and personal strength. You're in an excellent position to move onto the next platform for personal growth, and you may not even have to go far away to do it. In August, when the eclipse cycle moves into the Leo-Aquarius axis, you'll experience a time when the things you've been working toward reach a climax. Throughout the year, you're likely to sense that your life path is shifting and that it's time to incorporate a greater sense of purpose into your personal awareness.

If your Moon is from 0–4 degrees of Aquarius you're feeling the pressure of Saturn in square aspect to your Moon, while Neptune conjuncts your Moon. These combined influences indicate that you must be especially discriminating between the urging of your imagination and what you really need. If you can blend your responsibilities with your creativity, then you'll make progress. Every time you try to escape from fulfilling your highest needs you'll feel a tug from the reins of responsibility inhibiting your freedom.

If your Moon is between 5–15 degrees of Aquarius, you're experiencing a profound awakening while Uranus conjuncts your Moon and Pluto sextiles your Moon. You may move, change jobs, alter your relationship, and break out of restraints that have been in the way of your progress. If your Moon is between 15–29 degrees of Aquarius, you're benefiting from the transit of Saturn in sextile aspect to your Moon. It's time to focus, consolidate, and develop attitudes that allow you to feel stable and secure.

Regardless of the exact degree of your Aquarius Moon, you're experiencing a cycle of highly charged energy. It's like watching the world around you change while you feel the bonds that have held you back dropping away with each breath. Enjoy it!

Affirmation for the Year

"My soul is evolving in magnificent ways, and my spirit is renewed with each moment."

January

You're feeling inspired and have enough energy to carry your desires into manifestation—that means you can make things happen if you're putting your heart and soul into them. The pace is quick and the rapid changes may leave you out of breath. Take time during the Full Moon on January 12 to re-evaluate and regroup, seeking out practical solutions to any problems you've encountered. Make adjustments and complete significant steps that will help solidify your position and security from January 18–27. Let yourself reach out to others who are in accord with your needs and aims, but also look for ways to strengthen the lives of those who count on you for understanding. Then prepare to move into the next level during the Aquarius New Moon on January 28. Try to avoid becoming shortsighted, though, since it's easy to think that your position is the only one worth consideration. There may be other viable options!

February

You'll make significant headway in matters that are most important to you by expressing your thoughts and feelings with greater clarity. Your mental ingenuity is highly charged, and some of the ideas that pop into your mind can keep you busy for a while. Taking advantage of a surprising opening can make a big difference in a personal relationship from February 5 until the Full Moon on February 11. It's time to bring issues into the open and examine them honestly. You need to make a commitment that fits your situation now and leaves room for future growth; anything less will feel entirely too restraining. Be sure you're not hiding from the problems you need to address, since you may just discover them in another circumstance. Different situations develop after the solar eclipse on February 26 that may include power struggles, but unless they really involve you try not to get in the middle of them.

March

Your passion is kindled, and if you've been hoping for a time of emotional fulfillment, it's easier to create with the help of Venus transiting over your Moon. During the lunar eclipse on March 12 you may have an experience that underscores your true values, and if you want to show your appreciation for someone this is a great time to do so. A higher level of love emerges in your heart this and can alter your close relationships. This may also spur a desire to become more fully involved in humanitarian efforts, or you may feel more confident in your creative or artistic expression. Although there are a few restrictions emerging after the vernal equinox on March 20, most of them make sense and provide a focus for your energy and efforts. Let love determine your guidelines, and allow your special insights to guide you into a truly exhilarating period of self-realization.

April

If you stay on target you will most definitely succeed in fulfilling your hopes and desires, especially if you're focused on your highest needs. You may feel a little disappointed in others whose aims turn out to be selfish or unreasonable, and if you're watching for signals you'll discover the source of these problems during the Full Moon on April 11. You must also be sure you're paying attention to the reality of a situation from April 12–23, since it's easy to be deceived if you're taking something at face value (especially if the mask is misleading) or basing your feelings on unrealistic desires or expectations. Everything becomes rather clear during the New Moon on April 26, and this is a good time to deal directly with people or problems. In fact, you may not be able to move forward until you've satisfied these concerns. Try not to punish yourself if you're disappointed. After all, some things are just learning experiences.

May

Although you're pretty focused on what you need and want, there may be some explosive situations that rock the boat. If you're trying to clear up a messy situation, you may lose patience if the problems persist, but make every effort to be comprehensive so you don't have to carry on with this any longer than necessary. Frustrations build through the Full Moon on May 11, and after that there is a little cooling off period. Watch for misunderstandings from May 15–23, when maintaining a stubborn attitude or closed mind hurts your progress. You are also a little vulnerable to deception during this period, so try to be alert to situations that seem fishy—it's a fine line to walk, and you may have to allow a few extra hours for contemplation and reflection if you're going to keep your cool. The New Moon on May 25 ushers in a period of new hope and clear direction. Measure your pace, though, because there may still be a few potholes along the road to satisfaction.

June

In some situations your objectivity is functioning at 100 percent, but there are little glitches here and there that operate along the lines of wanting to have your cake and eat it too! Now there's nothing that dictates that you can't be happy and enjoy what you're doing, but you may have to sacrifice some of your desires for absolute freedom if you want to get closer to that person who's caught your eye. Letting your guard down for a while near the Full Moon on June 9 opens the door for all sorts of possibilities, especially if you're in a situation that feels familiar. You could be flirting with disaster if you're not paying attention to the signals that tell you something is just not right for you. Maybe you're ready for a change, but it helps if you know that's what's really happening!

July

The first few days of July can be simply fascinating. There are obstacles, but you probably don't mind them if you're delighted with the process of overcoming them. Emotionally sticky situations can be a bit problematic during the Full Moon on July 9, but you may not be paying much attention to them if you're distracted by a larger goal. You may be thinking that this would be one of those times when it would be nice to have a clone taking care of part of your life so you could be focusing all your attention on what you want to do. Or you could just ignore all the things you don't really want to get stuck with and do what you want to do anyway (the only problem is the effect it has on the people around you). Partners may demand more of your energy or they could withdraw their support. Try to get a good reading on the situation during the New Moon on July 23 when you can turn a situation around if you've carried things a little too far.

August

You're feeling a little more emotionally sensitive. Now, you don't really like to admit that, but darn it, you have feelings too! Just because you try to make emotions logical does not mean you're not a feeling, caring person. You just don't like to get bogged down in all that sentimental stuff. But wait, there's a lunar eclipse in Aquarius on August 7—there *is* hope that someone will understand how you feel and what you need. First, you have to come to grips with those needs, and if you want to address them with someone else in your life, this is the time. You're even willing to make some adjustments that will lead to a peaceful solution. Whether you're dealing with personal relationships or career issues, it's crucial that your aims fit your deepest needs. Work on those elements after the solar eclipse on August 21.

September

You may decide to alter your life in a significant way near the time of the Moon's eclipse on September 6 (yes, there's another lunar eclipse). If you've completed important obligations, then you may feel that it's time to step onto a different path. It's best to avoid burning all your bridges, though, because you may accidentally leave a few things undone. Reach closure when possible, but focus on transformation as the primary process—allowing yourself and the situations in your life to evolve and reach a different level. Those things that need to end will drop away once you tell them good-bye. There's no need to do anything drastic. More peaceful solutions arise after September 24, when a forgiving attitude permeates the atmosphere. This is also a better time to think about moving, redecorating or improving your environment.

October

The month begins on a positive note, and your attitudes are upbeat, allowing you to feel more confident about your choices and challenges. Others may also be more cooperative, and you'll have a chance to utilize that spirit of cooperation during the Full Moon on October 5, when mutual goals have a much better chance of succeeding than selfish motives. Refreshing possibilities stir your imagination from October 1–9, when you may also receive accolades for your special efforts. Stubborn attitudes can get in the way from October 13–16, but this also lets you know your source of resistance if you're hoping for change. Power plays from October 17–20 can pull you away from your detached perspective, but try not to sink to the level of those whose manipulations are destructive. After the New Moon on October 20 you have a golden opportunity to launch your ideas. You're most confident on October 28 and 29.

November

There are uncomfortable circumstances brewing near the time of the Full Moon on November 4. You've been in these situations before (you know, like the dinner party with the boring guests and dreadful food). If you really don't want to get stuck, then say "No," but you may have to do something you'd rather not do. Get it over with, keep your attitudes pleasant, and look for an opening. It's there on November 5 and 6 when you can take positive advantage of an unexpected change. After paying your dues, you have an excellent period of stabilization and confidence emerging on November 22. For the next few weeks you can enjoy rewards for your hard work and generosity, not that you did it for the goodies, but they are nice when they finally arrive! Plan to do something that brings you exceptional pleasure from November 24–30, since during this time your heart is open and you're ready to experience pure love.

December

This is a very satisfying month. Although you may feel a little overextended near the time of the Full Moon on December 3, you may decide it's for a good cause, and not resent the price you pay. If there are misunderstandings, you may be the one who seems to be able to settle them diplomatically and to the satisfaction of all concerned. Special interests and creative projects lift your spirits after December 11, when you may also feel like you're ready to make an important commitment that can positively alter the direction of your life. The New Moon on December 18 marks a wonderful time of fresh beginnings, and may also be a time when new friends emerge as old friendships are rekindled. Hold the vision of what you want to achieve and release it with love to your higher self. This is your time to be uplifted through hope.

Pisces Moon

You are capable of experiencing life from a different dimension—the space of vibration, where the spirit of all life begins. Through your Pisces Moon you can develop an exceptional sensibility that allows you to experience the essence of the Source. Perched on the fine line between reality and illusion, those sensibilities allow you to float beyond ordinary reality into the world of imagination. Dealing with everyday life is not always easy for you, though, and you may fight an eternal battle between knowing when to let go and when to hold on.

You can be compassionate, forgiving, and accepting of what others cannot tolerate. You appreciate the true diversity of life experience, and see from the place of "possibility." Maintaining your personal boundaries is not easy, and if you are to experience growth through your relationships you must develop an emotional filter. You may even respond just as strongly to the landscape of your imagination as you respond to the outside world. For this reason, it's important to give yourself time to learn what a person or situation is like before you emotionally immerse yourself.

The weight of stress and painful reality of life can overwhelm you, and it is then that you become the master of escape. Your home needs to provide a safe heaven where you can dream, feel safe and let go of the tensions of the world. You're vulnerable to being drawn into illusions and can go to far inside yourself, where it is warm, safe, and much more enchanting than the harsh world. You can also bring this world to life by creating an energy that emanates from your soul.

The Year Ahead for Pisces Moon

This is your year to manifest the fulfillment of your needs. Jupiter transits through Pisces during 1998, forming a conjunction to your Moon, lending the energy of optimism and opportunity to your emotional needs. It's been twelve years since you experienced the advantageous energy of this cycle, and the choices you make and opportunities to accept now can carry you far into the future. There are also a few tests (aren't there always?!), but you may feel much better about dealing with them. It's time to expand your horizons in harmony with your needs. Be careful: you can also overextend yourself be being unrealistically optimistic, so think before you make too many promises.

The eclipses complete their cycle in the Virgo-Pisces axis this year, marking a time of culmination. The situations in your life that are ready to change can reach their climax point this year, and you are operating from a level of greater awareness concerning your feelings and needs. You may feel that it's easier for you to forgive, let go, and move on with your life. Making those choices will open the way to enjoy positive personal growth. Saturn's energy is also adding to your need to release the past, and much like a series of stepping stones, you're creating a definite direction that will help you fulfill your hopes.

If your Moon is in the first 10 degrees of Pisces you're experiencing profound changes in your needs. You may decide to pull up your roots and transplant yourself—physically and emotionally. The outer planets—Uranus, Neptune, and Pluto—are all stimulating a deep need to change. If you've been hanging onto situations that are counterproductive, or even if you've been holding onto illusions, it's time to break free and experience a true period of renewal and rebirth. Some situations may change beyond your control, but the manner in which you respond makes a crucial difference in the outcome!

Keep in mind that you are ready to expand your reach and open your heart. Regardless of the exact degree of your Moon, you can feel the yearnings of your heart calling you. Let yourself have the life you deserve. It's your turn!

Affirmation for the Year

"The Universe provides true abundance in all things. My life is filled with love, joy, and all that I need."

January

An undercurrent of excitement can throw you off balance, so try to stay focused on the things in front of you instead of jumping too far ahead. Do something that helps you feel more grounded during the Full Moon on January 12. You might even enjoy having lunch with someone special and touching base during this time, because it's a wonderful period of emotional renewal. Practical considerations add structure to your time after January 13, and you might even enjoy the consistency. However, there is an increase of tension building around you, and you need positive ways to diffuse it. Creative expression, romantic interludes, and regular periods of contemplation and meditation can be helpful after January 18. Mars enters Pisces on January 25, adding a quality of intensity and directness to manner in that you express your emotions.

February

Navigate through the land mines of emotionally charged situations with care from February 1–7, because you can get caught in the squeeze of other people's emotional garbage. It's really not a pretty place, so try to keep your emotional filters working, and give yourself ample time to rejuvenate. You may also feel some angry dragons of your own raising their heads, and if so, then take a look at any unresolved feelings you've been trying to ignore and deal with them immediately and directly. The intensity factor calms a bit after the Full Moon on February 11, but the effects may take a while to cool. Listen to your inner urging and honor your needs now, because this is the time to come to grips with your deepest desires. The Pisces solar eclipse (that means it's also a new Moon) adds special emphasis to your needs on February 26, and this is an excellent time to look at your life. If you like what you see, stabilize it. If not, get started on those changes.

March

Some of your expectations may come crashing down before the lunar eclipse on March 12, especially if you've based your hopes on unrealistic possibilities. This is also a good time to eliminate things that just don't fit any longer. If you're uncertain about the best place to start, explore your options with a trusted counselor. Spend time in reflection, listen to your dreams. Consider taking a few days away from your everyday schedule from March 1–8, when travel stimulates your imagination. Your confidence is stronger after March 15, but you may decide to focus on getting everything in order before you make more sweeping changes in your life. Initiating change will be easier next month, after you've dealt with your obligations and finished the things that are already clamoring for your attention.

April

After a few jam-packed days from April 1–6, you're ready to give yourself a break. However, there are still obligations, and if you disappear before the Full Moon on April 11 you may get pulled back into the situation just to be sure you've fulfilled your responsibilities. Venus moves into Pisces on April 6 and through the remainder of the month you'll enjoy an enhanced sense of beauty. This energy can be quite helpful in relationships, and you also feel much more inclined to use your best assets when necessary. If you're unhappy in a love relationship those feelings emerge from April 11–15, when you really must deal with your deeper needs. Change what you can, but take a good look. You know in your heart if there's hope. If not, set your sights on new possibilities—and there are some on the horizon beginning April 16. Check it out, and put your plans in motion after the New Moon on April 26.

May

This is a great month to get yourself organized. Changes in your personal environment need to reflect your needs for comfort and sense of style, and whether you need to move, rearrange the furniture, or redecorate, you may feel inspired to make your house more of a home. During the Full Moon on May 11 you're in the mood for love, and might prefer to share the experience in your freshly revamped surroundings. (The days just before the Full Moon are a build-up to this energy, so think about your plans for that weekend!) Putting your plans into motion for your worldly concerns, like positive changes in your work situation, shows progress from May 10–21, when your performance can definitely make a mark on someone who counts. Try not to distract yourself from your priorities after May 22.

June

So much to do, so little time! You may bemoan your fate if you've made too many promises, since there's definitely something sweet on the horizon for the Full Moon on June 9. Before you decide to indulge, be sure you really want it, though, because you could be sacrificing something more important for a momentary delight. The choices may appear to be easier after June 15, but there are little traps along the way. One of them is the illusion of something (or someone) appearing to be better than it really is. Test the situation by asking yourself what you'll have to pay for the pleasure of the experience. Think about it. Bargain a little. Then, take action after the New Moon on June 23 when you have more facts. You're still not sure? That's okay, too, because you may need a little more time to tell exactly how far you'll have to go to get what you think you want. What a devilish dilemma!

July

Your intentions seem to be quite honorable, but you may not be judging some of your choices carefully enough. The apparently playful energy from July 1–7 can have drastic consequences if you promise what you cannot deliver, and you may be stretched by things you had not even anticipated. Give yourself a break during the Full Moon on July 9 to regroup. You may also fall victim to unrealistic expectations from others, and since you hate to disappoint anyone you could cave in and do something even though it's not what you want. You're in a better position to navigate the maze of emotionally charged situations after July 19, when there are more resources available, including better support from others. Until then it will be easier to maintain your sanity by learning to say "No" when possible. It's easy. *No*. Practice.

August

Things around you may be happening at a dizzying pace, but you are in pretty good shape emotionally. During the lunar eclipse on August 7 you might feel most content if you take a little time for yourself, or spend your hours with friends you truly enjoy. You're in a loving mood from the August 9–18, and you'll benefit from doing something special for those who have your heart. This is also a good time to mend fences and heal old emotional wounds, particularly if you've been neglecting the people who mean the most to you. The solar eclipse on August 21 opens the way for a few adjustments that will help you get your life back on track. After August 23 you can feel the wheels of motion turning again, but you may also need to target changes in your relationships. Reflect upon the way you respond to the needs and demands of others, and compare this with what you really want and need. You're starting to bridge the gap.

September

The lunar eclipse in Pisces on September 6 marks a significant period of awareness and opens the possibility for change. Integrating your needs and wants can be challenging, but now you're ready to concentrate your energy on experiences that will uplift and empower your creativity and spirituality. Since your journey through life involves interaction with others your consciousness and experience is shaped not only by what you feel within yourself but also by what you encounter. Take a careful look at the people and situations you're encountering now, because you can be more objective. If you want to shift your attitudes to reflect your true needs while allowing room in your life for the others who share your journey, this is the time to do it. Even if nothing seems to be noticeable on the "outside," your inner resolve can shift and you can free yourself as you open to fresh possibilities during the New Moon on September 20.

October

You may feel like you're dabbling with a situation that does not fully suit your desires or needs, but you could just be in it for the learning experience. That's okay, too. Think of the period near the Full Moon on October 5 as a time of outreach and experimentation, and try to remain objective if you're involved in something that seems transitional. The real transition is happening within you! Confrontations can be explosive after October 7 when Mars moves into the opposition to your Moon, and you may feel more vulnerable. If you listen to your inner voice you may discover that you're the one who needs a few confrontations, and that you're ready to release anger or frustration. Communicating what you feel is easier after October 12, when you may also run into excessive control from others. After October 26 you feel more in the flow, but you may still feel forced to take a stand for what you really want.

November

It's easy to be caught in the squeeze of expectations, and it's crucial that you send the messages you intend to send to others. Saying one thing and doing another will only lead to headaches. You need to be close to the ones you love during the Full Moon on November 4, and even if you can't be together you'll feel much better if you make some kind of contact. Demonstrative exchanges solidify relationships, and it's that feeling of definition you're after. If someone else is sending double messages—saying one thing and doing another—confront them. All you have to lose is confusion. Of course, you could also find out that you have a problem on your hands, and that can be surprisingly empowering. Moving into unfamiliar territory can be a positive challenge during the New Moon on November 18, and that includes emotional spaces as well as physical ones!

December

You're feeling restless and may also be a bit anxiety-ridden from December 1–10 if you allow your insecurities to get the best of you. Stop for a moment and ground yourself during the Full Moon on December 3, since there are plenty of distractions that can keep your head spinning. Once you've established a firm foothold you can take steps that are more assuring, even if you are dealing with something or someone out of the ordinary. Friends emerge to offer support and guidance after December 11, and if you'll put your talents into motion you may even discover new avenues of self-confirmation. The hectic pace can wear you down if you forget to take care of yourself, so remember to take care of ordinary practices like eating and sleeping. You feel much more emotionally centered after December 23, when you can let go of all that spinning energy and just relax for a while—sounds like a good way to celebrate the holidays!

Directory of
Products
&
Services

Llewellyn's Computerized Astrological Services

Llewellyn has been a leading authority in astrological chart readings for more than 30 years. We feature a wide variety of readings with the intent to satisfy the needs of any astrological enthusiast. Our goal is to give you the best possible service so that you can achieve your goals and live your life successfully. **Be sure to give accurate and complete birth data on the order form. This includes exact time (A.M. or P.M.), date, year, city, county and country of birth. Note: Noon will be used as your birthtime if you don't provide an exact time. Check your birth certificate for this information! Llewellyn will not be responsible for mistakes from inaccurate information.** An order form follows these listings.

SIMPLE NATAL CHART

Learn the locations of your midpoints and aspects, elements, and more. Discover your planets and house cusps, retrogrades, and other valuable data necessary to make a complete interpretation. Matrix Software programs and designs The Simple Natal Chart printout.

APS03-119 .... $5.00

PERSONALITY PROFILE

Our most popular reading also makes the perfect gift! This 10-part profile depicts your "natal imprint" and how the planets mark your destiny. Examine emotional needs and inner feelings. Explore your imagination and read about your general characteristics and life patterns.

APS03-503 .... $20.00

LIFE PROGRESSION

Progressions are a special system astrologers use to map how the "natal you" develops through specified periods of your present and future life. With this report you can discover the "now you!" This incredible reading covers a year's time and is designed to complement the Personality Profile Reading. **Specify present residence.**

APS03-507 .... $20.00

COMPATIBILITY PROFILE

Are you compatible with your lover, spouse, friend, or business partner? Find out with this in-depth look at each person's approach to the relationship. Evaluate goals, values, potential conflicts. This service includes planetary placements for both individuals, so send birth data for both. **Indicate each person's gender and the type of relationship involved** (romance, business, etc.).

APS03-504 .... $30.00

PERSONAL RELATIONSHIP INTERPRETATION

If you've just called it quits on one relationship and know you need to understand more about yourself before testing the waters again, then this is the report for you! This reading will tell you how you approach relationships in general, what kind of people you look for and what kind of people might rub you the wrong way. Important for anyone!

APS03-506 .... $20.00

TRANSIT REPORT

Keep abreast of positive trends and challenging periods in your life. Transits are the relationships between the planets today and their positions at your birth. They are an invaluable timing and decision-making aid. This report starts on the first day of the month, devotes a paragraph to each of your transit aspects and their effective dates. ***Be sure to specify your present residence.***

APS03-500 – 3-month report $12.00
APS03-501 – 6-month report $20.00
APS03-502 – 1-year report $30.00

BIORHYTHM REPORT

Some days you have unlimited energy, then the next day you feel sluggish and awkward. These cycles are called biorhythms. This individual report accurately maps your daily biorhythms and thoroughly discusses each day. Now you can plan your days to the fullest!

APS03-515 – 3-month report $12.00
APS03-516 – 6-month report $18.00
APS03-517 – 1-year report $25.00

TAROT READING

Find out what the cards have in store for you with this 12-page report that features a 10-card "Celtic Cross" spread shuffled and selected especially for you. For every card that turns up there is a detailed corresponding explanation of what each means for you. Order this tarot reading today! ***Indicate the number of shuffles you want.***

APS03-120 .... $10.00

LUCKY LOTTO REPORT (State Lottery Report)

Do you play the state lotteries? This report will determine your luckiest sequence of numbers for each day based on specific planets, degrees, and other indicators in your own chart. Give your full birth data and middle name. ***Tell us how many numbers your state lottery requires in sequence, and the highest possible numeral. Indicate the month you want to start.***

APS03-512 – 3-month report $10.00
APS03-513 – 6-month report $15.00
APS03-514 – 1-year report $25.00

NUMEROLOGY REPORT

Find out which numbers are right for you with this insightful report. This report uses an ancient form of numerology invented by Pythagoras to determine the significant numbers in your life. Using both your name and date of birth, this report will calculate those numbers that stand out as yours. With these numbers, you can tell when the important periods of your life will occur. ***Please indicate your full birth name.***

APS03-508 – 3-month report $12.00
APS03-509 – 6-month report $18.00
APS03-510 – 1-year report $25.00

ULTIMATE ASTRO-PROFILE

More than 40 pages of insightful descriptions of your qualities and talents. Read about your burn rate (thirst for change). Explore your personal patterns (inside and outside). The Astro-Profile doesn't repeat what you've already learned from other personality profiles, but considers the natal influence of the lunar nodes, plus much more.

APS03-505 .... $40.00

ASTROLOGICAL SERVICES ORDER FORM

SERVICE NAME & NUMBER ____________________________________

____

Provide the following data on all persons receiving a service:

1ST PERSON'S FULL NAME, including current middle & last name(s)

____

Birthplace (city, county, state, country) ____________________

____

Birthtime ______ ❒ A.M. ❒ P.M. **Month** ______ **Day** _____ **Year** ________

2ND PERSON'S FULL NAME (if ordering for more than one person)

____

Birthplace (city, county, state, country) ____________________

____

Birthtime ______ ❒ A.M. ❒ P.M. **Month** ______ **Day** _____ **Year** ________

BILLING INFORMATION

Name ____

Address ____

____

City ____________________ **State** _______ **Zip** __________

Country ____________ **Day phone:** ____________________

Make check or money order payable to Llewellyn Publications, or charge it!
Check one: ❒ Visa ❒ MasterCard ❒ American Express

Acct. No. ____________________________ Exp. Date __________

Cardholder Signature ______________________________________

Mail this form and payment to:

LLEWELLYN'S PERSONAL SERVICES

P.O. BOX 64383-K933 • ST. PAUL, MN 55164-0383

Allow 4-6 weeks for delivery.

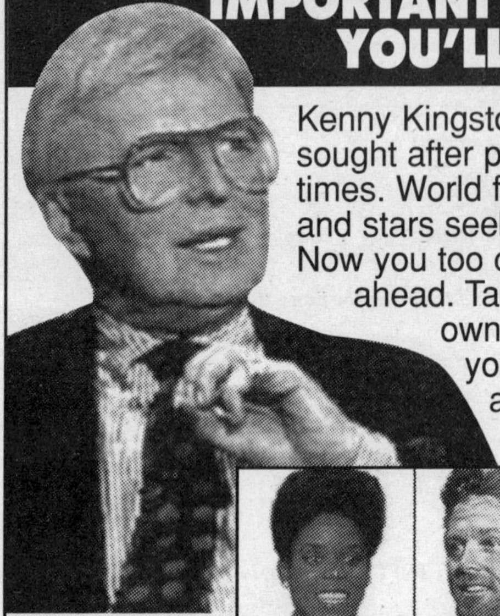